CONTEMPORARY ORCHESTRATION

Contemporary Orchestration: A Practical Guide to Instruments, Ensembles, and Musicians teaches students how to orchestrate for a wide variety of instruments, ensembles, and genres, while preparing them for various real-world professional settings ranging from the concert hall to the recording studio. It integrates instrument characteristics, technique, and performativity with professional and practical considerations.

Beginning with practical problem solving, the book outlines issues that need to be addressed before beginning the orchestration process. A section on score preparation offers a guide to preparing concert scores, transposed scores, condensed scores, recording-studio scores, and hybrid scores. Addressing both contemporary and traditional instruments and ensembles, it demonstrates how to prepare scores and parts for both acoustic and recording-studio environments, how to incorporate and notate world music instruments in a western European orchestral setting, how to incorporate and notate jazz and pop elements, and how to score for musical theater.

Features

- Practical Considerations: Practical suggestions for choosing a work to orchestrate, and what to avoid when writing for each instrument.
- In the Profession: A guide to the courtesies, considerations, and expectations in the professional environment.
- Building the Score: Step-by-step procedures for orchestrating a variety of ensembles and genres.
- Scoring Examples: Multiple scoring examples for each instrument and ensemble.
- Suggested Exercises: Orchestration exercises that use problem- solving techniques to review and reinforce chapter material.
- Companion Website: Video resources and discussion of additional instruments and ensembles.

RJ Miller has composed, orchestrated, arranged, conducted and/or produced recordings with the London Philharmonic and the St. Petersburg Philharmonic, and for such films as the digital re-release of the original *The Last of the Mohicans* and *The Lost World*. His credits appear on over 300 CDs, videos, film, and television productions. His courses at the Metropolitan State University of Denver include Arranging and Orchestration, Arranging for Music Educators, and Scoring for Film and Television.

CONTEMPORARY ORCHESTRATION

A Practical Guide to Instruments, Ensembles, and Musicians

RJ Miller

NEW YORK AND LONDON

First published 2015
by Routledge
711 Third Avenue, New York, NY 10017

and by Routledge
2 Park Square, Milton Park, Abingdon, Oxon, OX14 4RN

Routledge is an imprint of the Taylor & Francis Group, an informa business

© 2015 Taylor & Francis

The right of RJ Miller to be identified as author of this work has been asserted by him in accordance with sections 77 and 78 of the Copyright, Designs and Patents Act 1988.

All rights reserved. No part of this book may be reprinted or reproduced or utilized in any form or by any electronic, mechanical, or other means, now known or hereafter invented, including photocopying and recording, or in any information storage or retrieval system, without permission in writing from the publishers.

Trademark notice: Product or corporate names may be trademarks or registered trademarks, and are used only for identification and explanation without intent to infringe.

Library of Congress Cataloging-in-Publication Data
Miller, R.J. (Robert Joseph), 1953– author.
  Contemporary orchestration: a practical guide to instruments, ensembles, and musicians/RJ Miller.
  pages cm
  1. Instrumentation and orchestration. I. Title.
  MT70.M57 2015
  781.3'74—dc23
  2014019576

ISBN: 978-0-415-74190-3 (hbk)
ISBN: 978-0-415-74191-0 (pbk)
ISBN: 978-1-315-81500-8 (ebk)

Typeset in Baskerville 2
by Florence Production Ltd, Stoodleigh, Devon, UK

CONTENTS

List of Musical Examples — xvi
Preface — xix

1 Preliminary Considerations — **1**
   The Physics of Sound — *1*
   The Overtone Series — *2*
   Implied Fundamental — *6*
   Instrumental Balances — *9*
   Instrumental Combinations — *10*

2 Scores, Parts and Notation — **13**
   Score Preparation — *13*
   Score Order — *19*
   Concert, Transposed and Condensed Scores — *21*
   Preparation of Instrumental Parts — *23*
   Preparation of Recording-studio Scores — *27*
   Preparation of Hybrid Studio Scores — *28*
   Recording-studio Parts — *29*
   Instrument Transposition Guide — *32*
   Instruments and Abbreviations — *34*
   General Notation Considerations — *35*
   Traditional Terminology — *36*
   Rhythmic Subdivisions within the Measure — *44*
   Notes — *46*

3 Practical Problem Solving — **47**
   Measures One and Two — *50*
   Measures Three, Four and Five — *51*
   Measures Six, Seven, Eight and Nine — *53*
   Completed Revoicing — *54*

4 The Violin Family — 57

- THE ESSENTIALS — 57
  - *The Bridge* — 57
  - *The Bow* — 57
  - *Rosin* — 58
  - *Basic Bowing Terms and Descriptions* — 58
- THE INSTRUMENTS — 66
  - *Violin* — 66
  - *Viola* — 70
  - *Violoncello* — 75
  - *Double Bass* — 79
- THE ENSEMBLES — 82
  - *String Quartet* — 82
  - *Chamber Strings* — 82
  - *Orchestral Strings* — 82
  - *Symphony Orchestra Strings* — 83
- PRACTICAL CONSIDERATIONS — 83
- IN THE PROFESSION — 83
- BUILDING THE SCORE — 84
- SCORING EXAMPLES — 90
  - *Scoring Examples for String Quartet* — 90
  - *Scoring Examples for Orchestral Strings* — 94
- SUGGESTED EXERCISES — 102
  - *Scoring Exercise for String Quartet* — 102
  - *Scoring Exercise for Orchestral Strings* — 104

5 The Brass Family — 107

- THE ESSENTIALS — 107
  - *Cylindrical and Conical Classifications* — 107
  - *Whole-tube Brass Instruments* — 107
  - *Half-tube Brass Instruments* — 108
  - *Single-tonguing* — 108
  - *Double-tonguing* — 108
  - *Triple-tonguing* — 108
  - *Slurs* — 108
  - *Flutter-tonguing* — 108
  - *Trills* — 108
  - *Shakes* — 109

CONTENTS

Brass Glissandi	*109*
1/2-valve Glissando	*109*
Trombone Glissando	*109*
Valve Tremolo	*109*
Mutes	*110*
Brass Embouchure Considerations	*111*
THE INSTRUMENTS	111
Trumpet	*111*
Cornet	*113*
Flugelhorn	*114*
Trumpet in D	*115*
Piccolo Trumpet	*115*
E♭ Soprano Cornet	*117*
Bass Trumpet	*117*
Horn	*118*
Tenor Trombone	*121*
Bass Trombone	*122*
Valve Trombone	*123*
Alto Trombone	*123*
Cimbasso	*124*
E♭ Alto Horn (Tenor Horn)	*125*
Euphonium	*126*
Baritone	*126*
Tuba	*127*
Sousaphone	*128*
THE ENSEMBLES	129
Brass Quintet	*129*
Chamber Ensembles	*129*
Orchestral Brass	*130*
Wind Ensemble and Concert Band Brass	*130*
British-style Brass Band	*131*
PRACTICAL CONSIDERATIONS	140
IN THE PROFESSION	140
BUILDING THE SCORE	141
SCORING EXAMPLES	147
Scoring Examples for Brass Quintet	*147*
Scoring Examples for Orchestral Brass	*150*
Scoring Examples for Wind Ensemble/Concert Band Brass	*154*
Scoring Examples for British-style Brass Band	*158*

	SUGGESTED EXERCISES	162
	Scoring Exercise for Brass Quintet	*162*
	Scoring Exercise for Orchestral or Wind Ensemble Brass	*163*
6	**The Woodwind Family**	**165**
	THE ESSENTIALS	165
	Cylindrical and Conical Classifications	*165*
	Edge-blown Aerophones	*166*
	Single Reed Instruments	*166*
	Double Reed Instruments	*166*
	Saxophone Mouthpieces	*166*
	Single-tonguing	*166*
	Double-tonguing	*167*
	Triple-tonguing	*167*
	Flutter-tonguing	*167*
	Slurs	*167*
	Trills	*167*
	Tremolos	*168*
	Glissandi (Portamenti)	*168*
	Saxophone Subtone	*169*
	THE INSTRUMENTS	169
	THE FLUTE FAMILY	*169*
	Flute	*169*
	Piccolo	*170*
	Alto Flute	*171*
	Bass Flute	*172*
	Contra-Alto Flute	*173*
	Contrabass Flute	*173*
	Subcontrabass Flutes	*174*
	D♭ Piccolo	*175*
	THE SINGLE REED FAMILY	*176*
	Clarinets	*176*
	E♭ Clarinet	*176*
	B♭ Clarinet	*177*
	Clarinet in A	*178*
	E♭ Alto Clarinet	*178*
	B♭ Bass Clarinet	*179*
	E♭ Contralto Clarinet	*180*
	B♭ Contrabass Clarinet	*180*

THE SAXOPHONE FAMILY	*181*
B♭ Soprano Saxophone	*181*
E♭ Alto Saxophone	*182*
B♭ Tenor Saxophone	*183*
E♭ Baritone Saxophone	*184*
E♭ Sopranino Saxophone	*184*
B♭ Bass Saxophone	*185*
E♭ Contrabass Saxophone	*186*
THE DOUBLE REED FAMILY	*186*
Oboe	*186*
English Horn	*187*
Oboe d'amore	*188*
Baritone (Bass) Oboe	*188*
Bassoons	*189*
Contrabassoons	*190*
THE ENSEMBLES	191
Flute Choir	*191*
Flute Orchestra	*191*
Clarinet Choir	*192*
Wind Quintet	*193*
Chamber Woodwinds	*194*
Orchestral Woodwinds	*195*
Wind Ensemble and Concert Band Woodwinds	*195*
PRACTICAL CONSIDERATIONS	196
IN THE PROFESSION	196
BUILDING THE SCORE	196
SCORING EXAMPLES	207
Scoring Example for Flute Choir	*207*
Scoring Example for Flute Orchestra	*208*
Scoring Examples for Clarinet Choir	*213*
Scoring Examples for Wind Quintet	*215*
Scoring Examples for Orchestral Woodwinds	*220*
Scoring Examples for Wind Ensemble/Concert Band Woodwinds	*227*
SUGGESTED EXERCISES	232
Scoring Exercise for Wind Quintet	*232*
Scoring Exercise for Orchestral Woodwinds or Wind Ensemble Woodwinds	*234*

7 The Percussion Family   **237**

Instruments Classifications   *237*
Synthetic and Sampled Sounds   *237*
Notation and Score Order   *238*

THE ESSENTIALS   242
Rudiments   *242*

THE INSTRUMENTS   253

MEMBRANOPHONES   253
Timpani   *253*
Snare Drum   *255*
Bass Drum   *256*
Tambourine   *257*
Tenor Drum   *258*
Tom-toms   *258*
Bongos   *259*
Conga   *259*
Timbales   *260*
Drum Set   *261*

IDIOPHONES OF DEFINITE PITCH   263
Orchestra Bells   *263*
Crotales   *263*
Xylophone   *264*
Marimba   *265*
Vibraphone   *266*
Chimes   *267*

IDIOPHONES OF INDEFINITE PITCH   268
Triangle   *268*
Hand Cymbals (Piatti)   *268*
Suspended Cymbal   *268*
Sizzle Cymbal   *269*
Finger Cymbals   *269*
Tam-tam   *270*
Woodblocks   *270*
Temple Blocks (Tempo Blocks)   *270*
Ratchet   *271*
Shakers   *271*
Sleigh Bells   *271*
Mark Tree   *271*
Wind Chimes   *272*

Bell Tree	*272*
Flexatone	*272*
Vibraslap	*273*
Anvil	*273*
Brake Drum	*273*
Thunder Sheet	*274*
Cowbells and Agogo Bells	*274*
Claves	*275*
Maracas	*275*
Cabasa and Afuche-Cabasa	*275*
Guiro	*276*
Castanets	*276*
Rainstick	*276*
AEROPHONES	277
Slide Whistle	*277*
Coach's Whistle	*277*
Samba Whistle	*277*
Siren	*278*
CHORDAPHONES	278
Celesta	*278*
Piano	*278*
THE ENSEMBLES	280
Percussion Ensemble	*280*
Orchestral (and Wind Ensemble/Concert Band) Percussion	*280*
PRACTICAL CONSIDERATIONS	281
IN THE PROFESSION	281
BUILDING THE SCORE	282
SCORING EXAMPLES	285
SUGGESTED EXERCISES	290
Scoring Exercise for Membranophones and Idiophones	*290*
Scoring Exercise for Mallet Instruments	*291*

8   Voices   295

THE ESSENTIALS	295
Vocal Notation	*295*
Vocal Ranges	*296*
Vowel Considerations	*297*
Difficult Intervals	*298*

Voicings		*298*
PRACTICAL CONSIDERATIONS		299
THE ENSEMBLES		299
Unaccompanied Choir		*299*
Choir with Keyboard Accompaniment		*300*
Choir with Orchestra (or Wind Ensemble)		*300*
IN THE PROFESSION		300
BUILDING THE SCORE		301
SCORING EXAMPLES		303
Scoring Examples for Adult Choir		*303*
Scoring Examples for Choir and Orchestra		*305*
Scoring Example for Children's Choir		*309*
SUGGESTED EXERCISE		310

9 Pedal Harp — 313

THE ESSENTIALS	313
The Grand Staff	*314*
Playing Position and Range of Hands	*314*
Pedals	*315*
Pedal Diagrams	*316*
Pedal Changes	*316*
Enharmonics	*317*
Arpeggios	*317*
Sustain	*318*
Glissandi	*318*
Repeated Notes	*319*
Harmonics	*319*
PRACTICAL CONSIDERATIONS	332
IN THE PROFESSION	332
BUILDING THE SCORE	332
SUGGESTED EXERCISE	335

10 Guitar — 337

THE ESSENTIALS	337
Tuning	*337*
Guitar Range and Transposition	*337*
Guitar Notation	*338*
Sample Chords in C	*339*

Sample Chords in C♯ — *340*
Sample Chords in D♭ — *340*
Sample Chords in D — *341*
Sample Chords in D♯ — *341*
Sample Chords in E♭ — *342*
Sample Chords in E — *342*
Sample Chords in F — *343*
Sample Chords in F♯ — *343*
Sample Chords in G♭ — *344*
Sample Chords in G — *344*
Sample Chords in G♯ — *345*
Sample Chords in A♭ — *345*
Sample Chords in A — *346*
Sample Chords in B♭ — *346*
Sample Chords in B — *347*
Harmonics — *347*

THE ENSEMBLES — 349
Guitar Ensemble — *349*
Guitar Orchestra — *349*

IN THE PROFESSION — 349

BUILDING THE SCORE — 349

SCORING EXAMPLES — 355
Scoring Example for Solo Guitar — *355*
Scoring Examples for Guitar in an Orchestral Setting — *356*

SUGGESTED EXERCISE — 360

11 Scoring for Orchestral Tutti — 363

PRACTICAL CONSIDERATIONS — 363

BUILDING THE SCORE — 363

SCORING EXAMPLES — 380

SUGGESTED EXERCISE — 382

12 Scoring for the Wind Ensemble/Concert Band Tutti — 383

Wind Ensemble — *383*
Concert Band — *384*

PRACTICAL CONSIDERATIONS — 385

BUILDING THE SCORE — 387
Scoring for Wind Ensemble/Concert Band Tutti — *387*

	SCORING EXAMPLES	392
	SUGGESTED EXERCISE	395
13	**Scoring for Musical Theater**	**397**
	Attrition	*397*
	Bandstation	*397*
	Books	*398*
	Conductor's Score	*398*
	Instrumentation	*398*
	Alternate Instrumentation	*400*
	PRACTICAL CONSIDERATIONS	402
	BUILDING THE SCORE	402
	Scoring the Chorus	*403*
	Creating the Piano/Vocal Part	*404*
	Scoring the Rhythm Section	*405*
	Scoring the Brass Section	*406*
	Scoring the Woodwind Section	*407*
	Scoring the String Section	*407*
	Piano/Conductor's Score	*408*
	Piano/Vocal Part	*409*
	Two-piano Arrangement	*409*
	Full Score	*409*
	SUGGESTED EXERCISE	411
14	**Instrument Substitution and Quick Reference Guides**	**413**
	Practical Ranges and Registers for the Orchestral String Family	*416*
	Practical Ranges and Registers for Brass Quintet	*419*
	Practical Ranges and Registers for Wind Quintet	*421*
	Practical Ranges and Registers for Saxophones	*423*
	Practical Ranges and Registers for the Orchestral Percussion Family	*426*
	Practical Ranges and Tessitura for Voices	*428*
15	**Suggested Listening and Analysis**	**429**
16	**Parting Thoughts**	**439**
	Common Sense	*439*
	Step One	*439*
	Awareness of Acoustical Balances	*439*
	Scoring for Orchestral Tutti	*439*
	Cross-voicing of like Timbres	*440*

Cover the Seams	*441*
Passing Melodies from Instrument to Instrument	*441*
Not Everyone Needs to Play all the Time	*442*
Avoid Exact Repeats	*442*
Importance of Voice-leading and Rhythmic Interest within Parts	*442*
Importance of Clear/Clean Notation	*443*
Know the Capabilities and Limitations of Every Instrument	*443*
Ask a Player	*443*
Think Like a Player	*444*
Know What to Avoid	*444*
Learn from Your Mistakes	*444*
Find Your Voice	*444*
Seven Traits of a Great Orchestrator	*444*
Credits	*447*
Index	*451*

MUSICAL EXAMPLES

Chapter 2

Edvard Grieg, *Arietta*, mm. 1–12, 20–23
RJ Miller, *Callisto* (from *The Galilaen Moons of Jupiter*, Movement II), mm. 1–11
RJ Miller, *Io* (from *The Galilaen Moons of Jupiter*, Movement I), flute part, mm. 1–40, 61–68
RJ Miller, *Moments*, mm. 1–17
RJ Miller, *The Processional*, violin part, mm. 1–55
Austin Wintory, *Captain Abu Raed* (score), mm. 1–11
Austin Wintory, *Captain Abu Raed* (violin parts), mm. 1–11

Chapter 3

Peter Ilyich Tchaikovsky, *Chanson Triste*, mm. 1–9

Chapter 4

Camille Saint-Saëns, *Danse Macabre*, mm. 14–21
Frédéric Chopin, *Prélude*, Op. 28 No. 20, mm. 1–13
Felix Mendelssohn, *War March of the Priests* (from *Athalie*), mm. 1–16
Georg Friedrich Händel, *Sarabande*, mm. 1–20
Ludwig van Beethoven, *Quartet No. 8 in E minor*, Op. 59 No. 2, mm. 1–8
RJ Miller, *Elegy*, mm. 23–41
Gabriel Fauré, *Pavane*, Op. 50, mm. 1–9
Ludwig van Beethoven, *Quartet in B Flat Major*, Op. 130, mm. 347–361
Alexander Borodin, *String Quartet No. 1*, Scherzo, mm. 1–12
Joseph Haydn, *Symphony No. 101 in D Major* (Hoboken 1/101), Movement I, mm. 1–23
Franz Schubert, Symphony in B Major, Op. posth., Movement I, mm. 1–8
W. A. Mozart, *Symphony in G Minor*, K. 550, Movement I, mm. 1–18.
Peter Ilyich Tchaikovsky, *Romeo and Juliet*, Overture-Fantasy, mm. 388–403.
RJ Miller, *The Wilderness Suite*, Movement VIII (*The Balance of Nature*), mm. 58–65
Claude Debussy, *La Mer*, Movement III (*Dialogue du vent et de la mer*), mm. 168–178
A. Ilyinsky, Cradle Song (from "Noure and Anitra" Suite), Op. 13, mm. 1–38
E. A. Mcdowell, The Flow'ret (Forest Idyl No. 1), mm. 1–57

Chapter 5

Genari Karganov, *Arabeske*, mm. 1–24
Carl Bohm, *La Zingana*, mm. 1–9

Sir Arthur Sullivan, *The Lost Chord*, mm. 1–11
Georg Friedrech Händel, "Largo" (from *Xerxes*), mm. 1–15
Jean-Philippe Rameau, Tambourin (from *Les Fêtes d'Hébé*), mm. 1–17
Peter Ilyich Tchaikovsky, *Capriccio Italien*, mm. 1–16
Antonin Dvořák, *Slavonic Dances*, Op. 46 No. 4 in F Major, mm. 9–16
Serge Prokofiev, "Noces de Kijé" from *Lieutenant Kijé*, Movement III, mm. 81–92
Cecil Effinger, *Silver Plume*, mm. 107–114
H. Owen Reed, "Mass," Movement II from *La Fiesta Mexicana*, mm. 68–84
RJ Miller, *The Summit*, mm. 12–30
W. J. Westbrook, *Pleyel's Hymn*, mm. 1–12
Ede Poldini, *In the Wood*, m. 1–10
Franz Schubert, *Marche Militaire*, Op. 51 No. 1, mm. 1–28
Theodore Lack, *Cabaletta*, mm. 1–16
Carl Maria von Weber, *Prayer* (The Hunter), mm. 1–38

Chapter 6

George Gershwin, *Rhapsody in Blue*, mm. 1–5, orchestrated by Ferde Grofé (transposed solo B♭ clarinet part)
Edvard Grieg, *Spring Dance*, Op. 38 No. 5, mm. 1–41
John Field, *Nocturne*, mm. 1–22
J. S. Bach, *Acknowledge me, my Keeper*, mm. 1–12
Edvard Grieg, *Sylph*, Op. 62 No. 1, mm. 58–90
Ludwig van Beethoven, *Prayer*, Op. 48 No. 1, mm. 1–28
Fannie Blumenfeld Zeisler, *Près de L'Eau*, Op. 38 No. 3, mm. 1–17
Joseph Haydn, *Gipsy Rondo*, mm. 1–18
Anton Reicha, *Two Andantes and Adagio (II. Andant pour le Cor Anglais)*, mm. 1–22.
Antonio Rosetti, *Quintet in E flat*, mm. 17–35
Joseph Haydn, *Symphony No. 100 in G Major*, Movement I, mm. 24–31
Franz Schubert, *Symphony in B Flat Major*, Movement I, mm. 118–134
Ludwig van Beethoven, *Symphony No. 9*, Op. 125 *(Finale)*, mm. 343–358
Peter Ilyich Tchaikovsky, *Nutcracker Suite (Dance of the Sugarplum Fairy)*, mm. 4–20
Alfred Reed, *A Sacred Suite*, mm. 1–22 (transposed score)
Norman Dello Joio, *Fantasies on a Theme by Haydn*, mm. 37–54
Vaclav Nelhybel, *Chorale*, mm. 72–86
Vaclav Nelhybel, *Festivo*, mm. 43–63
Renaud de Vilac, *Adeste Fideles*, mm. 1–53
Halfdan Kjerulf, *Berceuse*, mm. 1–45

Chapter 7

RJ Miller, *Ba-Da-Ka-Dup!*, mm. 1–17
RJ Miller, *Akumal* (drum set part), mm. 1–53
RJ Miller, *The Circus is in Town* (marimba part), mm. 72–80
RJ Miller, *Zounds*, mm. 1–22
Alan Hovhaness, *October Mountain*, Op. 135, Movement I, mm. 1–80
RJ Miller, *Yellowstone*, mm. 165–181
RJ Miller, *Cadence #1*, mm. 1–12
RJ Miller, *Your Heart's Desire*, mm. 1–69

Chapter 8

Robert Franz, Wolfgang Müller, *Widmung*, m. 1–8
Traditional, *Auld Lang Syne*, m. 1–8
Dimitri Bortnianski, *Cherubic Hymn*, m. 1–38
Ludwig van Beethoven, *Gloria*, from *Mass in C*, Op. 86, mm. 1–28
RJ Miller, *Good Tidings*, mm. 1–13
Edward MacDowell, *The Brook*, mm. 1–46

Chapter 9

Jules Massenet, *Last Dream of the Virgin*, Prelude, mm. 59–64
Carlos de Mesquita, *Esmeralda* (excerpt), mm. 1–37
Eduard Schütt, *En Berçant*, mm. 1–32

Chapter 10

Traditional, *Greensleeves*, mm. 1–65
Ferninando Sor, *Sonata in C Major for Guitar*, Op. 15b
Antonio Vivaldi, *Concerto in D major*, Movement I
RJ Miller, *Zoot Suit* (guitar part), mm. 1–40
Victor Hollaender, *Canzonetta*, mm. 1–49

Chapter 11

John Antes, *Christ the Lord, the Lord Most Glorious*, mm. 1–9
RJ Miller, *Promises*, from *The Wedding Suite*, mm. 98–105
RJ Miller, *Celebration Waltz*, from *The Wedding Suite*, mm. 73–105
Franz Schubert, *Symphony in C Major*, Movement IV, Op. posth., mm. 15–25
RJ Miller, *Processional*, mm. 5–11
Moritz Moszkowski, *Spanish Dance*, Op. 12 No. 1, mm. 1–19

Chapter 12

John Antes, *Christ the Lord, the Lord Most Glorious*, mm. 1–9
J. S. Bach, *O Haupt voll Blut und Wunden*, mm. 1–13
RJ Miller, *Yuletide*, mm. 111–120
RJ Miller, *Recessional*, mm. 41–49.
Xaver Scharwenka, *Polish Dance*, Op. 3 No. 1, mm. 1–16

Chapter 13

RJ Miller, *Sarah's Song*, mm. 1–8
RJ Miller, *Lullaby for Ethan*, mm. 1–16

Chapter 16

RJ Miller, *Concerto for Unaccompanied Trumpet Trio*, Movement II, mm. 36–40
RJ Miller, *Berceuse*, mm. 13–20
Marie Auguste Durand, *Valse*, Op. 83 No. 1, mm. 223–231

PREFACE

I have always found that a practical approach to orchestration yields the most favorable results. An extensive knowledge of scoring techniques and instrument capabilities, tempered with common sense, empowers one to produce superior orchestrations that will be enjoyed by both the audience and the performers. Creating each part within an orchestration through the "eyes of a player" ensures that every part within the orchestration is playable, logical, and idiomatic of the instrument. In other words, to achieve the best result when writing a trumpet part, think like a trumpet player; when writing a violin part, think like a violinist, and so on. Using this approach will produce an orchestration where all parts work well both individually and as an ensemble. The overall effect is an orchestration that flows well, reads well, performs well, and requires less rehearsal time and less individual practice time. In the professional world, time quite literally is money. The more effort and attention to detail the orchestrator expends during the creation of a work, the lesser the amount of time that could potentially be wasted during the rehearsal or in the studio.

Having begun my professional career as a player, I had numerous occasions to encounter studio parts that were obviously written by orchestrators with little or no understanding of my instrument. On one hand, that was incredibly sad; on the other hand, it was fortuitous as my professional writing career actually began by re-writing these types of parts so that recording sessions could proceed as scheduled. It was this experience of trying to sight-read non-idiomatic, illogical parts (while trying to make them sound plausible) that initiated my quest to create a practical orchestration guide.

Reading about an instrument is no substitute for the practical knowledge gained by playing the instrument or seeking the insight of professional players. For well over four decades I have had the good fortune to have worked and interacted with some of the world's finest musicians, academicians, and studio engineers, and the vast majority of information upon which I base my approach to orchestration is the direct result of conversations with, and the critical input of these learned colleagues. The remainder of the information contained in this text was garnered from listening analytically to performances (both live and recorded), analyzing scores, studying with brilliant academicians, making mistakes, and documenting what worked well and what didn't work well.

Goals

Contemporary Orchestration began as a series of reference graphics consisting of fingering charts, practical ranges and registers, transpositions, sample scoring examples, and other elements I found useful and pertinent. The text has evolved significantly through the course of teaching university orchestration classes and thereby encountering the needs of the beginning orchestrator. It is my hope that this text will provide the orchestrator with salient information and a practical approach to orchestration that will be of value in both the academic and the professional environment.

The main goal of this text is to prepare the student for the "real world" environment of a professional orchestrator. With the intent to impart an understanding and appreciation that ultimately we, as orchestrators, are writing for musicians, not just for instruments, the text fosters the development of textural creativity, tempered with common sense.

Features

Rarely does a professional orchestrator make a living strictly from scoring for traditional orchestras and/or chamber ensembles. It is far more likely that one will need the ability to score for a vast assortment of instruments and ensembles, in a variety of genres, and for performance environments ranging from the concert hall, to the stage, to the recording studio.

Contemporary Orchestration provides:

1) the essential information on instruments and ensembles one would expect to find in a traditional orchestration textbook, combined with information on how to prepare scores and parts for both the concert hall and recording studio environments;
2) how to incorporate and notate world music instruments in a western European orchestral setting;
3) how to incorporate and notate jazz and pop elements,
4) how to score for musical theatre, pedal diagrams and practical glissando combinations for pedal harp, additional instruments, additional ensembles, scoring techniques, genres, international components, professional courtesies, and recording studio considerations. All of which are skills required of an orchestrator in the professional environment;
5) over 800 instrument specific graphics, plus 185 musical examples and score excerpts.
6) suggested scoring exercises at the end of each chapter;
7) "Practical Considerations," an outline of elements to contemplate when scoring for specific instruments, including "What to Avoid";
8) "Building the Score," a step-by-step approach to scoring for specific instrumentation;
9) access to a companion web site containing fingering charts, discussions of additional instruments, discussions of addition ensembles, extensive video content on percussion rudiments, and supplemental suggested scoring exercises.

Organization

The first three chapters of the text address preliminary elements such the overtone series and its relevance to orchestration, instrumental balances and combinations, notation, standards for scores and parts, and problem solving.

As the text progresses through the instrumental families, the chapters address requisite information on each instrument (The Essentials), professional courtesies, considerations and expectations (In the Profession), problem solving and practical scoring approaches (Building the Score), plus scoring examples and suggested exercises are provided.

Following the chapters on instrumental families, orchestral tutti, wind ensemble/concert band tutti, and musical theater (pit orchestra) scoring is addressed. Practical guidelines for scoring each ensemble are presented (Practical Considerations), followed by problem solving and practical scoring approaches (Building the Score), and scoring examples and suggested exercises are provided.

The text culminates with quick reference guides and suggestions for instrument substitution, listening and analysis, and parting thoughts (including "Seven Traits of a Great Orchestrator").

To the Instructor

The instructor may consider teaching from this text using a traditional, "teacher-centered" approach, a more contemporary "learner-centered" approach, or a hybrid of these two approaches. No matter the chosen approach, the culture should be cooperative, collaborative, and supportive. Being a good orchestrator is a combination of orchestration skills and the sum of all of one's musical experiences. As such, active student participation in the learning process is encouraged.

I also encourage instructors to add their personal experiences, both as performers and orchestrators, to the presentation of this material. A collaborative effort (between author and instructor) results in a more balanced, realistic, and personal learning experience for the student.

For every preference, suggestion, and caution I've expressed in this text one can find a published example to the contrary. It is not my intent to imply that the methods and techniques presented in this text are the only correct ones. They are not. Presented herein are the approaches I have found to be the most practical, most productive, most concise, and most logical during a professional career spanning more than four decades.

Some reviewers of this text have suggested that I provide examples of poorly scored works to demonstrate the difference between those and well-scored works. I find this a valid suggestion and I have often used this approach in my classroom lectures. However, it simply seemed an unwieldy inclusion for this text. Additionally, there's always the possible that including such examples would lend a tacit credence to these works.

To the Student

Students are encouraged to transfer knowledge from their current musical understanding and performance experiences to the orchestration environment. When participating in a performance ensemble, one is literally inside the orchestra. Drawing upon that broad experience while studying the specifics presented in this text will give one a more comprehensive perspective on the orchestration process.

Students should strive to "write through the eyes of a player." For example, when one orchestrates for brass, the parts should lie on the instruments so idiomatically that the musicians assume that the orchestrator is a brass player. By following the guidelines presented in this text, one will embark upon this journey. Accepting and honestly evaluating the critical feedback from one's players will ensure that one stays on course.

Companion Website: www.routledge.com/cw/miller

It is impossible to cover everything one should know about orchestration in the scope of a few hundred pages. Therefore, supplemental information can be found on the companion website. Addition items include:

- fingering charts for many of the instruments discussed in the text;
- discussions of additional instruments, both common and archaic (with fingering charts included); and
- discussions of addition ensembles, and extensive video content on percussion rudiments.

Acknowledgments

I would be remiss if I did not acknowledge the exceptional individuals who contributed their time and personal expertise to aid my understanding of instruments and orchestration. My most sincere thanks to: (Woodwinds:) Sonny Stitt, Robert F. Rebholz, Jeff Kashiwa, Tim Weisberg, Lew Tabackin, Jane Lyman, Holly Cornik, Philip Tarlton, Dr. Nancy Andrew, Dr. Gregory Dufford, Prof. Mark Harris, (Brass:) Clark Terry, Don Ellis, Prof. Ron Miles, Rich Matteson, Jerry Hey, Harvey Phillips, Dr. Glen Fifield, Dr. Michael Hengst, Dr. Hoyt Andres, Daniel Kuehn, Dr. Walter Barr, Michael Allen, (Percussion:) Louie Bellson, Joe Morello, Steve Reid, Anatoly Ivanov, Larry Thompson, Gary Sosias, Ty Burhoe, Prof. Mark Foster, (Piano:) Eric Gunnison, Inga Dzektser, Dr. Fernanda Nieto-Pulido, Dr. Tamara Goldstein, Peter Friesen, (Voices:) Pearl Bailey, Ella Fitzgerald, Dr. William C. Ramsey, Dr. MeeAe Nam, Prof. M. B. Krueger, (Harp:) Lysa Rytting, Lisa Coffey, Caryl Thomas, (Strings:) Ron Bland, Gigori Sedukh, Eugenia Alikhanova, Tatyana Kokhanovskaya, Olga Ogranovich, Dr. Gregory Walker, Cedra Kuehn, (Guitar:) Tom Doenges, Russ Freeman, Randy Chavez, Prof. Alex Komodore, (MIDI, Samplers & Synthsizers:) Tom Capek, (Studio Production:) Jeff Shuey, Kevin Clock, Steve Avadis, Victor Dinov, Glen Neivaur, (Orchestration, Arranging, Composition, and Theory:) Don Sebesky, Toshiko Akiyoshi, Phil Wilson, Dave Grusin, Dr. Alma Dittmer, Dr. Louis Gonzales, Dr. Larry Smith, Prof. Cherise Leiter, Dr. David Farrell, and Dr. Fred Hess. I wish I could thank Count Basie for his response to my questions, but when I met him I was so star-struck that all I could manage to say was, "Thank you." He simply smiled at me from his wheelchair and said, "You're very welcome." . . . an opportunity missed.

I would also like to thank the following friends for their learned input, assistance, encouragement, support and proofreading during creation of this text: Dr. Joice Gibson, Dr. Trudi Wright, Prof. Katie Flannery, Prof. Michael Christoph, Dr. Lisa Cook, Dr. Larry Worster, Dr. Michael J. Kornelsen.

Finally, this text would not exist without the understanding, support, constant proofreading, and critical input of my brilliant and beautiful wife, Heidi. She is both the love of my life and the most valuable contributor to this work. I would also like to extend my thanks and apologies to my sons, Q. and Mason, for allowing me to work on this text when I should have been in the backyard playing catch.

—RJ Miller

1

PRELIMINARY CONSIDERATIONS

An intimate understanding of the potential, the complexities and the response to stimuli of one's chosen medium is the foundation of artistic expression. For those whose art is music, the chosen medium of expression is sound. As such, an awareness of the characteristics of sound affords one the opportunity to manipulate these attributes to one's benefit. A skilled orchestrator is mindful of the acoustical implications of every note in the score.

The Physics of Sound

Acoustics is the science of sound and acoustical physics is the mathematical laws governing the properties, production and manipulation of sound. As such, acoustical physics is the scientific basis of music. It both governs and explains the fundamental elements of music, namely:

1. The nature of musical sound.
2. The overtone series.
3. The construction and function of intervals.
4. The physical properties of the sound-producing media.

A musical sound is generated by the vibration of an elastic body (something capable of movement), such as a stretched string (string family, harp, selected keyboard instruments), a metal bar or disk (pitched percussion, tuning fork), or an enclosed column of air (wind instruments). A simple vibration is characterized by its frequency (the number of vibrations, or cycles per second, expressed as hertz (Hz)) and its amplitude (the intensity of its vibration, i.e. the height and depth of cycle, as in the movement of a plucked string). These two characteristics are directly related to two basic properties of the resulting sound: pitch and amplitude.

The greater the frequency, the higher the pitch.
The greater the amplitude, the louder the sound.

Utilizing acoustical properties advantageous to the overall resonance of one's work, while avoiding acoustical properties detrimental to the work, is the goal of every skilled composer, orchestrator and arranger. An intimate understanding of these acoustical properties is critical to achieving that goal.

The Overtone Series

An overtone is an acoustic effect produced by a vibration (tone). Every tone generates a series of ascending, acoustically generated sympathetic vibrations. To the untrained ear, these sympathetic vibrations are not heard distinctly because their intensity (amplitude) is much less than that of the fundamental. Nevertheless, they are extremely important, since they account for the different tone colors (timbre) produced when the same pitch is played on different instruments. (*Note*: Trained musicians have little difficulty hearing at least some of these overtones.)

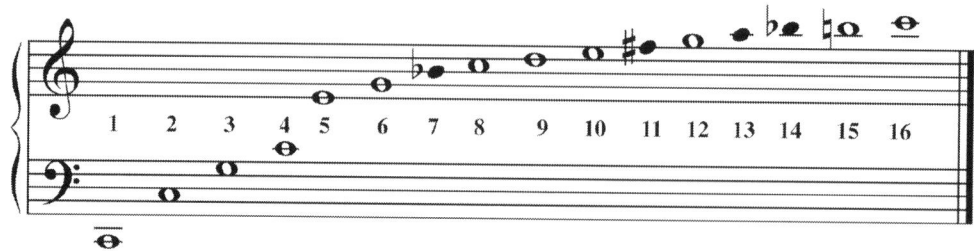

The lowest tone represented above is the fundamental (or first partial). This is the frequency identified by the ear as the pitch of the musical tone. The frequencies of the overtones (upper partials) are multiples of the frequency of the fundamental. This mathematical relationship is governed by specific laws of acoustical physics (some of which were discovered by the Greek philosopher and mathematician Pythagoras), and most commonly expressed as ratios. The intervallic relationships between partials are exactly the same for any given fundamental.

For a given tone, with a frequency of 440 Hz, the frequency of the tone one octave higher in pitch is 880 Hz. Thus, the ratio of these two tones constituting an interval of an octave is 2:1. The ratio of a given interval is calculated based upon the relationship of the partials at the first occurrence of the interval in the overtone series. Calculating the applicable intervallic relationships contained within a major scale would result in the following set of ratios:

The first occurrence of the interval of a major 2nd resulting in the second note of the ascending major scale is between partials 8 and 9. Since the ratio is representing an increase in frequency it is expressed as 9:8.

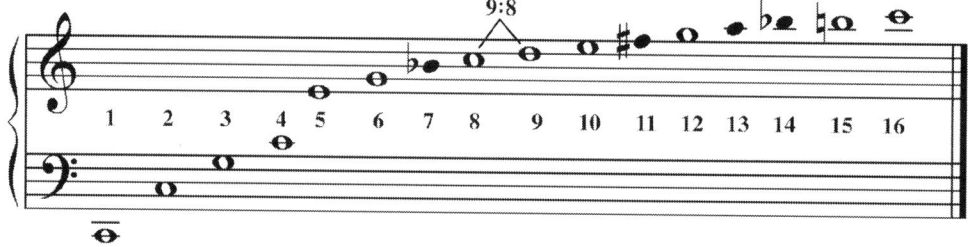

The first occurrence of the interval of a major 3rd is between partials 4 and 5, represented by the ratio 5:4.

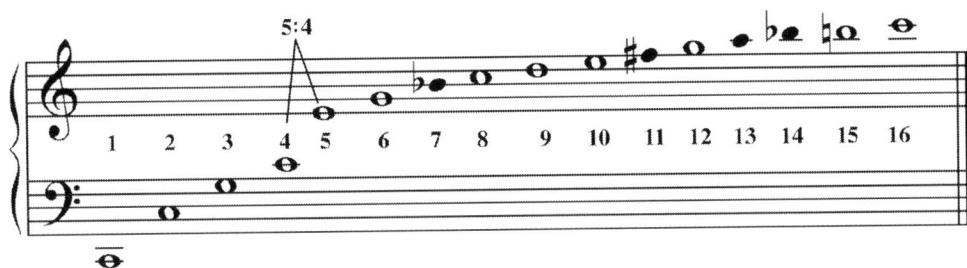

The first occurrence of the interval of a perfect 4th is between partials 3 and 4, represented by the ratio 4:3.

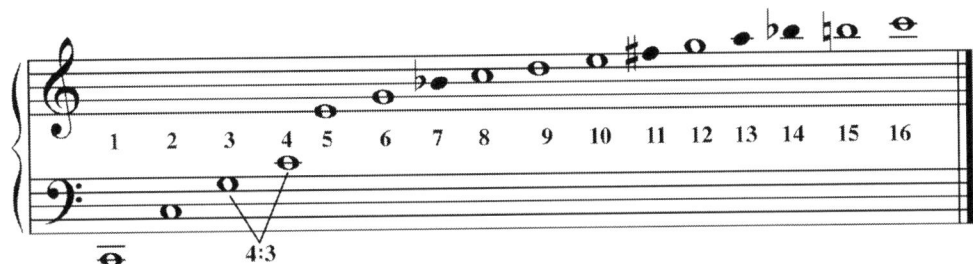

The first occurrence of the interval of a perfect 5th is between partials 2 and 3, represented by the ratio 3:2.

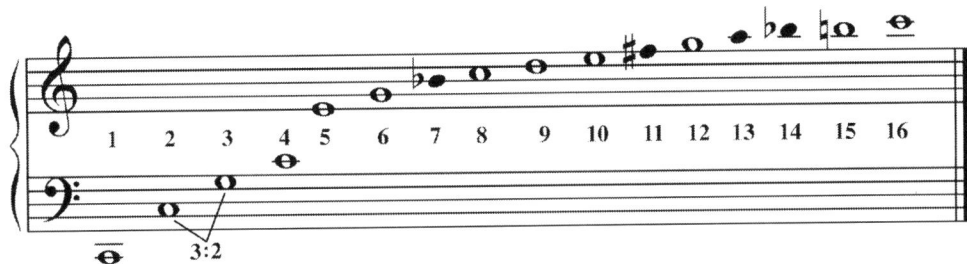

The first occurrence of the interval of a major 6th is between partials 3 and 5, represented by the ratio 5:3.

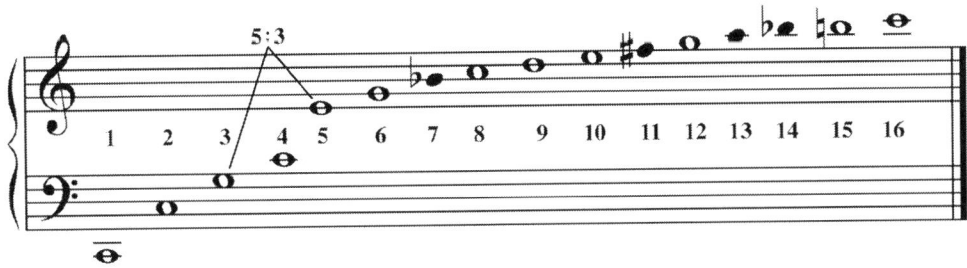

The first occurrence of the interval of a major 7th resulting in the seventh note of the ascending major scale is between partials 8 and 15, represented by the ratio 15:8. *Note*: There are occurrences of a major 7th between lower partials in the overtone series, such as between partials 6 and 11, and between partials 7 and 13. However (as implied by the black-note notation), these intervals are quite out-of-tune and do not result in the 7th degree of the ascending major scale.

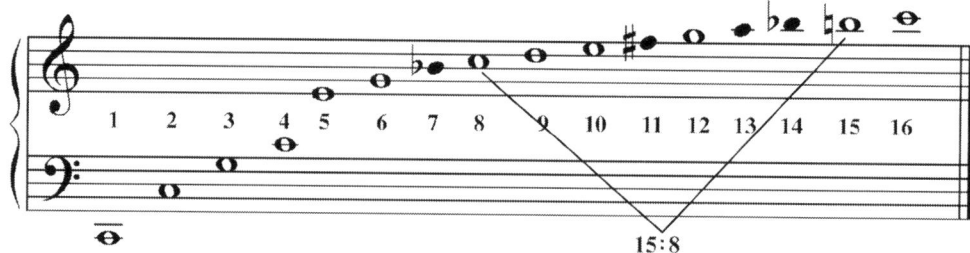

The first occurrence of the interval of a perfect octave is between partials 1 and 2, represented by the ratio 2:1.

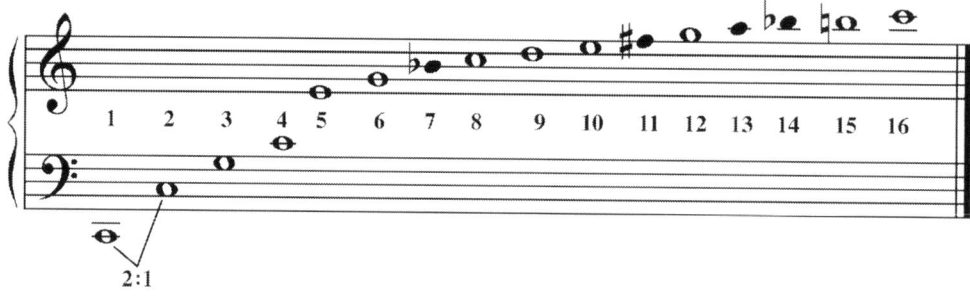

The scoring of a dominant 7th chord requires the inclusion of a minor 7th. The first occurrence of the interval of a minor 7th is between partials 4 and 7, represented by the ratio 7:4.

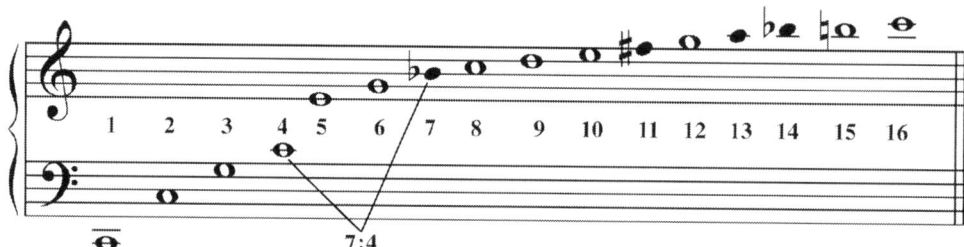

These ratios apply directly to the method by which instruments produce different pitches (the length of a string, the position of finger holes, the length of the pipe, etc.). The frequency of a pitch is in inverse proportion to the length of the medium producing the sound. If a vibrating string producing the pitch c' is 1 foot in length, the length of the string necessary to produce c" (ratio 2:1) would be 6 inches, and length of the string necessary for the perfect 5th (3:2) would be 4 inches.

Since, as previously stated, the intervallic relationships between partials are identical for any given fundamental, one might well wonder how the overtone series contributes to the production of different instrumental timbres. Musical instruments actually produce a "composite sound" resulting from the simultaneous sounding of multiple partials at varied amplitudes. The shape, construction, vibrating medium, etc. of the instrument cause certain partials to be accentuated or suppressed. The timbre of an instrument is the result of these varied amplitudes of the generated partials.

PRELIMINARY CONSIDERATIONS 5

The following is a sample of the overtone spectrum (the relative strength of partials) generated by various instruments playing an A–440 at *mf*.

Flute:

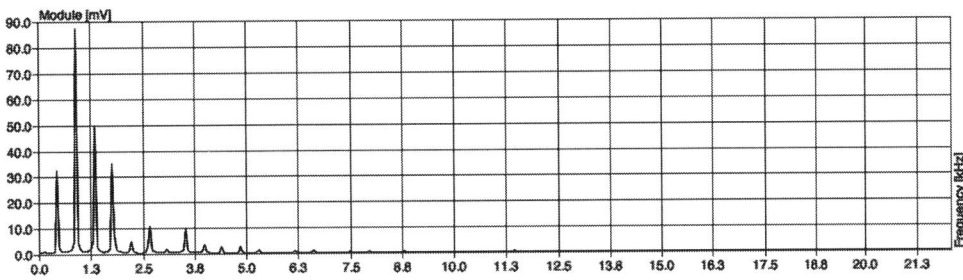

Oboe:

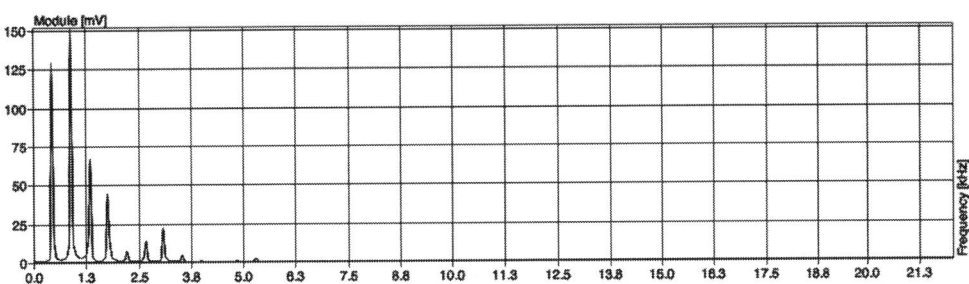

B♭ Clarinet:

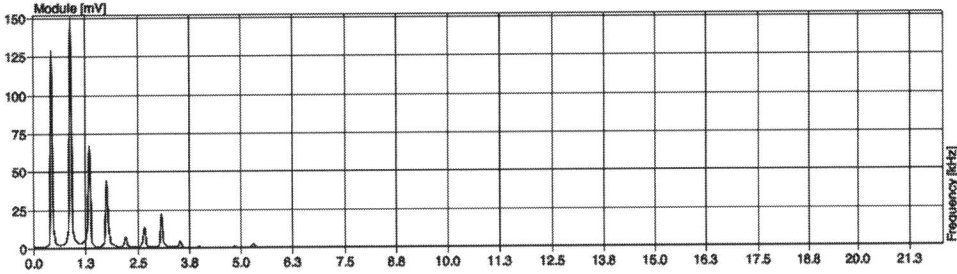

Horn:

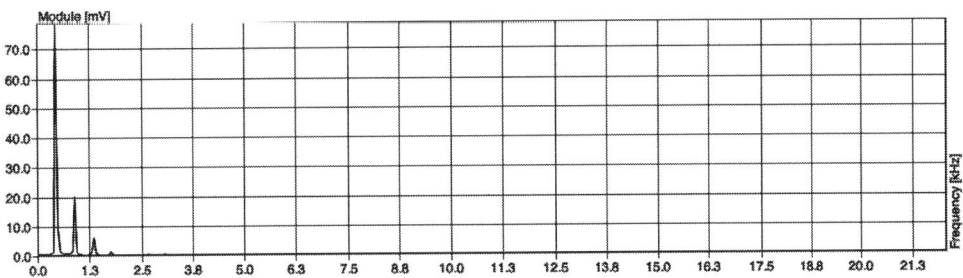

B♭ Trumpet:

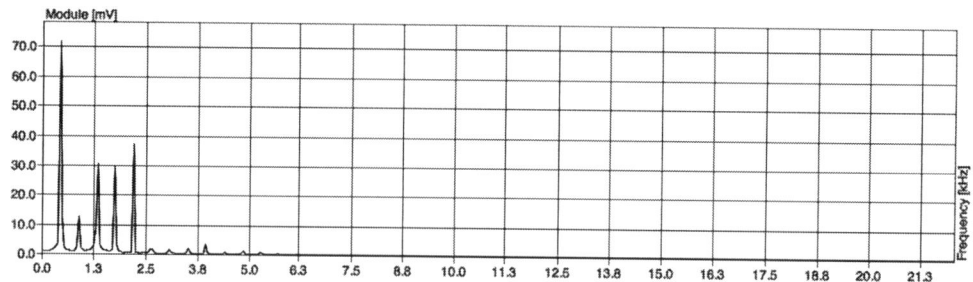

Combining instruments will produce a new timbre unlike that of any singular instrument. When combining instruments of different timbres, the intensities of the generated partials are merged, resulting in a new, combined instrumental timbre. The following is the overtone spectrum (the relative strength of partials) generated by the combined texture of a flute and oboe, both playing an A–440 at ***mf***.

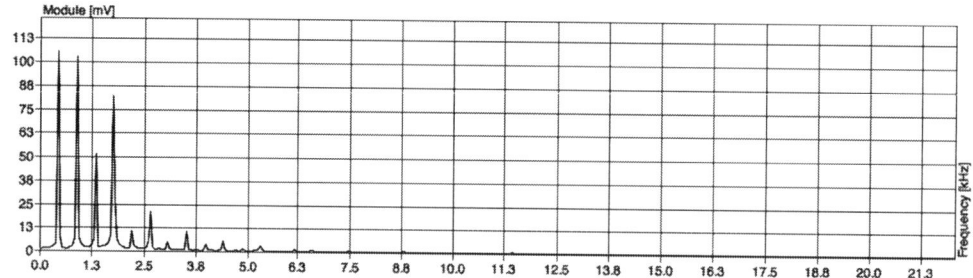

(A new timbre generated by the resultant merged strength of partials.)

Implied Fundamental

Just as for any generated tone a series of sympathetic vibrations are generated above the given pitch, for any generated interval, a series of sympathetic vibrations are generated below until they reach the implied fundamental frequency.

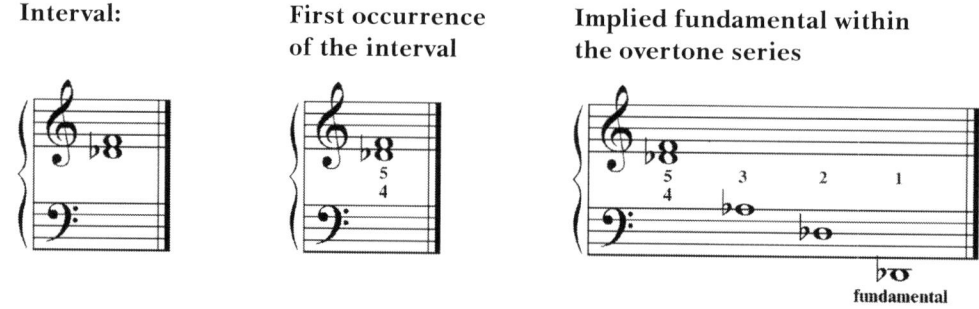

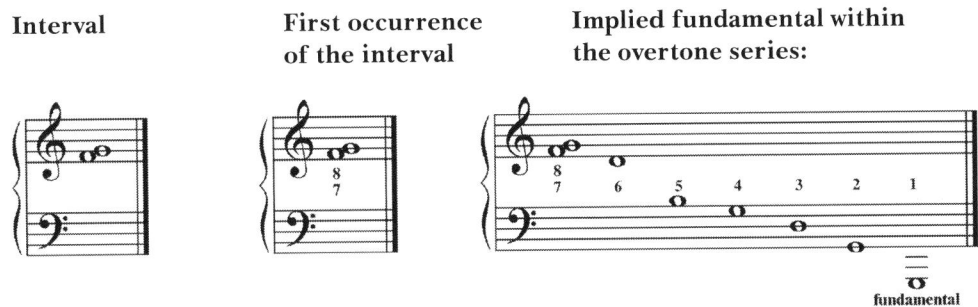

The human ear can perceive an approximate frequency range of 20 Hz to 20,000 Hz. Pitches above 20 kHz simply are not perceivable by the human ear (or mind). Pitches below 20 Hz begin to be perceived as individual pulses or beats. (*Point of reference*: The lowest A on the piano is 27.5 Hz and the highest C is 4186.01 Hz.) This perception of sound is one of the key considerations when voicing chords within a work. When a scored interval implies a fundamental frequency below the perceptional hearing range of the human ear (brain), the voicing lacks clarity and sounds "muddy." By insuring that all voicing imply a fundamental within the perceptional hearing range of the human ear (brain), one's work is aided by the naturally occurring acoustics. The end result is not only clarity in the work, but also a work that sounds fuller and richer due to the enhancement of these naturally occurring acoustics.

Voicing Chords

By taking the lowest voiced interval in a given chord and calculating the implied fundamental, one can insure that the voicings within one's work generate implied fundamentals within the perceptible hearing range.

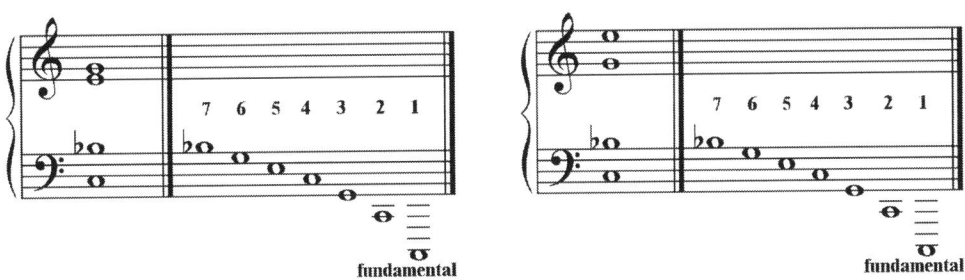

Deleting or Adding Chord Elements

The more dominant (or reinforced) a sympathetic frequency is in the overtone series, the less it is needed in the voicing of the chord. By referencing the overtone series implied by a chord (in both directions), the orchestrator/arranger can determine which chord elements can best be deleted.

When scoring a four-note chord (such as a C7 chord) for four voices in close harmony, all four chord-members may be used. (*Note*: The implied fundamental is well within the perceptional hearing range.)

When scoring the same C7 chord for three voices, a chord-member must be deleted. The 3rd of the chord is necessary for the recognition of major or minor tonality, and the 7th is necessary for the recognition of the dominant 7th (and for the voice-leading of the cadence). The 5th of the chord is reinforced throughout the overtone series and will be generated sympathetically. Retaining the root of the chord helps solidify the implied fundamental.

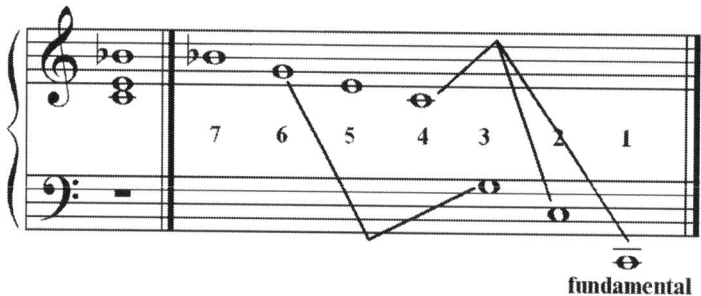

When scoring the same C7 chord for two voices, two chord-members must be deleted. The 3rd of the chord is necessary for the recognition of major or minor tonality, and the 7th is necessary for the recognition of the dominant 7th (and for the voice-leading of the cadence). The 5th of a chord is always one's first (and most preferable) choice and deleting the root of the chord is the second most preferable choice. Both the root and the 5th of the chord are reinforced throughout the overtone series and will be generated sympathetically. By utilizing the strength of acoustically generated overtones it is possible to voice or at least imply any basic chord with as few as two notes.

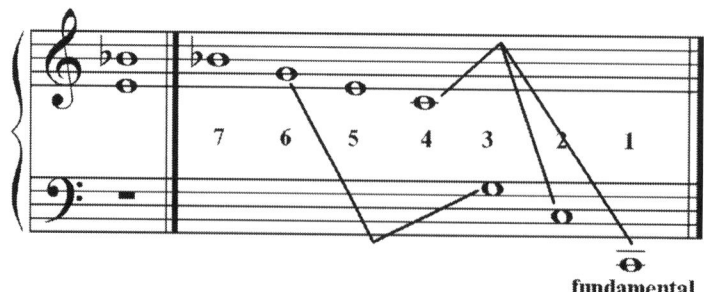

In the equal temperament musical world a case could be made that the interval F♭ (the enharmonic spelling of E♮) to B♭ could result in an implied fundamental of G♭. This is a technically valid argument. However, the lower in the overtone series an interval occurs, the stronger the implication of the fundamental. The first occurrence of the F♭ to B♭ interval in the G♭ overtone series is between partials 7 and 10. The first occurrence of the E♮ to B♭ interval in the C overtone series is between partials 5 and 7. As such, the implication of a C fundamental would be stronger than the implication of a G♭ fundamental.

When adding notes to a chord, one follows a similar process. One should add notes that are predominate within the overtone series, with the exception of doubling the 3rd of the chord. In order of preference, one should first double the root, then the 5th and finally the 7th. Adding non-chord notes and octave reinforcements of the melody will be addressed later in this text.

Instrumental Balances

The art of orchestration demands a beautiful and well-balanced distribution of chords forming the harmonic texture. Moreover, transparence, accuracy and purity in the movement of each part are essential conditions if satisfactory resonance is to be obtained.

(Nikolay Rimsky-Korsakov, *Principles of Orchestration*)

At soft dynamic levels relatively few balance problems exist between instruments. However, as the dynamic level increases, certain instruments should be doubled (even tripled) to obtain a satisfactory balance within the ensemble.

Approximate Instrumental Balances at Louder Dynamic Levels

2 flutes (unison)	balances with 1 clarinet
2 flutes (unison)	balances with 1 oboe
2 flutes (unison in the high register)	balances with 1 trumpet
2 flutes (unison in the high register)	balances with 1 trombone
3 flutes (unison)	balances with 1 horn
2 clarinets (unison)	balances with 1 horn
2 oboes (unison)	balances with 1 horn
2 bassoons (unison)	balances with 1 horn
2 horns (unison)	balances with 1 trumpet
2 horns (unison)	balances with 1 trombone
2 horns (unison)	balances with 1 tuba
4 horns (unison)	balances with 1 bass trombone (low register)
1 trumpet	balances with 1 trombone
1 trumpet	balances with 1 tuba
2 trumpets	balances with 1 bass trombone (low register)
2 trombones	balances with 1 bass trombone (low register)
2 tubas	balances with 1 bass trombone (low register)
2 flutes (unison in the high register)	balances with 1 string section (1st violins, 2nd violins, viols)
2 bassoons (unison)	balances with 1 string section (celli, basses)
1 trumpet	balances with 1 string section (1st violins, 2nd violins, viols)
1 trombone	balances with 1 string section (1st violins, 2nd violins, viols)
2 horns	balances with 1 string section (1st/2nd violins, viols, celli)
1 bass trombone (low register)	balances with 2 low string sections (celli and basses)
1 tuba	balances with 1 low string section (celli, basses)

At loud dynamic levels, the two loudest instruments in the ensemble are the bass trombone (in the low register) and the piccolo (in the high register).

At a loud dynamic level, sustained passages will overpower staccato parts. Balance between simultaneously occurring sustained and staccato parts can be achieved by marking the sustained parts two, possibly three dynamic levels below that of the staccato parts.

There are a few exceptions, but generally it is difficult, if not impossible for any wind instrument to play softly in the extreme altissimo register.

When orchestrating tutti sections, scoring a complete, well-balanced harmony within each instrumental family (woodwind, brass, strings) has a tendency to produce a satisfactory overall balance within the combined ensemble.

When scoring crescendi and decrescendi, ensemble balances should be calculated based upon the loudest dynamic level.

Instrumental Combinations

As earlier stated, combining instruments of different timbres, the generated overtones are merged resulting in a new combined instrumental timbre. However, combining two instruments of like timbre (2 flutes, 2 oboes, 2 trumpets, etc.) in unison results in a thicker and more powerful sound. Be aware that this combined sound is less capable of expressiveness than that of a singular instrument.

Combining Woodwinds

Combining flute and oboe (in unison) results in a timbre more resonant than the flute timbre and less nasal than that of the oboe. At a soft dynamic, the flute timbre will be slightly more dominant in the low register, while the oboe timbre will be slightly more dominant in the high register.

Combining flute with clarinet (in the middle registers) results in a timbre fuller and rounder than that of the flute, and darker than that of clarinet (due to the accentuated lower harmonics generated by the flute). However, the clarinet timbre will dominate the flute in the high register.

Combining oboe with clarinet produces a uniquely beautiful timbre that seems to accentuate the best qualities of both instruments. Combining clarinet (in unison) with bassoon adds a fullness and richness to the bassoon timbre. However, the bassoon timbre will dominate the clarinet timbre in the clarinet's weak register (throat tones).

Combining Brass

In general, when combining brass instruments, the timbre of a cylindrical instrument (trumpet, trombone, bass trombone) will dominate the timbre of a conical instrument (cornet, horn, tuba).

Combining instruments of like construction (cylindrical or conical) usually requires the doubling to be at the octave rather than in unison, due to the limited overlapping ranges. Combining trumpets with trombones (at the octave) can produce a powerful, majestic sound. Combining horns with tuba (again, at the octave) can produce a mellow, rounded timbre, often haunting, melancholy or thought provoking. Combining cornet with horns can produce a soaring, yet lyrical timbre.

Combining Strings

Combining 1st and 2nd violins results in an increase of richness, resonance and power. However, this combination produces no alteration to the overall timbre.

Combining violins with viols will, once again, result in an increase of richness, resonance and power of sound. However, there will be little noticeable change of color, as the timbre of the violins will dominate the timbre of the viols.

Combining viols with celli produces a rich and full resonance, along with a noticeable increase in presence and power. While the viola timbre is still quite audible, the cello timbre will be the dominant timbre.

Combining violins in unison with celli produces a timbre similar to that of the viols–celli combination. Due to the differences of registers required for this combination to play a unison line (violins in the low register, celli in the high register), the cello timbre will, once again, be the dominant timbre.

While octave doubling of the string bass results in a full and reinforced foundation, unison doubling of the string bass with other members of the string family is neither practical, nor desirable.

Combining Woodwinds with Brass

Combining reeds with brass can produce different effects, depending upon the dynamic level. When reeds are combined with brass at identical dynamic levels, the reeds will soften any brashness of the brass. When soft brass are combined with loud reeds, the brass will add strength and reinforce the color of the reeds.

In general, the timbre of woodwind instruments blends well with that of the brass family. In woodwind–brass combinations, the brass timbre will be predominant, with the woodwind timbre softening and sweetening the color of the brass.

Doubling is accomplished between instruments with common or overlapping registers:

- Trumpet doubled with flute.
- Trumpet doubled with oboe.
- Trumpet doubled with English horn.
- Trumpet doubled with clarinet.
- Horn doubled with clarinet.
- Horn doubled with English horn.
- Horn doubled with bass clarinet.
- Horn doubled with bassoon.
- Trombone doubled with English horn.
- Trombone doubled with bass clarinet.
- Trombone doubled with bassoon.
- Tuba doubled with bassoon.
- Tuba doubled with contrabassoon.

Combining Woodwinds with Strings

The timbre of woodwind instruments blends wonderfully with that of the string family. In woodwind–string combinations, the woodwind timbre causes the string timbre to become more resonant, while the string timbre softens the quality of the woodwinds.

Doubling is best accomplished between instruments with common or overlapping registers:

- Violins doubled with flute.
- Violins doubled with oboe.
- Violins doubled with clarinet.
- Viols doubled with clarinet.
- Viols doubled with English horn.
- Viols doubled with bassoon.
- Celli doubled with clarinet.
- Celli doubled with bass clarinet.
- Celli doubled with bassoon.
- Basses doubled with bass clarinet.
- Basses doubled with bassoon.
- Basses doubled with contrabassoon.

Combining Brass with Strings

The timbres of the brass and string families are so dissimilar that (with one notable exception) the combination does not result in a blended sound. Even when combined, the instruments are perceived as separate, simultaneously occurring timbres. This is not to imply that the combination of brass and strings is not effective, simply that one family has little effect on the timbre of the other. The above-mentioned exception is the combination of horn with celli, which produces a smooth and blended timbre.

Doubling is best accomplished between instruments with common or overlapping registers:

- Trumpet doubled with violins.
- Horns doubled with viols.
- Trombones doubled with celli.
- Tuba doubled with basses.

Combining Woodwinds, Brass and Strings

Though the timbres of the brass and strings families have little effect upon each other, adding woodwinds to the mix imparts a fuller resonance and a more even blend to the ensemble.

Doubling is best accomplished between instruments with common or overlapping registers:

- Violins doubled with flute and trumpet.
- Violins doubled with oboe and trumpet.
- Violins doubled with clarinet and trumpet.
- Viols doubled with clarinet and horn.
- Viols doubled with English horn and horn.
- Viols doubled with bassoon and horn.
- Celli doubled with clarinet and horn.
- Celli doubled with bass clarinet and trombone.
- Celli doubled with bassoon and trombone.
- Basses doubled with bass clarinet and tuba.
- Basses doubled with bassoon and tuba.
- Basses doubled with contrabassoon and tuba.

Which timbre will be the dominant timbre in these combinations is dependent upon the number of instruments employed and the instrumental balances therein (see "Instrumental Balances" above).

2
SCORES, PARTS AND NOTATION

Score Preparation

There is no definitive set of rules governing the layout of the conductor's score, with each publisher having its own individual publication guidelines. However, there are specific, common elements expected from every score. The following parameters serve as a practical guide to the expected content, and all listed elements are compatible with the parameters suggested by the Major Orchestras Librarians' Association.

Cover Page

- Designation of concert, transposed, or condensed score.
- The title of the composition (plus subtitle, if any).
- The type of ensemble.
- The name of the composer.
- The name of the orchestrator, arranger, or transcriber (if any).
- The name of the lyricist (if any).
- Statement of copyright and publisher information.

Transposed Score

Lyric Pieces Suite
for Flute Orchestra

Composed by
Edvard Grieg

Adapted and Orchestrated by
RJ Miller

Copyright © MMVI by Appassionata Music

SCORES, PARTS AND NOTATION 15

Inside Cover Page

- Explanations.
- Special instructions.
- Interpretation of special signs or symbols.
- Detailed information about the instruments to be used (e.g. list of percussion).
- Translation of text (if applicable).

Lyric Pieces Suite
for Flute Orchestra

Instrumentation:

- (1) 1st Piccolo
- (1) 2nd Piccolo
- (1) 3rd Piccolo
- (8) 1st C Flute
- (8) 2nd C Flute
- (8) 3rd C Flute
- (8) 4th C Flute
- (8) 1st Alto Flute (in G)
- (8) 2nd Alto Flute (in G)
- (8) 1st Bass Flute
- (8) 2nd Bass Flute
- (4) Contra Alto Flute (in G)
- (4) Contrabass Flute

Instrumentation List

Includes doublings, complete percussion listing & assignments (if applicable)

Instructions:

Performance instructions, Translation of text (if applicable), other pertinent information

Blah, blah.

16 SCORES, PARTS AND NOTATION

First Page of Music

- *Always* a "right-hand" page.
- All information from the cover page, plus first system of music.
- Title should be at the top margin (centered).
- Composer name (above music, aligned to right margin).
- Orchestrator, arranger, transcriber (as applicable) below composer.
- System is indented (indented from left margin).
- All instruments with full instrument names, in score order.
- Choirs (families) are connected by brackets.
- All instrumental doubles are listed.
- Copyright notice.

SCORES, PARTS AND NOTATION

17

Subsequent Pages

- Same systems as on first page of music.
- Abbreviated instrument names.
- Not indented.
- Name of composition.
- Page numbers.
- While not mandatory, one may delete staves of tacet instruments.
- Rehearsal letters/numbers.
- Measure numbers.
- Double bars (as needed).

SCORES, PARTS AND NOTATION

Last Page of Score

- Measures in the last system of the work must be proportional to the measures in the rest of the score. *Never* allow one or two measures to encompass the entire width of the page. *Always* adjust the right margin to provide proportional measures.

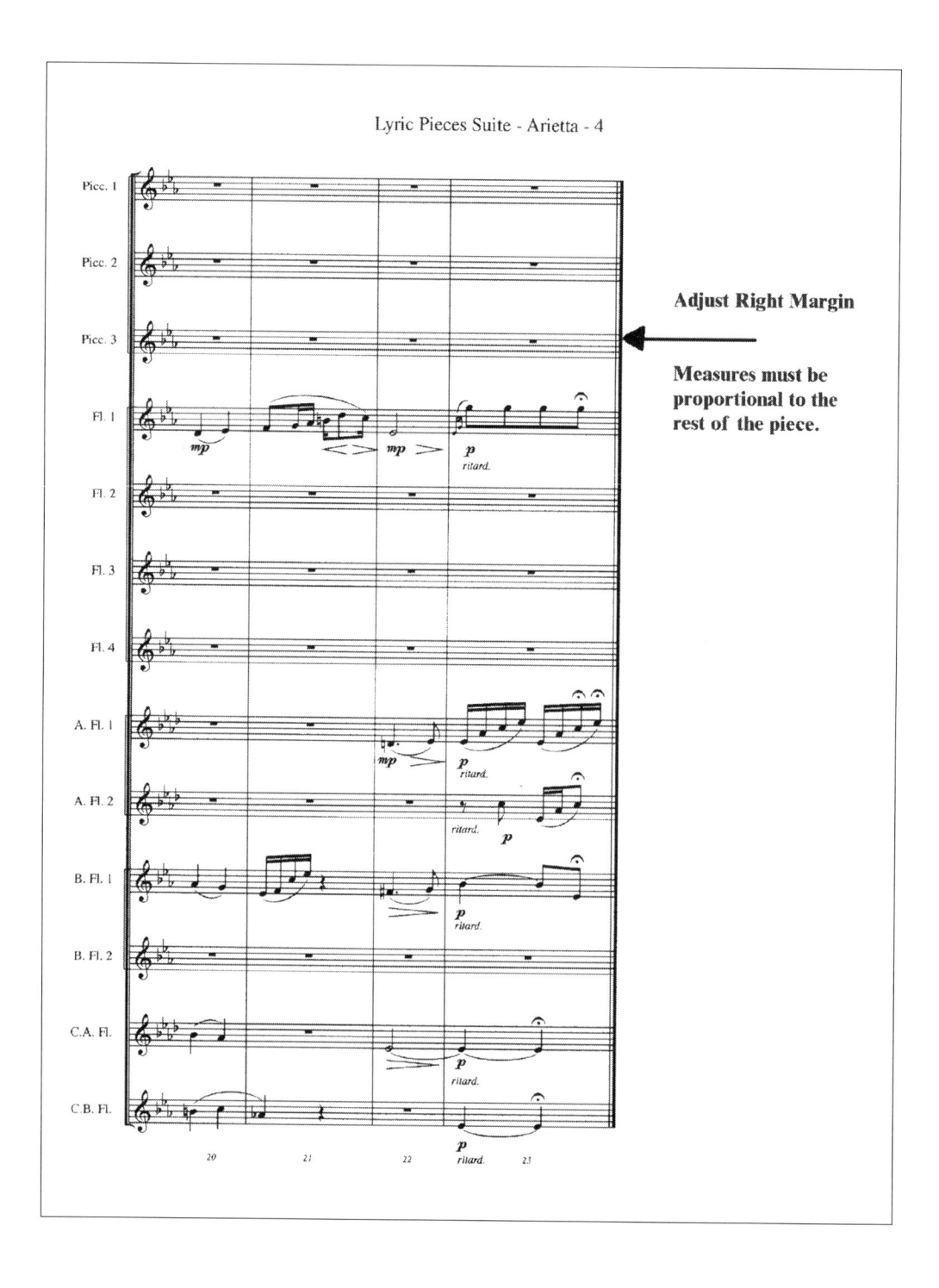

Measure Numbers and Rehearsal Marks in the Score

Though not a "traditional" practice, providing measure numbers under every measure in the score and using measure numbers for rehearsal marks (instead of the "traditional" letter rehearsal marks) provides a great service to the conductor, accommodating concise and succinct rehearsals. This system is also invaluable in recording-studio sessions where wasted time is wasted money.

Some publishers place rehearsal marks in the score and parts at ten-measure intervals (some even at five-measure intervals). While this is certainly a functional approach, a more musically useful and practical method is to place rehearsal marks (with double bars) at significant musical events, e.g. at the end of melodic phrases, key changes, significant tempo changes, solo sections, etc. Since rehearsals focus on these musical events, this approach better supports the manner in which rehearsals are generally conducted.

Score Order

The term "score order" refers to the organization of instruments, as they are distributed from top of the page to the bottom of the page in the conductor's score. As with the elements discussed under score preparation, there is no definitive set of rules governing the exact order of appearance of the instruments, with each publisher, composer, arranger and orchestrator having slightly different approaches. Generally, the instruments are divided into families (woodwinds, brass, percussion, strings) and listed with the instruments of highest register at the top of the applicable family, descending to the instruments of lowest register at the bottom. The following score order serves as a practical guide to the acceptable configurations.

Score Order of Instrumental Families
- Woodwinds
- Brass
- Percussion
- Auxiliary instruments
- Vocalists
- Strings

Choir w/piano
- Sopranos
- Altos
- Tenors
- Basses
- Piano/accomp. instruments

String Quartet
- Violin 1
- Violin 2
- Viola
- Violoncello

Piano Trio
- Violin
- Violoncello
- Piano

Wind Quintet
- Flute
- Oboe
- Clarinet
- Horn
- Bassoon

Brass Quintet
- Trumpet 1
- Trumpet 2
- Horn
- Trombone
- Tuba

Brass Sextet
- Trumpet 1
- Trumpet 2
- Horn
- Trombone
- Euphonium
- Tuba

Concert Band/Wind Ensemble
- Flutes
- Oboes
- Bassoons
- Clarinets
- Saxophones
- Cornets
- Trumpets
- Horns
- Trombones
- Euphoniums (baritones)
- Tubas
- Timpani
- Percussion

Jazz Ensemble
- Voices/solo instrument
- Saxophones (w/doubles)
- Trumpets (w/doubles)
- Trombones
- Piano/keyboards
- Guitar
- Bass
- Trap Set (drum set)
- Percussion/auxiliary instruments

Orchestra
- Flutes
- Oboes
- Clarinets
- Bassoons
- Horns
- Trumpets
- Trombones
- Tuba
- Timpani
- Percussion
- Piano
- Harp
  - Other instruments
  - Solo instrument
  - Voices
- Violins 1
- Violins 2
- Viols
- Violoncelli
- Contrabass

Concert, Transposed and Condensed Scores

The conductor's score is usually prepared in one of three formats. The usage, purpose and publisher's dictate determine the format of choice.

Concert Score

A concert score is the full score, containing most of the instruments of the ensemble displayed in concert pitch. Instruments that are transposed at the octave (piccolo, bass flute, contrabassoon, xylophone, double bass) or at two octaves (glockenspiel, crotales) are displayed in their transposed form in concert scores to eliminate the need of excessive ledger lines or octavo markings. Concert scores are the preferred format for composers, orchestrators and arrangers, and is the standard for recording sessions. By displaying all instruments in concert pitch, the harmonic content is more easily determined, and thereby easier and quicker to troubleshoot. Some publishers refer to this type of score as a "Score in C." While "Concert Score" remains the term most commonly used in the industry, both terms refer to the same type of score, and both terms are considered acceptable.

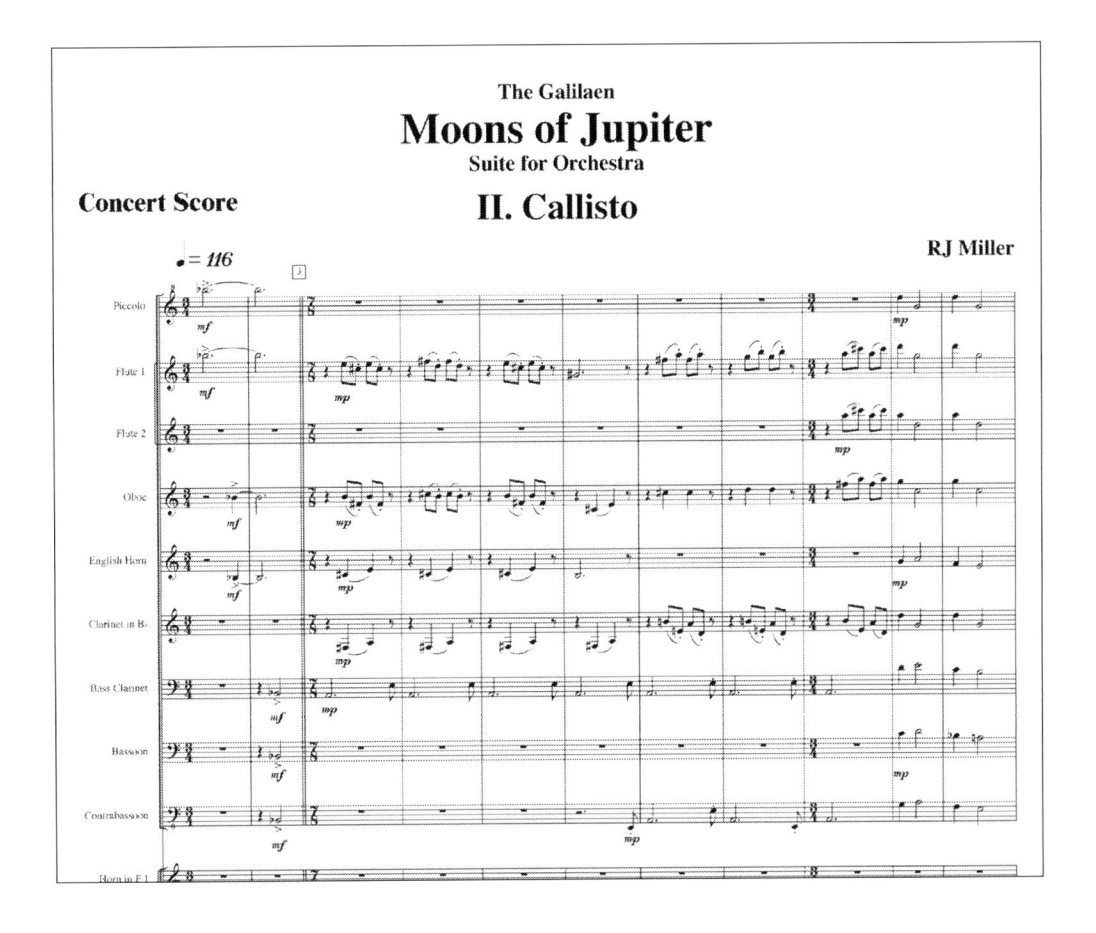

All the previously mentioned elements of score preparation apply to concert scores, including the formatting of the title page, instruction page, page one of the score, subsequent score pages and format of the final page of the score (see "Score Preparation" above).

Transposed Score

A transposed score is the full score, containing all the instruments of the ensemble displayed in their transposed form. Transposed scores are the preferred format for most conductors and publishers. By displaying all instruments in transposed pitch, the conductor sees exactly that which the players see on their parts. Assuming the score contains no errors, the transposed score can aid rehearsals, as the conductor need not transpose the written notes when communicating with the players. Publishers prefer transposed scores because the parts exist in the final form, thus requiring less time for preparation of the individual parts.

All the previously mentioned elements of score preparation apply to transposed scores, including the formatting of the title page, instruction page, page one of the score, subsequent score pages and format of the final page of the score (see "Score Preparation" above).

Condensed Score

The condensed score (sometimes referred to as a "short score") is a reduction of the full concert score. The music is reduced to fit on approximately four to six staves, and usually combines similar parts on the same staff. The instruments assigned to a particular section of music are designated with text placed appropriately in the score. Publishers are often fond of this format because it greatly reduces printing costs. Conductors not used to reading full instrumental scores (as well as those of lesser experience) find that this format adequately accommodates their needs.

Depending upon the situation, an orchestrator/arranger may be required to create multiple scores. If the score is for use in the recording studio, a concert score will normally suffice. If the score is for live performance, the conductor may prefer a transposed score. If the score is for publication, the publisher will often require both a transposed score and a condensed score. The orchestrator/arranger must be able and prepared to produce any or all of these formats with equal ease.

Preparation of Instrumental Parts

Generating competently notated, edited and formatted parts from an orchestral score is nothing less than an art. In years past, "copyists" were retained by publishers to extract the individual parts from the conductor's score, apply the appropriate transposition and either write out the parts by hand or typeset the parts in preparation for publication. The standard process was for the copyist to spend a number of years as apprentice to a "master copyist," learning the rules and execution of notation before rising to the status of copyist and eventually becoming a master copyist.

Notation software, while a great aid to the part-generating process, is not a substitute for a working knowledge of musical notation and formatting. The default settings available in most commercially available notation software are geared to the most common usage (as viewed by the software designer) and not necessarily suited for the specific needs of a given composition. One must expend the time and effort to either customize these settings, or be willing to edit the extracted part to meet requirements of a given piece. This can be a time-consuming process, usually requiring more time than the novice might project. Always allow adequate time for editing parts. Improperly prepared parts will not only be difficult to read and increase the needed rehearsal time, but also bias the perception of the conductor, players and publisher against the quality of the orchestration (and orchestrator).

One should also be aware that the standard page size for ensemble parts is not the letter size page of 8.5 × 11 inches. Professional standards dictate that ensemble parts are provided in formats of either 9.5 × 12.5 inches, or 10 × 13 inches. The margin from the edge of the page to the edge of the systems should be at least 0.75 inches, and the area of the page dedicated to the notation and systems of music should be no less than 8.5 × 11 inches.

Page One of the Part

- Title (plus subtitle, if applicable, top centered).
- Credits (right margin alignment, lower than title).
- Instrument name (left margin alignment, lower than title).
- First system indented.
- Approximately eight systems on first page.
- Clef and key signature at the beginning of every system.
- Measure number at beginning of system.
- Copyright information (bottom centered).

Subsequent Pages of the Part

- No system indentation.
- Approximately nine to ten systems on page.
- Clef and key signature at the beginning of every system.
- Measure number at beginning of system.
- Title, instrument and page number on every subsequent page (either top or bottom).

Last Page of Part

- No system indentation.
- Clef and key signature at the beginning of every system.
- Measure numbers at beginning of system.
- Measures in last system must be proportional to the measures in the rest of the piece. Never allow one or two measures to span the entire width of the page.
- Title, instrument and page number on every subsequent page (either top or bottom).

Preparation of Recording-studio Scores

Certain procedures in score and part preparation have become accepted practice in the film industry in many locations (particularly in Los Angeles, California) and are worthy of mention. As previously stated, the following is not a globally standardized practice and is rarely used in commercially published materials.

In the following film score[1] one will note the oversized time signatures, measure numbers placed (centered) under every measure, the queue number and start time is indicated, and, although this is a transposed score, no key signatures are used (the parts are presented in transposed form through the use of accidentals).

Preparation of Hybrid Studio Scores

Since the advent of MIDI technology, film and television scores have often contained both "live" players and sampled (or electronically produced) sounds controlled by MIDI data. When constructing a hybrid studio score, the parts to be performed by live players are placed (in orchestral score order) at the top of the score, and the parts to be performed using MIDI technology are placed (in orchestral score order) at the bottom of the score.[2]

RJ Miller, *Moments*, mm. 1–17.

Copyright © 2007 by Appassionata Music. Used by permission.

Recording-studio Parts

All of the previously stated formatting parameters apply to studio parts, with the following exceptions:

- Measure numbers are placed (centered) under every measure.
- Systems are slightly further apart to allow space for measure numbers and to accommodate any last-minute instructions that may need to be written in the part.

It is the practice in many locations that key signatures are not used in studio parts. The parts are appropriately transposed, but one uses accidentals for any needed chromatic alterations. This is not a globally standardized practice. One should inquire as to the current practice used where one will be recording. This practice is rarely used for commercially published materials.

Parts should be taped together in a bifold format. Up to three pages can be taped together to eliminate the need for page turns. Parts longer than three pages long should be formatted as a booklet with appropriate editing to accommodate page turns.

Additionally, selected studio parts may be combined to aid synchronization between instruments/sections.[3]

Instrument Transposition Guide

Instrument	Transposition	Clef
Piccolo	Down a Perfect Octave	Treble
Flute (C Flute)	Non-transposing	Treble
Alto Flute (in G)	Up a Perfect 4th	Treble
Bass Flute	Up a Perfect Octave	Treble
Contra Alto Flute (in G)	Up a Perfect 11th	Treble
Contrabass Flute	Up a Perfect 15th	Treble
Oboe	Non-transposing	Treble
Oboe d'amore	Up a minor 3rd	Treble
English Horn	Up a Perfect 5th	Treble
Heckelphone	Up a Perfect Octave	Bass and Tenor
Bassoon	Non-transposing	Bass and Tenor
Contrabassoon	Up a Perfect Octave	Bass
E♭ Clarinet	Down a minor 3rd	Treble
B♭ Clarinet	Up a Major 2nd	Treble
Clarinet in A	Up a minor 3rd	Treble
E♭ Alto Clarinet	Up a Major 6th	Treble
B♭ Bass Clarinet	Up a Major 9th	Treble
E♭ Contra Alto Clarinet	Up a Major 13th	Treble
B♭ Contrabass Clarinet	Up a Major 16th	Treble
E♭ Sopranino Saxophone	Down a minor 3rd	Treble
B♭ Soprano Saxophone	Up a Major 2nd	Treble
E♭ Alto Saxophone	Up a Major 6th	Treble
B♭ Tenor Saxophone	Up a Major 9th	Treble
E♭ Baritone Saxophone	Up a Major 13th	Treble
B♭ Bass Saxophone	Up a Major 16th	Treble
E♭ Contrabass Saxophone	Up a Major 20th	Treble
Sopranino Recorder	Down a Perfect Octave	Treble
Soprano Recorder	Down a Perfect Octave	Treble
Alto Recorder	Non-transposing	Treble
Tenor Recorder	Non-transposing	Treble
Bass Recorder	Up a Perfect Octave	Bass
Great Bass Recorder	Up a Perfect Octave	Bass
Contrabass Recorder	Non-transposing	Bass
B♭ Piccolo Trumpet	Down a minor 7th	Treble
Piccolo Trumpet in A	Down a minor 6th	Treble
E♭ Trumpet	Down a minor 3rd	Treble
D Trumpet	Down a Major 2nd	Treble
C Trumpet	Non-transposing	Treble

Instrument	Transposition	Clef
B♭ Trumpet	Up a Major 2nd	Treble
E♭ Cornet	Down a minor 3rd	Treble
B♭ Cornet	Up a Major 2nd	Treble
Flügelhorn	Up a Major 2nd	Treble
E♭ Bass Trumpet	Up a Major 6th	Treble
B♭ Bass Trumpet	Up a Major 9th	Treble
Horn (French Horn)	Up a Perfect 5th	Treble (occasionally in Bass Clef)
F Alto Horn, Mellophonium	Up a Perfect 5th	Treble
E♭ Alto Horn, Mellophonium	Up a Major 6th	Treble
Baritone (Treble Clef)	Up a Major 9th	Treble
Baritone (Bass Clef)	Non-transposing	Bass
Alto Trombone	Non-transposing	Bass and Alto
Tenor Trombone	Non-transposing	Bass and Tenor
Bass Trombone	Non-transposing	Bass
Cimbasso	Non-transposing	Bass
Euphonium	Non-transposing	Bass
Tuba	Non-transposing	Bass
Sousaphone	Non-transposing	Bass
Serpent	Non-transposing	Bass
Alto Ophicleide	Non-transposing	Bass and Treble
Bass Ophicleide	Non-transposing	Bass
Double Bass Ophicleide	Non-transposing	Bass
Orchestra Bells	Down a Perfect 15th	Treble
Chimes (Tubular Bells)	Non-transposing	Treble
Crotales	Down a Perfect 15th	Treble
Xylophone	Down a Perfect Octave	Treble
Marimba	Non-transposing	Treble and Bass
Timpani	Non-transposing	Bass
Piano	Non-transposing	All
Harp	Non-transposing	All
Guitar	Up a Perfect Octave	Treble
Bass (Guitar)	Up a Perfect Octave	Bass
Banjo	Non-transposing	Treble
Tenor Banjo	Up a Perfect Octave	Treble
Violin	Non-transposing	Treble
Viola	Non-transposing	Alto and Treble
Violoncello	Non-transposing	Bass, Tenor and Treble
Double Bass	Up a Perfect Octave	Bass

Instruments and Abbreviations

Instrument	Abbreviation	German	French	Italian
Piccolo	Picc.	Kleine Flöte	Petite Flûte	Ottavino (or) Flauto piccolo
Flute	Flt. (or) Fl.	Flöte	Flûte	Flauto
Oboe	Ob.	Oboe (or) Hoboe	Hautbois	Oboe
English Horn	Eng. Hn.	Englisches Horn	Cor anglais	Corno inglese
Clarinet	Cl. (or) Clar.	Klarinette	Clarinette	Clarinetto
Bass Clarinet	Bs. Cl. (or) Bs. Clar.	Bassklarinette	Clarinette basse	Clarinetto basso
Bassoon	Bssn. (or) Bsn.	Fagott	Basson	Fagotto
Contrabassoon	Cbssn. (or) Cbsn.	Kontrafagott	Contrebasson	Contrafagotto
Saxophone	Sax (or) Sx.	Saxophon	Saxophone	Sassofono
Horn (in F)	Hn.	Horn	Cor	Corno
Trumpet	Trpt. (or) Tpt.	Trompete	Trompette	Tromba
Trombone	Trbn. (or) Trb.	Posaune	Trombone	Trombone
Tuba	Tba. (or) Tb.	Tuba	Tuba	Tuba
Timpani	Timp.	Pauken	Timbales	Timpani
Glockenspiel (or) Orchestral bells	Glsp.	Glockenspiel	Carillon	Campanelli
Xylophone	Xylo. (or) Xyl.	Xylonphon	Xylophone	Xilofono
Marimba	Mar.	Marimbaphon	Marimba	Marimba
Vibraphone	Vib.	Vibraphon	Vibraphone	Vibrafono
Chimes (or) Tubular bells	Chm.	Röhrenglocken	Jeu des claches	Capane tubolari
Crotales	Crot.	Glocken Zimbeln	Cymbales antiques	Crotali
Flex-a-tone	Flex.	Flexaton	Flexatone	Flessatono
Crash Cymbals	Cymb. (or) Cym.	Becken	Cymbales	Piatti
Suspended cymbal	Susp. Cymb.	Hängendes Becken	Cymbale suspendue	Piatto sospeso
Finger cymbals	Fing. Cymb.	Fingerzimbeln	Cymbales digitales	Cimbalini
Triangle	Trgl.	Triangel	Triangle	Triangolo
Tam-Tam	Tam-Tam	Tamtam	Tam-tam	Tamtam
Wood blocks	W. Bl.	Holzblöke	Blocs de bois	Blocci di legno cinese
Temple blocks	T. Bl.	Tempel-Blöcke	Tempel-blocs	Blocci di leno coreano
Claves	Claves	Holzstab	Claves	Claves
Castanets	Cast.	Kastagnetten	Castagnettes	Castagnette
Ratchet	Ratch.	Ratsche	Crécelle	Raganella

Instrument	Abbreviation	German	French	Italian
Snare drum	S. Dr. (*or*) Sn. Dr.	Kleine Trommel	Caisse claire	Tamburo piccolo
Bass drum	Bs. Dr.	Grosse Trommel	Grosse caisse	Gran cassa
Tambourine	Tamb.	Tamburin	Tambour de basque	Tamburo basco
Piano	Pno.	Kavier	Piano	Pianoforte
Celesta	Cel.	Celesta	Céleste	Celesta
Harpsichord	Hpschd.	Cembalo	Clavecin	Cembalo
Organ	Org.	Orgel	Orgue	Organo
Harp	Hp. (*or*) Hrp.	Harfe	Harpe	Arpa
Violin	Vn. (*or*) Vln.	Violine (*or*) Geige	Violon	Violino
Viola	Va.	Bratsche	Alto	Viola
Violoncello	Vc. (*or*) Vlc.	Violoncell	Violoncelle	Violoncello
Double bass	D. B.	Kontrabass	Contrebasse	Contrabasso

General Notation Considerations

There is no "bible" of notation. In other words, there is no definitive reference book that addresses all of the notation issues one is likely to encounter in the course of a professional or academic career. However, there are two accepted premises to guide one through the musical notation labyrinth, namely:

Clarity of part

Ease of reading

Music notation has evolved over many centuries, often in somewhat haphazard ways. Prior to the age of computer technology, the art of notation was the realm of publishers and copyists. Each publishing house had its own set of notation rules and these rules varied, sometimes significantly, from publisher to publisher. The publisher's master copyist was charged with codifying these rules and conveying them to apprentice copyists. These apprentices would eventually become master copyists themselves, and thus perpetuate these rules from generation to generation. Over the centuries, certain elements of notation became, more or less, standard practice. However, even today, for any given notation "rule" one can easily find exceptions to that "rule" in commercially published music. It is for this reason that the above stated premises (clarity of part and ease of reading) constitute the mantra of all notation specialists.

The music notation guidelines published here are a combination of those notation practices that are most universally accepted and those practices that the author learned during his own apprenticeship, though, as previously stated, one will undoubtedly find published exceptions to virtually every "rule" presented here. However, following these guidelines will result in scores and parts that are professional competent and internationally viable.

Traditional Terminology

Tempo

Since the traditional tempo designations listed below existed long before the invention of the metronome, precise definitions of each are, at best, speculative. For example, at various times the term "andantino" has been interpreted as meaning "slightly slower than andante," while at other times it has been interpreted as "slightly faster than andante." Interpretations of these tempo markings differ greatly from conductor to conductor (as well as from musicologist to musicologist, and from theorist to theorist). Should one choose to utilize traditional tempo terminology rather than metronome markings, one must accept the reality that tempos will be interpreted differently (sometimes drastically so) by different conductors.

Traditional Terms

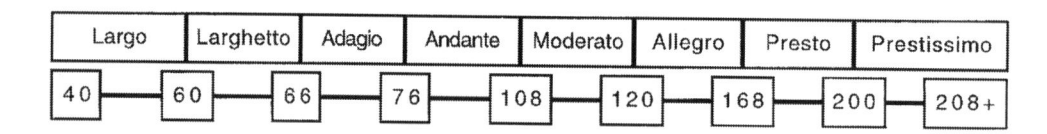

Largo	Larghetto	Adagio	Andante	Moderato	Allegro	Presto	Prestissimo
40	60	66	76	108	120	168	200	208+

Approximate MM Equivalent

Term	Description	Tempo	Approximate MM
Grave	Slowly and solemnly; in a stately manner	Very slow	~40–52 beats per min.
Largo	Slowly; in a broad and dignified manner	Very slow	~40–60 beats per min.
Larghetto	Slowly; in a broad and dignified manner; faster than Largo, but slower than Andante	Slowly	~60–72 beats per min.
Adagio	Slowly; at ease; faster than Largo, but slower than Andante	Slow	~64–76 beats per min.
Adagietto	Slightly faster than Adagio	Slow	~68–80 beats per min.
Lento	Tempo and style of a slow Andante	Slow	~72–84 beats per min.
Andante	"Moving" in a leisurely, unhurried manner	Moderately slow	~76–92 beats per min.
Andantino	Slightly faster than Andante	Moderately slow	~84–108 beats per min.
Moderato	At a moderate tempo; may also be used as a qualifying term—lessening the force of the stated term, i.e. Allegro Moderato	Moderate tempo	~108–120 beats per min.
Allegretto	Lively, playful; faster than Andante, but slower than Allegro	Moderate tempo	~108–120 beats per min.
Allegro	Joyful, cheerful, briskly	Moderately fast	~120–168 beats per min.

Term	Description	Tempo	Approximate MM
Vivace	Brisk and lively; a fast Allegro, or a slow Presto	Fast	~148–172 beats per min.
Presto	Very quick, nimble	Very fast	~168–200 beats per min.
Prestissimo	The quickest tempo possible	Extremely fast	~200+ beats per min.

Changes of Tempo

Term	Abbreviation	Definition
accelerando	*accel.*	Gradually increase speed
stringendo	*string.*	Gradually increase speed; tightening or pressing on
rallentando	*rall.*	Gradually decrease speed
ritardando	*rit.*	Gradually decrease speed
lentando	N/A	Gradually decrease speed
meno mosso	N/A	Less motion; immediately slower
piu mosso	N/A	More motion; immediately faster
incalzando	N/A	Increasing in speed and tone
calano	N/A	Diminishing in speed and amplitude
perdendosi	N/A	Dying away and becoming slower
slentando	N/A	Delaying; retarding
zurückhaltend	N/A	Slowing in speed

Notes

In today's world, it is quite probable that an orchestrator will work internationally. Knowledge of musical terminology used by composers, conductors and performers in other parts of the world is a valuable commodity. The following tables present selected terminology an orchestrator will undoubtedly encounter on the international rostrum.

Notes

Note	U.S.	English	German	French	Italian
𝄆𝅝𝄇	double-whole note	breve	doppeltakt (*m.*)	carrée (*f.*) or brevis	breve (*f.*)
𝅝	whole note	semibreve	ganze takt (*m.*) or ganze (*f.*)	semi-brève or ronde (*f.*)	semibreve (*f.*) intero (*m.*)
𝅗𝅥	half note	minim	halbe (*f.*) or halbe takt (*m.*)	blanche (*f.*)	minima (*f.*) or metà (*f.*)
𝅘𝅥	quarter note	crotchet	viertel (*f.*)	noire (*f.*)	semiminima (*f.*) or quarto (*m.*)
𝅘𝅥𝅮	eighth note	quaver	achtel (*f.*)	croche (*f.*)	croma (*f.*) or ottavo (*m.*)
𝅘𝅥𝅯	sixteenth note	semiquaver	sechzehntel (*f.*)	double croche (*f.*)	semicroma (*f.*) or sedicesimo (*m.*)
𝅘𝅥𝅰	thirty-second note	demisemiquaver	zweiunddreißigstel (*f.*)	triple croche (*f.*)	biscroma (*f.*) or trentaduesimo (*m.*)
𝅘𝅥𝅱	sixty-fourth note	hemidemisemiquaver	vierundsechzigstel (*f.*)	quadruple croche (*f.*)	semibiscroma (*f.*) or sessantaquattresimo (*m.*)
𝅘𝅥𝅲	one hundred twenty-eighth note	semihemidemisemiquaver or quasihemidemisemiquaver	hundertundacht-undzwanzigstel	cent-vingt-huitième or quintuple croche	centoventottavo (nota)

Rests

Rest	U.S.	English	German	French	Italian
	double-whole rest	breve rest	doppel pause (f.)	Baton (m.) or pause de brève (f.)	pausa di breve (f.)
	whole rest	semibreve rest	ganze pause (f.)	pause (f.)	pausa di semibreve (f.)
	half rest	minim rest	halbe pause (f.)	demi-pause (f.)	pausa di minima (f.)
	quarter rest	crotchet rest	viertelpause (f.)	soupir (m.)	pausa di semiminima (f.)
	eighth rest	quaver rest	achtelpause (f.)	demi-soupir (m.)	pausa di croma (f.)
	sixteenth rest	semiquaver rest	sechzehntelpause (f.)	quart de soupir (m.)	pausa di semicroma (f.)
	thirty-second rest	demisemiquaver rest	zweiunddreißigstelpause (f.)	huitième de soupir (m.)	pausa di biscroma (f.)
	sixty-fourth rest	hemidemisemiquaver rest	vierundsechzigstelpause (f.)	seizième de soupir (m.)	pausa di semibiscroma (f.)
	one hundred twenty-eighth rest	semihemidemisemiquaver rest	hundertundachtundzwanzigstelpause (f.)	cent-vingt-huitième de soupir (m.)	pausa di centoventottavo (f.)

Articulations

Symbol	Name	Description
staccato	staccato	Shorter than notated (approximately half the notated duration) and separated from subsequent notes
staccatissimo	staccatissimo	An exaggerated short duration (approximately one quarter the notated duration) with a light accent
marcato	marcato	A normal accent; moderately sharp attack
martelato	martelato	A strong accent; usually meant for attacks at loud dynamic levels
legato (tenuto)	legato (tenuto)	Note held to full duration; with or without a slight stress
martelato-staccato	martelato-staccato	Percussive attack and shorter than notated
martelato-staccatissimo	martelato-staccatissimo	Very percussive attack with an exaggerated short duration
martelato-legato	martelato-legato	Percussive attack with full duration of notation
legato-staccato	legato-staccato	Slightly stressed, moderately short, and separated from subsequent notes
legato-staccatissimo	legato-staccatissimo	Slightly stressed and exaggerated short duration
marcato-staccato	marcato-staccato	A normal accent with a moderately sharp attack; shorter duration than notated
marcato-staccatissimo	marcato-staccatissimo	A normal accent with a moderately sharp attack; and exaggerated short duration
marcato-legato	marcato-legato	A normal accent with a moderately sharp attack; with full duration of notation

Registers

It is always necessary for an orchestrator to competently converse in common terminology. This is especially true in the designation of registers. The following are commonly used designations for notes occurring in the various registers:

Sub Contra Octave
C_2 —— B_2

Contra Octave
C_1 —— B_1

Great Octave
C —— B

Small Octave
c —— b

One-line Octave
c′ —— b′

Two-line Octave
c″ —— b″

Three-line Octave
c‴ —— b‴

Four-line Octave
c⁗ —— b⁗

Five-line Octave
c′′′′′ —— b′′′′′

Clefs

Without a clef the lines and spaces of the staff are rendered tonally meaningless. All of the clefs currently used in common practice are available in contemporary music notation software applications. Depending upon the specific application, many rarely used or obsolete clefs are also available.

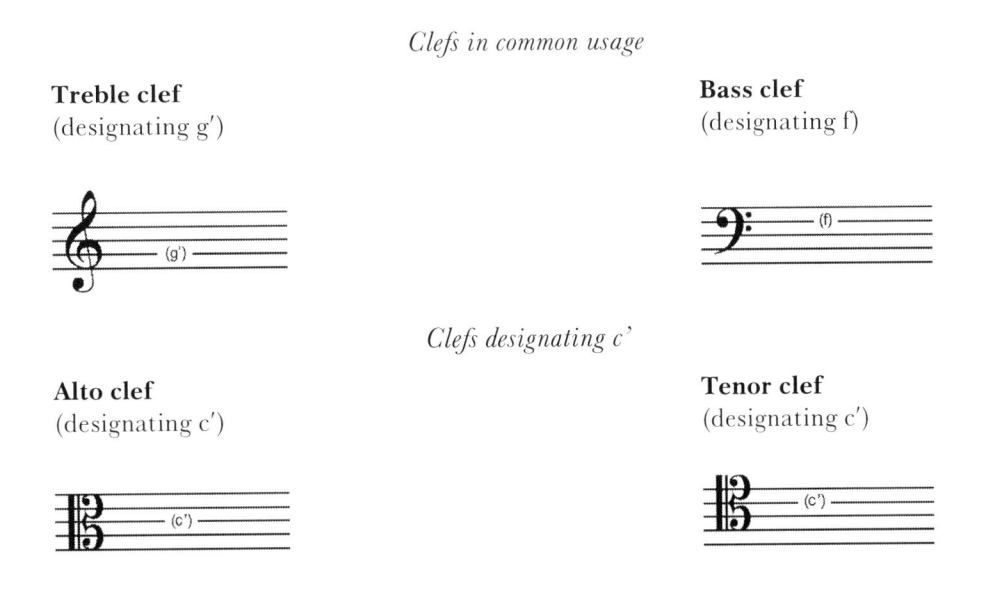

Clefs in common usage

Treble clef
(designating g′)

Bass clef
(designating f)

Clefs designating c′

Alto clef
(designating c′)

Tenor clef
(designating c′)

Hybrid Clefs

Tenor clef
(vocal only)

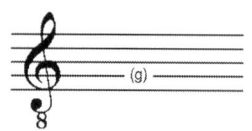

Double (tenor) clef
(vocal only, rarely used)

Treble clef octava
(piccolo, xylophone)

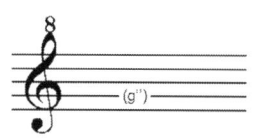

Treble clef quindicessima
(glockenspiel, rarely used)

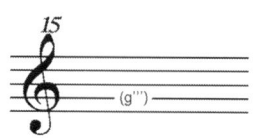

Bass clef ottava
(bass and baritone voices,
euphonium, tuba, rarely used)

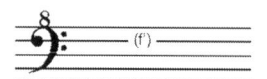

Bass clef ottava bassa
(contrabassoon, double basses)

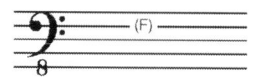

Percussion Clef

Non-pitch (percussion) clef

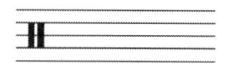

As it is not uncommon for composers, orchestrators and arrangers to utilize works containing antiquated notation as source material, one may on occasion encounter the following (now obsolete) clefs:

French violin clef

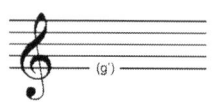

Soprano clef

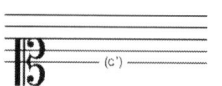

Mezzo-soprano clef

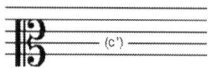

Baritone clef

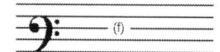

Vertical Alignments

Dynamics are always placed directly under notes, never under rests.

incorrect

correct

Horizontal Alignments

Whenever possible, it is advantageous not only to be cognizant of vertical alignments, but horizontal alignments as well. Horizontal alignments add to the clarity of the part and ease of reading, as well as the overall appearance of the part.

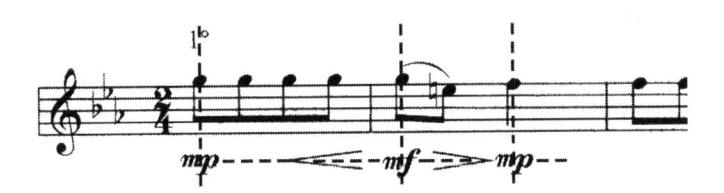

Note: When orchestrating a piano (or similar instrument) for an instrumental ensemble, one *must* define the scope of crescendi and decrescendi, whether or not it is defined in the original. Simply designating a crescendo and/or decrescendo will not suffice as one is coordinating dynamic interpretation for multiple performers.

Phrasing

In instrumental parts, all phrase markings are placed above the staff. Ties and slurs, on the other hand, go from notehead to notehead.

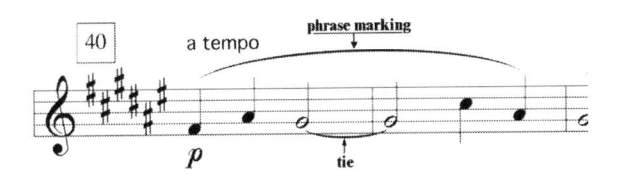

Rehearsal Marks

As previously stated, using measure numbers for rehearsal marks (instead of the "traditional" letter rehearsal marks) provides a great service to both conductor and performers, accommodating concise and succinct rehearsals. Additionally, one should always place double bars at rehearsal marks.

Rehearsal marks should always be placed within an enclosure. When occurring at the beginning of a system, the rehearsal mark enclosure should be aligned with the clef. When occurring elsewhere in the system, the rehearsal mark should be centered over the double bar.

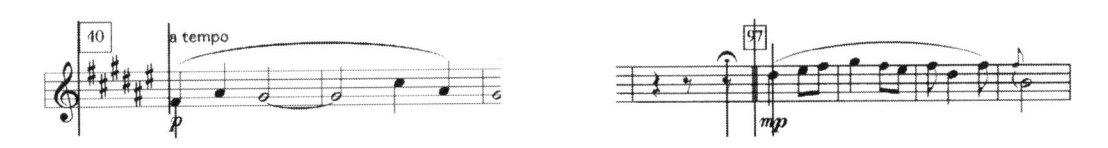

Vocal Parts vs. Instrumental Parts

In vocal parts all expression marks (dynamics, *rit.*, *accel.*, *cresc.*, *decresc.*, etc.) go above the staff to accommodate the placement of the lyrics below the staff. In (non-grand staff) instrumental parts the vast majority of expression marks are placed under the staff. The only items consistently placed above the staff are tempo markings (allegro, andante, a tempo, Tempo Primo, etc.) and rehearsal marks. Other expression marks may, under certain circumstances, be placed above the staff only if such placement accommodates clarity of part and ease of reading.

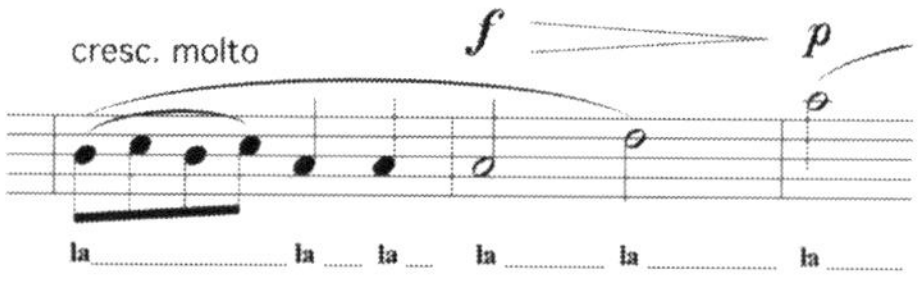

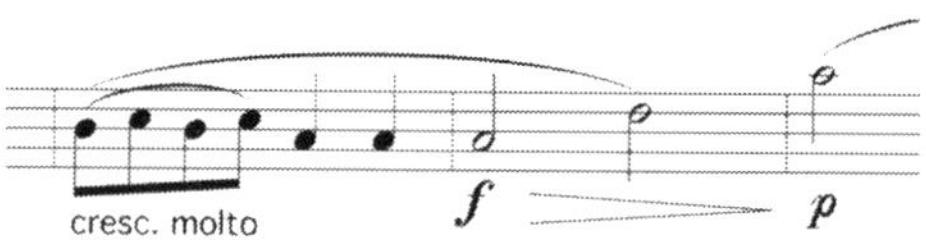

While there are rare circumstances when it is unavoidable, one should always attempt to keep notes, articulations, slurs, phrasing, dynamics, measure numbers, rehearsal marks, staff expressions, 8va markings, etc. from touching, colliding or overlapping. Colliding or overlapping elements detract from the clarity of part and ultimately invite confusion.

Rhythmic Subdivisions within the Measure

Unlike piano music (or similar grand staff instrument) where many liberties are taken with notation, strict notational practices must be exercised with ensemble or solo instrumental parts. Piano parts often contain multiple layers of rhythms, and since they exist within a "merged" part, notational shortcuts are often used to accommodate ease of reading for that specific instrument. Ensemble parts, on the other hand, do not contain those multiple layers that aid in the recognition of rhythm. Therefore, ensemble and solo parts require rhythmic subdivisions in virtually every measure to aid the player in sight-reading and performance. These rhythmic subdivisions occur on the strong beats of the measure.

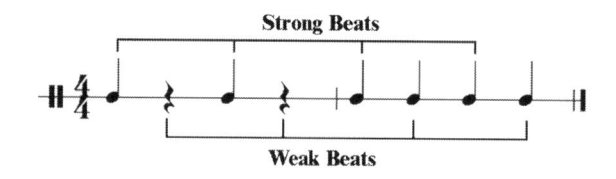

Rhythmic subdivisions, usually accomplished with the use of tied notes, provide a visual reference as to the position of the strong beats.

incorrect (no visible subdivision)   **correct (visible subdivision showing beat 3)**

incorrect (no visible subdivision) 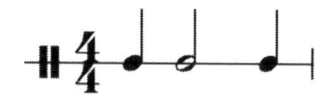   **correct (visible subdivision showing beat 3)**

incorrect (no visible subdivision)    **correct (visible subdivision showing beat 3)**

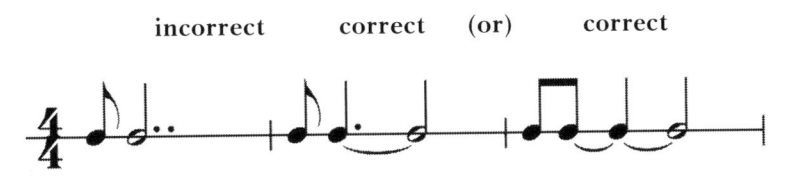

Even though the strong beat in triple meter usually only occurs on count one, it is advantageous to the player to see the individual beats within the measure. Being able to see a visual representation of the beats greatly aid the sight-reading process. Other possible subdivisions of 3/4 meter are 2 beats/1 beat, or 1 beat/2 beats. This technique of subdivision can be useful when the pattern (2 beats/1 beat, or 1 beat/2 beats) is repetitive for extended periods of time.

Compound meter should also be subdivided on the strong beats. In 6/8 meter (with the strong pulses on the 1st and 4th eighth-notes), the measure should be subdivided accordingly.

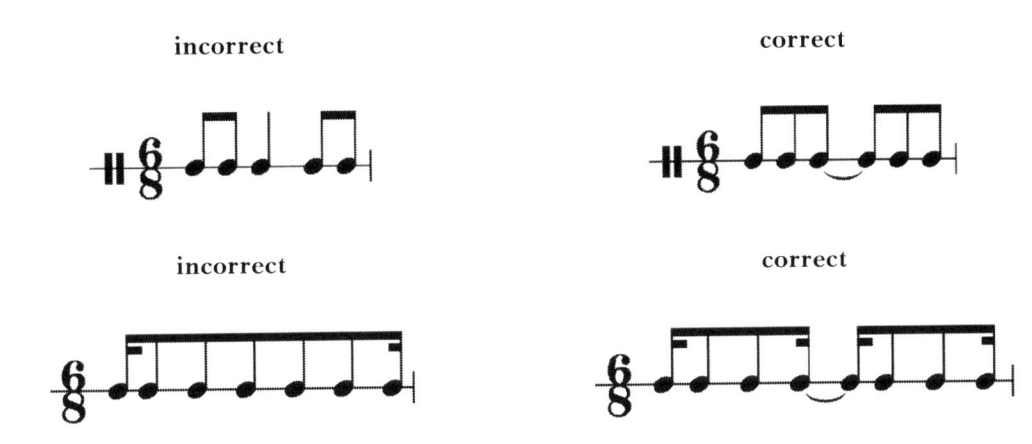

Odd meters are, most commonly, combinations of duple and triple meter in repetitive patterns. The following example is in 5/4 meter, comprising repetitive patterns of 3/4 and 2/4. The rhythmic subdivisions within the measure should follow the exact same repetitive pattern.

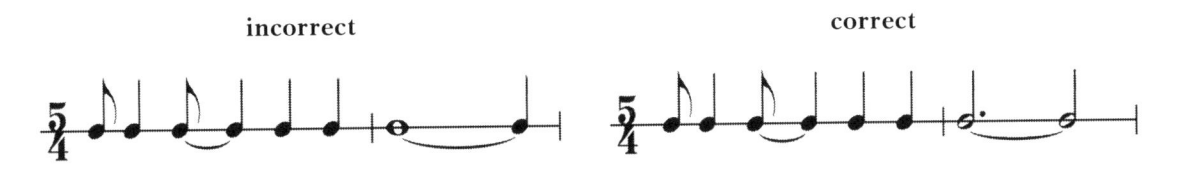

It is not uncommon in odd meters, especially in jazz, to place dotted vertical lines and the subdivision to aid the performer.

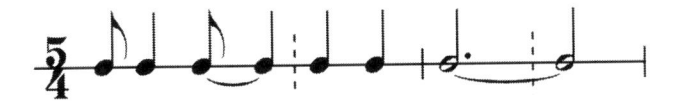

Notes

1. Excerpt from the film score to *Captain Abu Raed*—Winner of the Audience Award—World Cinema—Dramatic—2008 Sundance Film Festival—original music composed and orchestrated by Austin Wintory. Copyright © MMVII by Austin Wintory. Reprinted with permission of the composer.
2. Though the colloquial terminology may be somewhat inappropriate, in this context composers will often refer to the live players as "the live guys" and the MIDI parts as "the dead guys."
3. Sample violin part from the film score to *Captain Abu Raed*—composed and orchestrated by Austin Wintory. Copyright © MMVII by Austin Wintory. Reprinted with permission of the composer.

# 3
PRACTICAL PROBLEM SOLVING

Once a composition has been selected for orchestration, orchestrators expend significant amounts of time analyzing and problem solving before committing notes to the ensemble score. A number of elements must be addressed prior to beginning the orchestration process. Among those are:

- Is the selected composition idiomatically appropriate for the chosen ensemble?
- Can the selected composition be orchestrated without compromising the original compositional intent of the composer?
- Is the selected composition in an appropriate key for the chosen ensemble?
- Does the key of the selected composition need to be altered to accommodate the ranges and registers of the instruments in the chosen ensemble?
- Does the name of the selected composition prohibit altering the key? (Compositions with specific keys indicated in the titles, such as "Fugue in G minor," should be orchestrated in the original keys.)
- Are there elements within the notation of the selected composition that must be addressed or altered to work for the instruments of the chosen ensemble? (Pedal markings, arpeggios, elements that are idiomatically pianistic, rhythmic subdivisions, etc. all need to be considered.)
- Does the selected composition contain textual possibilities?
- If orchestrating with winds, does the selected composition accommodate the performer's need to breathe?

To demonstrate the problem-solving process, an orchestration for string quartet will be created from the following piano excerpt.

Peter Ilyich Tchaikovsky, *Chanson Triste*

Chanson Triste
(Excerpt)

P. Tchaikovsky (Op. 40, No. 2)

Note: The cadence at measure nine is not part of the original piece. It was added here simply to accommodate an ending for the exercise. The instrumentation of the traditional string quartet is 1st violin, 2nd violin, viola and cello. No double, triple or quadruple stops will be used in this exercise.

There are a number of issues that are immediately apparent, the first of which is an undefined crescendo mark beginning in measure three and culminating at count one of measure five. This is not an issue in piano music, since there is only one performer. The performer simply executes a crescendo, as the performer sees fit, accommodating the expressive nature of the performance. However, when scoring for an ensemble, the orchestrator *must* define the scope of crescendi and decrescendi. Multiple performers must be coordinated, and it is the responsibility of the orchestrator to define these elements of interpretation and expression. For the purposes of this exercise, a dynamic level of mezzo piano has been selected.

Chord members will need to be deleted in order to accommodate an orchestration for four voices. To determine which chord members may be deleted, one must perform a harmonic analysis of the piece. One of the important contributors to harmonic content in piano music is the use of the damper (sustaining) pedal. Use of this pedal causes notes to sustain through until the pedal is released.

PRACTICAL PROBLEM SOLVING

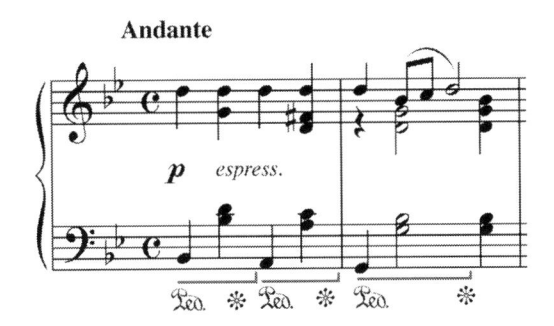

The damper pedal causes the note in the bass line to sustain longer than notated. These durations must be taken into account when orchestrating piano music. The following notation reflects the actual durations implied by the pedal markings.

Now that a true representation of the harmonic content exists, a chordal analysis can be performed. This may be a formal analysis or simply a chordal analysis. One simply chooses the most comfortable method, as the end result will be identical.

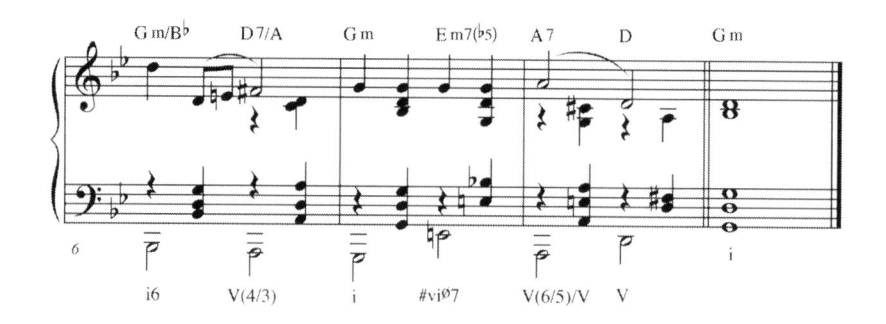

Once the harmonic analysis is complete, one may begin the revoicing (deleting) process. The melody line is paramount and must be retained. This will ultimately become the 1st violin part. The bass line is the second most important element, and its harmonic function must remain intact (in measures six through eight the notes of the bass line are below the range of the cello, so octave adjustments will be required). Now the inner voices must be reduced to two parts. Utilizing one's knowledge of the overtone series, one can delete those chord members that are acoustically reinforced while retaining those chord members necessary for the harmonic structure and competent voice-leading within the parts.

Measures One and Two

Measure One

Note that the opening chord (count one through count two) is a 1st inversion Gm chord (tonic) with 3rd of the chord doubled. One of the easiest methods of choosing which chord members to delete is to eliminate the octave doublings. Deleting the small octave B♭ reduces the chord to four voices without compromising the harmonic content.

The second chord (count three through count four) is a second inversion D7 chord (V4/3) with doublings of both the root and the fifth of the chord. Eliminating the octave doublings results in four voices, with all chordal members of the second inversion D7 chord (V4/3) represented. Additionally, the voice-leading of the inner voices is logical.

Measure Two

The harmonic content of the entirety of measure two is a root position Gm chord (tonic). On count two the melody briefly plays a (one-line octave) B♭, followed be a passing tone (c″), then sustains the d″ for two counts. Since the harmony is sustaining through this melodic movement, the sustained note in the melody is the one which should be considered when calculating the notes of the inner voices. Another consideration is that the bass line is interrupted on count

PRACTICAL PROBLEM SOLVING 51

four. While having the bass voice skip up an octave (from G to g) on count four is not unacceptable, choosing this option will result in a skip of a descending major ninth at the beginning of the next measure, resulting in very poor voice-leading. The best choice for the bass line is to sustain the G for three counts then rest on count four. This easily leads to the F at the beginning of measure three. (Allowing intervals between the inner voices to be greater than an octave results in a thin and less homogenous sound.)

Eliminating the doubled bass note (g) and the double 5th (d') resolves counts one through three. On count four, the cello (bass line) is resting and the melody is sustaining the d''. The root and 3rd are needed to complete the harmony on count four. The second voice in the piano part moves up to the one-line octave B♭, leaving the third voice with the root. Choosing the g for the third voice would result in a span of greater than an octave between the inner two voices, therefore g' becomes the best choice for the third voice.

Measures One and Two (Revoiced)

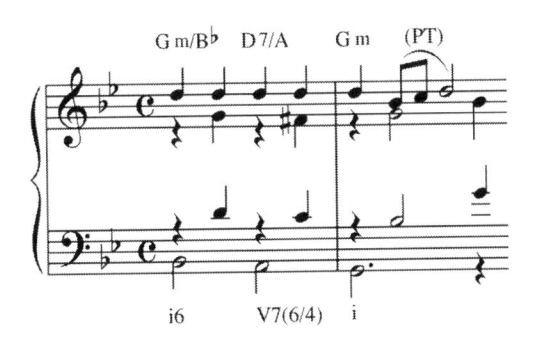

Measures Three, Four and Five

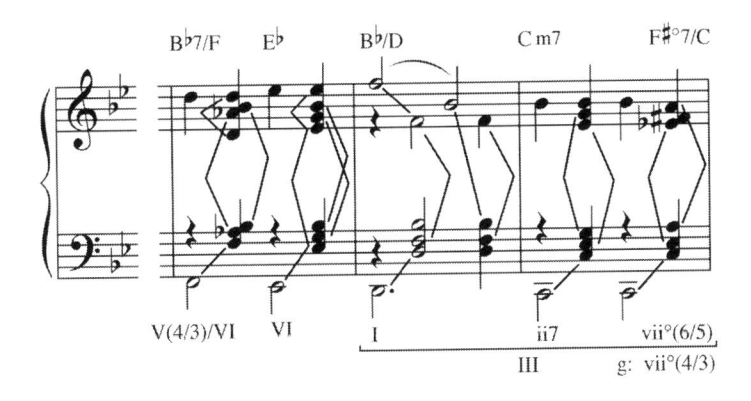

Measure Three

The opening chord (count one through count two) in measure three is a 2nd inversion B♭7 (V(4/3)/IV) with every member of the chord doubled. Eliminating the doubling reduces the chord to four voices without compromising the harmonic content. With the 5th in the bass and the 3rd in the melody, the root and 7th are left for the inner voices. Placing the 7th in the second voice, and the root in the third voice keeps the inner voices from spanning more than an octave and is the best choice. (This choice will ultimately result in a descending line in the second part, which will add to the color of the piece.)

The second chord (count three through count four) is a root position E♭ chord (VI), with the root quadrupled and the 3rd and 5th doubled. The melody and bass line are doubled and must remain so for the integrity of the composition. This leaves the 3rd and 5th of the chord for the inner voices. Logical voice-leading would suggest resolving the second voice to g′, which leaves the note in the third voice unchanged.

Measure Four

During measures four and five, the piece progresses through a brief tonicization in B♭ major (III of g minor), returning to g minor again in measure six through the use of an inverted diminished 7th chord common to both keys.

The harmonic content of the entirety of measure four is a first inversion B♭ chord (III in g minor, or I in the tonicization). As in measure two, the bass line is interrupted on count four. The best choice for the bass line is to sustain the G for three counts, then rest on count four. This provides consistency with the previous phrase, as well as voice-leading well into the C at the beginning of measure five.

Leaving voice two on the 5th (as in the original piano part) and placing the third voice on (small octave) B♭ on count two, moving to d′ on count four again resolves the issue of the inner voices spanning more than an octave (and is therefore the most effective choice).

Measure Five

Measure five presents an interesting situation for the bass line. The first C represents the end of the preceding descending bass line, and the second C represents the beginning of the next series of descending bass notes. The issue is that C is the lowest note on the cello and, as such, the instrument is not capable of playing the notes as written in measures six, seven and eight. To resolve this problem, the C on count one should remain as is (completing the descending line initiated at the beginning of the piece), while the C occurring on count three should be transposed up one octave. This skip of an octave in a bass line is perfectly acceptable and prepares the upcoming descending line to be realized in a playable register.

For both chords in measure five, the root is in the bass and the 7th is in the melody. Therefore, the 3rd and 5th (or the enharmonic spelling of the diminished 5th on count four) are placed in the inner voices. The 5th is already in the second voice (in the original piano part), so the 3rd is placed in the third voice (in a manner to accommodate voice-leading, while restricting the intervallic span to less than an octave between voices two and three).

Measures Three, Four and Five (Revoiced)

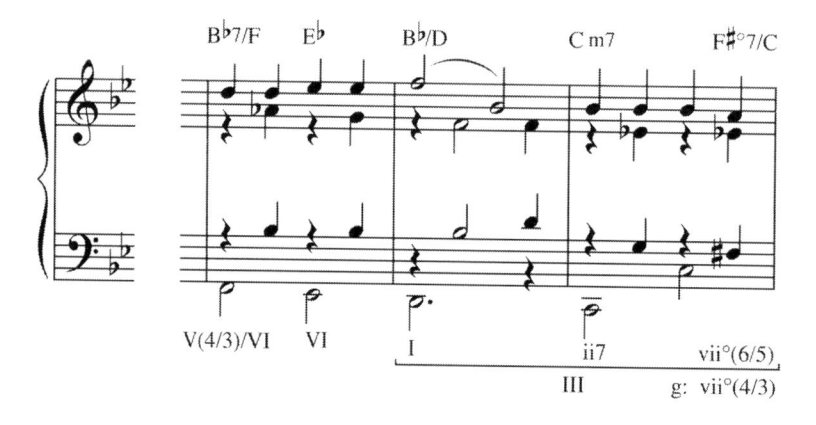

Measures Six, Seven, Eight and Nine

Measure Six

The melody remains as written in measure six, even though the line in the bass in now 8va. The b♭ in the second voice (on count two) is a doubling of the bass, but in this circumstance (where the available range between the melody and the bass is restricted because of the octave transposition in the bass) it functions better than leaving out the voice. The option of placing the second voice on g and the third voice on d would create an unacceptable voice-leading issue in the third voice. Therefore, by default, this is the best available option.

The chord on count three is a second inversion D7 (V(4/3)) chord. The 3rd is in the melody and the 5th is in the bass, so the inner voices must contain the root and 7th.

Measure Seven

Since the final cadence is approaching, one should exploit the low register of the cello. This lower register adds a sense of finality while still accommodating the II–V–i progression. The half note on count one should be G (transposed up an octave from the original, and continuing the descending line from the preceding measure). The half note on count three should go down to the E (utilizing the resonant lower register of the cello). The same procedure should occur in measure eight (this time, A to D).

The first chord in measure seven is a root position Gm (tonic) chord with the root in the melody and the root in the bass. The inner voices fill in the 3rd and 5th of the chord. The second voice in the piano part is a d' (5th of the chord) and should remain so here, with the third voice being placed on the 3rd of the chord.

In the following chord, the melody and the inner voice remain on the same pitches (g', d' and b♭, respectively) while the bass changes to E.

Measure Eight

The first chord of the measure is a root position A7 (V(6/5)/V) chord with the root doubled in the melody and bass. The second voice should be placed on the 3rd (c♯') and the third voice on the 7th (g). The 5th of the chord is reinforced acoustically and can be deleted without compromising the harmonic content.

The second chord of the measure is a root position D (V) chord with the root doubled in the melody and bass. Since there is no 7th in this chord, the second voice should be placed on the 5th (a) and the third voice on the 3rd (f♯).

Measure Nine

The final chord is a root position Gm (tonic) chord with the 5th in the melody and the root in the bass. The second voice should resolve to the 3rd and the third voice should resolve to the root (g).

Measures Six, Seven, Eight and Nine (Revoiced)

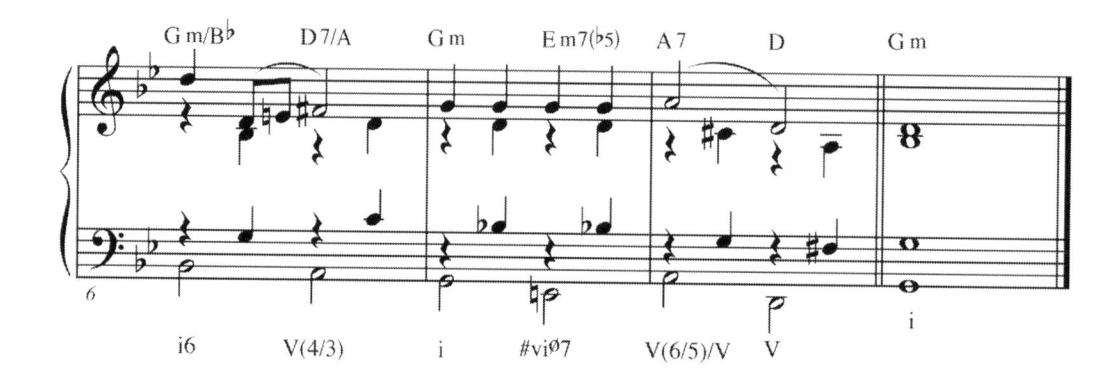

Completed Revoicing

The orchestration can be completed by placing the melody in the 1st violin, the second part in the 2nd violin, the 3rd part in the viola, and the bass line in the cello. Insert the dynamics in *all* parts, remembering that dynamics are only placed under notes (never under rests). Crescendi and descrendi also *must* be placed in *all* parts and their scope must be defined. Finally, change the bass line notation in measures two and four to reflect proper rhythmic subdivisions. The designation *express.* applies to the interpretation of the melody and thus should be placed above the staff (at the beginning of measure one) in the 1st violin part.

Chanson Triste
(Excerpt for String Quartet)

P. Tchaikovsky (Op. 40, No. 2)

Public Domain

    The final process, prior to the extraction of the individual parts, is designating elements of expression and interpretation by adding phrase markings and articulations. The notation of the original piano part may not specifically define these elements. However, by examining the melodic contour, pedal markings, dynamic shaping, etc., one can deduce the implied elements of expression and interpretation. When scoring for an ensemble, the orchestrator must define these elements, as applicable, in every part.

Chanson Triste
(Excerpt for String Quartet)

P. Tchaikovsky (Op. 40, No. 2)

4
THE VIOLIN FAMILY

Violin   Viola   Violoncello   Double Bass

The modern orchestral violin family consists of the violin, viola, cello, and double bass. Developed during the 16th century, these instruments were most likely the innovation of Andrea Amati of Cremona. The Amati family, along with the Stradivari and Guarneri families, refined and standardized these instruments (originally known as *violas da braccio*), resulting in the timbre that dominates the chamber music and orchestral palettes.

THE ESSENTIALS

The Bridge

The *bridge* is an apparatus that both supports the strings and transmits the vibrations generated by the strings to the top plate of the instrument. The sound produced by the strings alone is relatively quiet. However, when the vibrations are conveyed to the top plate by the bridge (then through the sound post to the back plate), the larger surface area of the body of the instrument displaces a much larger volume of air, resulting in greater amplitude. In essence, the bridge allows the body of the instrument to function as an amplifier.

The Bow

In simplest terms, the bow is a wooden stick with a length of horsehair that stretches from the tip to the frog (heel). A screw adjuster located at the end of the frog controls the tautness of the horsehair. Traditionally, the horsehair is from the tail of a male, grey horse (from such breeds as Arabian, American Quarter Horse, Andalusian, Percheron, Lipizzaner, etc.). Though the coat of these horses is typically grey, the tails are generally white in color. Younger players will often use less expensive bows that use a synthetic fiber in place of the horsehair.

Bow Stick — Tip — Hairs — Frog

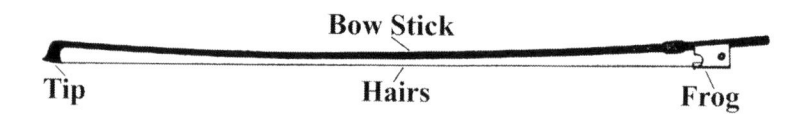

Rosin

To ensure suitable sound production, rosin is applied to the bow hairs to increase friction between the bow and the strings. Rosin is composed of conifer resin, often with various additives designed to modify or enhance the viscosity.

Basic Bowing Terms and Descriptions

One must be aware that the terms listed below are applicable to string bowing techniques only, and are not necessarily the terminology used when describing the articulation markings.

Down-bow

The down-bow stroke is initiated near the frog of the bow, then "pulled" across the string(s) to produce the sound. Being the stronger of the two bow strokes, it is most effective on strong beats and accented notes.

Up-bow

The up-bow stroke is initiated near the tip of the bow, then "pushed" across the string(s) to produce the sound. Being the weaker of the two bow strokes, it is effective on weak beats, pick-up notes, and unaccented notes.

Détaché

Détaché is the default bowing for any passage lacking bow markings, articulations and/or phrase markings. Contrary to what one might think, the term does not imply detached bow strokes. In détaché bowing, the bow alternates direction on each note, while performing the notes smoothly and without breaks between notes.

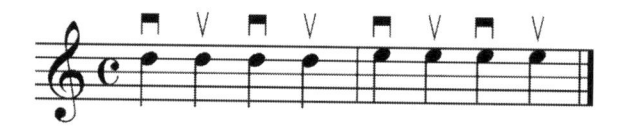

Legato

In legato bowing, several notes are played in one continuous movement of the bow (in one direction). Legato bowing produces a very smooth sound with no accentuated attacks or breaks between notes. The technique is notated with a slur connecting several notes.

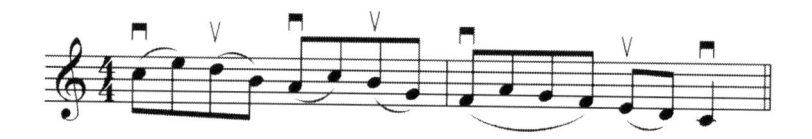

Portato (I.) or Louré (Fr.)

Portato or louré bowing is performed with a single bow stroke (duration of the phrase mark), but with a slight break between notes.

Jeté

Jeté bowing is performed with a bouncing motion towards the tip of the bow, creating repeated notes on one bow stroke. Jeté is notated by using slurred staccato.

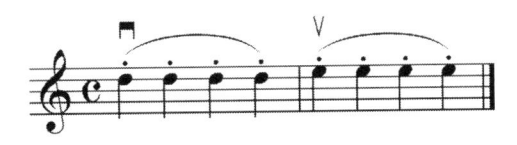

Staccato

With *staccato* bowing, the bow is stopped (remaining in contact with the string(s)) and the duration of the note is shortened to approximately half the notated value.

Spiccato (Saltando)

Spiccato (saltando) is a type of staccato where the bow is bounced upon the string(s). Spiccato is usually utilized in faster passages.

Marcato

Performance of marcato bowing is completely dependent upon the musical context. At slower tempi the bow is stopped between notes (like staccato), while at faster tempi the bow may be bounced (similar to jeté). No matter the tempo, there will be a separation between notes.

Martelé (Fr.) or Martellato (I.)

As with marcato, the actual performance of martelé is dependent upon the musical context. The spiccato marking designate a rougher separation between notes than that of the staccato marking. Grand martelé, indicated by the marking WB (standing for "whole bow") is an exaggerated bow stroke that, while still of short duration, results in forceful, accentuated notes

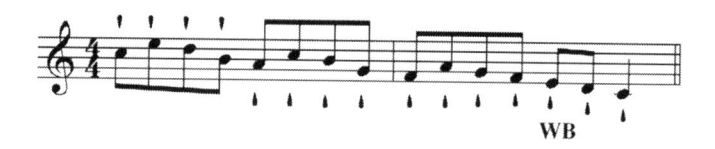

Trill

The actual performance of trills is dependent upon the genre of music being performed. In contemporary times, a trill is performed by rapidly alternating between the notated pitch and the upper neighboring pitch (diatonically, if not otherwise notated). Trills are performed smoothly, with no separation between notes. Unless the trill extends for multiple measures, it is performed with one bow stroke.

Tremolo (and Fingered Tremolo)

Tremolos are performed by rapidly moving the bow in a back-and-forth manner, generally in an unmeasured fashion, producing a vibrant effect. Fingered tremolos are performed in manner similar to a trill, but with an interval larger than a whole step.

tremolo   fingered tremolo

Sul Ponticello (I.), or Sur le chevalet (F.), or am Steg (G.)

Sul ponticello is the technique of bowing close to the bridge, creating a thin, less resonant sound. It is designated by placing the text *sul ponticello* above the note where the effect is to begin and cancelled by placing the text *ord.* or *norm.* above the staff where the effect ceases.

Flautando

Flautando is the technique of bowing close to the fingerboard, which produces a "flutelike" timbre. It is designated by placing the text *flautando* above the note where the effect is to begin, and cancelled by placing the text *ord.* or *norm.* above the staff where the effect ceases.

Sul Tasto (I.), or Sur la touche (Fr.), or am Griffbrett (G.)

Sul tasto is the technique of bowing over the fingerboard, creating a cloudy, less focused sound. It is designated by placing the text sul tasto above the note where the effect is to begin, and cancelled by placing the text *ord.* or *norm.* above the staff where the effect ceases.

Sul G

Sul G designates that all notes are to be performed upon the G string. Similar designations can apply to any string required (i.e. sul D, sul A, sul E, etc.).

Portamento (Glissando)

A portamento (or glissando) is performed by sliding from one note to the next, producing a continuous ascending (or descending) pitch. The effect is notated with a line between the two notes, and the text *gliss.* placed above or next to the line. Note that the effect can only be produced on a single string and never between notes on adjacent strings.

Pizzicato

The pizzicato effect is produced by plucking the string with the tip of the finger (some players use the thumb). It is notated by placing the text *pizz.* above the note where the effect is to begin and cancelled by placing the text *arco* above the staff where the effect ceases.

Arraché or Anreissen

An arraché or anreissen is a particularly forceful pizzicato effect. It is notated by placing the text arraché or anreissen above the note where the effect is to begin and cancelled by placing the text arco above the staff where the effect ceases.

Pizzicato Secco

A pizzicato secco is a dampened pizzicato effect. The player creates this effect by plucking the string, then immediately returning the finger to the string to mute the vibration. It is notated by placing the text *pizz. secco* above the note where the effect is to begin and cancelled by placing the text arco above the staff where the effect ceases.

Snap (or "Bartok") Pizzicato

A snap pizzicato (or "Bartok" pizzicato in homage to the inventor of the technique) is performed by pulling the string upwards and releasing it in a manner so that it "snaps" against the fingerboard. It is notated by placing the text snap above the note where the effect is to begin and cancelled by either placing the text *pizz.* above the staff where the effect ceases (if returning to a normal pizzicato) or placing arco above the staff (if returning to a bowed technique).

Col Legno

A col legno effect is produced by turning the bow upside down and using the wood of the bow (rather than the hair) to initiate sound. It is notated by placing the text col legno above the note where the effect is to begin and cancelled by placing the text *ord.* or *norm.* above the staff where the effect ceases.

Mutes

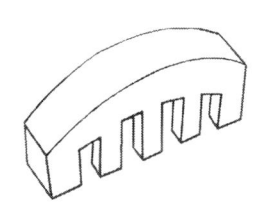

A mute (or sordino) is a device that may be attached to the bridge of the string instrument to produce a softer and mellower timbre by reducing (dampening) the audible overtones. Orchestrating the entire string section in mutes produces a quiet, almost whispering quality that proves quite effective when a subdued sound is desired. It is notated by placing the text mute (or *con sord.*) above the note where the effect is to begin and cancelled by placing the text without mute (or *senza sord.*) above the staff where the effect ceases.

Harmonics

String harmonics are divided into two separate classifications: *Natural harmonics*, where the resultant pitch is produced by lightly touching an open, vibrating string (the fundamental pitch) at one of the nodal points, and *artificial harmonics*, where the fundamental is artificially created by fingering the desired fundamental and lightly touching the nodal point with another finger.

Harmonics will occur at the lightly touched perfect octave, perfect 5th, perfect 4th, major 3rd, minor 3rd and major 6th. While technically possible, the harmonic generated at the major 6th is not only problematic, but also somewhat superfluous. It is problematic because of the physical distance of the interval on one string and superfluous because the range of harmonics generated by the major 6th is identical to that of the major 3rd. Harmonics at the major and minor 3rd are also problematic due to the tuning differences between equal temperament and just tuning. The harmonic generated at the major 3rd node is 14 cents flatter than an equal temperament major 3rd and the harmonic generated at the minor 3rd node is 16 cents sharper than an equal temperament minor 3rd.

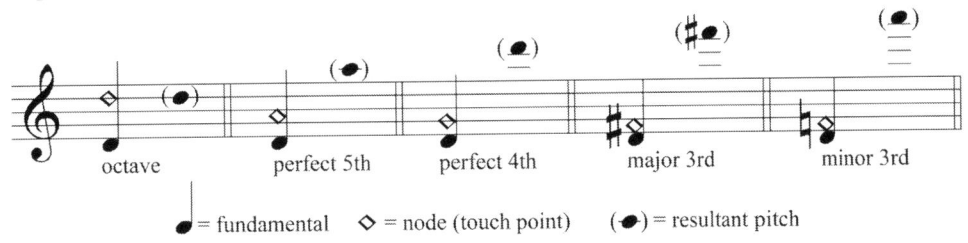

It goes without saying that there are professional players capable of competently performing any, if not all of the possible harmonic combinations; however, from a practical standpoint, harmonics generated at the intervals of a fourth, fifth, octave and two octaves yield the most stable and reliable results.

One should also note that harmonics function best at lower dynamic levels (*mezzo piano* or lower), with a maximum functional dynamic level of *mezzo forte*.

Practical Natural Harmonics

Interval	Overtone Partial	Resultant Pitch (above fundamental)
perfect 4th	4	2 octaves
perfect 5th	3	1 octave, plus a perfect 5th
perfect octave	2	1 octave
2 octaves	4	2 octaves

Double Stops

Double stops are performed by simultaneously bowing notes on adjacent strings. *Note*: This effect is only possible on adjacent strings due to the curvature of the bridge. Double stops (as well as triple stops and quadruple stops) should only be used for specific effects and never as avoidance for deleting chord members when orchestrating (particularly for orchestrating for string quartet or similar small ensemble).

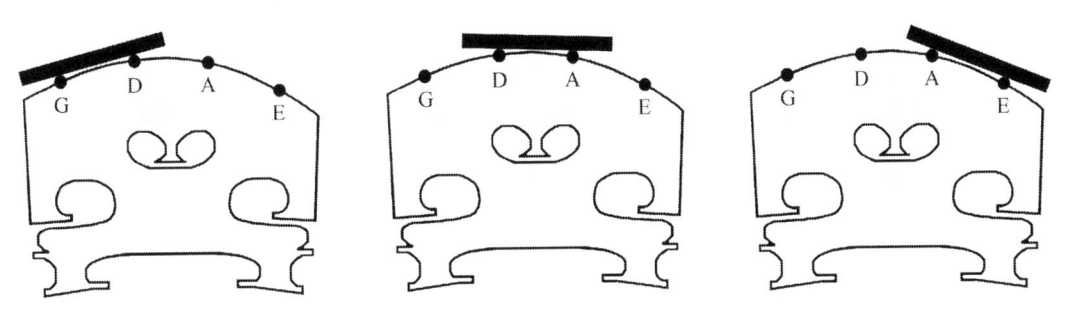

(Double stops as they would appear on the violin bridge)

Double stops are notated by placing both of the desired notes on the same stem.

Triple Stops

Triple stops are performed by briefly playing the lower two notes of the notated chord (on adjacent strings), allowing them to resonate, then quickly shifting the bow to simultaneously play the upper two notes. This gives the illusion that all three notes are sounding (as an appreggiated or broken chord). Again, this effect is only possible on adjacent strings due to the curvature of the bridge. *Note*: This technique requires more bow pressure to produce than that of standard bowing (or even that of double stops) and, as such, is not effective for softer passages.

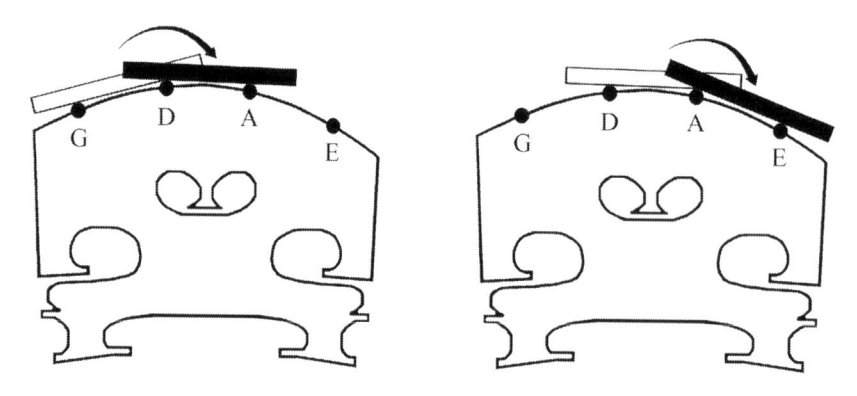

(Triple stops as they would appear on the violin bridge)

Triple stops may be notated as three vertically aligned notes (or three notes on a single stem), or as grace notes.

Quadruple Stops

Using the same technique as that of triple stops, quadruple stops are performed by briefly playing the lower two notes of the notated chord (on adjacent strings), allowing them to resonate, then quickly shifting the bow to simultaneously play the upper two notes, giving the illusion that all four notes are sounding (as an appreggiated or broken chord). As with triple stops, the technique requires more bow pressure to produce than that of standard bowing (or even that of double stops) and, as such, is not effective for softer passages.

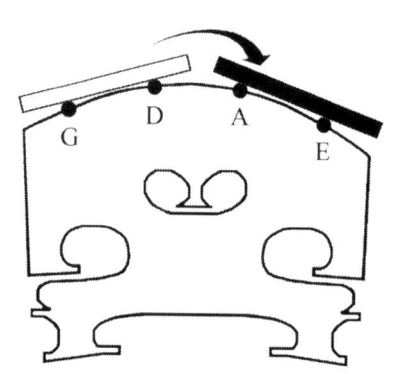

(Quadruple stops as they would appear on the violin bridge)

Quadruple stops may be notated as four vertically aligned notes (or four notes on a single stem) or as grace notes.

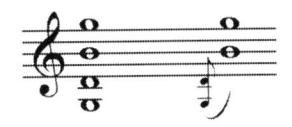

Scordatura

Occasionally, one may wish to detune one of the strings for a specific special effect. When one designates the "detuning" of a string it is referred to as *scordatura*. One should exercise caution while employing scordatura since the normal fingering patterns are disrupted when using this effect. While it is possible to lower the pitch of a string as much as a perfect fourth, intervals a minor 3rd (or more) will alter the timbre and resonance of the string. From a practical perspective, one should limit oneself to lowering the pitch a maximum of a major 2nd.

An example of solo violin scordatura can be found in the opening motif of *Danse Macabre* by Camille Saint-Saëns. In this selection, the violin's E-string is detuned a minor second (to E♭) creating a tritone between the upper two strings. This tritone is used as a double stop at various points throughout the piece.

Camille Saint-Saëns, *Danse Macabre*, **mm. 14–21 (solo violin)**

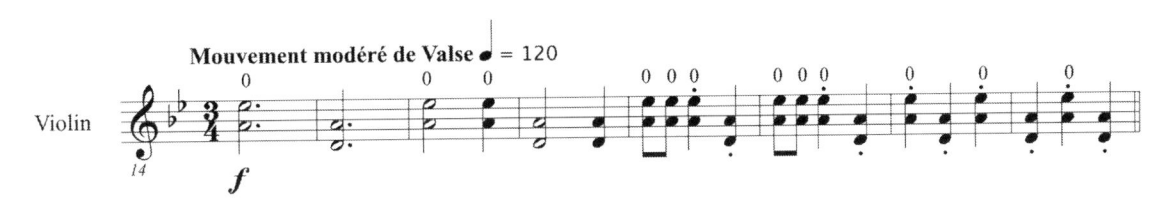

Wolf Tones

A *wolf tone* is an acoustic anomaly produced when the frequency (Hz) of a note played on the instrument matches the natural resonance of the body of the instrument. While wolf tones occur on all string instruments, they are most obvious on the cello and (to a lesser extent) on double bass. Notes that generate wolf tones are usually less resonant (due to frequency cancellation), produce an anomalous "howling" sound (hence the name) due to the amplification of certain overtones and can often produce an oscillating, "beating" sound (caused by the nodal intersections of the sympathetically generated waveforms).

Wolf tones can be reduced (or even completely alleviated) through the use of a *wolf tone eliminator*. The device consists of a rubber sleeve encased in a metal tube with a mounting screw that decreases the intensity of the offending vibrations.

Luthiers and Archetiers

A crafts-person who makes and/or repairs string instruments is called a "luthier." The history of lutherie encompasses several centuries, dating back to a time when the term referred to a maker of lutes. The term "archetier" refers to a crafts-person who is a maker of bows. While these terms are in general use throughout the world, on the North American continent, the terms "violin maker," "guitar maker," "bow maker," etc. are often used in their stead.

THE INSTRUMENTS

Violin

The smallest and highest pitched member of the traditional orchestral string family, the violin, is an expressive, dexterous and versatile instrument that is adept in a wide variety of genres. Players who specialize in classical repertoire tend to prefer the term "violinist." Players who specialize in popular or folk genres will often refer to themselves as a "fiddler." Technically, either term is correct. One should use the term most accepted for the genre and environment in which one is working.

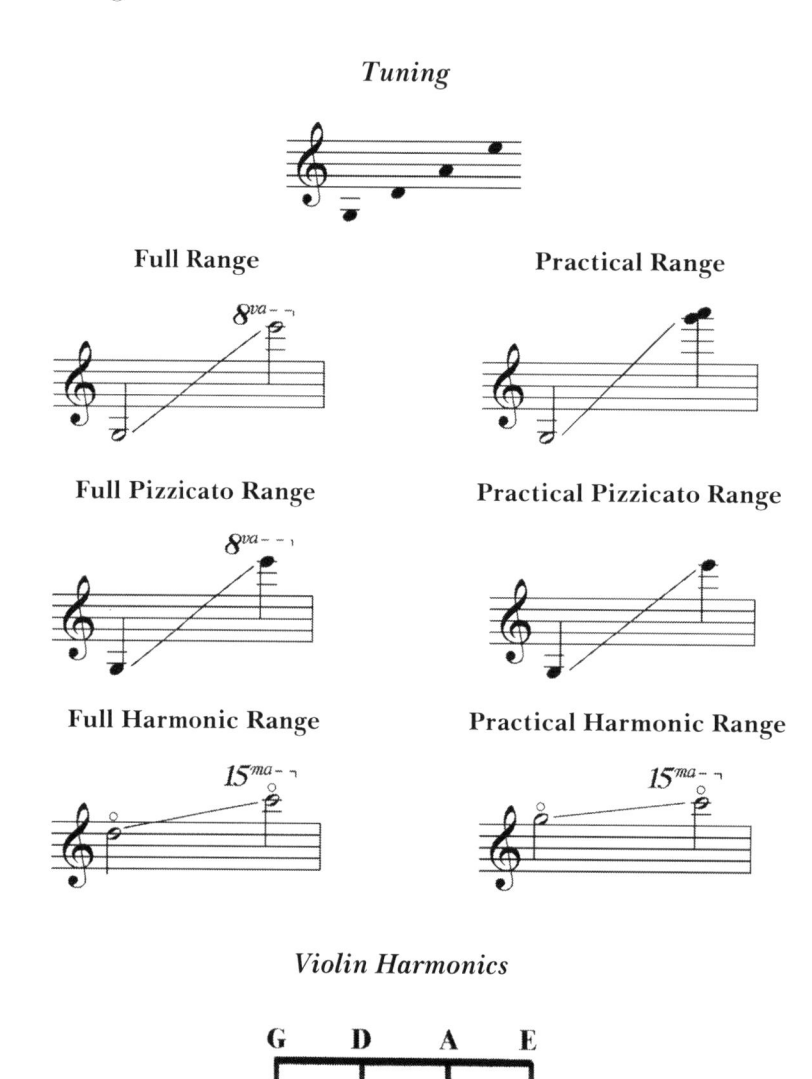

Tuning

Full Range **Practical Range**

Full Pizzicato Range **Practical Pizzicato Range**

Full Harmonic Range **Practical Harmonic Range**

Violin Harmonics

G   D   A   E
IV   III   II   I

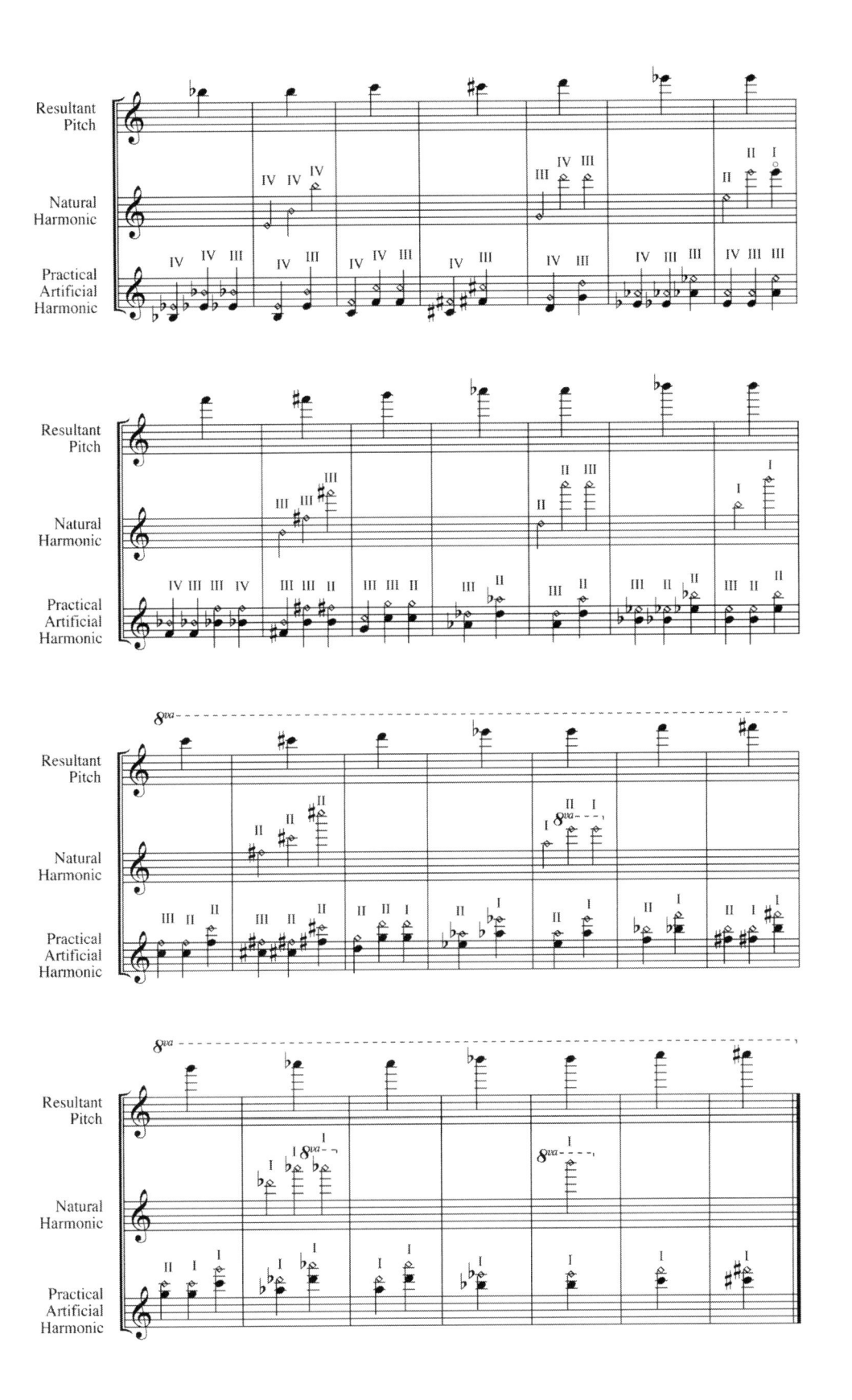

THE VIOLIN FAMILY

Violin Double Stops

The following represents a sampling of double stops available on the violin:

Violin Triple Stops

The following represents a sampling of triple stops available on the violin:

Violin Quadruple Stops

The following represents a sampling of quadruple stops available on the violin:

Viola

Similar in the design of the standard violin, the dimensions of a full-sized viola have not been standardized. Models may range from 25 mm to 100 mm larger than the standard full-sized violin. With strings tuned a perfect fifth lower than the violin, the body of the viola is not large enough to produce the same acoustical respond as the violin, resulting in the unique timbre of the instrument. (Increasing the size of the viola to the exact proportions of the violin would result in an instrument too unwieldy to be practical.) The viola bow is generally shorter and heavier, and the strings less responsive, than that of the violin. Bowing techniques are slightly different as a greater intensity is required, and fingering positions are further apart on the fingerboard than that of the violin. Viola parts are written in alto clef, with occasional forays into the treble clef to accommodate passages that would require extensive use of ledger lines. One typically refers to the person playing a viola as a *violist*, or *viola player*, and to the section as the *violas* or *viols*.

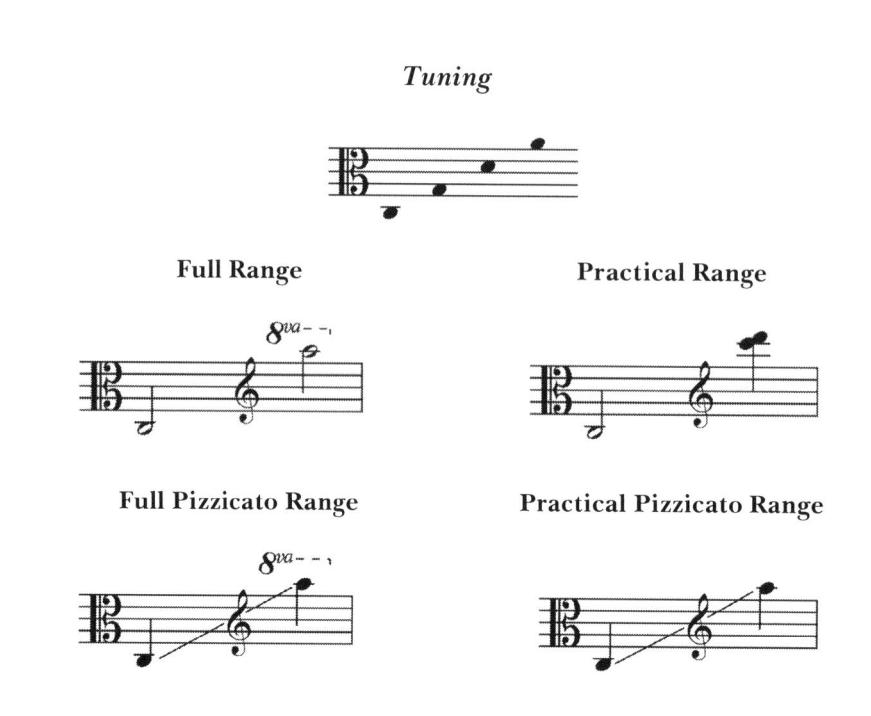

Tuning

Full Range　　　　　　　　　　**Practical Range**

Full Pizzicato Range　　　　　**Practical Pizzicato Range**

THE VIOLIN FAMILY

Full Harmonic Range **Practical Harmonic Range**

Viola Harmonics

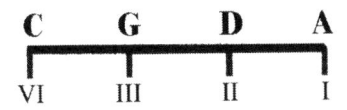

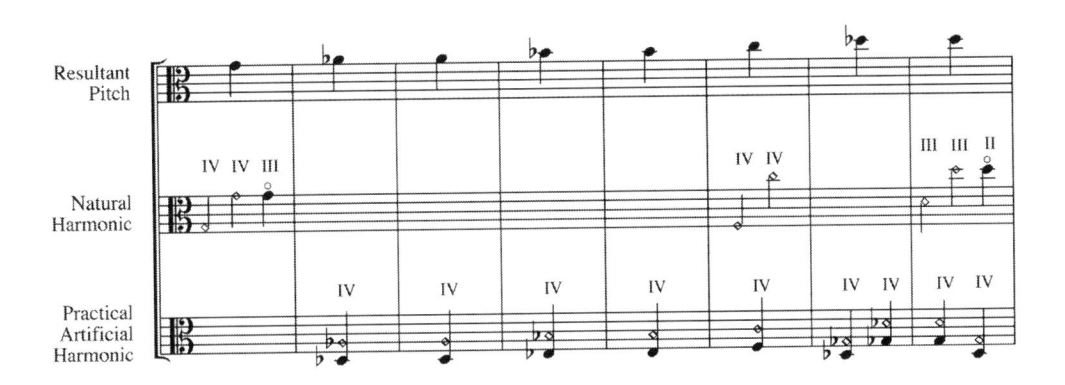

Viola Double Stops

The following represents a sampling of double stops available on the viola:

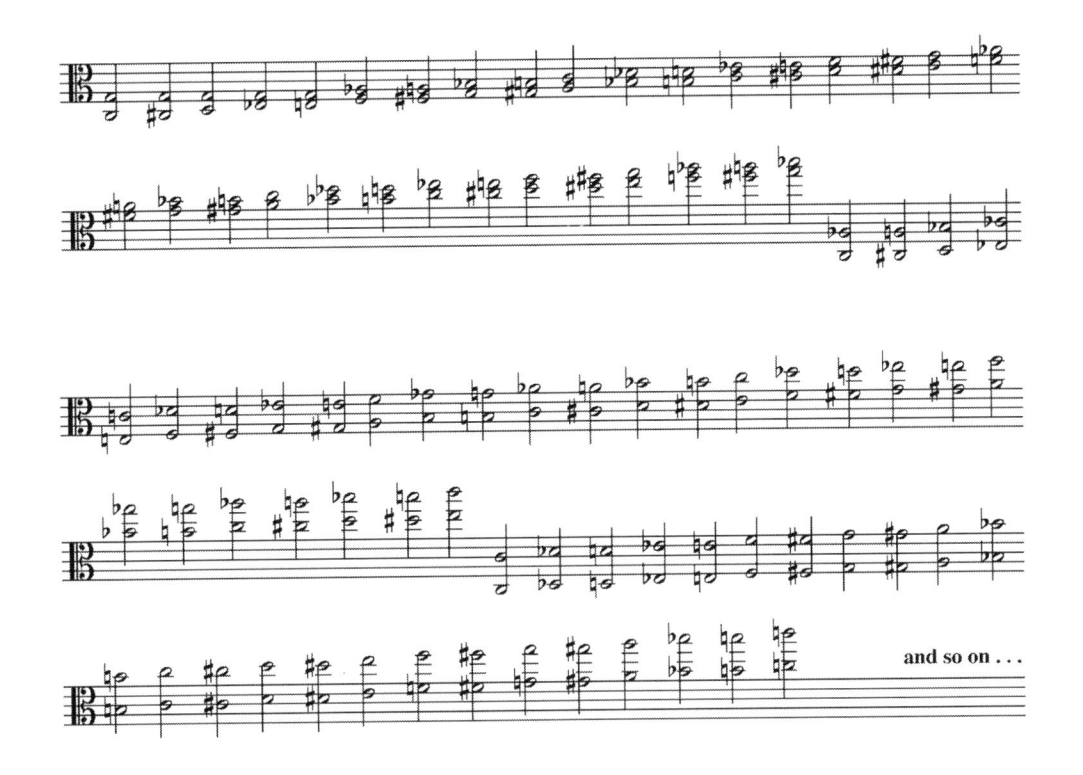

Viola Triple Stops

The following represents a sampling of triple stops available on the viola:

Viola Quadruple Stops

The following represents a sampling of quadruple stops available on the viola:

Violoncello

Commonly (and acceptably) referred to as a *cello*, the strings of the violoncello are tuned in perfect fifths (an octave below those of the viola). The cello is played in a seated position, with the body of the instrument resting between the knees and with the weight of the instrument supported by an endpin. Equally adept as a solo instrument or as a section member, the cello is a wonderfully versatile instrument capable evoking emotions, from sensitive and expressive, to playful and nimble, to dramatic and authoritative. One typically refers to the person playing a violoncello as a *cellist* and to the section as the *violoncelli*, *cellos* or *celli*.

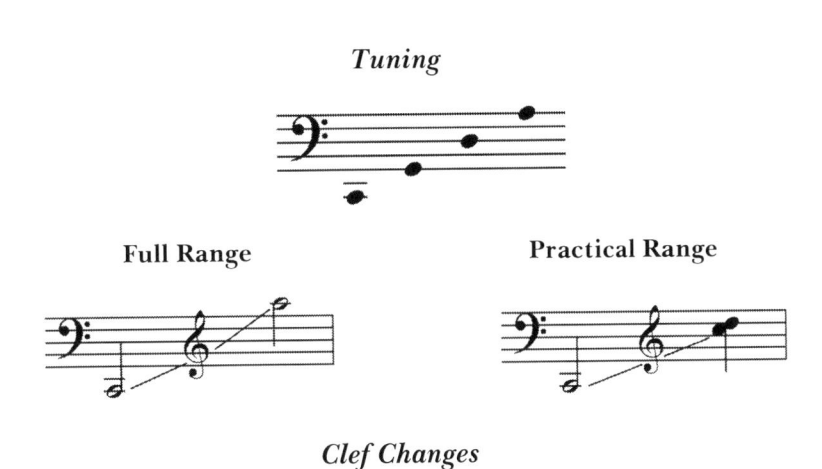

Tuning

Full Range *Practical Range*

Clef Changes

The range of the violoncello is such that it will often require clef changes to avoid excessive use of ledger lines. The default clef for the instrument is the bass clef, though parts may also be written in the tenor clef and, if needed, in the treble clef. In contemporary times it has become acceptable to shift from one clef to another as needed. However, there is a traditional practice about which one should be aware.

Traditional practices dictate that when clef changes are required in the cello part, a strict order of clef progression must be observed. The bass clef must be followed by the tenor clef prior to proceeding to the treble clef. Conversely, when descending from the treble clef, one must proceed to the tenor clef, before returning to the bass clef. On occasion, this practice will require the placement of a tenor clef at a place containing nothing more than rests and the treble clef placed prior the next entrance of notes. The reverse occurs for the return to the bass clef.

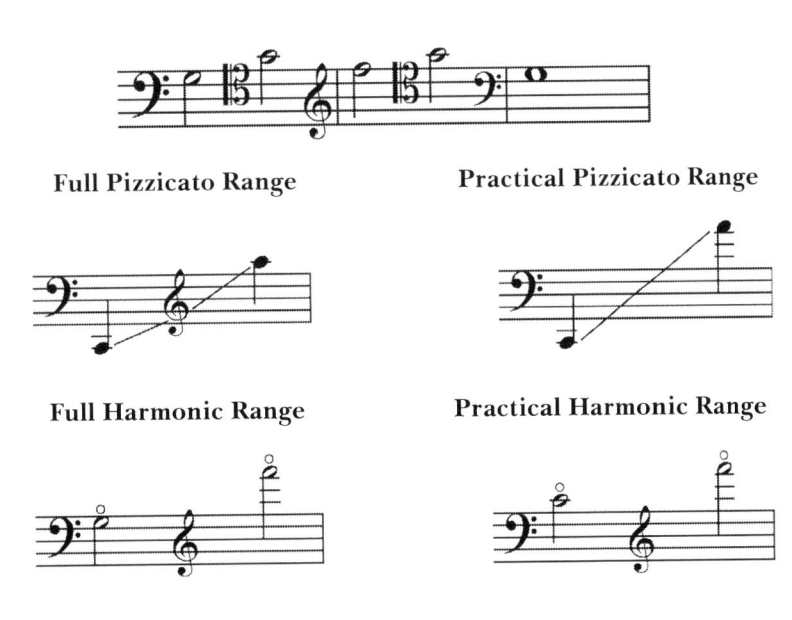

Full Pizzicato Range **Practical Pizzicato Range**

Full Harmonic Range **Practical Harmonic Range**

Violoncello Harmonics

Violoncello Double Stops

The following represents a sampling of double stops available on the cello:

Violoncello Triple Stops

The following represents a sampling of triple stops available on the cello:

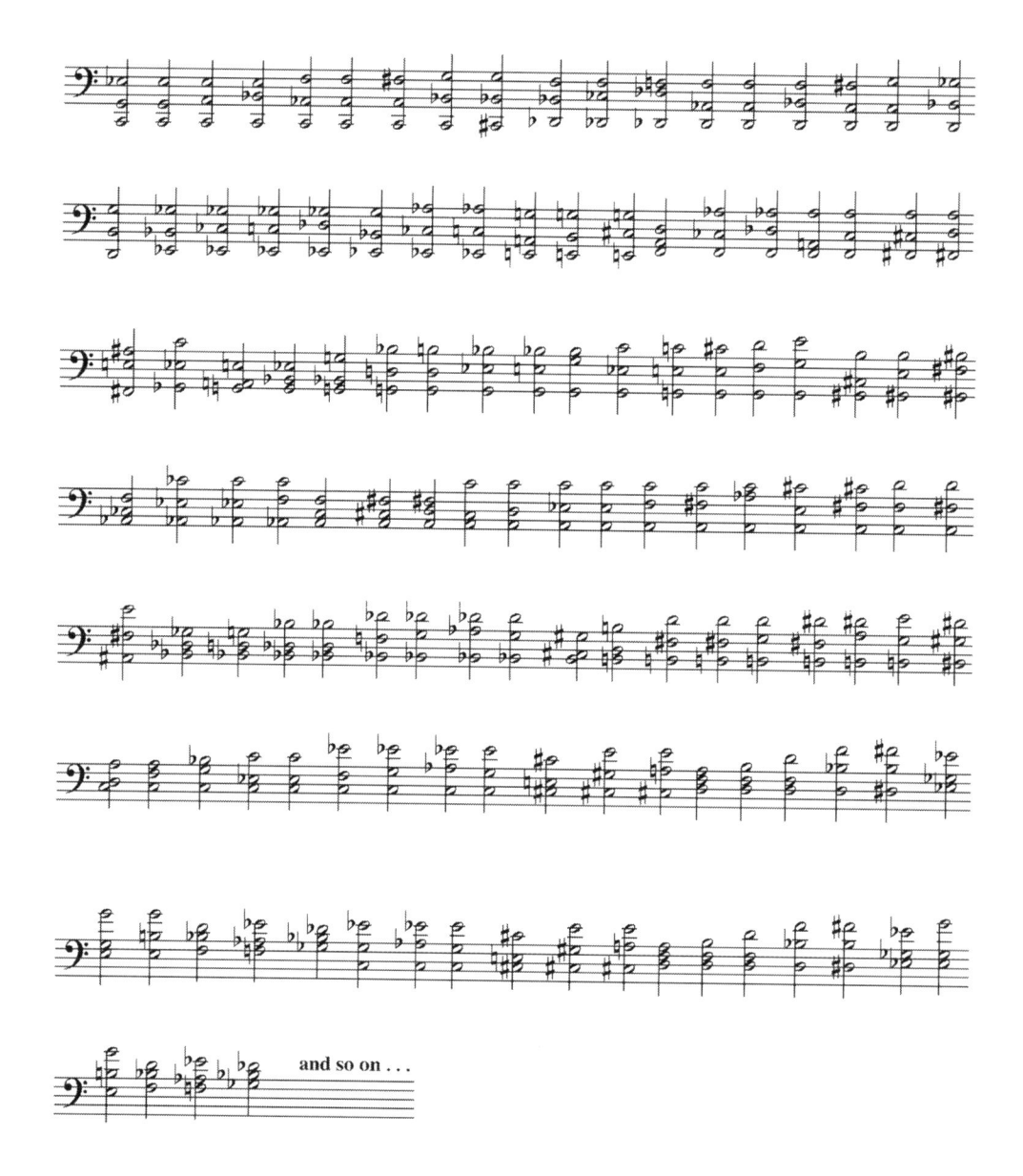

Violoncello Quadruple Stops

The following represents a sampling of quadruple stops available on the cello:

Double Bass

Depending upon the genre in which it appears, the double bass may be referred to by a variety of names. In the classical environment, the instrument is generally called a "double bass" or "contrabass," with occasional use of the term "bass viol"; in the wind ensemble/concert band environment it is usually called the string bass (to differentiate the part from the bass brass instruments); in the jazz environment it is call a "string bass," "upright bass", "acoustic bass," or simply "bass"; in country western, folk and other popular genres the names have become quite creative, and may include terms such as "doghouse bass" and "bull fiddle." Since all these terms refer to the same instrument, simply use a term appropriate for the genre in which one is working. One typically refers to the person playing a double bass as a "bassist," a "double bassist," a "contrabassist," a "bass player" or a "contrabass player," and to the section as the "basses," "double basses" or "contrabasses."

The shape and proportion of the double bass is unlike that of the upper strings, having sloped shoulders and a deeper body. The strings are larger and thicker, and the physical distance between intervals on the fingerboard is greater than that of the other string instruments. The strings of the double bass are tuned in perfect fourths and, as such, shifting fingering positions often required. Due to the physical demands placed upon the player and the somewhat cumbersome nature of the instrument, in general, one should avoid inordinately fast passages and large intervallic skips when writing for the double bass. If one is writing a solo selection or passage for a singular player of great skill, one can certainly employ a less conservative approach.

Tuning

Standard Tuning (4-String Bass)

**5-String Basses (or 4-String Basses with a C-attachment)
have the ability to play the low C**

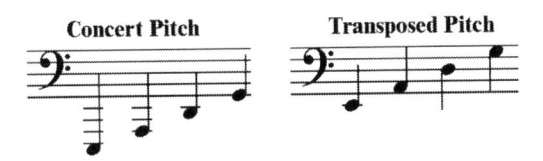

(Double bass always appears in transposed form, even in a concert score.)

Full Range (Transposed)

Practical Range (Transposed)

Full Pizzicato Range (Transposed)

Practical Pizzicato Range (Transposed)

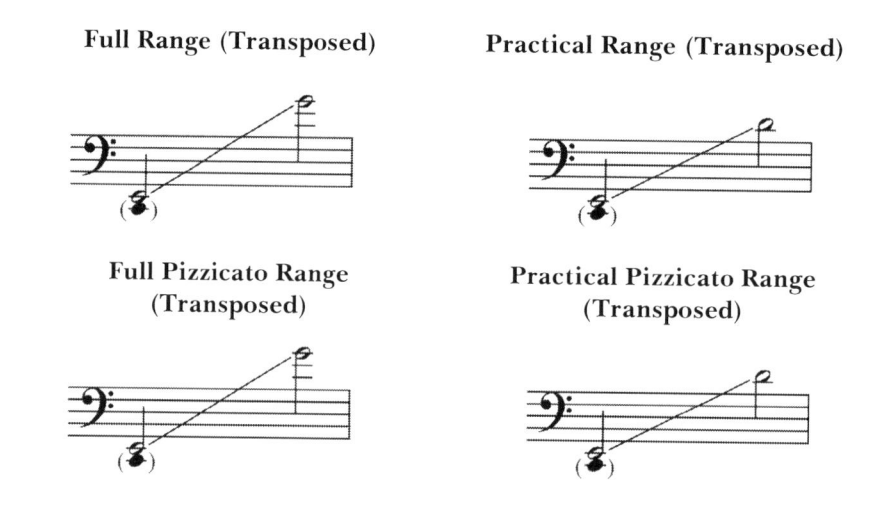

Harmonics

The use of harmonics on the bass is restricted to natural harmonics only. The physical distance between intervals renders the use of artificial harmonics virtually impossible (and at the very least, impractical). Bass harmonics, in an orchestral setting, lack significant projection and serve little purpose. The most practical use of bass harmonics would be in a solo or cadenza setting, where the harmonic timbre is exposed.

Practical Double Bass Harmonics

Multiple Stops

The physical dimensions of the bass, plus the low register in which it plays, render the use of multiple stops impractical in an orchestral setting. Double stops where one of the desired pitches is an open string are most feasible, with double-stop octaves being most useful. While technically possible, double stops in the upper register usually result in suspect intonation. Double stops containing close intervals in the middle and lower registers result in a muddy sound (see Implied Fundamental, p. 6). From a practical standpoint, if at all possible one should avoid writing multiple stops for double bass in an ensemble setting. If multiple notes are absolutely necessary, consider writing divisi.

Practical Double Bass Double Stops

French Bow

The French bow is held with the palm facing toward the bass. The thumb rests on the shaft of the bow (next to the frog) and the fingers grip the other side of the bow. The French bow is often the choice of soloists, as it offers greater dynamic range and control.

German Bow

With the German bow, players hold the bow with two fingers between the stick and the hair to maintain tension of the hair against the string. The German bow has a taller frog and is held with the palm angled upwards. The thumb rests on the side of the stick and the index finger balances the bow at the point where the frog meets the stick. The little finger supports the frog from underneath and the middle two fingers apply the force to move the bow across the strings. German bow proponents maintain that it is easier to use for light bow strokes as staccato, spiccato and detaché.

C Attachment

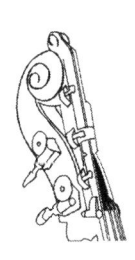

The C attachment (for double bass) is an apparatus allowing the low E string to be lowered four semitones to a low C. One of the benefits of this attachment is that it facilitates an exact doubling (at the octave) of the low register of the cello. One should be aware that this is considered "optional" equipment and it may or may not be readily available. One should never assume that this extended range will be at one's disposal. When bassists (without a C attachment) encounter notes written below the E, they will transpose the notes up an octave. There are also several manufacturers producing five-string double basses. However, one should not expect the five-string instrument to be readily available.

Practical Usage of Multiple Stops

As previously mentioned, multiple stops should be used for specific effects and never as avoidance for deleting chord members when orchestrating. They can be useful as a means to emphasize an accented chord by adding both fullness and power. In the following example, double stops will be utilized for this purpose in measure 1 and measure 3. *Note*: The chord is revoiced and double-stops avoided in measure 5 due the awkwardness of the descending interval (dim. 4th (g" to d#")).

THE ENSEMBLES

String Quartet

While evidence to the contrary exists, Franz Joseph Haydn is generally considered the "father of the string quartet." Haydn's 83 string quartets, along with those of Mozart and Beethoven, brought this ensemble (consisting of 2 violins, viola, violoncello) to the forefront of chamber music where it remains the preeminent ensemble in the genre to this day.

Chamber Strings

Though the string quartet is the dominant string ensemble in chamber music, a wealth of other chamber music ensembles containing strings exists in this genre. The following is but a sampling of the possible combinations.

Ensemble Name:	*Instrumentation:*
String Trio	violin, viola, violoncello
Piano Trio	violin, violoncello, piano
Piano Quartet	violin, viola, violoncello, piano
Piano Quintet	2 violins, viola, violoncello, piano (*or*) violin, viola, violoncello, contrabass, piano
String Quintet	2 violin, viola, violoncello with additional viola, violoncello, or contrabass
Pierrot Ensemble	flute, clarinet, violin, violoncello, piano
String Sextet	2 violins, 2 viols, 2 violoncelli
Piano Sextet	violin, 2 viols, violoncello, contrabass, piano (*or*) clarinet, 2 violin, viola, violoncello, piano
Wind and String Septet	clarinet, horn, bassoon, violin, viola, violoncello, contrabass
Wind and String Octet	clarinet, horn, bassoon, 2 violins, viola, violoncello, contrabass (*or*) clarinet, 2 horns, violin, 2 viols, violoncello, contrabass
String Octet	4 violins, 2 viols, 2 violoncelli (*or*) 4 violins, 2 viols, violoncello, contrabass
Double Quartet	4 violins, 2 viols, 2 violoncelli
Wind and String Nonet	flute, oboe, clarinet, horn, bassoon, violin, viola, violoncello, contrabass

Orchestral Strings

An orchestra comprised solely (or principally) of instruments of the violin family is referred to as a string orchestra. Occasionally, additional instruments (such as piano, harp, percussion or a singular wind instrument) are added to the basic ensemble for enhanced texture. The size of the string orchestra varies from ensemble to ensemble, but generally ranges from 12 or 13 instruments (4 1st violins, 3 or 4 2nd violins, 2 viols, 2 violoncelli and 1 double bass) to 21 or 22 instruments (6 1st violins, 5 or 6 2nd violins, 4 viols, 4 violoncelli and 2 double basses). It is not unusual for a string orchestra to perform without a conductor. When this is the case, the concertmaster serves as both player and conductor.

Symphony Orchestra Strings

In general, the string section of the symphony orchestra is considerably larger than that of the string orchestra. Additional string players are required to achieve an acceptable balance with the brass section, the percussion section and, to a lesser extent, the woodwind section. Typically, the string section of the symphony orchestra will contain approximately 60 players (16 1st violins, 14 2nd violins, 12 viols, 10 violoncelli and 8 double basses). Some orchestras will contain fewer and some will contain considerably more than 60 strings. In any case, the size of the sections will remain roughly proportional to that listed above.

PRACTICAL CONSIDERATIONS

Practical Guidelines for Choosing a Work to Orchestrate for Strings

- Choose pieces that stylistically apply to your chosen instrumentation.
- Choose pieces that are applicable to the ranges and registers (and key signatures) of your chosen instrumentation.
- Choose pieces that offer textual opportunities.

Practical Guidelines when Writing for Strings

- Avoid extended chromatic passages.
- Avoid large intervallic skips (exceeding an octave).
- Avoid awkward intervals (both ascending or descending) in tonal voice-leading, i.e. aug. 2nd, dim 4th, aug. 4th, dim 5th, major 7th, minor 9th, etc. (*Note*: As intrinsic elements of contemporary, free chromatic, serialized, avant-garde and atonal music, use of "awkward intervals" may be required to maintain the stylistic intent of these genres.)
- Always be cognizant of voice-leading in *all* parts.
- Avoid pieces that are specifically idiomatic of piano.
- Remember that piano arpeggios (generally) do not translate well to ensemble instrumentation.
- Always attempt to remain true to the (perceived) intent of the composer.
- Do not simply repeat sections, note-for-note; always attempt to add interest.
- Learn from the *masters*! *Listen to and analyze* as many different examples of string writing as possible.

IN THE PROFESSION

When scoring for strings, one should be aware of a professional courtesy involving bow markings within the score and parts. It falls within the jurisdiction of the concertmaster and principal string players to determine the specific applicable bowing for their section, and placing extensive explicit bow markings can be construed as an insult to the section leaders' abilities.

While it is a valid academic exercise to calculate and notate all the up-bows and down-bows in a given selection, doing so for the purposes of dictating the method of performance should be avoided. A skilled orchestrator implies bowing through slurs, phrasing, dynamics and articulations (and immense attention should be devoted to these details). Based upon these implications, the concertmaster and principal players will determine the appropriate bowing techniques for their section.

It is, however, acceptable to place bow markings in the part when specific bowing is require, such as in a section requiring repeated down-bows or up-bows. It is also appropriate to place extensive bow markings when scoring for elementary and, to a lesser extent, intermediate performers. However, when writing for college-level or professional level ensembles, one should respect the abilities of the section leaders unless an explicit bowing for a particular effect is required.

BUILDING THE SCORE

This example will demonstrate the process for creating a string quartet orchestration from an existing piano selection. Once an appropriate work has been selected, one should begin by performing a harmonic analysis. The analysis will determine harmonic elements that are to be deleted and the harmonic context, should harmonic elements need to be added. To aid in the demonstration of this process, no double, triple or quadruple stops will be used. For the purposes of the exercise the following selection will be used:

Frédéric Chopin, *Prélude*, Op. 28 No. 20, mm. 1–13

Upon completion of the analysis, one can delete the non-essential harmonic elements and octave doublings, reducing the selection to four voices. In the case of the violoncello part, one uses the instrument's range and register, and the context of the composition to determine the appropriate octave choice for the bass line.

One then examines the selection for elements within the notation that must be addressed or altered to work for the instruments of the chosen ensemble. These elements may include pedal markings, crescendi and decrescendi of undefined dynamic scope, dynamics that may need to be modified to be appropriate for the chosen instrumentation, ornamentation, rhythmic subdivisions, arpeggios, etc.

In this particular example, the scope of the crescendo in measures four and five is undefined. One could simply choose to crescendo one dynamic level resulting in a fortississimo on count 3 of measure 4. However, a dynamic level of this magnitude would be somewhat uncharacteristic for this type of chamber ensemble. A practical solution would be to modify the beginning dynamic, so that the crescendo will result in a more sensible dynamic. Therefore, the beginning dynamic will be altered to forte, with the crescendo culminating at fortissimo.

Since all of the remaining notational elements are appropriate for the chosen ensemble, one may proceed by assignment the top voice to the 1st violin, the second voice to the 2nd violin, the third voice to the viola, and bottom voice to the violoncello.

Largo
Violin I
Violin II
Viola
Cello
Vln. I
Vln. II
Vla.
Vc.
f
ff
p
pp

This example will demonstrate the process for adapting an existing piano selection for string orchestra. To aid in the demonstration of this process, no double, triple or quadruple stops will be used, and no divisi will be used. As always, one should begin by performing a harmonic analysis to determine the harmonic content and context to enable one to delete (or add) appropriate harmonic elements. For the purposes of the exercise the following selection will be used:

Felix Mendelssohn, *War March of the Priests* **(from** *Athalie***)**

Upon completion of the harmonic analysis, one can delete the non-essential harmonic elements, reducing the selection to five voices. Since piano parts are designed to be played within the physical span of the human hand, one may also seek alternate harmonic voicings to accommodate the ranges and registers of the chosen instruments. Creating a combination of voicings also alleviates potential harmonic monotony that may occur as a result of constant open (or constant closed) voicings. In this example, open voicings have been employed in measures 6 through 8, and measures 13 and 14. This "revoicing" allows the viola to remain in a more resonant register and provides a contrast of voicings without altering the original harmonic content.

Since all of the remaining elements are appropriate for the chosen ensemble, one may proceed by assigning the top voice to the 1st violins, the second voice to the 2nd violins, the third voice to the viols, the fourth voice to the violoncelli and the fifth voice to the contrabasses.

SCORING EXAMPLES

Scoring Examples for String Quartet

Scoring solutions for string quartet are extensive and limited only by one's creativity and knowledge of the instruments. The following examples are but a few of the possible approaches one might choose.

Georg Friedrich Händel, *Sarabande*, mm. 1–20, orchestrated for string quartet by RJ Miller

Ludwig van Beethoven, Quartet No. 8 in E minor, Op. 59 No. 2, Movement II, mm. 1–8

RJ Miller, *Elegy*, mm. 23–41.

Copyright © 2002 by Appassionata Music. Used by permission.

Gabriel Fauré, *Pavane*, Op. 50, mm. 1–9, orchestrated for string quartet by RJ Miller

Ludwig van Beethoven, Quartet in B flat major, Op. 130, Movement VI, mm. 347–361

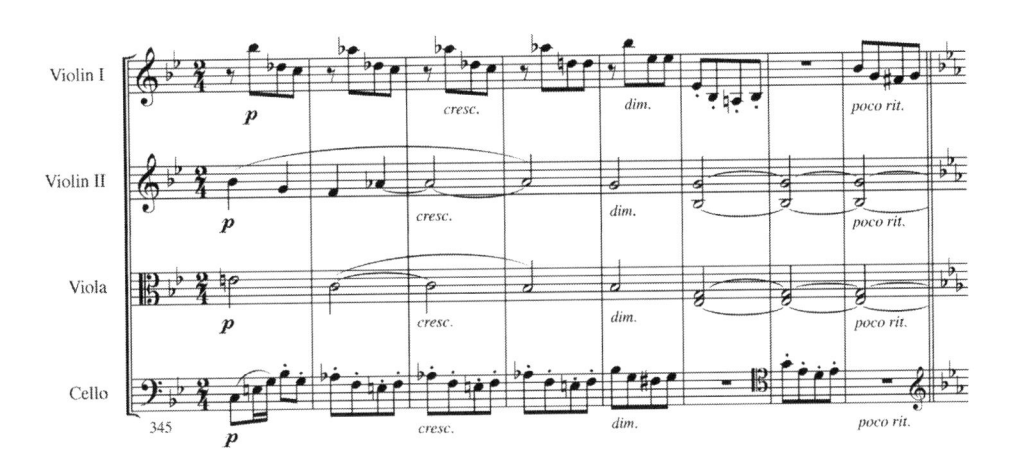

Alexander Borodin, String Quartet No. 1, *Scherzo*, mm. 1–12

Scoring Examples for Orchestral Strings

Scoring solutions one utilizes for the string quartet may also be applied to orchestral strings by doubling the contrabasses with the celli at the octave. With the additional players available per part and when combined with a multitude of additional instrumental textures available within the orchestra, the possible scoring solutions for orchestral strings are virtually endless. The following examples are but a few of the possible approaches one might choose.

Joseph Haydn, Symphony No. 101 in D major (Hoboken 1/101), Movement I, mm. 1–23

THE VIOLIN FAMILY

Franz Schubert, Symphony in B major, Op. posth., Movement I, mm. 1–8

W. A. Mozart, Symphony in G minor, K. 550, Movement I, mm. 1–18

Peter Ilyich Tchaikovsky, *Romeo and Juliet*, Overture-Fantasy, mm. 388–403

THE VIOLIN FAMILY

THE VIOLIN FAMILY

99

RJ Miller, *The Wilderness Suite*, Movement VIII (*The Balance of Nature*), mm. 58–65.

Copyright © 1992 by Appassionata Music. Used by permission.

Claude Debussy, *La Mer*, Movement III (*Dialogue du vent et de la mer*), mm. 168–178

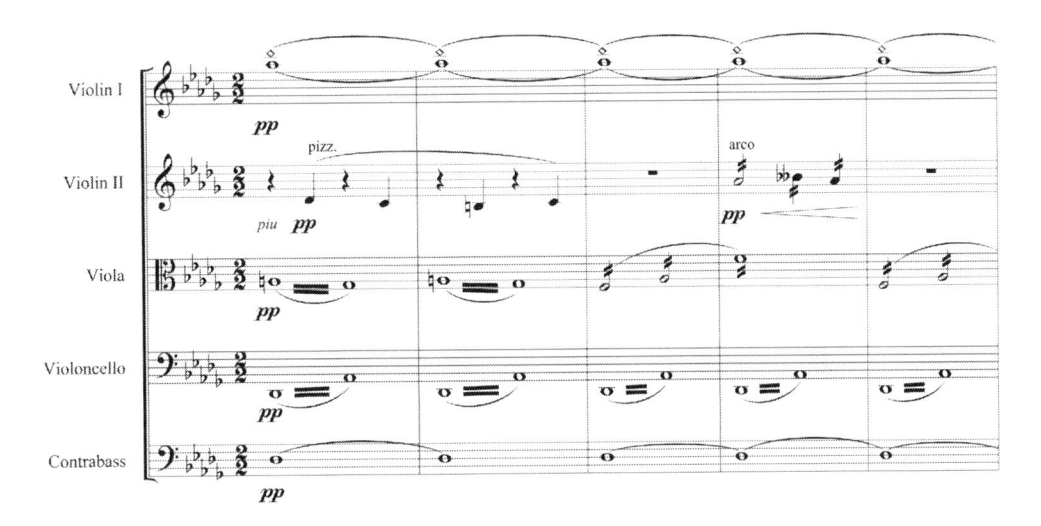

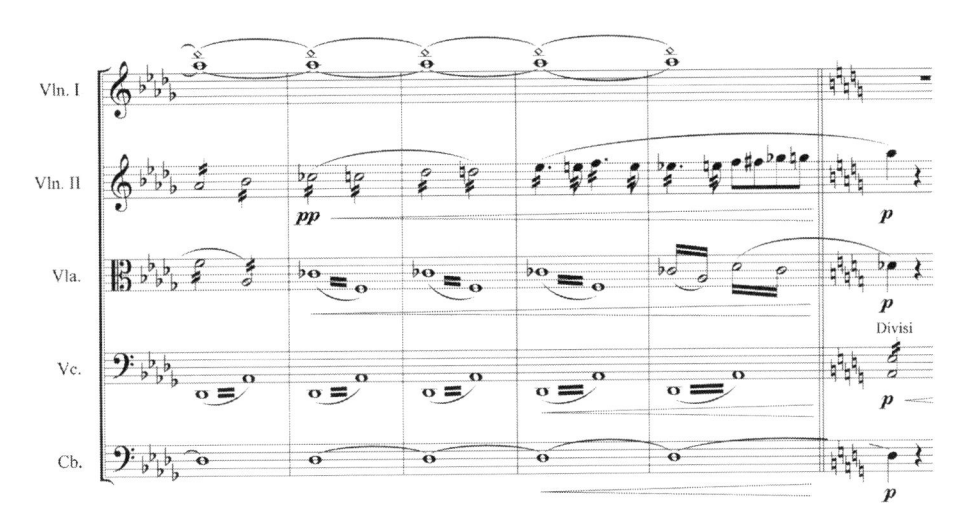

SUGGESTED EXERCISES

Scoring Exercise for String Quartet

Using the information and guidelines presented in this chapter and in Chapter 3 (Practical Problem Solving), orchestrate the following example for string quartet without the use of multi-stops. Perform a harmonic analysis and seek ways to add textural interest.

Alexander Ilyinsky, *Cradle Song* **(from the "Noure and Anitra" Suite), Op. 13**

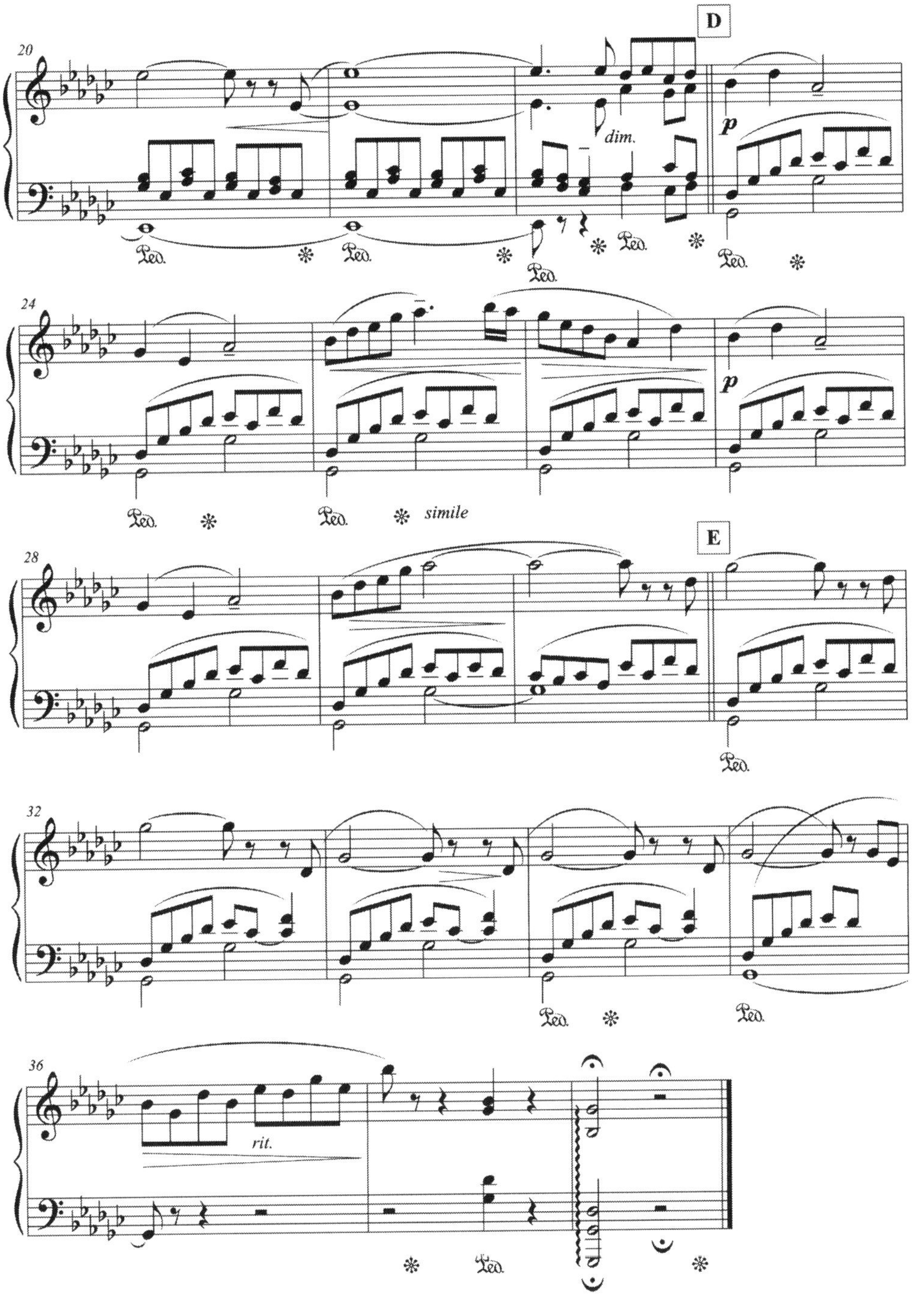

20
D
dim.
p
Ped.
24
simile
28
E
32
36
rit.

Scoring Exercise for Orchestral Strings

Using the information and guidelines presented in this chapter and in Chapter 3 (Practical Problem Solving), orchestrate the following example for string orchestra without the use of divisi or multi-stops. Perform a harmonic analysis and seek ways to add textural interest.

Edward Macdowell, *The Flow'ret* **(Forest Idyl No. 1)**

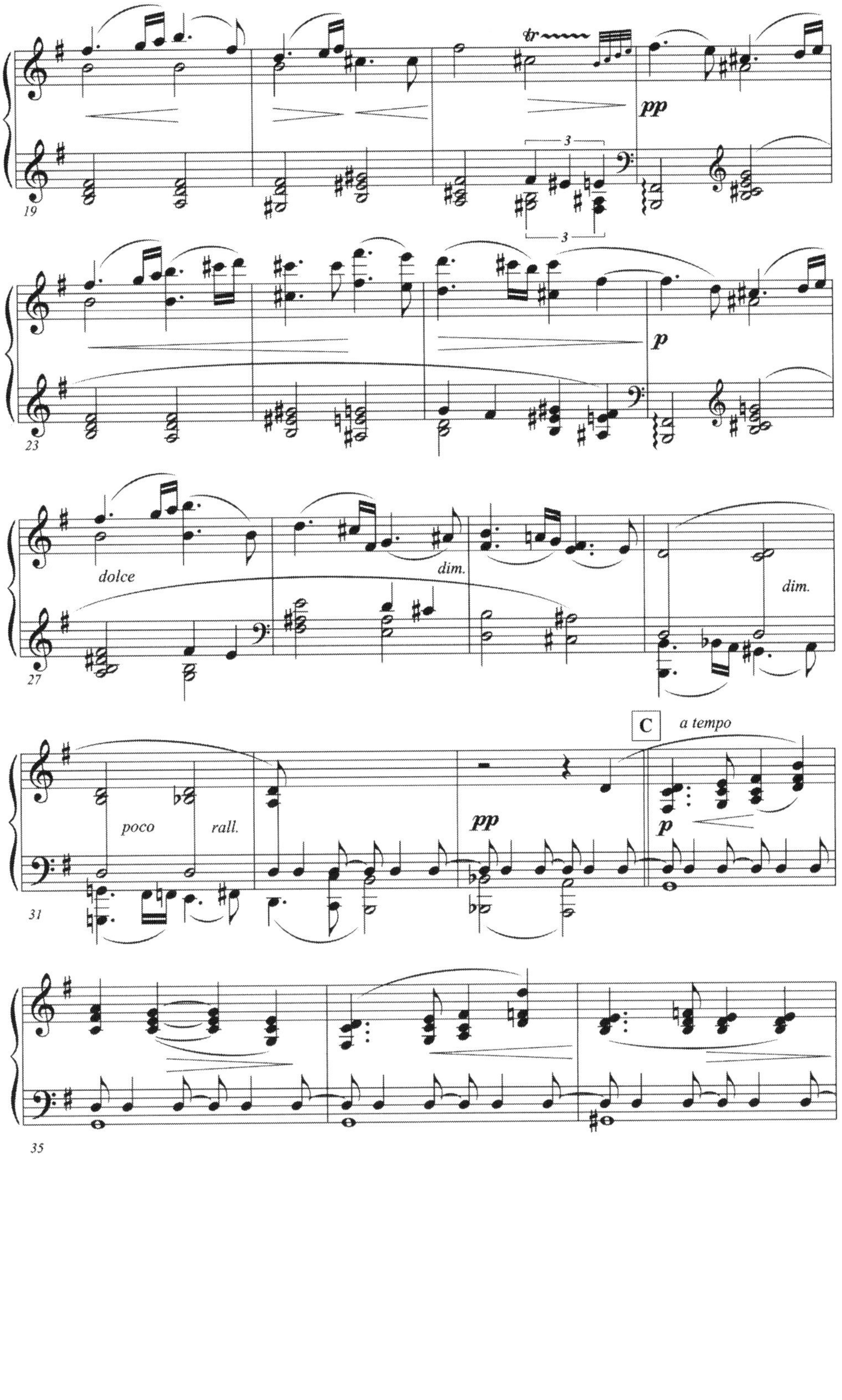
tr
pp
p
dolce
dim.
dim.
C
a tempo
poco
rall.
pp
p

106 THE VIOLIN FAMILY

5

THE BRASS FAMILY

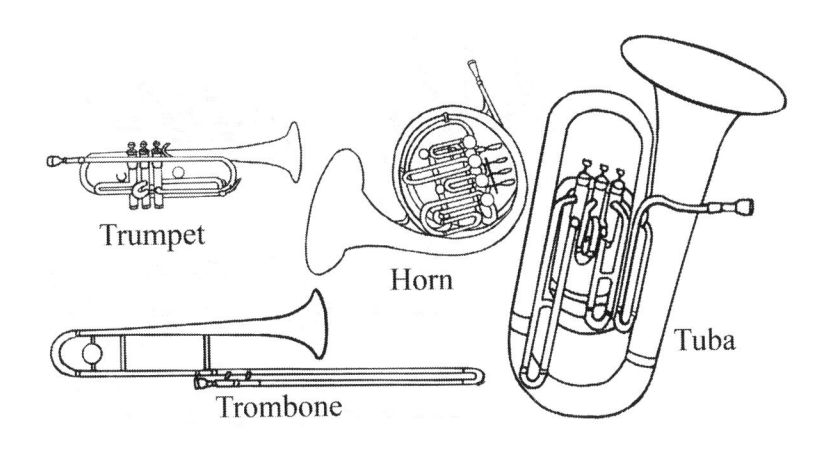

The classification of an instrument as a member of the brass family is not dependent upon the material from which it is made, but rather upon the means by which the player produces sound. Not all "brass instruments" are made of metal. The sound of a brass instrument is produced by the resonance of the air contained within the body of the instrument vibrating sympathetically with the "buzzing" of the player's lips upon the instrument mouthpiece.

THE ESSENTIALS

Cylindrical and Conical Classifications

A brass instrument is classified as cylindrical or conical based upon the proportion of the tubing that is of constant diameter, versus the proportion of tubing that constantly increases in diameter. Instruments containing a majority of tubing being of approximately constant diameter are classified as cylindrical. Instruments containing a majority of tubing being of constantly increasing diameter are classified as conical. Examples of cylindrical instruments include the trumpet and trombone; examples of conical instruments include the horn, euphonium and tuba.

Cylindrical brass instruments (containing tubing of constant diameter) generally have a bright and penetrating timbre. Conical instruments (containing tubing with constantly increasing diameter) generally have a timbre that is fuller and mellower than that of cylindrical instruments.

Whole-tube Brass Instruments

Instruments upon which the fundamental (1st partial) can be easily and precisely produced are referred to as whole-tube instruments. On these instruments the diameter of the tubing is proportionally larger in relation to the length of the tubing. Examples of whole-tube instruments include the euphonium and tuba.

Half-tube Brass Instruments

Instruments upon which the fundamental cannot be easily or precisely produced are referred to as half-tube instruments. On these instruments the diameter of the tubing is proportionally smaller in relation to the length of the tubing, and the second partial becomes the lowest practical note on the instrument. Examples of half-tube instruments include the horn in F and the trumpet.

Single-tonguing

Brass players commence notes by tonguing. The player places the tongue behind the upper front teeth and uses the syllable "ta" to begin the flow of air.

Double-tonguing

Double tonguing is a technique used to increase the speed at which a player can initiate the airflow. The player places the tongue behind the upper front teeth and uses the syllable "ta" to begin the flow of air followed by the syllable "ka" at the back of tongue to quickly initiate a second note. This can be done repeatedly, in quick succession: "ta-ka, ta-ka, ta-ka, ta-ka," etc.

Triple-tonguing

As with double-tonguing, triple-tonguing is a technique used to further increase the speed at which a player can initiate the airflow. The player places the tongue behind the upper front teeth and uses the syllable "ta" to begin the flow of air, followed by a second "ta" to quickly initiate a second note, followed by the syllable "ka" at the back of tongue to quickly initiate a third note. This can be done repeatedly, in quick succession, with the order of syllables at the discretion of the player: "ta-ta-ka, ta-ta-ka, ta-ta-ka, ta-ta-ka," or "ta-ka-ta ta-ka-ta ta-ka-ta ta-ka-ta," etc.

Slurs

Brass players (with the exception of trombonists) accomplish slurs by changing fingering without tonguing the note. In a group of notes that are slurred together, the first note is tongued and the remaining notes are initiated by changing the fingering. In situations where two adjacent notes are of different pitch but the same fingering, the player uses the embouchure to shift to the appropriate overtone (again, without tonguing). Due to the nature of the instrument, trombonists use very subtle tonguing between slurred notes (using the syllable "do"). This compensates for the natural portamento that would otherwise occur between slurred notes.

Flutter-tonguing

Flutter-tonguing produces a "growl-like" tone and is achieved by vibrating the tip of the tongue against the back of the upper front teeth, as if one were rolling a Spanish language "r."

Trills

The trill is accomplished by the rapid alternation between two adjacent notes. Without additional notation, the default trill is to the adjacent higher diatonic pitch. The upper note may be designated as a non-diatonic pitch by adding a sharp, flat or natural sign, as applicable, between the *tr* and the subsequent wavy line. Trills are relatively easy on all brass instruments with valves (they are not conducive to trombones).

Shakes

The shake is accomplished by the rapid alternation between two adjacent harmonics. Shakes are easier to accomplish and more effective in the upper registers as the harmonics are closer together. All brass instruments are capable of producing shakes, although they are most idiomatic of trumpets, cornets, flugelhorns and trombones.

Brass Glissandi

In the truest meaning of the term, the glissandi described below would technically and more accurately be described as portamenti. However, the long-established tradition of using the contrary terminology dictates usage of the term "glissando" when describing the following effects.

1/2-valve Glissando

Brass players of valve instruments can glissando smoothly between notes by depressing the valve(s) halfway and using the embouchure to create a portamento. While effective, this glissando (or portamento) effect is not full tone, lacking both timbre and amplitude until the target note is acquired.

Trombone Glissando

The unique construction of the trombone allows for smooth, full-toned glissandi up to the intervallic distance of an augmented fourth (though that interval is only available with a specific set of slide positions, i.e. 7th position to 1st position). One must often execute desired glissandi through the use of alternate slide positions.

Valve Tremolo

On brass instruments with valves, many notes can be played with alternate fingerings. Changing quickly, back and forth, from one fingering combination to an alternate fingering combination (on the same pitch) creates a tremolo effect. This effect is not available on trombones.

Mutes

The use of mutes significantly alters the timbre, amplitude and pitch accuracy of the instrument. Most mutes will cause the instrument to play slightly sharper than the open (non-muted) instrument, necessitating pitch compensation through the use of the tuning slides. Each type of mute is designed to create a specific (altered) timbre by suppressing certain overtones, while accentuating others. Since all mutes block the sound emanating from the bell of the instrument, amplitude is significantly decreased. While there is a multitude of brass mutes available, the following represents those most commonly used.

Straight Mute

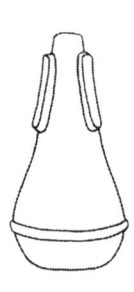

The most commonly used mute is the straight mute. Should an instrumental part not designate a specific mute, the straight mute is used by default. It is a cone-shaped, hollow mute that suppresses the lower harmonics, resulting in a nasal, almost metallic timbre. It has the widest dynamic range of any brass mute, and the metallic effect can be piercing when played at loud volumes. However, when played at normal volumes, the resultant timbre is useful both as a solo timbre, and as a timbre to be blended with others instruments in the ensemble. Straight mutes are available for all orchestral brass instruments (including tuba), and players are expected to have them at their disposal.

Cup Mute

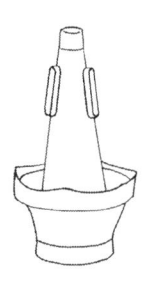

The construction of the cup mute is similar to that of the straight mute, with the addition of a flange that forms a cup over the bell. The mute is designed to suppress both the upper and lower harmonics, resulting in a timbre that is darker, richer and considerably more muffled than that of a straight mute. Cup mutes are available for all orchestral brass. Though available, cup mutes for horn and tuba are rarely used, and players are not expected to have them at their immediate disposal.

Wah-wah Mute (Harmon Mute)

The wah-wah mute (also known as the Harmon mute) is a hollow, spherical mute with a removable stem in the center. It has a solid ring of cork that completely blocks the bell, thereby forcing all of the sound through the mute. Placing the hand over the stem, then removing it, produces the idiomatic "wah-wah" sound, and extending the stem can alter this sound. A different "buzzing" timbre can be produced by removing the stem (a timbre popular with jazz players). One must specifically designate the desired configuration in the instrumental part. Wah-wah mutes are available for trumpets and trombones.

Bucket Mute

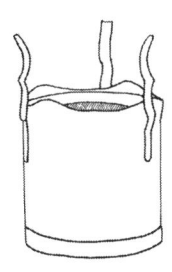

Bucket mutes are filled with cotton and clip to the rim of the bell. They are designed to suppress the upper-mid and high harmonics, resulting in a soft, mellow, muffled timbre. While useful for solo passages, the mute is extremely effective in creating a smooth and mellow blend of timbre within a section, or sections, of cylindrical brass instruments. The mute is also a useful aid in blending cylindrical brass instruments with strings. Bucket mutes are available for trumpets, trombones and tubas. They are not available for horns.

"In the Stand"

While not technically a mute, playing a cylindrical brass instrument into the music stand does produce a somewhat muted sound. The resultant, muffled sound is useful should one wish a less penetrating sound from cylindrical brass instruments. This technique is not practical on horn, euphonium and tuba.

"Stopped Horn"

Horn players can produce a unique "muted" timbre, sounding both nasal and distant, by employing a technique referred to as "stopped horn." The effect is accomplished by closing the bell with the right hand. To designate a "stopped horn" passage, one simply places the term "stopped" (gestopft (G.), bouché (Fr.), chiuso (I.)) above the note initiating the passage, and "open" (offen (G.), ouvert (Fr.), aperto (I.)) when the effect is to be terminated. In passages requiring quick alternations between stopped and open, one may use a plus sign (+) over the stopped notes. The stopped horn effect has a relatively limited practical range (from c′ to f″ in the transposed part) and produces the most characteristic timbre on the F "side" of the horn.

Brass Embouchure Considerations

When being played, brass instruments are in constant contact with the player's embouchure. Brass players spend years building and training the muscles in the embouchure to achieve accuracy and endurance. However, no matter the expertise of player, there will always be a certain amount of pressure against the lips (especially when playing in higher registers). This pressure adversely affects the blood-flow to lips, causing muscle fatigue. Once these muscles are fatigued, the lips will no longer "buzz" and tone production will cease until the blood-flow to lips is restored. One must always be aware of this situation when orchestrating for brass and allow adequate respites within the parts to accommodate this physical need.

THE INSTRUMENTS

Trumpet

The soprano member of the brass family is flexible, agile and at home in a broad range of genres. Trumpets are available in a wide variety of keys. The trumpet most commonly used in academia and in jazz is the B♭ trumpet, while the C trumpet dominates the orchestral field at the professional level. When scoring for symphony orchestra, one should orchestrate the trumpet parts to be functional on either instrument, as one can never be sure upon which instrument the part will be played. It is also wise to provide parts in both keys. Not doing so may force the

trumpet player to transpose the part for the instrument upon which the player is performing.
Note: Pianissimo passages are very difficult, if not impossible, to execute in the extreme registers.

Trumpet Range (Transposed)

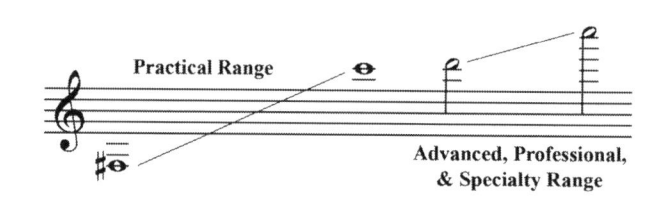

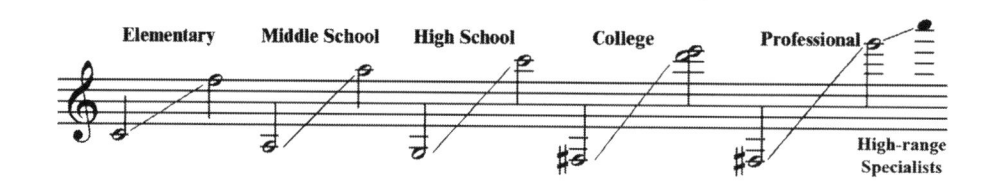

Trumpet Registers (Transposed)

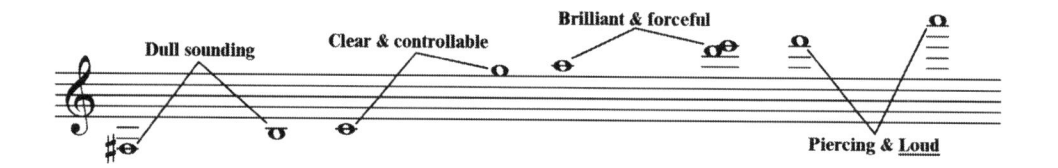

B♭ Trumpet Transposition

B♭ trumpets sound a major 2nd below the written note. Transposed parts are notated a major 2nd above concert pitch (adding two sharps to the key signature) and always notated in treble clef.

C Trumpet Transposition

C trumpet is a non-transposing instrument that is always written in treble clef.

Cornet

A close relative of the trumpet, and also a soprano voice in the brass family, the cornet is a conical instrument having a mellower timbre than that of the trumpet. Like trumpets, cornets are flexible, agile and at home in a wide range of genres. Though cornets are available in a variety of keys, the B♭ cornet is most frequently used (and most commonly available). Concert band music of the 20th century was regularly scored for separate cornet and trumpet sections. However, in recent years, and especially in the U.S., the trumpet has largely replaced the cornet in concert bands, wind ensembles and jazz ensembles. Cornets are still used as solo instruments in jazz, but not as part of a section. Cornets are not part of the standard orchestral instrumentation and would be considered an auxiliary instrument in an orchestration. To the orchestrator, the cornet offers a viable alternative to the penetrating and considerably more aggressive sound of the trumpet.

Cornet Range (Transposed)

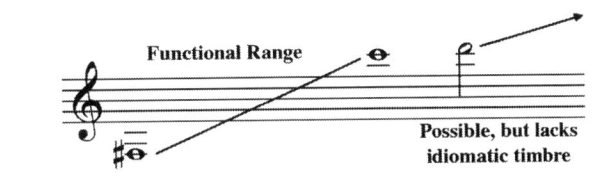

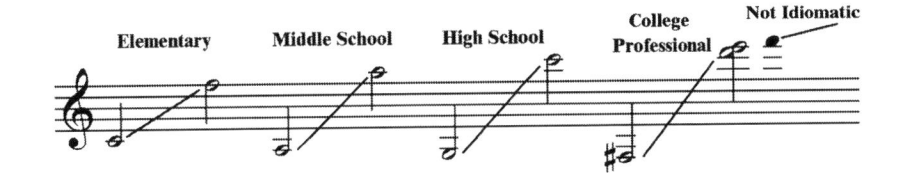

Cornet Registers (Transposed)

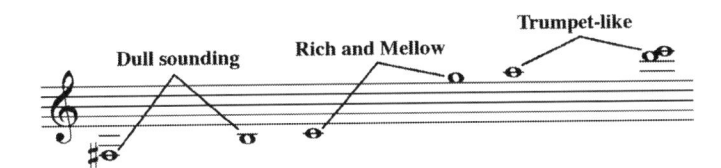

B♭ Cornet Transposition

B♭ cornets sound a major 2nd below the written note. Transposed parts are notated a major 2nd above concert pitch (adding two sharps to the key signature) and always notated in treble clef.

Flugelhorn

A close relative of both the trumpet and cornet, the flugelhorn is a conical instrument with a distinctive timbre that is fuller, darker and mellower than either the trumpet or cornet. The B♭ flugelhorn is the most commonly used instrument, though flugelhorns are available in a variety of keys. A favorite of jazz soloists and improvisers, the flugelhorn timbre is actually more similar to that of the horn than that of the trumpet. It is not uncommon for the entire trumpet section of a college or professional jazz ensemble to have flugelhorns at the ready. Flugelhorns have enjoyed sporadic popularity in wind bands throughout the years, but are not considered part of the standard instrumentation. Flugelhorns are not part of the standard orchestral instrumentation and would be considered an auxiliary instrument. To the orchestrator, flugelhorns offer a viable alternative to scoring horns in the extreme upper registers.

Flugelhorn Range (Transposed)

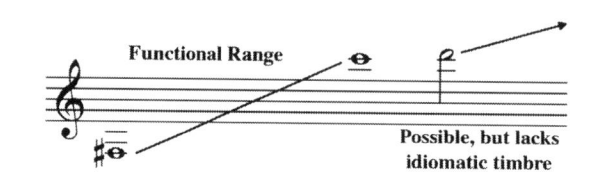

Flugelhorn Registers (Transposed)

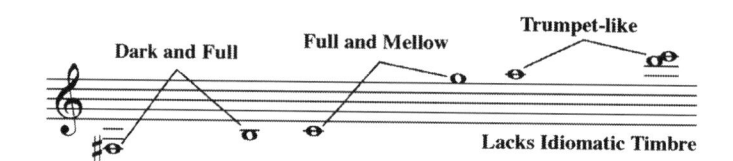

Flugelhorn Transposition

B♭ flugelhorns sound a major 2nd below the written note. Transposed parts are notated a major 2nd above concert pitch (adding two sharps to the key signature) and always notated in treble clef.

Trumpet in D

The trumpet in D has a lighter timbre and less aggressive sound than that of the B♭ or C trumpets. It was invented in the late 19th century as a replacement for the natural trumpet (trumpet without valves) of the Baroque era and specifically for use in the high trumpet parts in the music of J. S. Bach and G. F. Handel. While the instrument is perfectly suited for the technique and timbre required for music of the Baroque period, it is also a viable and useful timbre for contemporary orchestrations. Most professional trumpet players who specialize in classical repertoire will have a D trumpet in their arsenal. However, one cannot assume the instrument's availability at the amateur or academic levels.

D Trumpet Range (Transposed)

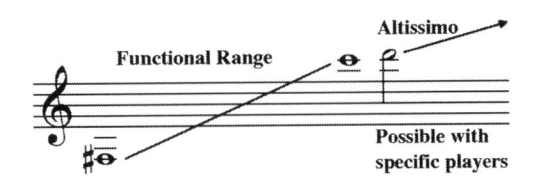

D Trumpet Registers (Transposed)

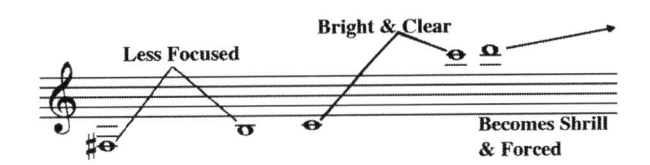

D Trumpet Transposition

D trumpets sound a major 2nd above the written note. Transposed parts are notated a major 2nd below concert pitch (adding two flats to the key signature) and always notated in treble clef.

Piccolo Trumpet

The most common piccolo trumpets are built in B♭, sounding an octave above that of the standard B♭ trumpet. These instruments often include a separate lead-pipe that, when substituted for the B♭ lead-pipe, allows the instrument to play in the key of A. There are also (rarely available) piccolo trumpets built to play in the keys of C, G, F, and E♭. Though the (B♭) instrument is one-half the size of the standard B♭ trumpet, it is rare that players can actually play notes higher than those they can play on the standard trumpet. One orchestrates for piccolo trumpet, not because of an availability of a higher register, but rather for the unique, clear and delicate timbre the instrument produces. Most piccolo trumpets are equipped with a fourth valve that extends the lower range of the instrument by a perfect fourth and increases the availability of alternate fingering combinations.

Piccolo Trumpet Range (Transposed)

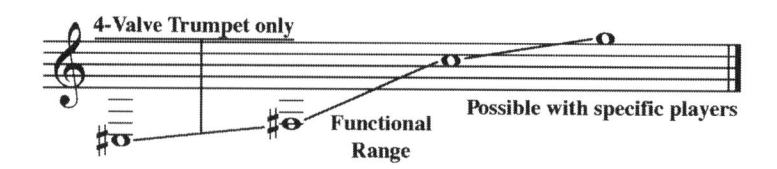

Piccolo Trumpet Overtones (Transposed)

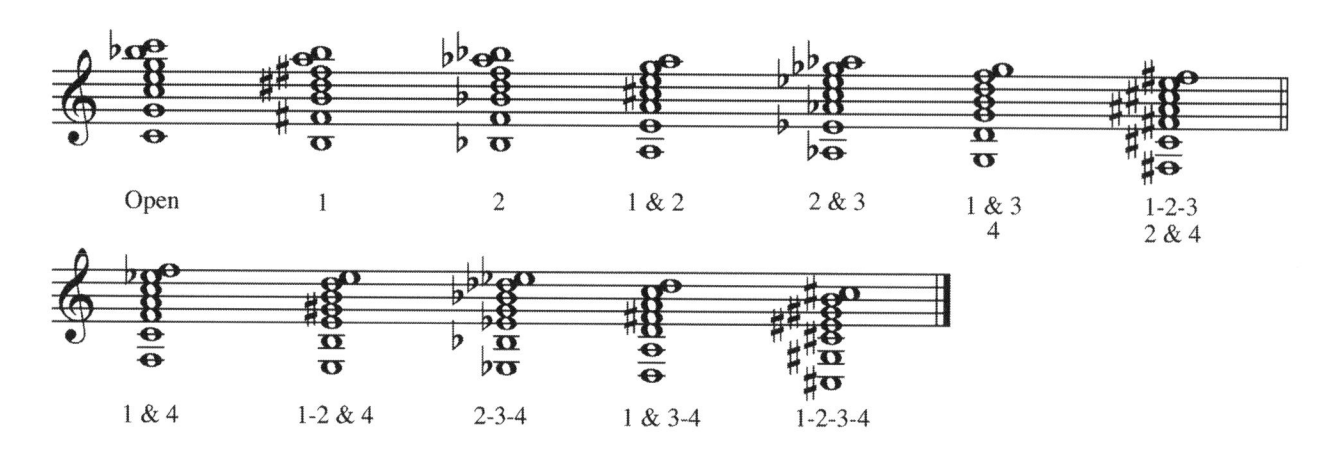

Piccolo Trumpet Transposition

Piccolo trumpets in B♭ sound a minor 7th above the written note. Transposed parts are notated a minor 7th below concert pitch (adding two sharps to the key signature) and always notated in treble clef.

Piccolo trumpets in A sound an octave and a major 6th above the written note. Transposed parts are notated a major 6th below concert pitch (adding three flats to the key signature) and always notated in treble clef.

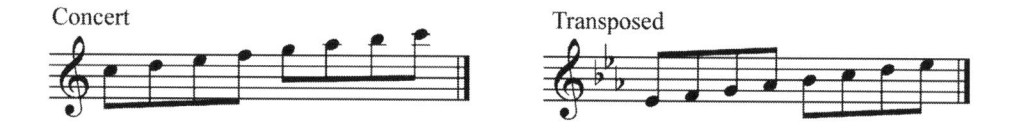

E♭ Soprano Cornet

The smallest and highest pitched cornet in the British-style brass band, the E♭ soprano cornet is pitched a perfect 4th higher than the B♭ cornet. It is regularly used to cover flute (and/or piccolo) parts found in works transcribed for the brass band medium. Its higher register and relative brightness of timbre allows a singular instrument to project well over a full section of B♭ cornets. While particularly useful for obbligato passages, the E♭ cornet may also be employed in combination with other instruments, or groups of instruments, to produce unique timbral textures.

E♭ Soprano Cornet Range (Transposed)

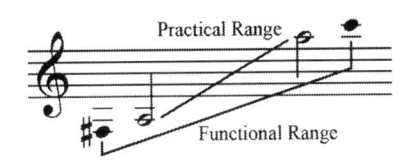

E♭ Soprano Cornet Registers (Transposed)

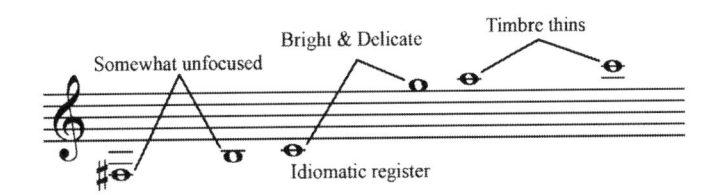

E♭ Soprano Cornet Transposition

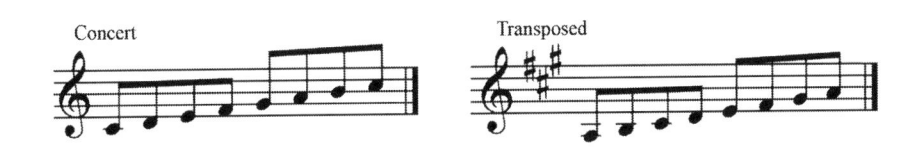

The E♭ soprano cornet sounds a minor 3rd above the written note. Transposed parts are notated a minor 3rd below concert pitch (adding three sharps to the key signature) and always notated in treble clef.

Bass Trumpet

Built in the key of B♭ and sounding an octave below the standard B♭ trumpet, the bass trumpet is most often played by a trombone player. Though the instrument plays in the same register and has the same range as a tenor trombone, bass trumpet parts are always written in the treble clef (transposed up a major 9th from the concert pitch). Orchestrating for bass trumpet in lieu of trombone may offer certain advantages, but it also demands certain technical sacrifices. One gains the facility and technique of a trumpet playing in the trombone register, but one no longer has the unique abilities of an instrument equipped with a slide at one's disposal. Therefore, when creating an orchestration, one should consider the bass trumpet as part of the trumpet section, and not as part of the trombone section.

Bass Trumpet Range (Transposed)

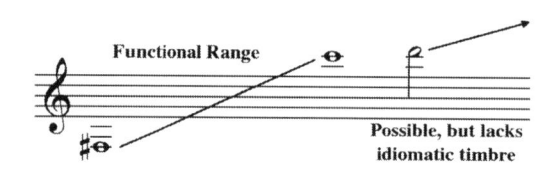

Bass Trumpet Transposition

B♭ bass trumpets sound an octave and a major 2nd below the written note. Transposed parts are notated an octave and a major 2nd above concert pitch (adding two sharps to the key signature) and always notated in treble clef.

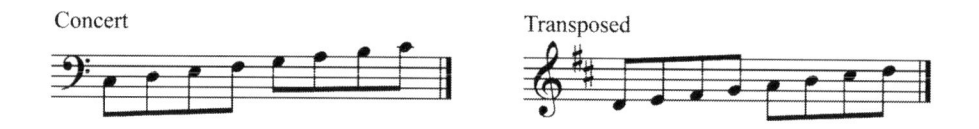

Horn

For centuries the English-speaking world has referred to this instrument as either the French horn or the horn in F. Since the instrument is neither French nor exclusively built in the key of F, the International Horn Society recommended (in 1971) that the instrument simply be referred to as the horn. As with most musical traditions, change comes slowly and the terms "French horn" and "horn in F," though technically misnomers, remain in common usage.

Though there are exceptions, horns are generally equipped with rotary valves. These valves are operated with the left hand, while the right is placed within the bell of the instrument. The right hand is used not only to balance and support the weight of the instrument, but also to control pitch and timbre.

Single Horn

Single horns are constructed with a singular set of tubing connected to a set of three rotary valves. The most common and readily available of these instruments is built in the key of F. The single horn is often found in academic environments (usually at the elementary and secondary levels) because it is easier to use, lighter in weight and less costly than the double horn. Additionally, the instrument produces the characteristic "horn" timbre throughout its entire playable range (as opposed to the B♭ "side" of the double horn). However, in spite of these advantageous features, the instrument does have a negative aspect. When playing above c" (in the transposed part), the harmonic partials are so close together that accuracy and pitch become major issues. These issues led directly to the development of the double horn. Unless one is scoring specifically for elementary or secondary school ensembles, one should assume that the horn parts will be played on double horns.

Double Horn

The double horn consists of two separate instruments of different keys (F and B♭) combined into a single assembly. These two separate sets of tubing are commonly referred to as "sides" of the horn. The player uses a fourth valve (or trigger), operated by the thumb on the left hand, to switch between the sides of the instrument. The F side (without trigger) of the instrument functions and sounds identical to the single horn. The B♭ side (with trigger) of the instrument contains shorter lengths of tubing and is therefore pitched higher. As such, in the upper registers on the instrument the harmonic partials are not as close together as on the F side of the horn, giving the player greater control over pitch and accuracy, as well as providing a wealth of alternate fingerings. One will notice a slight difference in timbre when using the B♭ side of the horn.

Using the fourth valve not only changes the basic length (and thus the harmonic series and pitch) of the instrument, it also causes the three main valves to use proportionate slide lengths.

Triple Horn

While extremely rare, one may encounter a triple horn. Triple horns are constructed with five valves (three main valves, plus two triggers) with sides tuned in F and B♭ (the same as the double horn), plus a descant side (in E♭ or F).

Transposition

Horn parts are always written transposed up a perfect 5th from concert pitch. It is left to the player to decide which side of the horn will be utilized on any given note. While horn players are capable of reading both treble and bass clefs, it is preferable to write the parts in treble clef, reserving the use of bass clef for those occasions when the number of ledger lines become prohibitive.

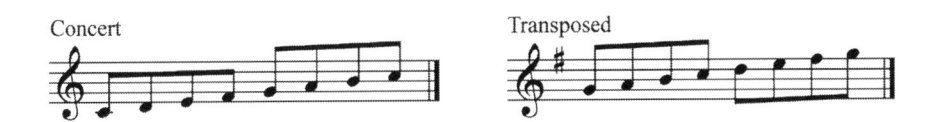

Transposed parts are notated a perfect 5th above concert pitch (adding one sharp to the key signature) and notated (preferably) in treble clef.

Historical vs. Contemporary Notation

Orchestrators should be aware of an inconsistency in notation for the extreme lower register of the horn. While the contemporary practice is to transpose the horn part up a perfect fifth from concert pitch, regardless of clef, many 19th-century scores transpose horn parts written in bass clef down a perfect 4th. Even though this practice has been discontinued, should one choose to write a horn part in bass clef, one should be prepared to inform the player about the notational practice employed.

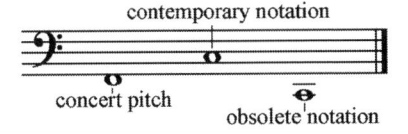

In many pre-20th-century scores, the transposed horn parts are written without a key signature. Accidentals are added as needed to accomplish the alterations required by the transposition. Though the practice is now viewed as antiquated and has been discontinued, one will inevitably encounter the practice when orchestrating historical works.

Horn Range (Transposed)

Horn Registers (Transposed)

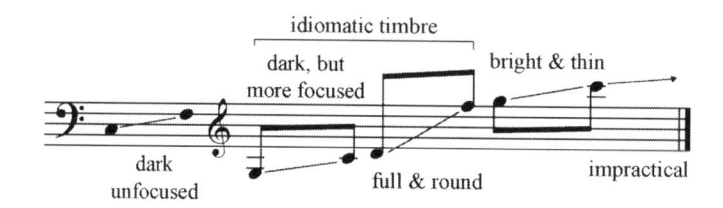

Division of Orchestral Horns

Traditionally, orchestral horns are divided into "high horns" and "low horns" with the 1st and 3rd horn parts being the high parts and the 2nd and 4th horn parts being the low parts. When scoring for horns in two parts, the 1st part is the high part and the 2nd part is the low part.

When scoring for horns in three parts, the 1st part is the high part, the 2nd part is the low part and the 3rd part is a high part (usually placed in between the 1st and 2nd parts).

When scoring for horns in four parts, the 1st and 3rd horn parts are the high parts, the 2nd part is the low part and the 4th part is the lowest part. (The 4th horn is usually expected to be a low range specialist.)

Tenor Trombone

The tenor trombone is the tenor voice of the brass choir, and though it is actually built in the key of B♭,[1] it is treated as a non-transposing (C) instrument. It is a cylindrical instrument using a slide, rather than valves, to achieve chromatic alterations of its overtone partials. Slide positions are approximations that require adjustment to compensate for inherent intonation. Rarely is a given note precisely that which one would find listed in a slide position chart. Alternate slide positions are frequently used to facilitate rapid or awkward passages, intonation adjustment and glissandi. While the range of the low register is readily definable, the functional span of the high register is entirely dependent upon the skill and expertise of the performer.

Trombone Range

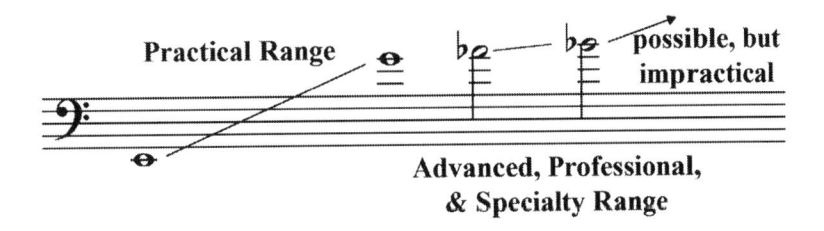

Trombone Registers

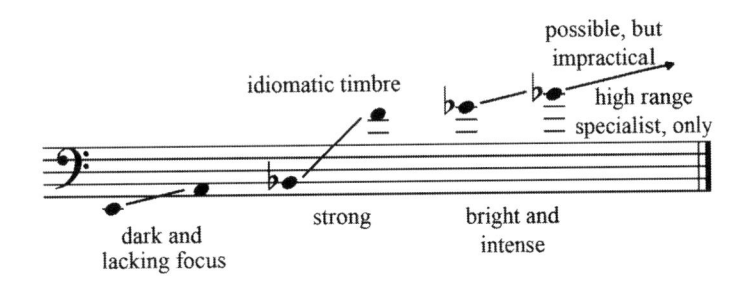

Trombone Transposition

Tenor trombones are non-transposing instruments that are written predominantly in the bass clef. Tenor clef may be utilized for passages where the number of ledger lines becomes prohibitive. Advanced players are equally adept at reading in either clef.

Trombone Slide Positions

1st position:	slide closed
2nd position:	approximately 3½ inches
3rd position:	approximately 7 inches
4th position:	approximately 10½ inches
5th position:	approximately 14 inches
6th position:	approximately 17½ inches
7th position:	approximately 21 inches

Bass Trombone

As is the case with the tenor trombone, the bass trombone is built in the key of B♭, but treated as a non-transposing (C) instrument. The length of its tubing is identical to that of the tenor trombone (9 feet in length). However, the diameter of the tubing (the bore) is wider, resulting in a full, strong timbre in the lower registers. Modern bass trombones are equipped with a valve (F trigger) that, when engaged, extends the length of the tubing by an interval of a perfect 4th, allowing the performer access to notes between the 2nd partial and the fundamental (1st partial) that would otherwise be unavailable on the instrument. Additionally, many newer bass trombones are equipped with a second valve (trigger) that extends the range even further. Depending upon the manufacturer and design, this second valve may be pitched in G, G♭, E, E♭ or D. When one is scoring for bass trombone, one may assume that the instrument will be equipped with an F trigger, but one should not arbitrarily assume that a second trigger, of whatever pitch, would be at one's immediate disposal.

Bass Trombone Range

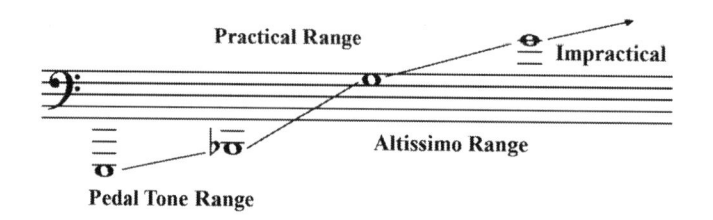

Bass Trombone Registers

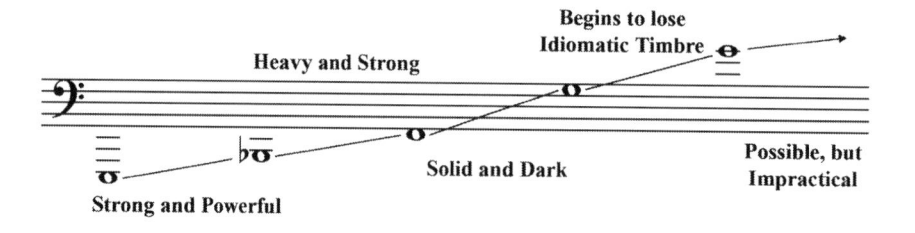

Valve Trombone

As with all brass instruments, the valve trombone has been produced in a variety of keys throughout its history. While one may (rarely) encounter other incarnations of the instrument, the tenor valve trombone has enjoyed the most universal acceptance. As such, the term "valve trombone" is now accepted as referring specifically to the tenor valve trombone. There are also bass and contrabass versions of the instrument presently available. However, the term "cimbasso" is used when referring to these lower-register instruments. While there are rare exceptions (Puccini, Verdi), the valve trombone has not acquired common acceptance as an orchestral instrument.

The valve trombone has the advantage of greater agility in fast or intricate passages than that of the slide trombone. This agility has resulted in the instrument enjoying substantial popularity in the realm of jazz. However, its timbre is not quite as full as that of the slide trombone and it lacks the abilities indigenous to the slide, i.e. glissando, microtonal pitches, etc.

Valve Trombone Range

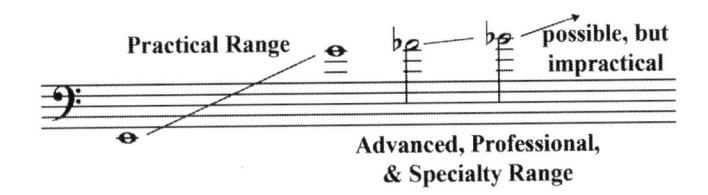

Valve Trombone Registers

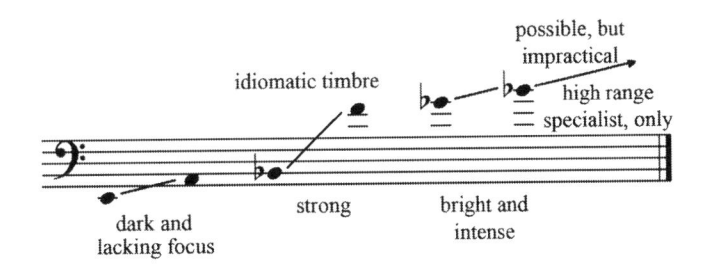

Valve Trombone Transposition

Valve trombones are non-transposing instruments that are written in the bass clef. Generally, octavo markings are used for passages where the number of ledger lines becomes prohibitive.

Alto Trombone

The alto trombone was in common usage from the 16th century through the 19th century and has even enjoyed occasional usage in the 20th century by composers such as Schoenberg, Berg and Britten. Because the timbre of the alto trombone is significantly brighter than that of the tenor trombone, trombonists in modern orchestras are expected to play alto trombones when performing well-known works originally scored for the instrument.

Though one may rarely encounter an instrument built in F, and even some equipped with a D or B♭ trigger, the standard alto trombone is built in the key of E♭. The total length of tubing is shorter, the slide is shorter and the slide positions differ from the tenor or bass trombones. There are also inherent intonation issues requiring the performer to compensate by adjusting slide positions. The amount of adjustment varies from instrument to instrument and from player to player, but rarely is a given note precisely that which one would find listed in a slide position chart.

Alto Trombone Range

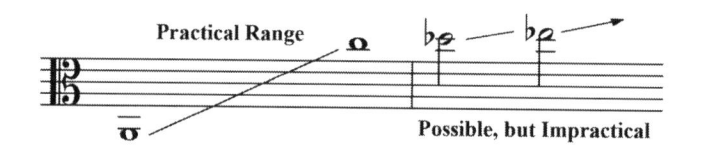

Cimbasso

Once relegated to playing the 4th trombone parts in the operas of such composers as Verdi, Bellini and Donizetti, the cimbasso has enjoyed a resurgence of popularity in the recording studio and film-scoring industries. The instrument has evolved from its original design, with the modern instrument technically being a contrabass valve trombone that plays in the same register as the tuba. This affords the orchestrator the opportunity to employ a brighter, more powerful cylindrical timbre in the lower registers of one's orchestrations. The cimbasso is also a suitable substitute when transcribing a selection that originally called for serpent or ophicleide. The timbre of the instrument ranges from rich and mellow at the softer and medium dynamic levels, to bright and powerful at the louder dynamic levels.

Most modern instruments are custom-made and, as such, are constructed in a variety of configurations. Depending upon the requested design parameters, it may be constructed with three to five piston or rotary valves, with or without triggers, and generally pitched in E♭, F, CC or BB♭. Unless one knows specifically the key and range of the cimbasso(s) available, one should restrict one's writing to the range common to all the instruments. One could designate "High Cimbasso" and "Low Cimbasso" to specify a preference for an F/E♭, or a CC/BB♭ cimbasso, respectively. The cimbasso part is always written in concert key (in bass clef) and one generally makes no distinction in the score as to specific key of the cimbasso to be used.

Cimbasso Range

Since the cimbasso is usually a custom-made instrument with various design possibilities, it is difficult to designate a definitive generic range for the instrument. However, since the instruments are designed to play in the same registers as the bass and contrabass tubas, the most practical approach is to assume that the instrument is capable of covering (at the very least) the same range as its tuba counterpart.

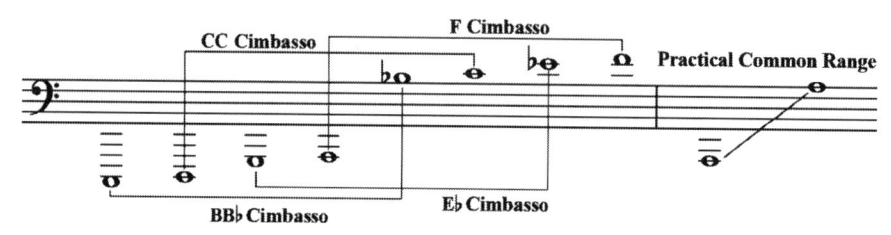

Cimbasso Registers

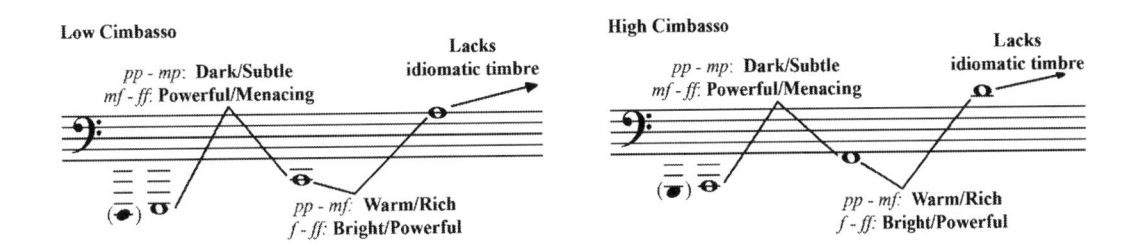

E♭ Alto Horn (Tenor Horn)

A stalwart member of the traditional British-style brass band, the E♭ alto horn (known as the alto horn in the U.S. and the tenor horn in the UK) is a three-valve brass instrument of predominantly conical bore that is pitched in E♭ and sounds an octave below the E♭ cornet. The instrument produces a rich, mellow timbre that is effectively used as a middle voice in the brass band and provides a suitable substitute for horns in F (French horns) in marching bands and similar ensembles where the latter is not a practical option. One should be aware that the instrument has somewhat less presence and projection than that of the more powerful cornets and trombones in the brass band setting and should orchestrate accordingly. Being a whole-tube instrument, the E♭ alto horn is capable of producing pedal tones, though this technique should be avoided in ensemble writing.

E♭ Alto Horn Range

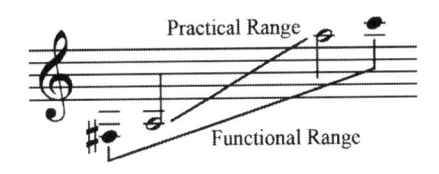

E♭ Alto Horn Registers

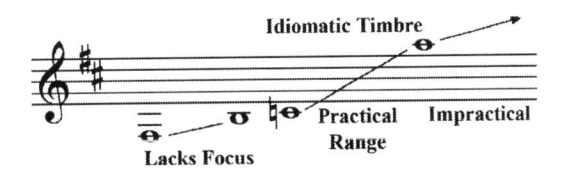

E♭ Alto Horn Transposition

The E♭ alto horn sounds a major 6th below the written note. Transposed parts are notated a major 6th above concert pitch (adding three sharps to the key signature), and always notated in treble clef.

Euphonium

The euphonium is a non-transposing, conical-bore instrument that serves as the tenor voice of the tuba family. Though there are exceptions, the euphonium is not generally found in orchestral settings. It does, however, enjoy prominence in ensembles such as concert bands, symphonic bands, wind ensembles, brass bands and other incarnations of the "band" setting. Its timbre is rich, mellow and more lyrical than cylindrical instruments that play in the same register and, as such, composers of "band" music often feature it as a solo instrument. One may think of the euphonium as occupying a niche in wind music similar to that of the cello in orchestral music.

Euphonium Range

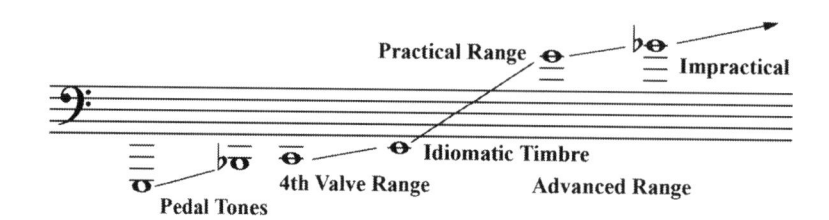

Euphonium Registers

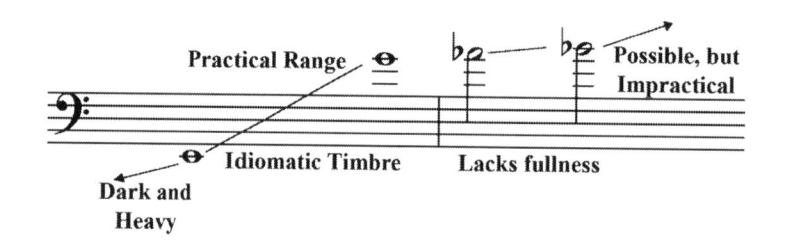

Baritone

The baritone horn (or simply "baritone") is a cylindrical-bore instrument commonly found in middle-school and high-school bands. Its timbre is slightly mellower than the trombone and slightly brighter than the euphonium. Though the instrument plays in roughly the same register and is often substituted for (and occasionally confused with) the euphonium, there are significant differences between the two instruments. The baritone has a tighter wrap of tubing, a smaller bore size, a smaller, curved, forward-pointing bell, and is manufactured exclusively in a three-valve configuration. This design results in an instrument whose weight, shape and configuration are advantageous to the needs of the marching band. However, it also results in an instrument lacking the full range and timbre of the four-valve euphonium needed for effective use in college and professional concert settings. Since the baritone has been a dominant instrument in school bands and marching bands for over a century, competent knowledge of the instrument is vital for the professional orchestrator.

Baritone Transposition and Clefs

Baritone parts are produced (and supplied) in both concert (bass clef) and transposed (treble clef) versions. In middle-school and high-school environments, baritone players are often converted trumpet players. By supplying a treble clef part (transposed up an octave and a major second from concert pitch, with the addition of two sharps to the key signature), the players can use the same fingerings they learned on the B♭ trumpet or cornet. All other players read non-transposed (bass clef) parts.

Baritone Range

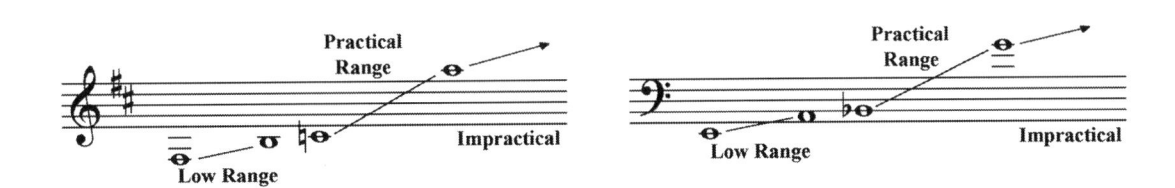

Baritone Registers

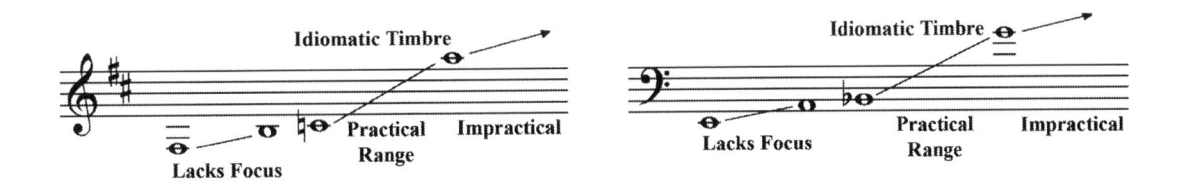

Tuba

The tuba is a conical-shaped instrument and the largest and lowest-pitched member of the brass family. Modern tubas are commonly available in four sizes. The smaller varieties of tubas are considered bass tubas and pitched in F or E♭. The larger (and thus lower-pitched) tubas are considered contrabass tubas, pitched in C (CC) or B♭ (BB♭). The orchestrator rarely makes a distinction in the score as to which tuba is to be used, leaving the choice of instrument to the player and the preference of a given location. In the U.S., the instrument of choice for the orchestral setting is the CC tuba, while the BB♭ is the preference in Russia, Germany and Austria. In England, the E♭ is considered the standard orchestral tuba, while on most of the European continent the F tuba is considered the standard orchestral instrument, complemented by the contrabass tubas only when the extended lower registers are required.

With only one exception, tuba parts are written in concert pitch (non-transposing) and in bass clef. The one exception to this convention exists in traditional British-style brass bands where the tuba parts are transposed into treble clef. The transposed parts for BB♭ tubas are written two octaves and a major 2nd above concert pitch, and transposed parts for E♭ tubas are written one octave and a major 6th above concert pitch.

Three-, Four-, Five- and Six-valve Tubas

In addition to being manufactured in a variety of keys, tubas are also manufactured with a variety of valve configurations. Three-valve tubas are the least expensive and generally relegated to the realm of beginning students. The four-valve tuba is the most common choice of the professional tubist, followed closely by the five-valve tuba. The six-valve configuration is relatively rare and usually only found on F tubas. The orchestrator need not be concerned about these configurations except when scoring specifically for middle-school or high-school level ensembles. One must be cognizant of the range restraints of three-valve tubas (as well as sousaphones) when scoring for these ensembles.

Tuba Range

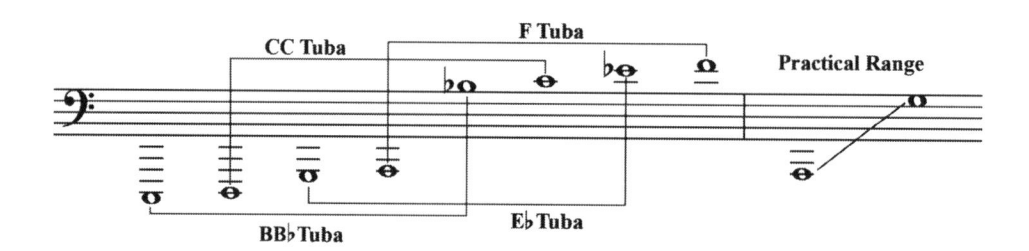

Tuba Registers

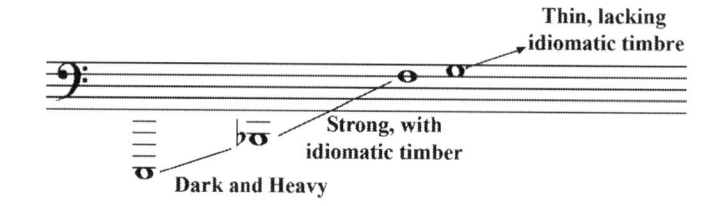

Sousaphone

Named in honor of John Philip Sousa, the sousaphone is a three-valve variation of the standard BB♭ tuba designed specifically for use in marching bands. Technically a member of the helicon family, the body of the instrument is designed to wrap around the performer, allowing the weight of the instrument to be supported by the performer's left shoulder. The bell of the instrument is above the performer's head and faces to the front, allowing for a forward projection of the sound. Sousaphones are often constructed using lighter materials (e.g. fiberglass) than that of standard tubas, reducing the weight of the instrument. This design accommodates the need to carry the instrument while performing in a marching band.

Sousaphone Range

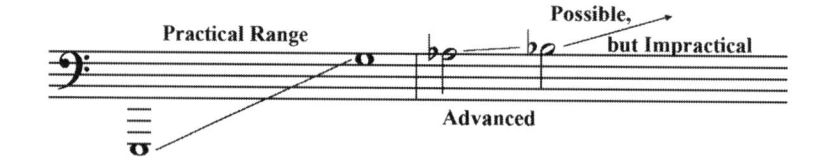

Sousaphone Registers

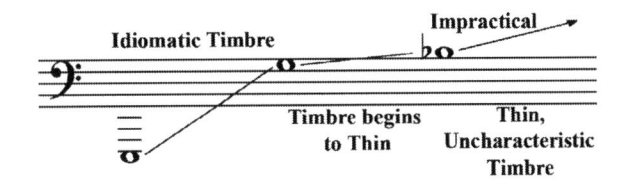

THE ENSEMBLES

Brass Quintet

The traditional brass quintet is a five-member ensemble consisting of two B♭ trumpets, one horn, one tenor trombone and one tuba. Though the ensemble is an incarnation of the late 1940s, the repertoire is expansive, encompassing eras ranging from the Renaissance to the 21st century, and genres from classical to jazz to pop. The instrumentation of the brass quintet may be altered to accommodate specific needs. Cornets or flugelhorns may be substituted for the trumpets; euphonium may be substituted for trombone; one trumpet part may be substituted for piccolo trumpet while the other is written for D trumpet; bass trombone may be substituted for tuba; and so on.

When orchestrating for brass quintet, one should strive for variety of timbres. This variety aids in providing interest to the orchestration. One should avoid repeating complete sections of a work using the same treatment and instrumentation. One can achieve interest by featuring a different instrument on the melody, contrasting conical instruments with cylindrical instruments, trading the melody from instrument to instrument, alternating registers, etc.

One must always be aware of the performer's need to breathe, as well as allowing adequate respites within the parts to accommodate the physical needs of the embouchure. Failure to do so will result in an unplayable orchestration of little (if any) value.

Chamber Ensembles

Chamber music ensembles perform music designed to be presented in an intimate setting. As such, the acoustical nature of cylindrical brass instruments generally precludes their involvement in the traditional chamber music environment. However, as a conical instrument with the ability to balance and blend well with woodwinds, the horn has a well-established position in the chamber music genre. The following is a sampling of the chamber music ensembles that include horn:

Horn Trio	horn, violin, piano
Voice, horn and piano	voice, horn, piano
Piano and Wind Trio	piano, clarinet, horn, bassoon
Wind Quintet	flute, oboe, clarinet, horn, bassoon
Piano and Wind Quartet	piano, oboe, clarinet, horn, bassoon
Wind Sextet	2 oboes, 2 horn, 2 bassoons (*or*) 2 clarinets, 2 horns, 2 bassoons
Piano and Wind Quintet	flute, oboe, clarinet, horn, bassoon, piano
Wind and String Septet	clarinet, horn, bassoon, violin, viola, violoncello, contrabass

Wind and String Octet	clarinet, horn, bassoon, 2 violins, viola, violoncello, contrabass (*or*) clarinet, 2 horns, violin, 2 viols, violoncello, contrabass
Wind and String Nonet	flute, oboe, clarinet, horn, bassoon, violin, viola, violoncello, contrabass
Double Wind Quintet	2 oboes, 2 English horns, 2 clarinets, 2 horns, 2 bassoons (*or*) 2 flutes, oboe, English horn, 2 clarinets, 2 horns and 2 bassoons

Since the Tuba–Euphonium Quartet also contains all conical instruments, it is conceivable that under the correct circumstances the ensemble could be considered a chamber music ensemble.

Tuba–Euphonium Quartet	2 Euphoniums, 2 Tubas (Standard Quartet) (*or*) 4 Tubas (*or*) 3 Euphoniums, 1 Tuba (*or*) 1 Euphonium, 3 Tubas (*or*) 4 Euphoniums

Orchestral Brass

The size of the brass section in the orchestral setting varies from ensemble to ensemble, but generally ranges from 9 to 13 instruments. The basic configuration is four horns, two trumpets, two trombones and one tuba. Since the first horn part can often be quite demanding, a fifth horn player is frequently employed and assigned to the first horn part to allow the first horn player an occasional respite. In contemporary music, including music for pops orchestra, it is not unusual to expand the orchestral brass section to include four trumpets, three trombones (plus bass trombone) and occasionally two tubas.

Wind Ensemble and Concert Band Brass

In a wind ensemble or concert band setting, the brass section offers the orchestrator a wealth of scoring opportunities. With more instruments at one's disposal than in the orchestral setting, one has more timbre and textures with which to work. All members of the brass section blend well with one another and, when scored as a full ensemble, produce a rich and homogeneous sound. The combination of multiple cylindrical and conical instruments offers a variety of textual combinations, and when combined with the varied timbres of the woodwind section, a plethora of timbral opportunities are available to the orchestrator.

Whether scoring for wind ensemble or for concert band (wind band, symphonic band, etc.) one may assume a relatively even distribution of parts within the brass section. This is not to say that there is a one-to-one balance between the various parts at all dynamic levels. One must exercise care when scoring for the horn section to insure proper balance with the rest of the brass section. At lower dynamic levels (*ppp–mp*) a singular horn will balance on a one-to-one basis with any other instrument in the brass section. However, at louder dynamic levels (*mf–f*) at least two horns are needed to balance with any other singular member of the brass section. While one may comfortably score four separate parts for horns at the lower dynamic levels (*ppp–mp*), one may wish to score the horns in two parts (1st and 3rd horns in unison and 2nd and 4th horns in unison) at *mf–f* levels, and place all four parts in unison at *ff–ffff* levels.

The upper members of the brass section tend to sound best when scored in close voicing, while the lower brass are most sonorous when scored in open voicing. One may score the tenor trombones in either close or open voicing if used in combination with the baritones/euphoniums and tubas in octaves or open voicing.

When the brass section is scored as part of the full ensemble, one must be aware that the woodwinds will be dominated by the power and fullness of the brass. If the woodwinds are used for providing added texture in this technique, balance between the sections is not overly critical. However, if part of the woodwind section has an independent role (i.e. an obbligato passage), one must be acutely aware of the acoustical balances, reinforcing the woodwind part with sufficient numbers of players to be heard over the brass.

The brass soloists in this genre are the 1st trumpet, 1st horn, 1st trombone and baritone/euphonium. The tuba is rarely featured as a soloist within the context of the ensemble, except for the occasional transitional passage of short duration.

Contrary to orchestral score order, the horns are placed below the trumpets/cornets in the wind ensemble or concert band conductor's score. The baritones/euphoniums are placed below the trombones. Occasionally, a string bass part will be provided as a supplement/reinforcement to the tuba part. Even though this part is an exact doubling of the tuba part (transposed for double bass), the orchestrator must designate whether a given passage is to be played pizzicato or arco.

Developed in the early 1950s by Frederick Fennell, the wind ensemble is a diminutive version of the concert band. In its original incarnation, the wind ensemble consisted of one player per part evincing more precise intonation and clarity of part. While one still finds numerous wind ensembles adhering to this configuration, many contemporary ensembles tend to favor two players per part. In either case, the distribution of parts is balanced within the ensemble.

The instrumentation of the brass section in the concert band can vary from ensemble to ensemble and from composition to composition. Some works separate trumpets and cornets into independent sections serving differing purposes. Some works treat baritones as instruments separate from euphoniums, while others assign them identical parts. The number of players per part also varies from ensemble to ensemble. As previously stated, the only assumption an orchestrator can make when scoring for this ensemble is that the sections will be relatively balanced. When scoring brass in this medium, one can expect the availability of the following instruments:

 Trumpets and/or Cornets in B♭ (scored in 3 parts)
 Horns (scored in 2–4 parts)
 Tenor Trombones (scored in 2–3 parts)
 Bass Trombone (scored in 1 part)
 Baritones/Euphoniums (generally scored in 1 part)
 BB♭ Tubas (scored in 1 part)

British-style Brass Band

Having a tradition dating back to the 19th century, the standardized instrumentation of the British-style brass band encompasses the broad range and timbres of the brass section. With the exception of tenor and bass trombones, the ensemble is composed of conical instruments, opting for cornets and flugelhorn instead of trumpets.

Though the number of brass bands in North America has declined in recent decades, it remains a popular and viable medium throughout the rest of world. As such, it behoves the orchestrator to be familiar with the scoring possibilities, opportunities and idiosyncrasies of this traditional ensemble. The unique instrumentation of the ensemble has been standardized as follows (in score order):

- (1) E-flat Soprano Cornet
- (10) Cornets
  - Solo (4-5 players)—**Front-row Cornets**
  - Repiano (1 player)⎤
  - 2nd (2 players)   ⎬ **Back-row Cornets**
  - 3rd (1-2 players)⎦
- (1) Flugelhorn
- (3) E-flat Alto Horns (Tenor Horns)
  - Solo (1 player)
  - 1st (1 player)
  - 2nd (1 player)
- (2) Baritones
  - 1st (1 player)
  - 2nd (1 player)
- (2) Tenor Trombones
  - 1st (1 player)
  - 2nd (1 player)
- (1) Bass Trombone
- (2) Euphoniums
- (2) E-flat Tubas
- (2) B-flat Tubas
- (1) Drum Set
  (or)
  Percussion (2-3 players)

When scoring for brass band, one traditionally writes within a restricted tessitura for each instrument. Since it is rare that the entire membership of a given band will consist entirely of professional musicians, one should write in such a manner that amateur musicians might play the selection. Additionally, instruments that would appear in concert key in the orchestral environment appear in a transposed form in the brass band setting. With the exception of the bass trombone and percussion, all of the instruments in the brass band are written in treble clef and in transposed form.

E♭ Soprano Cornet

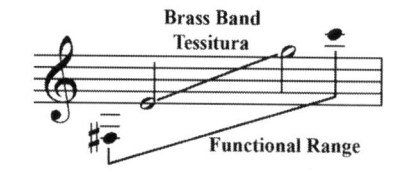

The above listed tessitura may be expanded if scoring for a specific player with more advanced abilities.

The E♭ soprano cornet sounds a minor 3rd above the written note. Transposed parts are notated a minor 3rd below concert pitch (adding three sharps to the key signature) and always notated in treble clef.

One approaches writing for the soprano cornet as one might approach writing for piccolo in the orchestral setting, using its brighter timbre for splashes of color, obbligato or countermelody passages and melodic reinforcement. One should use the soprano cornet sparingly, avoiding long extended passages, as the timbre can lose its effectiveness if overused.

The soprano cornet may be used in unison with the solo cornet line to brighten the timbre of the line, or doubled at the octave to add emphasis to the line. If a given melody line progresses beyond the comfortable tessitura of the solo cornet, it may be passed to the soprano cornet for the higher sections, then back to the solo cornet when the melody descends back to its comfortable tessitura. The soprano cornet may also be used, either in unison or at the octave, with the repiano cornet (see below) or solo horn to accentuate countermelody passages.

Cornets

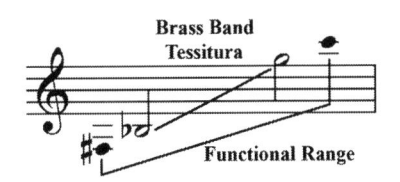

The above listed tessitura may be expanded if scoring for a specific player with more advanced abilities.

The cornet sounds a major 2nd below the written note. Transposed parts are notated a major 2nd above concert pitch (adding two sharps to the key signature) and always notated in treble clef.

Solo Cornet (Front-row Cornets)

Solo cornets are the primary melodic instruments in the brass band setting and may be scored in a tutti context or as a solo part for the principal player (if the texture of the selection so dictates). When scoring for a single solo player, one may expand the standard tessitura to exploit the technical abilities of the principal player, as the principal player is traditionally the strongest cornet player in the ensemble. When scoring for tutti, one should restrict the scope of one's writing to the standard tessitura for the instrument. Generally, the solo cornets are the most technically proficient players in the brass band, thus allowing for greater complexity than other parts in the ensemble.

Repiano Cornet

The term "repiano" is most likely a distorted form of "ripieno," meaning "supplementary." The term does not designate a unique instrument (the repiano cornet is a standard B♭ cornet), but rather the nomadic nature of the part. It will often serve multiple purposes within a singular selection. The repiano cornet may be used to add weight to either the front-row cornet melody or back-row cornet harmony parts, be doubled in unison or at the octave with the soprano cornet, flugelhorn, or E♭ horn on countermelodies, supplement harmonic parts contained in the ensemble or be featured as an independent solo voice.

2nd and 3rd Cornet (Back-row Cornets)

The 2nd and 3rd cornets are traditionally used for harmonic accompaniment. In an amateur setting, these parts are usually covered by the weakest of the cornet players. As such, one should restrict oneself to the lower and middle range, and the tessitura. While one should always attempt to avoid writing tedious, repetitious parts, it is not always possible to do so with these parts due to the limited available range. If the scope of a melody is contained within the lower to middle range of the cornet tessitura, one could opt to score the entire cornet section in unison tutti (and thereby add interest to the 2nd and 3rd cornet parts). However, at no time should one rely upon the 2nd and/or 3rd cornets to independently carry a melody or countermelody. In addition to avoiding the upper range of the tessitura, one must also exercise caution not to score these cornet parts below the range of the accepted tessitura, as these notes tend to be unfocused and of questionable intonation with amateur players.

Flugelhorn

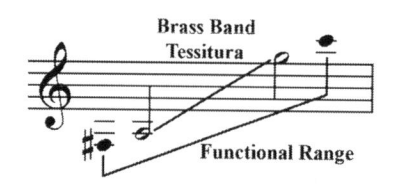

The flugelhorn sounds a major 2nd below the written note. Transposed parts are notated a major 2nd above concert pitch (adding two sharps to the key signature) and always notated in treble clef.

Traditionally, the flugelhorn doubles the repiano cornet part. Fortunately, contemporary composers and orchestrators have recognized the unique and flexible qualities of the instrument and expanded its use into other realms. The instrument may be used as a soloist, though the mellowness of its tone is easily dominated by the brightness of the cornets, thus restricting this usage to softer passages with predominately low brass accompaniment. The mellow, full timbre of the flugelhorn allows it to be used as the upper member of the horn section, as well as the upper member of the trombone section. It also may be used for doubling a trombone or euphonium passage at the octave.

E♭ Alto Horn (Tenor Horn)

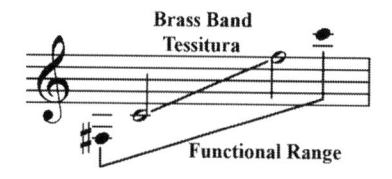

The alto horn sounds a major 6th below the written note. Transposed parts are notated a major 6th above concert pitch (adding three sharps to the key signature) and always notated in treble clef in the brass band setting.

The primary function of the horns is to provide accompaniment in the middle register of the ensemble, spanning the gap from the cornets to the low brass. Voicing these accompaniment parts in such a manner that they overlap with the lower cornets (rather than voicing them completely below the cornets) will result in a blended, homogeneous timbre. For best results horns should be voiced in close voicing with the top horn (solo or 1st) and the 2nd horn, spanning no more than an octave. Should one have need of a strong melody or countermelody in this register, scoring the three horns in unison (possibly doubled with flugelhorn or baritone, depending upon the register) will produce a full, rich sound.

Solo Horn

The solo horn is generally used as an accompaniment instrument, voiced as top voice in the horn section and often doubling the 2nd cornet. In the context of a soloist, the solo horn is generally assigned melodies (or countermelodies) that venture too low to be played by the flugelhorn and too high to be comfortably played by the euphonium. It may also play melodies (or countermelodies) that reside within the tessitura of the euphonium, but require a lighter timber. As a solo instrument, the solo horn is best utilized in quiet passages with lightly scored low brass accompaniment.

1st and 2nd Horns

Except for the rare occasion when all three horns are scored in unison, the 1st and 2nd horns are primarily accompaniment instruments. When scored in tandem with 2nd and 3rd cornet accompaniment, the 1st horn will often double the 3rd cornet part, with the 2nd horn score below and in close position. One should avoid cross-voicing between the 1st and 2nd horns, as this technique is not idiomatic of the brass band genre.

Baritone

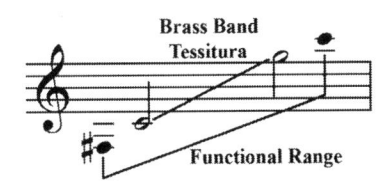

The baritone sounds a major 9th below the written note. Transposed parts are notated a major 9th above concert pitch (adding two sharps to the key signature) and always notated in treble clef in the brass band setting.

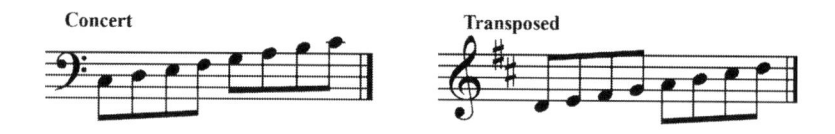

The baritone can be an agile and versatile instrument when performed by a technically proficient player. With a lighter timbre than that of the euphonium, the baritone may be used both as an accompaniment instrument and a melody (or countermelody) instrument. The 1st and 2nd baritones often play different parts, serving different functions and are usually treated as independent instruments.

1st Baritone

The 1st baritone may be used as an independent melody or countermelody instrument, or may double the solo cornet melody at the octave. It may double the 1st or 2nd horn parts to add fullness to the accompaniment, or be used as a "4th horn" in a horn quartet context. It is also double the euphonium line when reinforcement is needed.

2nd Baritone

The 2nd baritone is subordinate and supportive to the 1st baritone. Generally, the 2nd baritone player is not expected to have the technical prowess of the 1st baritone player and parts generally reflect that premise. It may be used in lieu of a euphonium if a lighter timbre is required, may be employed as a "4th horn" if the 1st baritone is otherwise engaged, or double the 1st baritone for fullness if the line is not overly elaborate.

Trombones

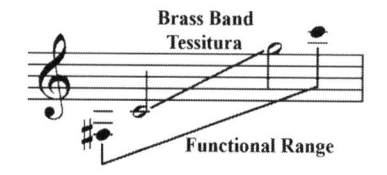

The three trombones are the most cylindrical instruments in the brass band, and capable of producing overpowering volume. While this may be a unique quality, exploiting this power of amplitude can be detrimental to the overall blend of the ensemble. As with all orchestrations, acoustical balances are of paramount concern to the orchestrator. One must also be aware of slide positions to avoid awkward or cumbersome slide patterns, and one should not assume the tenor trombones will be equipped with an F trigger. The tenor trombones and bass trombone may be scored as independent elements, with the tenor trombones performing one function and the bass performing a separate function; or as a 3-part section, thereby contrasting the cylindrical timbre of the trombones with the conical-timbre instruments residing in the lower register of the ensemble.

Tenor Trombone

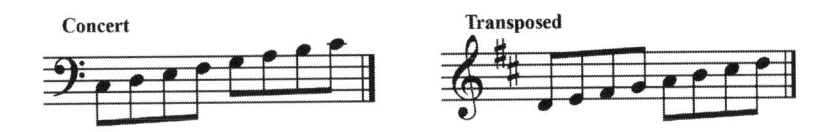

The trombone sounds a major 9th below the written note. Transposed parts are notated a major 9th above concert pitch (adding two sharps to the key signature) and always notated in treble clef in the brass band setting.

The 1st trombone may be treated as a solo instrument capable of both declamatory statements and smooth melodic interpretations, or may double the solo cornet melody at the octave. It may also be used to bring brightness to a countermelody, or as strictly an accompaniment instrument.

The 2nd trombone is supportive to the 1st trombone and generally considered an accompaniment instrument. Best results are achieved when the tenor trombones are scored in close voicings, with the 2nd trombone voiced less than an octave below the 1st trombone.

Bass Trombone

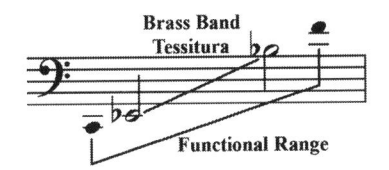

Unlike the remainder of the brass instruments in the ensemble, the bass trombone is always written in bass clef (and in concert key). In addition to the extended range provided by the trigger apparatus, players may be capable of producing pedal tones. Useful for isolated notes of limited duration (such as the last note of a selection), pedal tones should be used sparingly. In most cases the bass trombone is assigned to the bass line, either independently, in unison with the tubas, or in octaves with the tubas.

Euphonium

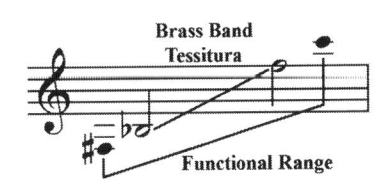

The euphonium sounds a major 9th below the written note. Transposed parts are notated a major 9th above concert pitch (adding two sharps to the key signature) and always notated in treble clef in the brass band setting.

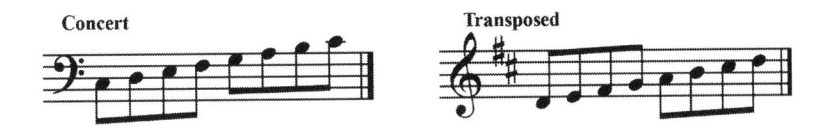

Depending upon the instrument's age and origin, the euphoniums found in brass bands may be equipped with either three or four valves. Instruments with a fourth valve have greater range capabilities than those with three valves. While becoming increasingly common, one should not assume the definitive availability of a four-valve instrument; one should restrict one's writing to the capabilities of the three-valve instrument.

The euphonium has a warm, full timbre and may be used for solos, melodic doublings, countermelodies and accompaniment passages. As a member of the tuba family, it is also well suited to doubling the tuba lines (either in unison or at the octave).

E♭ Tuba

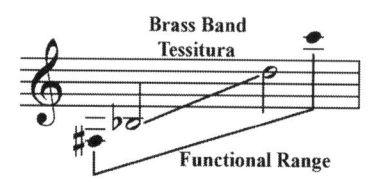

The E♭ tuba sounds an octave and a major 6th below the written note. Transposed parts are notated an octave and a major 6th above concert pitch (adding three sharps to the key signature) and always notated in treble clef in the brass band setting.

Though there are two E♭ tubas in the standard ensemble, they are generally assigned to one part. If a lighter texture is required, one may designate the part to be performed by one player (notated 1º or with the text "1 only"). It is possible to write two independent parts for the E♭ tubas, but this is rarely done and only under the most unique of circumstances. The E♭ tuba is a foundation instrument, assigned almost exclusively to the bass line. It may be used in unison or in octaves with the B♭ tubas, or as the sole bass presence when the timbre of the B♭ tubas is deemed too heavy for a particular passage. The E♭ tuba may also be used as a solo instrument. However, one should exercise caution in doing so as tuba solos can be perceived as comical if not appropriate for the genre of the selection. Since E♭ tubas are manufactured in a variety of configurations, one should not assume the availability of a four-valve instrument and restrict one's writing to the capabilities of the three-valve instrument.

B♭ Tuba

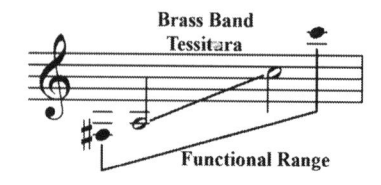

The B♭ tuba sounds two octaves and a major 2nd below the written note. Transposed parts are notated two octaves and a major 9th above concert pitch (adding two sharps to the key signature) and always notated in treble clef in the brass band setting.

Like E♭ tubas, B♭ tubas (BB♭ tubas in orchestral terminology) are manufactured in a variety of valve configurations and one may even occasionally encounter a sousaphone in a given band. As such, it is prudent to restrict one's writing to the capabilities of the three-valve instrument. Even with this restraint, the tessitura of the B♭ is quite low and the timbre is full, dark and occasionally heavy. While possible, it is not practical to write divisi lines for this part, as a singular line is far more functional and idiomatic.

Since its timbre can be somewhat heavy, one should avoid using the B♭ tuba in a continuous manner throughout a selection. The instrument can be far more effective when used within the context of the full ensemble (tutti) and at climatic points. Placing the bass line in the E♭ tubas and adding the B♭ tuba (8vb) at the appropriate moment can add to a sense of arrival by expanding the overall range of the ensemble into a lower register. Writing a continuous bass line for the B♭ tubas can result in plodding, monotonous orchestration, devoid of textual interest.

Percussion

The percussion section of the brass band generally falls into one of two classifications: a singular percussionist playing a drum set (and various other instruments that can be accessed while seated at the drum set) or multiple percussionists (2–3) capable of playing a variety of percussion instruments (including the drum set). If the section consists of a single percussionist, one may assume the availability of the following instruments: Instruments contained within the drum set (bass drum, snare drum, tom-toms, hi-hat, ride cymbal, crash cymbal), tambourine, triangle, wood block, cowbell and glockenspiel.

If the section consists of a solitary percussionist, one may assume the availability of the following instruments: Instruments contained within the drum set (bass drum, snare drum, tom-toms, hi-hat, ride cymbal, crash cymbal), tambourine, triangle, wood block, cowbell, glockenspiel, various Latin percussion instruments, and possibly timpani, chimes and tam-tam. It is rare to encounter a xylophone, vibraphone or marimba in the amateur environment. (See Chapter 7 for a detailed discussion of notation, sticks, mallets, brushes and scoring possibilities for all the above listed percussion instruments.)

Timpani

If the brass band percussion section consists of a singular player seated at a drum set, the availability of timpani is unlikely. If the section consists of multiple percussionists, one may assume access to a pair of timpani (usually a 29"/28" timpano and a 26"/25" timpano). It is rare to have access to a full set of timpani in this medium, and one cannot assume that the available timpani will be equipped with tuning pedals. Due to the cost of the instruments and limited funding available to amateur groups, encountering hand-tuned timpani is not an unusual occurrence. As such, one should restrict tuning changes to the absolute minimum. (See Chapter 7 for a discussion of timpani sizes, ranges, tessitura, tuning, notation and mallet possibilities.)

Scoring Opportunities within the Brass Band

As a distinctly unique ensemble, the brass band offers scoring possibilities not found in other traditional ensembles. The instruments that comprise the ensemble allow for the creation of diverse blended textures and distinctive soloist timbres. All members of the brass band blend well with one another and the fuller scored ensemble produces a rich, homogeneous sound. The combination of conical and cylindrical instruments offers the orchestrator a variety of textual combinations, and scoring for small groups of instruments within the ensemble presents many opportunities to add interest to one's orchestrations.

PRACTICAL CONSIDERATIONS

Practical Guidelines for Choosing a Work to Orchestrate for Brass

- Choose pieces that stylistically apply to your chosen instrumentation.
- Choose pieces that are applicable to the ranges and registers (and key signatures) of your chosen instrumentation (unless a selection specifically designates a key, such as "Minuet in G," one should feel free to alter the key to accommodate the instrumentation).
- Choose pieces that offer textural opportunities.
- Avoid pieces that are specifically idiomatic of piano.

Practical Guidelines when Scoring for Brass

- Avoid large intervallic skips (exceeding an octave).
- Avoid awkward intervals (both ascending or descending) in tonal voice-leading, i.e. aug. 2nd, dim 4th, aug. 4th, dim 5th, major 7th, minor 9th, etc. (*Note*: As intrinsic elements of contemporary, free chromatic, serialized, avant-garde and atonal music, use of "awkward intervals" may be required to maintain the stylistic intent of these genres.)
- Always be cognizant of voice-leading in *all* parts.
- Remember that piano arpeggios (generally) do not translate well to ensemble instrumentation.
- Always attempt to remain true to the (perceived) intent of the compose.
- Do not simply repeat sections note-for-note; always attempt to add interest.
- Learn from the *masters*! *Listen to and analyze* as many different examples of brass writing as possible.

IN THE PROFESSION

One never asks a player to employ a technique that could (even slightly) damage the instrument. Striking the bell of the instrument with the mouthpiece or other hard object does produce an interesting sound. However, a professional quality instrument is a significant financial investment and, as such, professional players simply will not use their instruments in a manner for which they were not designed. These types of effects are best left to the percussion section.

Unless needed for a very specific effect, one does not generally notate breath marks in a brass part. A skilled orchestrator implies an appropriate place to breathe through phrasing, slurs, rests and articulations (and immense attention should be devoted to these details). Based upon these implications, the players will determine the appropriate place to breathe. A brass part filled with breath marks would be considered offensive by advanced and professional players.

One does not notate alternate fingerings (or slide positions) in a brass part, unless needed for a very specific effect. While this may be acceptable for beginning students, it is considered offensive by advanced and professional players.

BUILDING THE SCORE

This example will demonstrate the process for creating a brass quintet orchestration from an existing piano selection. Once an appropriate work has been selected, one should begin by performing a harmonic analysis. This analysis will determine the harmonic content and context. These elements are decisive factors when determining the deletion or addition of harmonic elements.

For the purposes of the exercise the following selection will be used:

Genari Karganov, *Arabeske*

Upon completion of the analysis, one can delete the non-essential harmonic elements (or add appropriate harmonic elements, if needed). One then examines the selection for elements within the notation that must be addressed or altered to work for the instruments of the chosen ensemble. These elements may include pedal markings, crescendi and decrescendi of undefined dynamic scope, dynamics that may need to be modified to be appropriate for the chosen instrumentation, ornamentation, rhythmic subdivisions, arpeggios, etc.

In this particular example, the pedal markings affect the duration of certain notes and are addressed by notating those specific element with the implied durations. Since the melody is passed from the bass clef to the treble clef (and back) the melody is transferred from instrument to instrument in a logical manner. The result is an interplay of registers and textures.

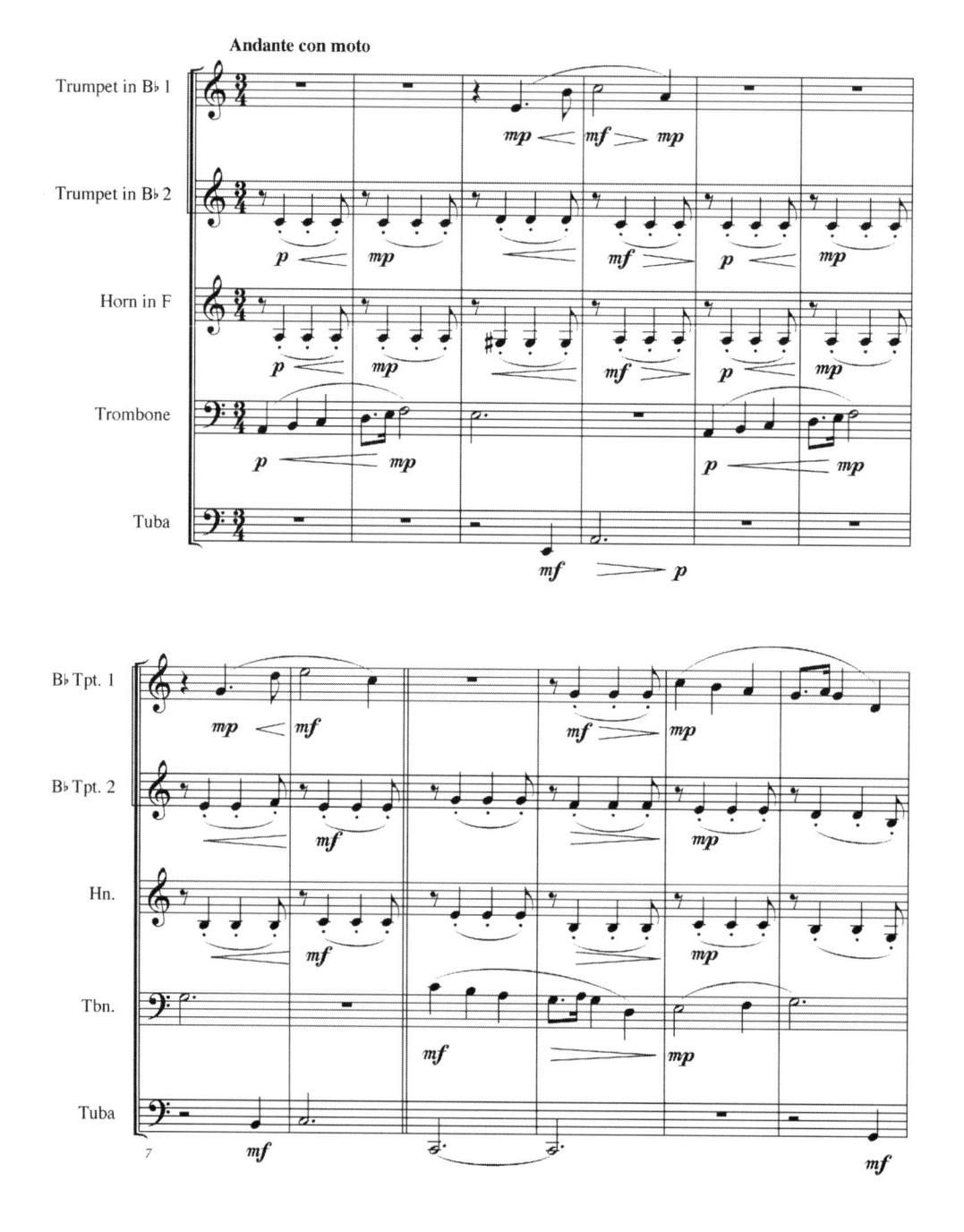

This example will demonstrate the process for adapting an existing piano selection for orchestral brass. As always, one should begin by performing a harmonic analysis to determine harmonic content and context. This enables one to competently add or delete appropriate harmonic elements. For the purposes of the exercise, the following selection will be used.

Carl Bohm, *La Zingana*

Upon completion of the harmonic analysis, one can add appropriate harmonic elements that are appropriate for the genre to accommodate the expanded instrumentation. Since piano parts are designed to be played within the physical span of the human hand, one may also seek alternate harmonic voicings appropriate for the ranges and registers of the chosen instruments.

This particular selection contain several chords that lend themselves to expanded voicings, as well as numerous options to transfer melodic elements from instrument to instrument and register to register. One should always pursue opportunities to add interest to the texture of the work (within the context of the original composition).

THE BRASS FAMILY

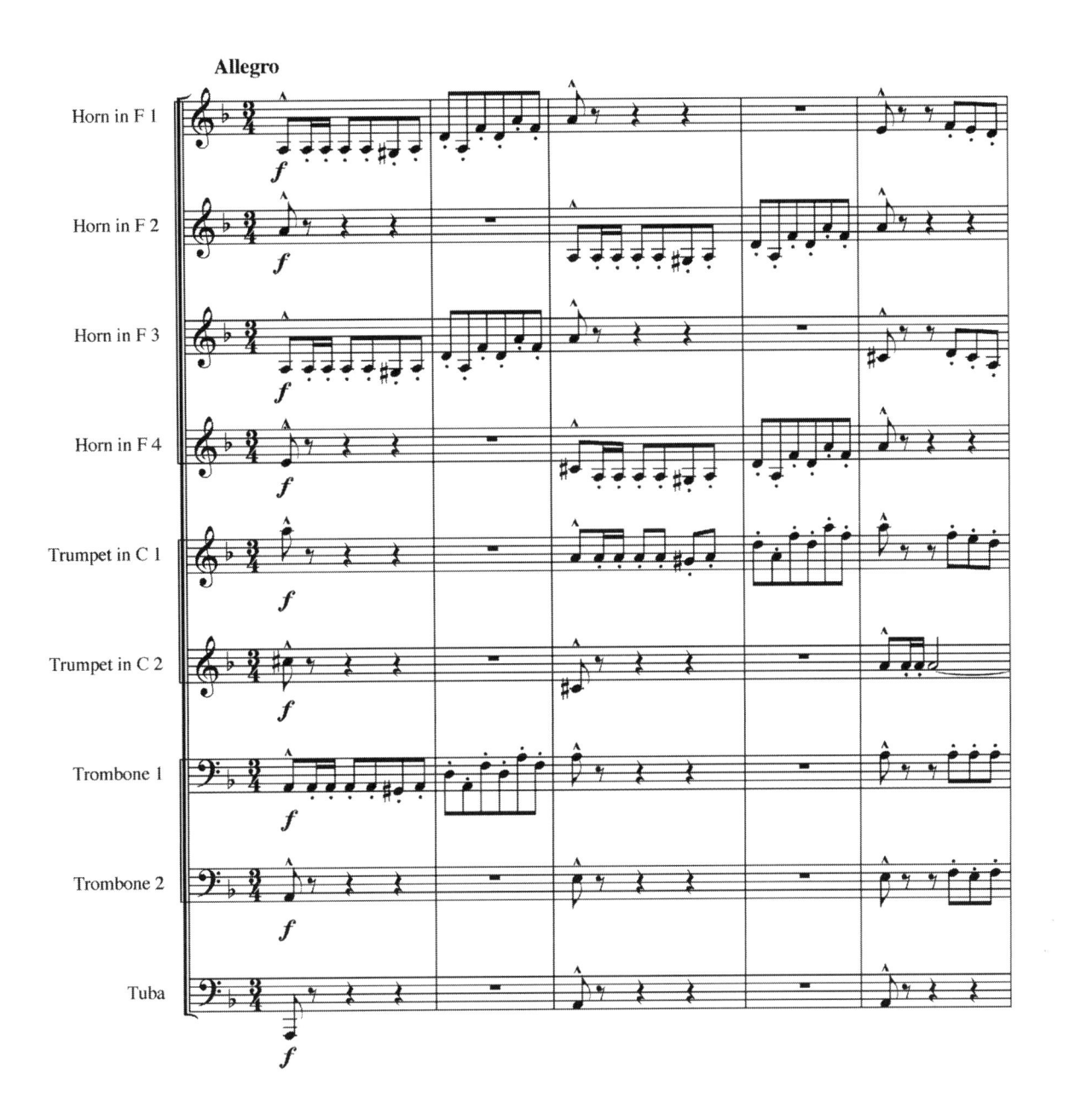

THE BRASS FAMILY

SCORING EXAMPLES

Scoring Examples for Brass Quintet

Sir Arthur Sullivan, *The Lost Chord*, mm. 1–11 (arranged and orchestrated by RJ Miller, transposed score)

Georg Friedrech Händel, "Largo" (from *Xerxes*), mm. 1–15 (arranged and orchestrated by RJ Miller, transposed score)

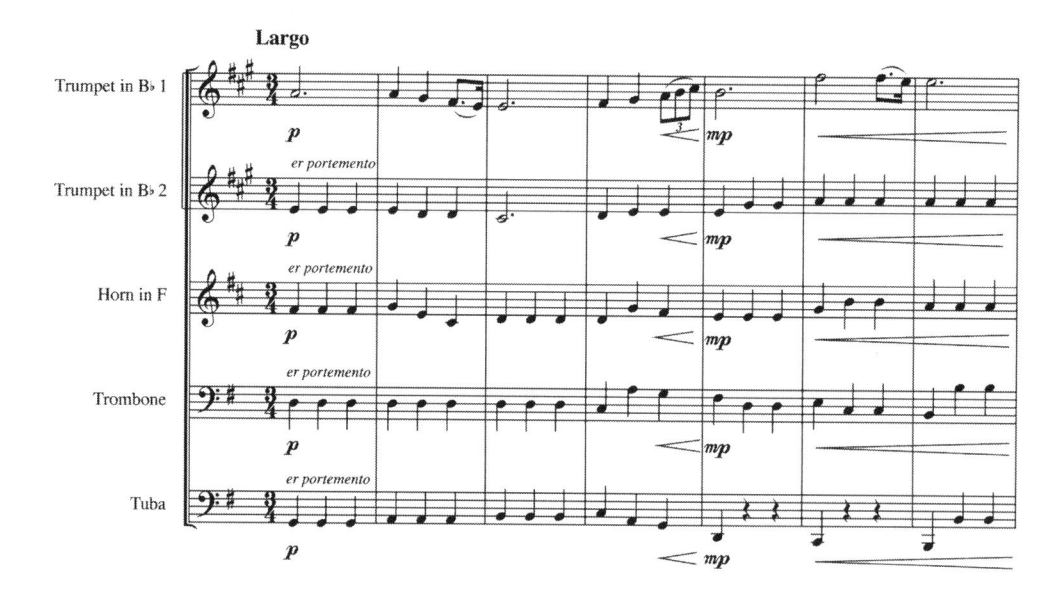

Jean-Philippe Rameau, Tambourin (from *Les Fêtes d'Hébé*), mm. 1–17 (arranged and orchestrated by RJ Miller, transposed score)

Scoring Examples for Orchestral Brass

Scoring for orchestral brass presents certain problems not encountered by other sections of the orchestra. As previously stated, the timbres of the brass and strings families are so dissimilar that (with the exception of the horn) the combination does not result in a well-blended sound. Even when combined, the instruments are perceived as separate, simultaneously occurring timbres. However, if one includes the woodwind section (as an acoustic catalyst) in one's sonic palette, one can achieve a homogeneous blend between all the sections.

Scoring solutions one utilizes for brass quintet may also be applied to orchestral brass only in the loosest of terms. With additional instruments, additional players and parts available per section, and the multitude of additional instrumental textures available within the orchestra, acoustical balances are of paramount concern. However, the availability of these additional elements offers a virtually endless palette from which to choose. The following examples are but a few of the possible approaches one might choose.

Peter Tchaikovsky, *Capriccio Italien*, mm. 1–16 (transposed score)

THE BRASS FAMILY

151

Antonín Dvořák, *Slavonic Dances*, Op. 46 No. 4 in F Major, mm. 9–16 (transposed score)

Serge Prokofiev, "Noces de Kijé" from *Lieutenant Kijé*, Movement III, mm. 81–92 (transposed score)

Scoring Examples for Wind Ensemble/Concert Band Brass

Cecil Effinger, *Silver Plume*, mm. 107–114.

Copyright © 1961 by Elkan Vogel, Inc. Used by permission of the Cecil Effinger estate, Corinne Effinger Owen, Executor.

H. Owen Reed, "Mass," Movement II from *La Fiesta Mexicana*, mm. 68–84.

Copyright © 1954 (renewed) Beam Me Up Music. All rights controlled and administered by Alfred Music. All rights reserved. Used by permission of Alfred Music.

RJ Miller, *The Summit*, mm. 12–30.

THE BRASS FAMILY

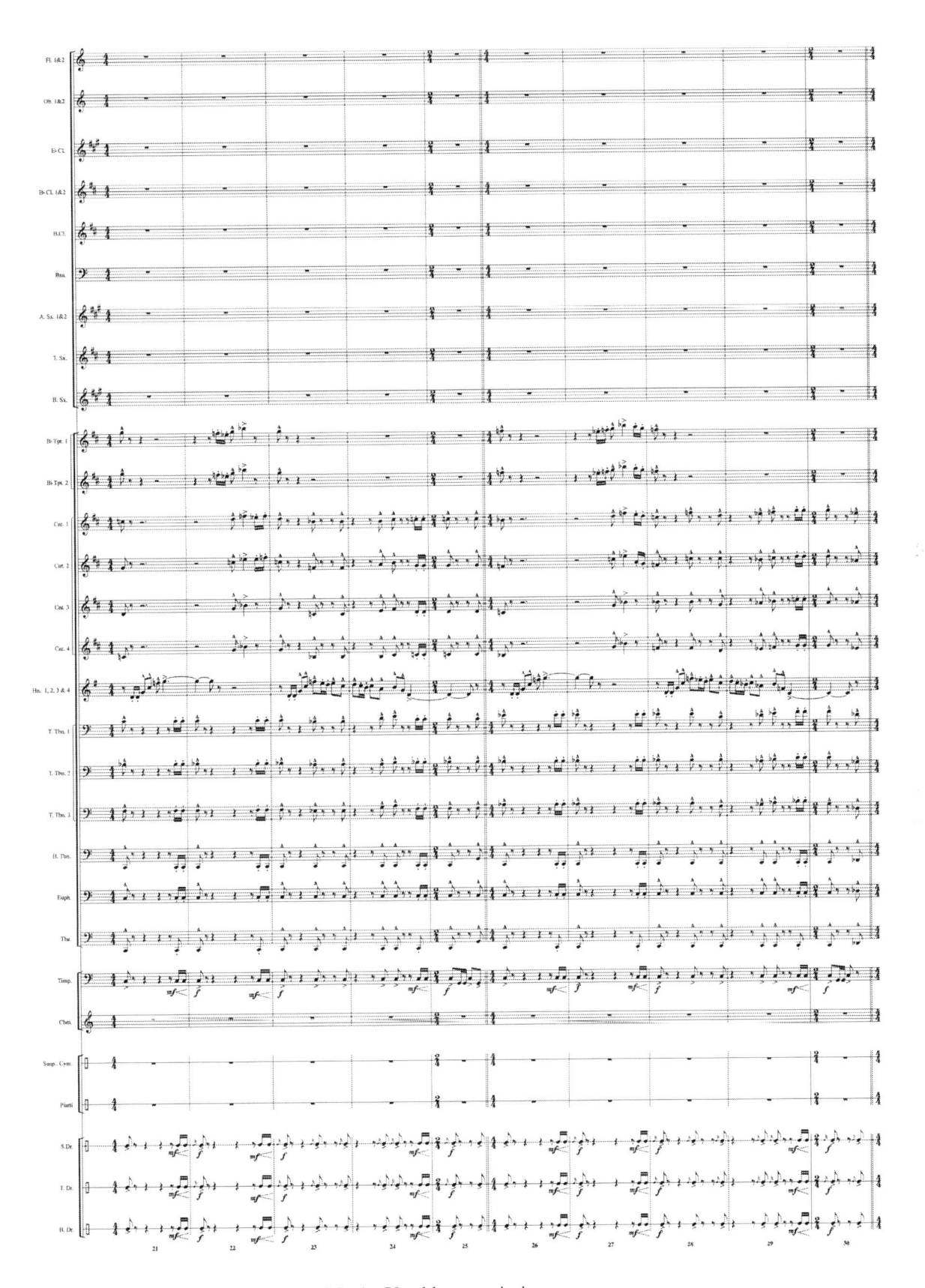

Copyright © 2004 by Appassionata Music. Used by permission.

Scoring Examples for British-style Brass Band

W. J. Westbrook, *Pleyel's Hymn*, mm. 1–12 (orchestrated by RJ Miller, transposed score)

Ede Poldini, *In the Wood*, mm. 1–10 (orchestrated and arranged by RJ Miller, transposed score)

Franz Schubert, *Marche Militaire*, Op. 51 No. 1, mm. 1–28 (orchestrated by RJ Miller, transposed score)

THE BRASS FAMILY

SUGGESTED EXERCISES

Scoring Exercise for Brass Quintet

Using the information and guidelines presented in this chapter and in Chapter 3 (Practical Problem Solving), orchestrate the following example for brass quintet. Perform a harmonic analysis and seek ways to add textural interest.

Theodore Lack, *Cabaletta*

THE BRASS FAMILY

Scoring Exercise for Orchestral Brass or Wind Ensemble Brass

Using the information and guidelines presented in this chapter and in Chapter 3 (Practical Problem Solving), orchestrate the following example for orchestral brass or wind ensemble brass. Perform a harmonic analysis and seek ways to add textural interest.

Carl Maria von Weber, *Prayer* **(The Hunter)**

Note

1. In 1st position (without trigger), the fundamental (1st partial) of the trombone is Bb_1 (contra octave).

6
THE WOODWIND FAMILY

Flute

Oboe

Clarinet

Bassoon

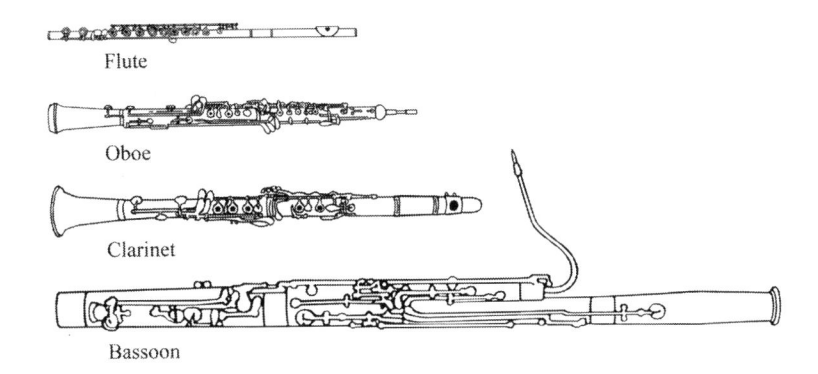

The classification of an instrument as a member of the woodwind family is not dependent upon the material from which it is made, but rather upon the means by which it produces sound. Not all "woodwind instruments" are made of wood. The sound of woodwinds is produced by the vibration of the air-column contained within the body of the instrument. This vibration is created by directing the airflow across the edge of an opening (edge-blown aerophone), between a reed and a fixed surface (single reed instrument), or between two reeds (double reed instrument).

THE ESSENTIALS

Cylindrical and Conical Classifications

As with brass instruments, one can readily observe that woodwind instruments (with the exception of the flute family) contain both cylindrical and conical properties. A woodwind instrument is classified cylindrical or conical based upon the proportion of the resonating tube that is of constant diameter, versus the proportion of tube that constantly increases in diameter. Though all woodwind instruments tend to accentuate the odd-numbered harmonic partials, cylindrical woodwind instruments generally have a bright and penetrating timbre, while the conical woodwind instruments generally have a timbre that is fuller and darker than that of cylindrical instruments. Cylindrical woodwind instruments include the members of the flute and clarinet families. Conical woodwind instruments include the members of the oboe and bassoon families. Despite their agility, flexibility and uniqueness of timbre, saxophones (also considered conical woodwinds) have yet to be fully accepted as part of the standard orchestral palette.

Edge-blown Aerophones

Edge-blown aerophones (Hornbostel-Sachs classification: 421.121.12) produce their sound by directing the flow of air across an opening in the instrument, causing the column of air within the tube to vibrate. Amplitude is a direct result of airflow velocity, as the minimal vibration of the instrument offers little appreciable enhancement.

Single Reed Instruments

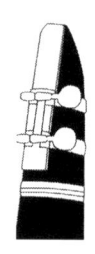

Single reed instruments produce sound with the vibration of a singular reed against the instrument mouthpiece. The reed is roughly rectangular in shape, with the thin, rounded, vibrating tip and a flat side that rests against the mouthpiece. These reeds are generally made of cane, though reeds made of synthetic materials are also readily available.

Double Reed Instruments

Double reed instruments produce sound by directing the flow of air between two reeds of equal flexibility that vibrate against each other. The standard orchestral double reed instruments are not used in conjunction with a mouthpiece. Rather, the two reeds are tightly bound together with waxed silk and attached to the cylindrical staple (or tube) that is inserted into the body of the instrument (in the case of the oboe), or on to the bocal (in the case of the bassoon). As with single reeds, double reeds are generally made of cane (reeds made of synthetic materials are also readily available).

Saxophone Mouthpieces

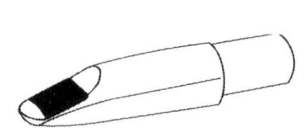

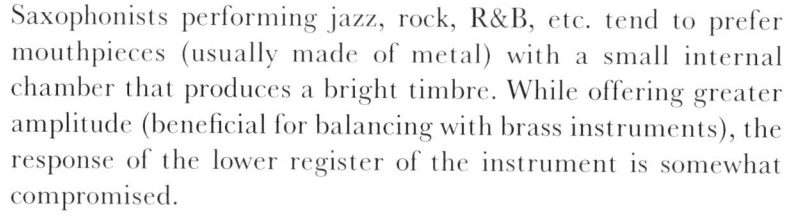

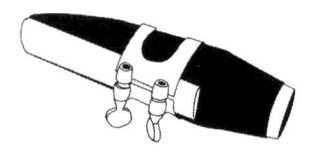

Saxophonists performing jazz, rock, R&B, etc. tend to prefer mouthpieces (usually made of metal) with a small internal chamber that produces a bright timbre. While offering greater amplitude (beneficial for balancing with brass instruments), the response of the lower register of the instrument is somewhat compromised.

Classical saxophonists generally prefer mouthpieces (usually made of ebonite or plastic) with a concave internal chamber that produces a softer, less piercing timbre. This type of mouthpiece offers greater response in the lower register of the instrument.

Single-tonguing

Woodwind players commence notes by tonguing. In the case of the flute, the player places the tongue behind the upper front teeth and uses the syllable "ta" to initiate the flow of air. In the case of the reed instruments, the player places the tip of the tongue on the tip of the reed (or reeds) and uses the syllable "ta" to initiate the flow of air.

Double-tonguing

Double-tonguing is a technique used to increase the speed at which a player can initiate the airflow. While technically possible on all woodwind instruments, the effect is most practical when applied to the flute. The flautist places the tongue behind the upper front teeth and uses the syllable "ta" to begin the flow of air followed by the syllable "ka" at the back of tongue to quickly initiate a second note. This can be done repeatedly, in quick succession: "ta-ka, ta-ka, ta-ka, ta-ka," etc. Double-tonguing on reed instruments generally yields less than adequate results. While the tongue contacts the reed(s) on the "ta" syllable, it does not contact the reed(s) on the "ka" syllable resulting in a somewhat inconsistent attack. From a practical perspective one should avoid requiring double-tonguing of reed instruments unless one is scoring specifically for a performer who is exceptionally skilled in the technique.

Triple-tonguing

Triple-tonguing is a technique used to further increase the speed at which a player can initiate the airflow. As with double-tonguing, the effect is most practical when applied to the flute. The flautist places the tongue behind the upper front teeth and uses the syllable "ta" to begin the flow of air, followed by a second "ta" to quickly initiate a second note, followed by the syllable "ka" at the back of tongue to quickly initiate a third note. This can be done repeatedly, in quick succession, with the order of syllables at the discretion of the player: "ta-ta-ka, ta-ta-ka, ta-ta-ka, ta-ta-ka," or "ta-ka-ta ta-ka-ta ta-ka-ta ta-ka-ta," etc. Triple-tonguing on reed instruments generally yields less than adequate results. As with double-tonguing, one should avoid requiring triple-tonguing of reed instruments unless one is scoring specifically for a performer who is exceptionally skilled in the technique.

Flutter-tonguing

In the case of the flute, flutter-tonguing produces a "growl-like" tone and is achieved by vibrating the tip of the tongue against the back of the upper front teeth, as if one were rolling a Spanish language "r." For reed instruments the effect is achieved by vibrating the tip of the tongue against the tip of the reed(s).

Slurs

Woodwind players accomplish slurs by not tonguing when initiating a note. In a group of notes that are slurred together, the first note is tongued and the remaining notes are initiated by simply changing the fingering.

Trills

The trill is accomplished by the rapid alternation between two adjacent notes. Without additional notation, the default trill is to the adjacent (higher) diatonic pitch.

The upper note may be designated as a non-diatonic pitch by adding a sharp, flat or natural sign, as applicable, between the *tr* and the subsequent wavy line. Trills are relatively easy on all woodwind instruments. However, if one is not intimately familiar with a given instrument, it is wise to reference a trill-fingering chart to confirm the specific trill desired is possible (or feasible).

Tremolos

The tremolo is accomplished by the rapid alternation between two non-adjacent tones. Tremolos are relatively easy on all woodwind instruments. However, as with trills, if one is not intimately familiar with a given instrument, it is wise to reference a fingering chart to confirm that the specific tremolo desired is not unwieldy.

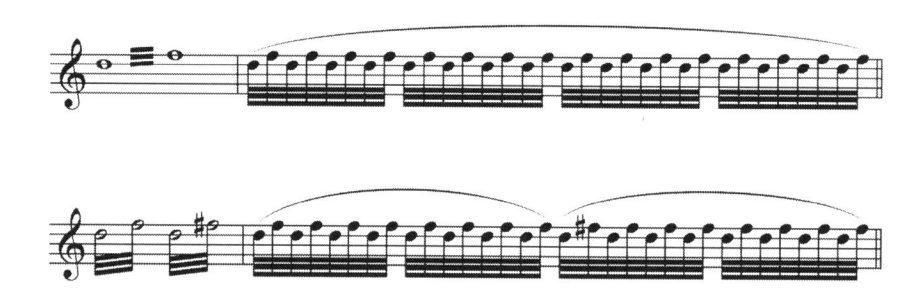

Glissandi (Portamenti)

Glissandi (portamenti), such as that heard in the opening statement of George Gershwin's *Rhapsody in Blue*, are possible only on clarinets (and saxophones), and only in an ascending direction. This is a tremendously difficult technique and should be used only with the utmost discretion. While the remaining woodwind instruments are technically capable of glissandi, the practical approach is to restrict the intervallic span of the glissandi to an octave or less, and avoid writing glissandi pass across the fingering break of the instrument.

George Gershwin, *Rhapsody in Blue*, mm. 1–5, orchestrated by Ferde Grofé (transposed solo B♭ clarinet part).

Copyright © 1924 (Renewed) WB Music Corp. All rights reserved. Used by permission of Alfred Music.

Saxophone Subtone

Subtone is a style of producing a soft, warm timbre on the instrument. Many great jazz saxophonists (such as Paul Desmond and Stan Getz) mastered and utilized this technique to produce a fluid, lyrical, less edgy sound. This technique is most effective in the lower register and involves the production of a "breathy" sound, often by allowing air to "leak" from the embouchure around the mouthpiece.

THE INSTRUMENTS

THE FLUTE FAMILY

Flute

The standard concert flute (typically referred to simply as the "flute") is a soprano voice of the woodwind choir and, with the exception of the piccolo, the highest voice of the orchestral winds. While one may occasionally encounter various alternate designs (particularly in Europe), Western concert flutes typically conform to the design (and fingerings) developed by Theobald Boehm in 19th century.

Standard concert flutes are manufactured in both closed-hole and open-hole configurations. Open-hole (or French model) flutes have holes in the centers of five of the keys that are covered by the fingers when depressed. Western European and North American orchestral flautists prefer the open-hole configuration, believing it results in greater clarity and amplitude in the lowest octave of the instrument range. Eastern European orchestral flautists disagree with this premise and have a tendency to prefer closed-hole models.

Flute Range

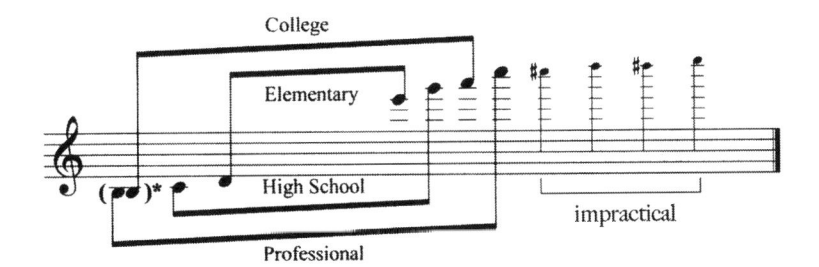

Many professional and intermediate model flutes have a "low B-foot" which extends the range of the flute down half a step to B♮. (Be aware that, while popular in North America, many professional flautists in European orchestras prefer not to play flutes with a B-foot, feeling that the added length adversely alters the timbre of the instrument.)

Flute Registers

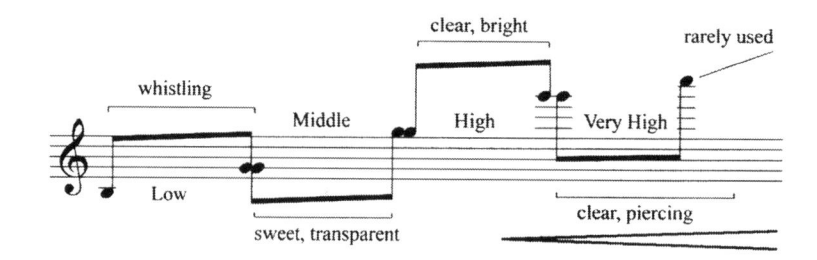

Flute Transposition

The standard concert flute is a non-transposing instrument that is always written at concert pitch in the treble clef.

Piccolo

The piccolo is the smallest and highest pitched member of the flute family, being approximately one-half the size of the standard concert flute. Piccolo parts sound one octave above the written pitch. If the flautist is doubling (playing part of the piece on flute and part of the piece of piccolo) the piccolo part is usually assigned to the 2nd flute part (or 3rd flute part, if scoring for woodwinds in threes). If the player is not doubling on flute, the piccolo should appear as a separate part in the score.

The piccolo has a brilliant, piercing timbre in the upper register, a soft and refined timbre in the middle register, and a thin, airy, somewhat haunting timbre in the lowest register. One should use restraint when scoring for piccolo in the orchestral setting. It is best used for accentuating selected melodic lines, obbligato figures and for "splashes" of color. The piccolo in the upper register can easily be heard over an entire tutti orchestra. If not used conservatively, the piercing timbre of the upper register quickly becomes tiresome to the ear.

Piccolo Range

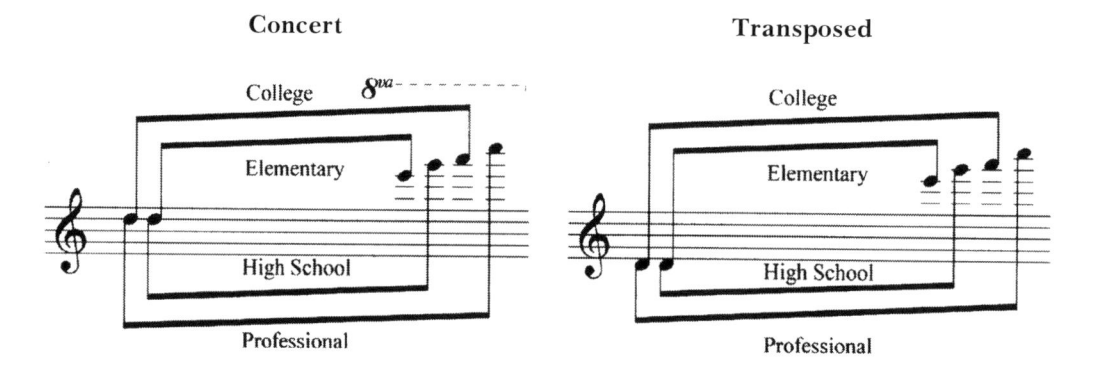

Piccolo Registers

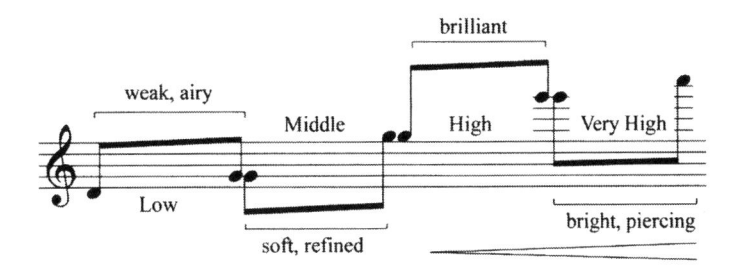

(musical notation showing piccolo register ranges: Low "weak, airy"; Middle "soft, refined"; High "brilliant"; Very High "bright, piercing")

Piccolo Transposition

(musical notation showing Concert vs. Transposed examples)

Written piccolo parts are transposed down one octave from concert pitch. Piccolo parts appear in transposed form in both concert and transposed scores. Piccolo parts are always notated in treble clef.

Alto Flute

The alto flute is a transposing instrument, pitched in the key of G and sounding a perfect 4th lower than written. It has a distinctive, warm, mellow tone when used in the lower octave and a half of its range. Higher registers, while certainly possible, cease to yield the distinctive tone for which the instrument is known. Since the body of the alto flute has a greater length and bore diameter than that of the standard concert flute (C flute), the instrument requires more airflow to produce and sustain its sound. As such, one's phrases and note durations should be written in a manner to accommodate this circumstance. One should also be aware that alto flutes are not equipped with a B-foot.

One may occasionally encounter British repertoire that refers to this instrument as a bass flute (or bass flute in G). If referred to as a bass flute in G, the desired instrument is an alto flute. If simply referred to as a bass flute, one should reference the key signature of the transposed part to determine if the instrument desired is indeed a bass flute in C, or an alto flute in G. If working from a concert score, one should refer to the range and register of the part to confirm the identity of the desired instrument.

Alto Flute Range/Practical Register

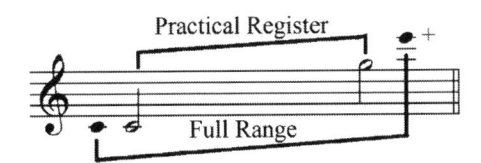

(musical notation showing Practical Register and Full Range of the alto flute)

If one is scoring the instrument as part of an ensemble, the practical register listed above is the region that produces the tone most unique to the instrument and best serves the expanded timbres of the flute choir. Should one score the instrument in a soloistic context, one may certainly venture into the upper register. However, the instrument ceases to produce its characteristic rich, full sound as it ascends from the middle register.

Alto Flute Transposition

Alto flutes sound a perfect 4th below the written note. Transposed parts are notated a perfect 4th above concert pitch (adding one flat to the key signature) and always notated in treble clef.

Bass Flute

The bass flute is a transposing instrument, pitched in the key of C and sounding a perfect octave lower than written. It has a haunting, almost hollow-sounding timbre in the lower octave and a half of its range. Higher registers are not practical as the instrument lacks agility and fails to produce the unique tone for which the instrument is best known. As with alto flutes, bass flutes are not equipped with a B-foot.

Due to its the extended length and large bore, the instrument requires significant airflow. As such, the bass flute is not capable of long, sustained note durations or extended phrases without breaths. Its sound has little project and will not penetrate in lightly scored orchestrations. While this is of little concern in the recording-studio environment, the instrument is best used as an unaccompanied (or very lightly accompanied) solo instrument in orchestral settings.

Bass Flute Range/Registers

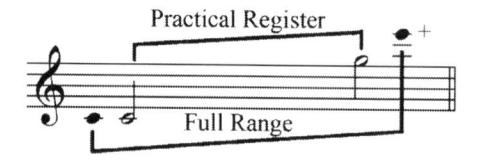

The practical register listed above is the region that produces the tone most unique to the instrument and best serves the expanded timbres of the flute choir. In a soloistic context, one may venture into the upper register, knowing that the instrument will cease to produce its characteristic rich, full sound as it ascends from the middle register.

Bass Flute Transposition

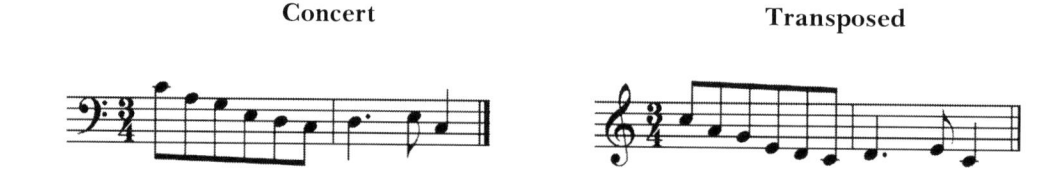

Bass flutes sound a perfect octave below the written note. Transposed parts are notated a perfect octave above concert pitch and always notated in treble clef.

Contra-Alto Flute

The contra-alto flute (contralto flute, contrabass flute in G) is a transposition instrument sounding an octave, plus a perfect 4th below the notated pitch. While the instrument has also been manufactured in the key of F, the contra-alto flute in G is the standard. Rarely, if ever, found in an orchestral setting (and never in the wind ensemble/concert band environment), the instrument has become a staple of the flute orchestra. The size and configuration of the instrument typically require the player to stand while playing. The tone is round, full and poignant, but because of the amount of air required to generate the tone, notes of long, sustained duration are impractical. Should one be inclined to use the instrument outside the flute orchestra, one must confirm the availability of the instrument.

Contra-Alto Flute Range

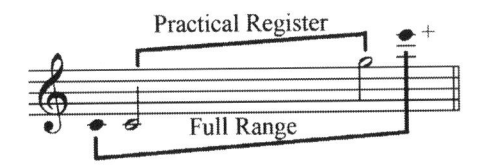

If one is scoring the instrument as part of an ensemble, the practical register listed above is the region that produces the tone most unique to the instrument and best serves the expanded timbres of the flute choir. Should one score the instrument in a soloistic context, one may certainly venture into the upper register. However, the instrument ceases to produce its characteristic rich, full sound as it ascends from the middle register.

Contra-Alto Flute Transposition

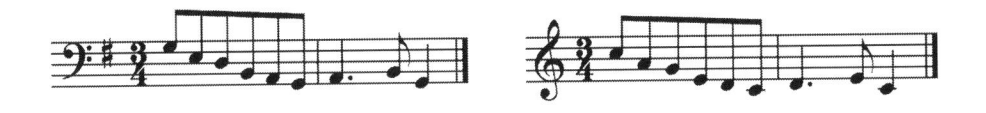

Contra-alto flutes sound an octave, plus a perfect 4th below the written note. Transposed parts are notated an octave, plus a perfect 4th above concert pitch (adding one flat to the key signature) and always notated in treble clef.

Contrabass Flute

The contrabass flute is rarely used outside the flute orchestra environment, though its unique timbre is occasionally employed in film scores. Some contrabass flutes are equipped with a B-foot. However, one should not assume its availability unless scoring for a specific player on a specific instrument. The lower and middle registers have a rich, haunting timbre capable of conveying great compassion and lyricism. In the flute orchestra environment, the lower and middle registers provide a solid harmonic foundation for the ensemble. The upper register should be avoided as it lacks the strength of tone needed for both solo and ensemble usage. The size and configuration of the instrument requires the player to stand while playing.

Contrabass Flute Range

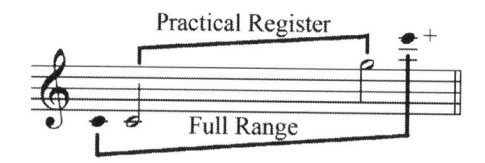

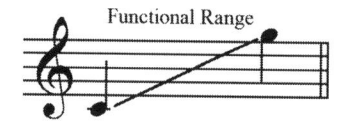

Contrabass Flute Transposition

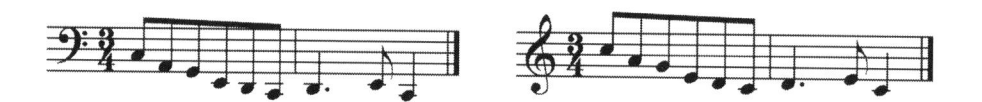

Contrabass flutes sound two octaves below the written note. Transposed parts are notated two octaves above concert pitch and always notated in treble clef.

Subcontrabass Flutes

Though extremely rare, there are two additional members of the low flute family. The subcontrabass flute in G is pitched an octave below the contra-alto flute, and the double contrabass flute (also known as the subcontrabass flute in C, or the octobass flute) is pitched an octave below the contrabass flute. The functional range of these instruments is quite restricted, but their unique tone offers textual possibilities not afforded by other instruments.

Subcontrabass Flute in G Range

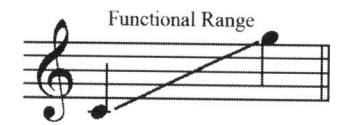

Subcontrabass Flute in G Transposition

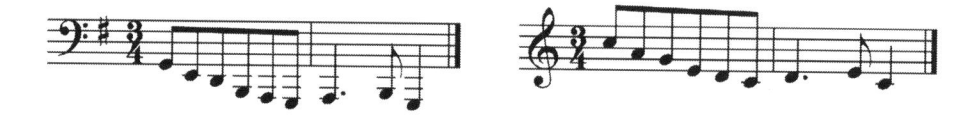

The subcontrabass flute in G sounds two octaves, plus a perfect 4th below the written note. Transposed parts are notated two octaves, plus a perfect 4th above concert pitch (adding one flat to the key signature) and always notated in treble clef.

Double Contrabass Flute Range

Double Contrabass Flute Transposition

The double contrabass flute sounds three octaves below the written note. Transposed parts are notated three octaves above concert pitch and always notated in treble clef.

D♭ Piccolo

Though the D♭ piccolo is now considered obsolete, standard band music in the first half of the 20th century always contained parts for the D♭ piccolo (i.e. John Philip Sousa's "The Stars and Stripes Forever" was originally written for D♭ piccolo.)

D♭ Piccolo Range

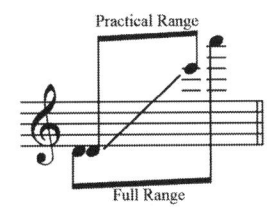

D♭ Piccolo Transposition

D♭ piccolos are built in the key of D♭, sounding a minor 9th above the written note. Transposed parts are notated a minor 9th below concert pitch, and always notated in treble clef.

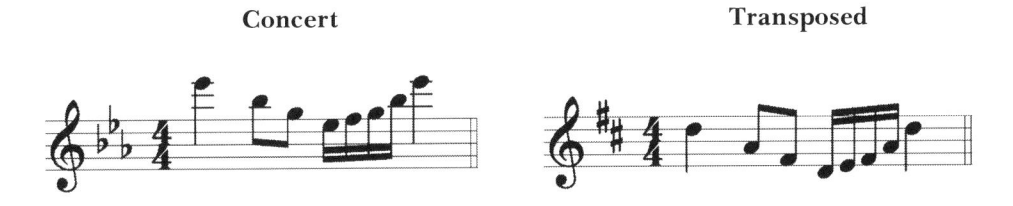

Concert **Transposed**

To convert a D♭ piccolo part to standard (C) piccolo, transpose the written D♭ piccolo part up a minor 2nd.

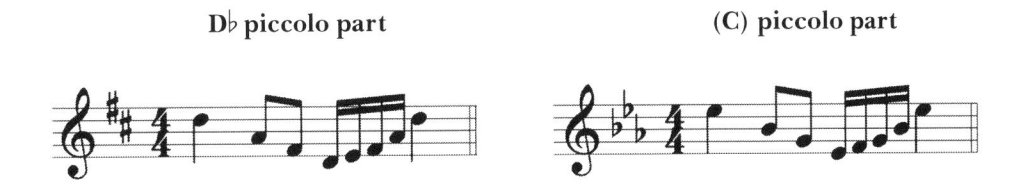

D♭ piccolo part **(C) piccolo part**

THE SINGLE REED FAMILY

Clarinets

Clarinets are cylindrical bore, single reed aerophones with the widest practical range of all the wind instruments. This is a direct result of the shape, construction and acoustical properties of the instrument. When a woodwind instrument crosses from its lowest register into its middle register it is referred to as crossing "the break." This is the point where the instrument shifts from generating fundamental pitches to generating pitches based upon overtones. It is also the point where fingering patterns transition from few, if any, holes covered (or keys depressed) to most of the holes covered (or most of the keys depressed). With most woodwind instruments the break occurs at the interval of an octave. However, on the clarinet the break occurs at the interval of a twelfth. Due to these unique acoustical attributes, clarinets have no difficultly with entrances in their lowest (chalumeau) register and respond well throughout most of their practical range.

The registers of the clarinet are divided into three separate classifications. The lowest register is classified as the chalumeau register, the middle register as the clarino register and the upper register as the altissimo register. The orchestrator should be aware of two problematic regions within the range of the instrument. First, the notes spanning g′ to b♭′ are called "throat tones" and have a somewhat hoarse or unfocused timbre, particularly with younger players. This register also presents intonation challenges for the beginning and intermediate player. Advanced and professional players will have mastered the means to compensate for this discrepancy of timbre and intonation, and generally have little difficulty in this register. Second, as with most woodwinds, the notes in upper altissimo register are shrill and piercing, with fingering combinations that tend to be somewhat awkward. Writing rapid, extended passages in this register will yield disappointing results.

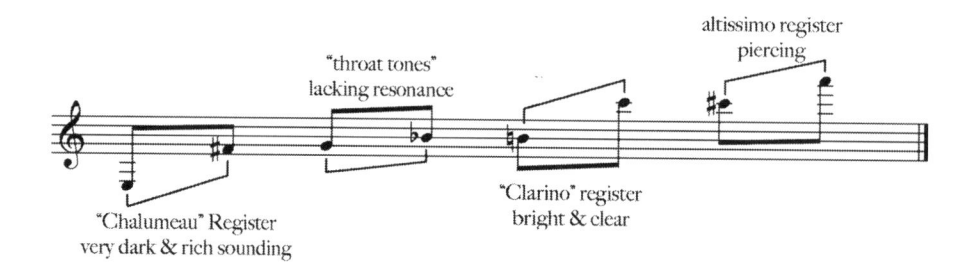

E♭ Clarinet

The E♭ clarinet is a transposing instrument sounding a minor third higher than notated. Being smaller in size than the B♭ (soprano) clarinet, it is commonly referred to as a "sopranino" clarinet. Unlike most "auxiliary" instruments, the upper register possesses the most distinctive timbre of the E♭ clarinet. This register can be quite piercing and is most effective when used for "splashes" of color. It can also be used to cover high passages that would be perilous for the B♭ clarinet. One generally orchestrates for this instrument in a manner similar to that one would use when scoring for the piccolo.

While one may occasionally encounter an E♭ clarinet in the orchestral setting, the instrument is a staple in wind ensembles, concert bands and marching bands. In all ensembles, a singular player plays the E♭ clarinet part. One should only assume the availability of this instrument at college and professional levels.

E♭ Clarinet Range

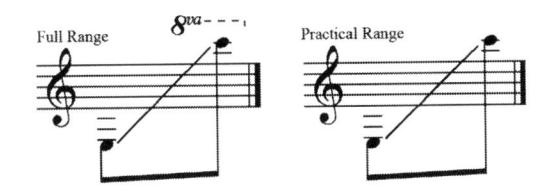

E♭ Clarinet Transposition

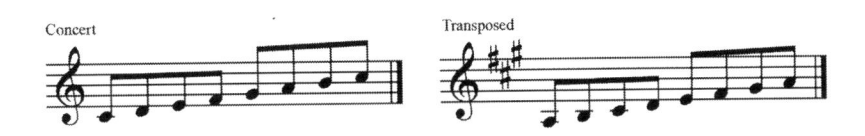

E♭ clarinets sound a minor 3rd above the written note. Transposed parts are notated a minor 3rd above concert pitch (adding three sharps to the key signature), and always notated in treble clef.

B♭ Clarinet

The B♭ (soprano) clarinet is a transposing instrument sounding a major second lower than notated. It is the most common of the clarinets and a stalwart of the wind section in the orchestral, wind ensemble/concert and marching band settings. Its wide range and distinctive timbre has also afforded forays into the jazz environment as a solo voice and occasionally as a lead instrument when combined with saxophones. Equally adept as a solo, section or tutti voice, the B♭ clarinet offers the orchestrator great versatility in its usage.

B♭ Clarinet Range

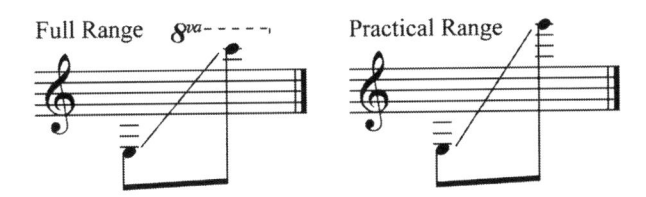

B♭ Clarinet Transposition

B♭ clarinets sound a major 2nd below the written note. Transposed parts are notated a major 2nd above concert pitch (adding two sharps to the key signature), and always notated in treble clef.

Clarinet in A

One usually encounters the clarinet in A only within the orchestral environment. It is a transposing instrument sounding a minor 3rd below the notated pitch. The instrument is slightly larger than the B♭ clarinet, with a somewhat darker tone. Having the transposition of the minor 3rd (adding 3 flats to the key signature) allows the instrument to play in the concert keys containing multiple sharps that would be considerably more difficult on the B♭ clarinet (whose transposition adds 2 sharps to the key signature). In contemporary times, it is rare for an orchestrator to require the use of the clarinet in A as its availability cannot be assumed. When scoring for wind ensemble/concert band it is advisable for the orchestrator to choose concert keys that accommodate the multiple B♭ and E♭ instruments within the ensemble, thereby circumventing the need for the clarinet in A.

Clarinet in A Range

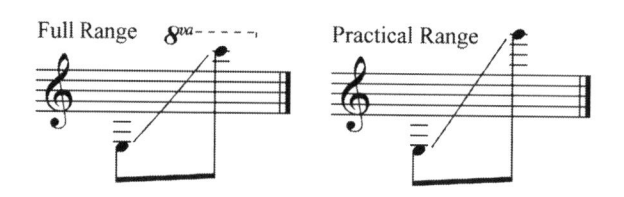

Clarinet in A Transposition

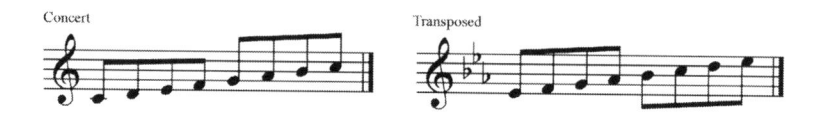

Clarinets in A sound a minor 3rd below the written note. Transposed parts are notated a minor 3rd above concert pitch (adding three flats to the key signature) and always notated in treble clef.

E♭ Alto Clarinet

The E♭ alto clarinet is a transposing instrument sounding a major 6th lower than notated. It is rarely used in the orchestral setting, except as a substitute for the now antiquated basset horn and basset clarinet, and within this context may be featured as a soloistic voice. However, in contemporary times it is more often used for its textural qualities and as a 3rd clarinet part. The instrument is more established as a member of the wind ensemble/concert band (and occasionally the marching band) where it may serve as an independent voice, a unison doubling of 3rd clarinet part, or as an textual quality when doubled with other instruments of the ensemble that play in the same register.

E♭ Alto Clarinet Range

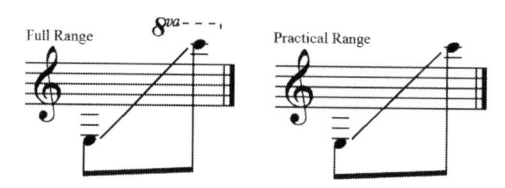

E♭ Alto Clarinet Transposition

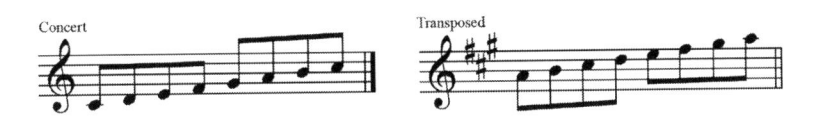

E♭ alto clarinets sound a major 6th below the written note. Transposed parts are notated a major 6th above concert pitch (adding 3 sharps to the key signature) and always notated in treble clef.

B♭ Bass Clarinet

The B♭ bass clarinet is a transposing instrument sounding a major ninth lower than notated. It is an established member of the clarinet section in wind ensembles/concert bands with occasional usage in marching bands. In the orchestral setting, the B♭ bass clarinet is generally added to the ensemble when the selection is scored for woodwinds in threes. The instrument is a particularly useful timbre when scoring for film and television, and can occasionally be a valuable, unexpected timbre in jazz and contemporary popular music. As with all of the larger clarinets, the harshness of the throat tone timbre is more pronounced than on the smaller clarinets. While it is certainly permissible to pass through the throat tone area, as well as to use the register in tutti sections, one should strive to avoid exposing this problematic region of the instrument's range in soloistic passages. The chalumeau and clarino registers yield the most characteristic timbre and are the most viable registers on the instrument.

B♭ Bass Clarinet Range

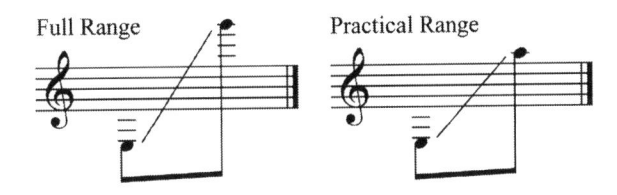

B♭ Bass Clarinet Transposition

B♭ bass clarinets sound an octave, plus major 2nd (major 9th) below the written note. Transposed parts are notated a major 9th above concert pitch (adding two sharps to the key signature) and always notated in treble clef.

E♭ Contralto Clarinet

The E♭ contralto clarinet (E♭ contra-alto clarinet, E♭ contrabass clarinet) is a transposing instrument, sounding an octave and a major 6th lower than notated. Often used in conjunction with, or in lieu of the BB♭ contrabass clarinet, and is best used as a unison doubling or an octave doubling of that part. When scoring for the instrument in the wind ensemble/concert band setting, it is wise to score the part in unison with the BB♭ contrabass clarinet and provide an optional double bass part that duplicates the part.

E♭ Contralto Clarinet Range

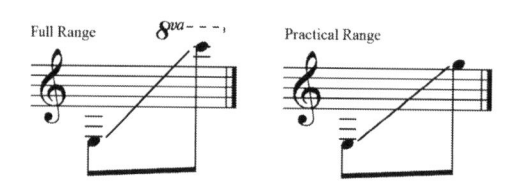

E♭ Contralto Clarinet Transposition

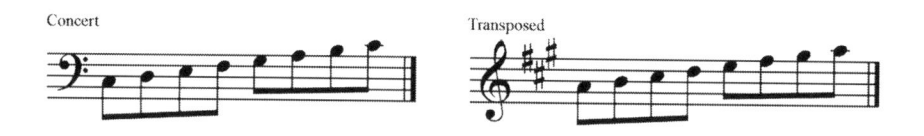

E♭ contralto clarinets sound an octave, plus major 6th below the written note. Transposed parts are notated an octave, plus major 6th above concert pitch (adding three sharps to the key signature), and always notated in treble clef.

B♭ Contrabass Clarinet

The largest member of the standard clarinet family, the BB♭ contrabass clarinet is a transposing instrument, sounding two octaves and a major 2nd below the notated pitch. Some instruments have an extended lower register, ranging from an additional minor 2nd (E♭) to an additional major 3rd (C) below the standard range. One cannot assume the availability of this extended range unless writing for a specific player with a specific instrument. One is better served by restricting one's writing to the capabilities of the standard instrument. As with the B♭ bass clarinet, the throat tone register is problematic, and the chalumeau and clarino registers yield the most characteristic timbre.

The B♭ contrabass clarinet is generally found in works requiring expanded instrumentation. However, it is not part of the standard orchestral palette and should be considered an "auxiliary" instrument in the orchestral setting. When scoring for the instrument in the wind ensemble/concert band setting, it is wise to provide an optional double bass part that duplicates the part. The size and weight of the instrument precludes its usage in the marching band environment. In the recording-studio environment one should be aware that rapid passages often produce a significant amount of "clattering" noise from the keys.

B♭ Contrabass Clarinet Range

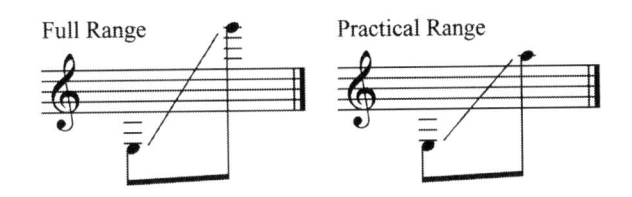

B♭ Contrabass Clarinet Transposition

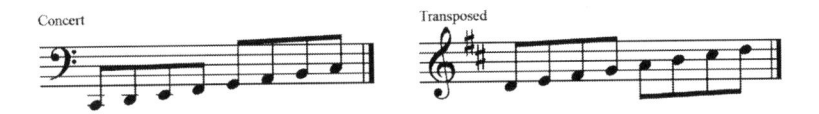

B♭ contrabass clarinets sound two octaves, plus a major 2nd below the written note. Transposed parts are notated two octaves, plus a major 2nd above concert pitch (adding two sharps to the key signature) and always notated in treble clef.

THE SAXOPHONE FAMILY

Invented in 1838 (and patented in 1846) by Adolphe Sax, the saxophone was originally designed to enhance the low voices of the orchestra. Ironically, despite their agility, flexibility, and uniqueness of timbre, saxophones have yet to be fully accepted as part of the standard orchestral palette. These instruments, however, gained favor in band repertoire and quickly became a fixture in military bands, marching bands, jazz ensembles and concert bands.

B♭ Soprano Saxophone

The upper voice of the traditional saxophone quartet, the soprano saxophone is a transposing instrument in the key of B♭. With a transposition of a Major 2nd (same as that of the B♭ clarinet), it is pitched one octave above the tenor saxophone. Most modern instruments are equipped with a high F# key, and some also have a high G key (concert E''' and F''' respectively). However, even if these keys are available on the instrument, one should not assume these notes are readily at one's disposal. The instrument has a tendency to have intonation problems (due its proportionally smaller bore) and these problems are accentuated in the higher register. From a practical perspective, the orchestrator/arranger is best served writing soprano saxophone in comfortable registers (low to upper middle), where the player can more easily compensate for intonation discrepancies.

B♭ Soprano Saxophone Range

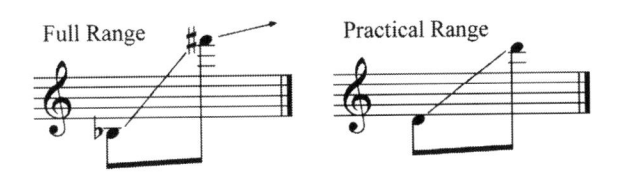

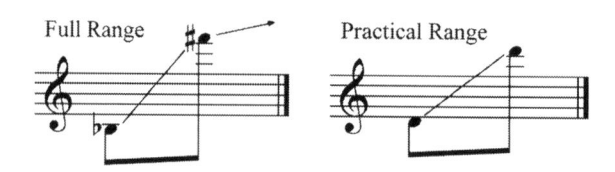

B♭ Soprano Saxophone Registers

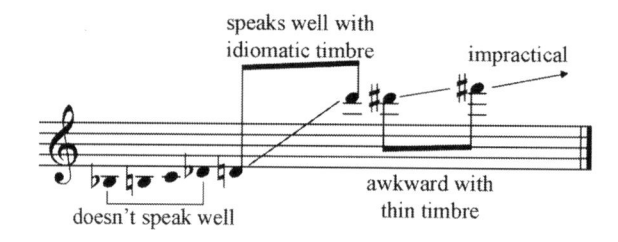

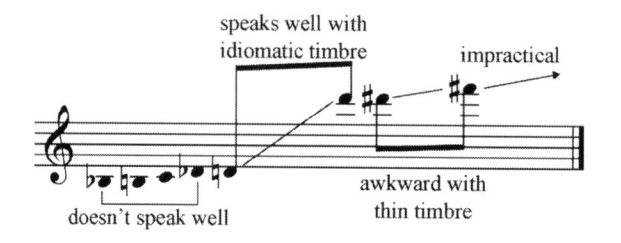

B♭ Soprano Saxophone Transposition

B♭ Soprano saxophones sound a major 2nd below the written note. Transposed parts are notated a major 2nd above concert pitch (adding two sharps to the key signature) and always notated in treble clef.

E♭ Alto Saxophone

Somewhat larger than the soprano saxophone, the alto saxophone is a transposing instrument in the key of E♭. With a transposition of a major 6th, it is pitched a perfect fifth below the soprano saxophone, and one octave above the baritone saxophone. Like the soprano saxophone, most modern alto saxophones are equipped with a high F♯ key (concert a″), and some professional models also have a high G key (concert a♭″). The alto saxophone has a proportionally larger bore, and therefore a greater stability of intonation than the soprano saxophone. However, the upper register is still somewhat difficult to control and is accessed best by approaching the high notes in an ascending manner, rather than by scoring abrupt altissimo entrances.

E♭ Alto Saxophone Range

E♭ Alto Saxophone Registers

E♭ Alto Saxophone Transposition

E♭ alto saxophones sound a major 6th below the written note. Transposed parts are notated a major 6th above concert pitch (adding three sharps to the key signature) and always notated in treble clef.

B♭ Tenor Saxophone

Somewhat larger than the alto saxophone, the tenor saxophone is a transposing instrument in the key of B♭. With a transposition of an octave plus a major 2nd (same as that of the B♭ bass clarinet), it is pitched one octave below the soprano saxophone and a perfect fourth below the alto saxophone. Most modern tenor saxophones are equipped with a high F♯ key, and some professional models have a high G key (concert e″ and f″, respectively). In a concert score, tenor saxophone parts are often written in bass clef. However, transposed tenor saxophone parts (like those of all saxophones) are always written in the treble clef.

B♭ Tenor Saxophone Range

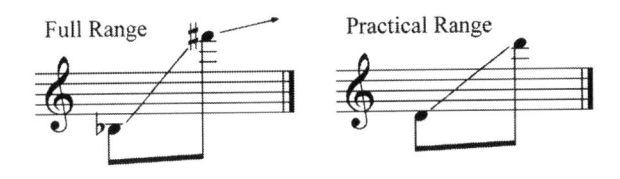

B♭ Tenor Saxophone Registers

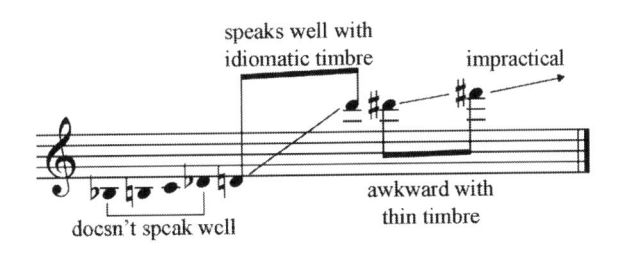

B♭ Tenor Saxophone Transposition

B♭ tenor saxophones sound a major 9th below the written note. Transposed parts are notated a major 9th above concert pitch (adding two sharps to the key signature) and always notated in treble clef.

E♭ Baritone Saxophone

The lowest voice of the traditional saxophone quartet, the baritone saxophone is a transposing instrument in the key of E♭. With a transposition of an octave plus a major 6th, it is pitched one octave below the alto saxophone. Most modern instruments are equipped with both a high F♯ key and a low A key (concert a' and c, respectively). The baritone saxophone is the only saxophone in standard production with this low A key. This low A (concert C) is very stable, speaks easily and is textually full and round. One should not shy away from its use, as it can be quite effective. In a concert score, baritone saxophone parts are usually written in bass clef. However, transposed baritone saxophone parts (like those of all saxophones) are always written in the treble clef.

E♭ Baritone Saxophone Range

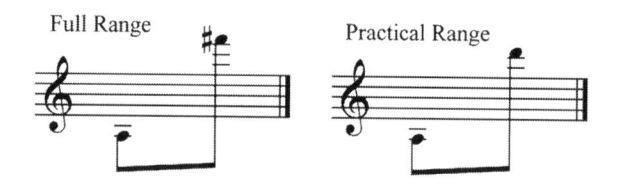

E♭ Baritone Saxophone Registers

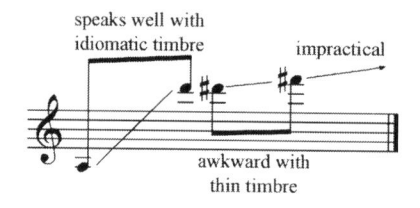

E♭ Baritone Saxophone Transposition

E♭ baritone saxophones sound an octave plus a major 6th below the written note. Transposed parts are notated an octave plus a major 6th above concert pitch (adding three sharps to the key signature) and always notated in treble clef. Most baritone saxophones are now equipped with a low A key (concert C).

E♭ Sopranino Saxophone

The sopranino saxophone is the smallest practical member of the saxophone family. While the B♭ sopranissimo ("soprillo") saxophone is indeed smaller than the sopranino, it offers little practical functionality to the orchestrator/arranger (other than use as a novelty). The sopranino saxophone is a transposing instrument in the key of E♭, pitched one octave above the alto saxophone. Transposed parts are written down a minor 3rd from concert pitch. As with the soprano saxophone, the orchestrator/arranger is best served writing soprano saxophone in comfortable registers (low to upper middle), where the player can more easily compensate for intonation discrepancies.

E♭ Sopranino Saxophone Range

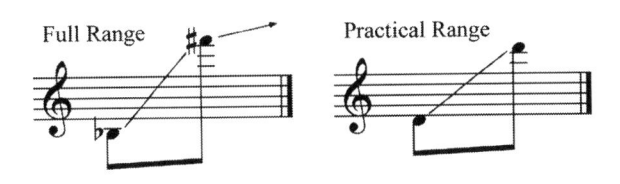

E♭ Sopranino Saxophone Registers

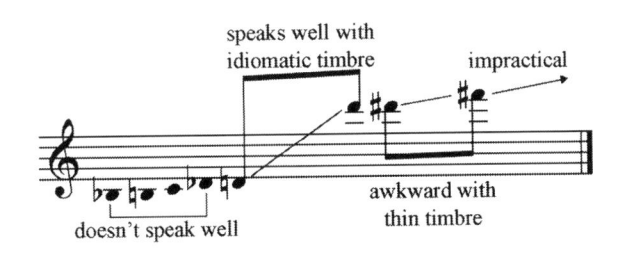

E♭ Sopranino Saxophone Transposition

E♭ sopranino saxophones sound a minor 3rd above the written note. Transposed parts are notated a minor 3rd below concert pitch (adding three sharps to the key signature) and always notated in treble clef.

B♭ Bass Saxophone

While similar in design to the baritone saxophone, the bass saxophone is neither in common use nor readily available. It is a transposing instrument in the key of B♭, with a transposition of two octaves plus a major 2nd. (One may occasionally encounter scores written for bass saxophone in C; however, that instrument is now obsolete.) Should one have access to a bass saxophone, one should be aware that these instruments have neither a high F♯ key nor a low A key. The instrument is most effective in the low and middle registers, as the upper register is sated with intonation problems.

B♭ Bass Saxophone Range

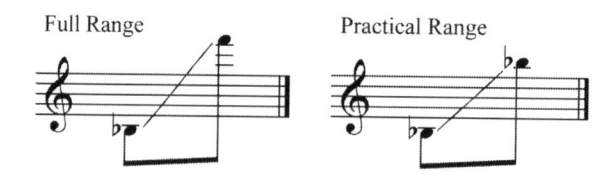

B♭ Bass Saxophone Registers

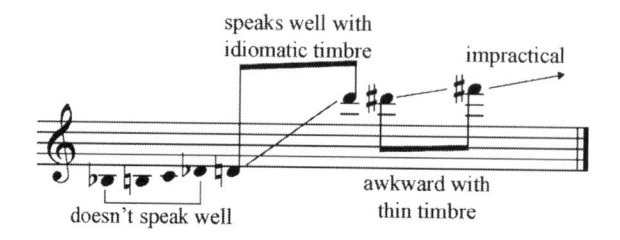

B♭ Bass Saxophone Transposition

B♭ bass saxophones sound an octave plus a major 9th below the written note. Transposed parts are notated an octave plus a major 9th above concert pitch (adding two sharps to the key signature) and always notated in treble clef.

E♭ Contrabass Saxophone

Even less common than the bass saxophone, the contrabass saxophone is rarely used, except as a novelty. Pitched in the key of E♭, and playing an octave lower than the baritone saxophone, the contrabass saxophone is extremely large and heavy. Like the bass saxophone, the contrabass saxophone is equipped with neither a high F♯ key, nor a low A key. Should one choose to write for this instrument, one should restrict oneself to the low and middle registers.

THE DOUBLE REED FAMILY

Oboe

The oboe is the soprano voice of the double reed family noted for its bright and lyrical timbre. It is a non-transposing instrument with a predominantly conical bore. In a soloistic context, the oboe projects well over other woodwinds and strings in the orchestral setting. In an ensemble framework, the instrument blends well with all other instruments in the orchestra. There are multiple incarnations of the instrument, each with a unique timbre and keywork system. However, the French-style model is the most ubiquitous and renders the timbre the modern ear most commonly associates with the instrument. As such, it is the qualities, capabilities and fingerings of that model to which this text refers.

Oboe Range

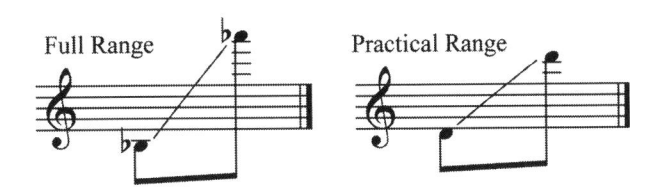

Oboe Registers

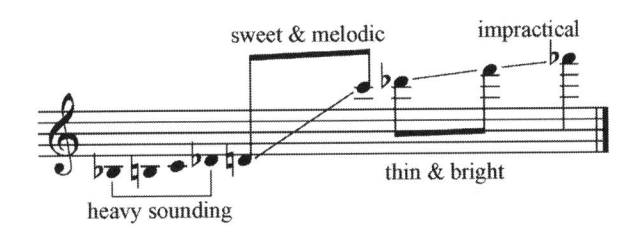

Oboe Transposition

The oboe is a non-transposing instrument that is always written in treble clef.

English Horn

The English horn (cor anglais) is generally considered the alto member of the double reed family. It is a transposing instrument pitched a perfect 5th below the oboe. Renowned as an eloquent solo texture capable of great expressiveness, the instrument's full, rich timbre also blends well within the ensemble. Within the ensemble setting, one would generally use the instrument as a 3rd oboe part, covering notes in the lower oboe register as well as those just below oboe range. Depending upon the genre and the desired texture, one could also consider substituting the English horn for the horn in F in the wind quintet. The instrument is generally built with the same keywork and uses the same fingering as the oboe.

English Horn Range

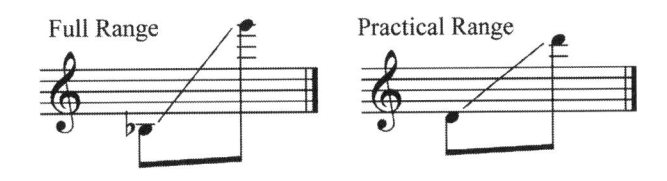

English Horn Registers

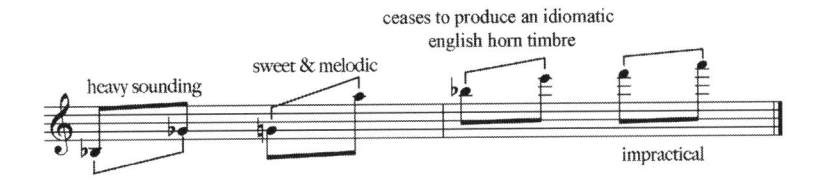

English Horn Transposition

English horns are built in the key of F, sounding a perfect 5th below the written note. Transposed parts are notated a perfect 5th above concert pitch (adding one sharp to the key signature), and always notated in treble clef.

Oboe d'amore

The oboe d'amore (Italian for "oboe of love") is a double reed instrument, slightly larger than the oboe and slightly smaller than the English horn. If one accepts the premise that the oboe is the soprano voice of the double reed family and the English horn is the alto voice, one would consider the oboe d'amore the mezzo-soprano voice of the double reed family. It is a transposing instrument (pitched in A), sounding a minor third lower than notated. The instrument uses a bocal and has a bulbous bell. It is generally built with the same keywork and uses the same fingering as the oboe and English horn.

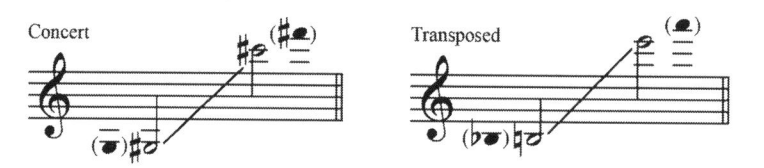

Oboe d'amore Range

Oboe d'amore Transposition

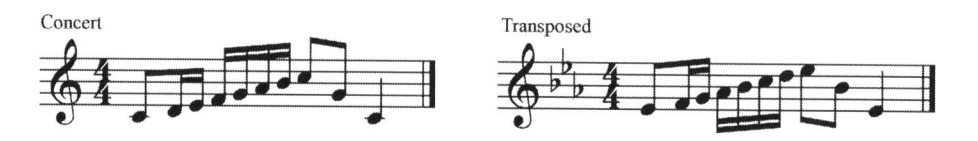

The oboe d'amore sounds a minor 3rd below the written note. Transposed parts are notated a minor 3rd above concert pitch (adding three flats to the key signature) and always notated in treble clef.

Baritone (Bass) Oboe

The baritone oboe (also known as the hautbois baryton or the "bass oboe") is a transposing double reed instrument pitched an octave below the oboe (in C). It has a timbre that is darker and richer than that of the English horn. It is always notated in the treble clef and has its most distinctive timbre in the middle and lower registers. The instrument is conical shaped, with a bulbous bell and equipped with a bocal. As previously mentioned, it is difficult to determine whether the composer intends usage of the baritone oboe or the heckelphone when "bass oboe" is designated in the score. Though more baritone oboes are extant than heckelphones, one's orchestration is still best served by substituting a contemporary instrument of greater availability. (See Chapter 14, Instrument Substitution.)

Baritone (Bass) Oboe Range

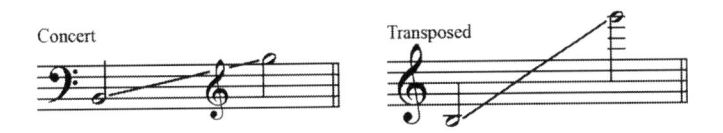

Baritone (Bass) Oboe Transposition

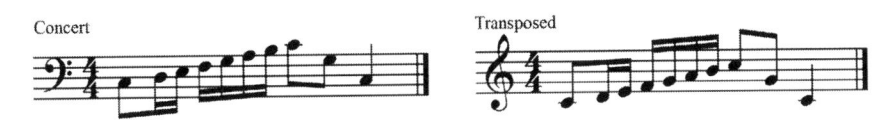

The baritone oboe sounds an octave below the written note. Transposed parts are notated an octave above concert pitch.

Bassoons

The bassoon is a non-transposing double reed instrument known for its unique and varied timbre, agility and extensive range. In an orchestral setting one can liken its diverse registers and usage to that of the violoncello. Outfitted with a relatively complicated keywork, the bassoon (depending upon the model) may have as many as nine keys operated by the left thumb only. Pitch can be adjusted significantly with breath support, embouchure, reed profile, or by altering the relative position of the bocal. The weight of the instrument requires the player to support the bassoon by using either a seat strap or a neck strap or shoulder harness.

Bassoon Range

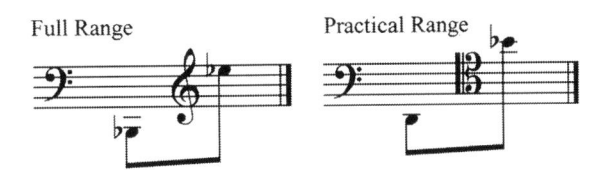

Bassoon Registers

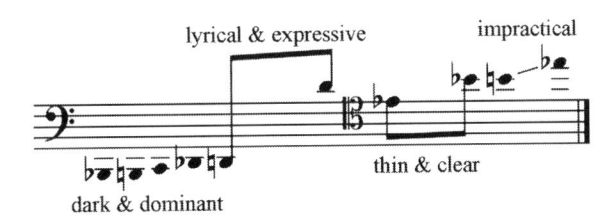

Bassoon Transposition

The bassoon is a non-transposing instrument that is usually written in bass clef. However, tenor clef and/or treble clef may be used to accommodate register.

Contrabassoons

The contrabassoon is a transposing double reed instrument; pitched an octave below the bassoon. The written part is notated an octave above the concert pitch in bass clef. While the contrabassoon is technically capable of playing in registers where the tenor, or even treble clef would be more appropriate, writing in these registers is not a practical usage of the instrument. Serving as the lowest voice of the woodwind section, the contrabassoon is best used in the lower registers to exploit its distinctive timbre and provide a solid foundation for the woodwinds. One generally orchestrates for this instrument in a manner similar to that one would use when scoring for the tuba or bass trombone in the brass section. Due to its weight and configuration, the contrabassoon employs an endpin rather than a seat strap supports its weight. It is equipped with a bocal that can be adjusted for fine-tuning, as well as a tuning slide for larger pitch adjustments.

Contrabasson Range

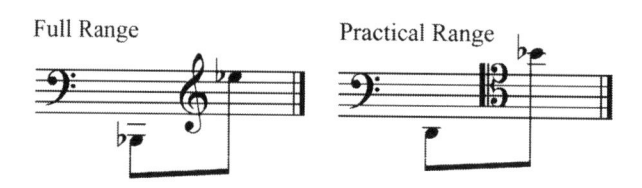

Contrabasson Registers

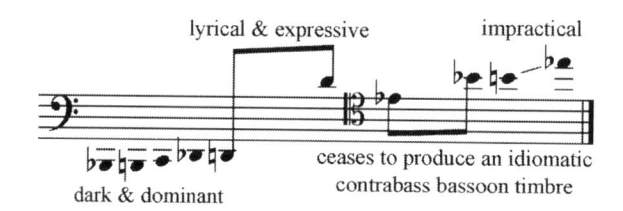

Contrabassoon Transposition

Contrabassoons are built in the key of C, sounding a perfect octave below the written note. Transposed parts are notated a perfect octave above concert pitch and usually notated in bass clef.

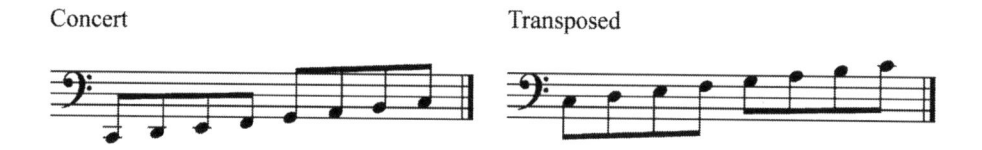

THE ENSEMBLES

Flute Choir

The term "flute choir" can be applied to a variety of flute ensembles, but generally it refers to a group of upper range flutes spanning the instruments from the bass flute to the piccolo. The contra and subcontra instruments are typically not part of the flute choir. The sound of the flute choir is quite homogeneous and, when scored in a manner similar to that of the vocal choir, can often resemble the sound of the flute stop on a pipe organ. Though certainly not definitive, the following instrumentation serves well for flute choir configurations:

Ensemble:	*Sextet:*	*Quintet:*	*Quartet:*
Piccolo	Piccolo	Piccolo	Piccolo
1st C Flutes (multiple)	1st C Flute	1st C Flute	C Flute
2nd C Flutes (multiple)	2nd C Flute	2nd C Flute	Alto Flute
3rd C Flutes (multiple)	3rd C Flute	Alto Flute	Bass Flute
Alto Flutes (multiple)	Alto Flute	Bass Flute	(*or*)
Bass Flutes (multiple)	Bass Flute	(*or*)	1st C Flute
		1st C Flute	2nd C Flute
		2nd C Flute	Alto Flute
		3rd C Flute	Bass Flute
		Alto Flute	
		Bass Flute	

One should use restraint when scoring the piccolo part, as the instrument is quite piercing in the altissimo register. The use of this register can easily overpower the rest of the ensemble and damage the balance and blend of the selection. One's orchestration is best served when using the instrument for "splashes of color," as an obbligato part, or as an octave doubling of a lower (melodic) part.

Flute Orchestra

The term "flute orchestra" is generally applied to large ensembles (30–80 players) containing flutes, spanning instruments from the contrabass flute to the piccolo. If available, the contra and subcontra instruments are also considered part of the flute orchestra. The sound of the flute orchestra has been described as a cross between the human voice and the flute stops on the pipe organ. Though certainly not definitive, the following instrumentation serves well for flute orchestra configurations:

Piccolo (1, or more if needed)	Piccolo (1, or more if needed)	Piccolo (1, or more if needed)
1st C Flutes (multiple)	1st C Flutes (multiple)	1st C Flutes (multiple)
2nd C Flutes (multiple)	2nd C Flutes (multiple)	2nd C Flutes (multiple)
3rd C Flutes (multiple)	3rd C Flutes (multiple)	3rd C Flutes (multiple)
1st Alto Flutes (multiple) (*or*)	1st Alto Flutes (multiple) (*or*)	Alto Flutes (multiple)
2nd Alto Flutes (multiple)	2nd Alto Flutes (multiple)	Bass Flutes (multiple)
1st Bass Flutes (multiple)	1st Bass Flutes (multiple)	Contra-alto Flutes (usually 2–4)
2nd Bass Flutes (multiple)	2nd Bass Flutes (multiple)	Contrabass Flutes (usually 2–4)
Contra-alto Flutes (usually 2–4)	Contra-alto Flutes (usually 2–4)	
Contrabass Flutes (usually 2–4)	Contrabass Flutes (usually 2–4)	
Sub Contrabass Flute in G (1)		
Double Contrabass Flute (1)		

The combination of the diverse distribution of registers (resultant varied timbres) throughout the ensemble, and the expanded lower range available from the contrabass and subcontrabass instruments, offers the orchestrator a wealth of orchestration opportunities. Options include (but are not limited to) scoring the entire ensemble as a harmonized block of sound (similar to an SSAATTBB vocal choir), contrasting the upper flutes with the lower flutes, creating a melodic interplay between different instruments in similar registers or contrasting registers, orchestrating the ensemble in independent layers (upper voices, middle voices and lower voices), passing melody content from instrument to instrument, etc.

Clarinet Choir

The exact instrumentation of the clarinet choir has never been clearly defined. Generally, any combination of B♭ and E♭ clarinets has been classified as a choir. The size of the choir can range from as few as 3 or 4 players, to as many as 40 or more, and the distribution of instruments varies from ensemble to ensemble. Normally, one attempts to span as wide a range as possible with the instruments at one's disposal and defines the ensemble based upon that criterion. Though certainly not definitive, the following instrumentation serves well for clarinet choir configurations:

Octet:
E♭ Clarinet
1st B♭ Clarinet
2nd B♭ Clarinet
3rd B♭ Clarinet

E♭ Alto Clarinet
B♭ Bass Clarinet
E♭ Contralto Clarinet
B♭ Contabass Clarinet

Septet:
E♭ Clarinet
1st B♭ Clarinet
2nd B♭ Clarinet
3rd B♭ Clarinet
   (*or* E♭ Alto Clarinet)
B♭ Bass Clarinet
E♭ Contralto Clarinet
B♭ Contabass Clarinet

Sextet:
E♭ Clarinet
1st B♭ Clarinet
2nd B♭ Clarinet
3rd B♭ Clarinet
   (*or* E♭ Alto Clarinet)
B♭ Bass Clarinet
E♭ Contralto Clarinet

Quintet:
E♭ Clarinet
1st B♭ Clarinet
2nd B♭ Clarinet
E♭ Alto Clarinet
B♭ Bass Clarinet

Quartet:
E♭ Clarinet
1st B♭ Clarinet
2nd B♭ Clarinet
   (*or* E♭ Alto Clarinet)
B♭ Bass Clarinet
   (*or*) 1st B♭ Clarinet
2nd B♭ Clarinet
E♭ Alto Clarinet
   (*or* B♭ Bass Clarinet)
B♭ Bass Clarinet
   (*or* E♭ Contralto Clarinet)

Trio:
E♭ Clarinet
1st B♭ Clarinet
B♭ Bass Clarinet
   (*or*) 1st B♭ Clarinet
2nd B♭ Clarinet
B♭ Bass Clarinet
   (*or*) B♭ Clarinet
E♭ Alto Clarinet
B♭ Bass Clarinet

The sound of the choir is quite homogeneous and can often resemble the sound of a pipe organ when scored in a manner similar to that of the vocal choir. The diverse distribution of registers throughout the ensemble, and the resultant varied timbres offer the orchestrator an abundance of scoring opportunities. Options include (but are not limited to) scoring the entire ensemble as a harmonized block of sound (similar to an SSAATTBB vocal choir), contrasting the upper clarinets with the lower clarinets, creating a melodic interplay between different instruments in similar registers or contrasting registers, orchestrating the ensemble in independent layers (upper voices, middle voices and lower voices), passing melody content from instrument to instrument, etc.

One should use restraint when scoring the E♭ clarinet part, treating it much as one would the piccolo. The instrument is quite piercing in the altissimo register and extended passages in this register quickly becomes taxing on the ear. One's orchestration is best served when using the instrument for "splashes of color," as an obbligato part, as an octave doubling of a lower (melodic) part, or by scoring the instrument primarily in the chalumeau and clarino registers.

The lower clarinets (B♭ bass clarinet, E♭ contralto clarinet, and B♭ contrabass clarinet) yield the best results and most characteristic timbre when scored in the chalumeau and clarino registers. When scored in these registers the instruments provide a solid foundation for the ensemble. Throat tones are problematic on the lower clarinets and one should avoid sustained notes in this region, as the resultant timbre is less than desirable. One should also remember that the larger instruments are somewhat less agile than the smaller instruments and, in a recording-studio environment, the noise generated by the keys in quick passages can be detrimental to the recording.

Wind Quintet

The traditional wind quintet (also referred to as a woodwind quintet) is a five-member ensemble consisting of one flute, one oboe, one clarinet, one horn and one bassoon. The ensemble dates to the 18th century and comprises instruments of the "wind section" of the Classical period orchestra. As such, the "woodwind" quintet traditionally contains a horn, a decidedly "non-woodwind" instrument. These five, distinctly different timbres offer the orchestrator textural opportunities not available in the other traditional chamber music ensembles.

If desired, the instrumentation of the woodwind quintet may be altered to accommodate specific needs. English horn may be substituted for the oboe, clarinet or the horn; bass clarinet may be substituted for the horn or bassoon; bassoon and contrabassoon, or bass clarinet and contrabass clarinet may be substituted for the horn and bassoon combination; E♭ clarinet or piccolo may be substituted for the flute, and so on.

When orchestrating for the woodwind quintet, one should exploit the variety of available timbres to add interest to one's orchestration. As always, one should avoid repeating complete sections of a work using the same treatment and instrumentation. One can achieve said interest by featuring a different instrument on repeated melodies, contrasting instruments of darker timbre with instruments of brighter timbre, trading the melody from instrument to instrument, alternating registers, etc.

One must always be aware of the performer's need to breathe and phrase the work appropriately to accommodate this need. One should also provide adequate respites within the horn part to accommodate the physical needs of the brass embouchure.

Using Saxophone in the Wind Quintet

Many contemporary wind quintets have opted to substitute alto saxophone for the traditional horn. Doing so converts the traditional "wind quintet" ensemble into a true "woodwind quintet." This practice offers both advantages and disadvantages.

If one is often adapting a horn part of an existing quintet for alto saxophone, one may encounter range and register issues, as the horn is technically capable of playing in ranges/

registers not available on the alto saxophone. Be aware that simply transposing sections of the horn part to a different octave to accommodate the saxophone range may not be a viable solution, as it alters the relationship with the other ensemble parts. Additionally, effects and techniques that are idiomatically brass, such as double-tonguing, triple-tonguing, rips, half-valve effects, mutes, stopped horn, etc. do not translate well to the saxophone. So one must exercise caution, scrutiny and creativity to insure that the orchestration remains true to the original intent of the composer. One must also accept the fact that audiences accustomed to the traditional wind quintet sound on a particular selection may be reluctant to accept this altered ensemble timbre.

If one is scoring a new selection, the saxophone offers many possibilities (generally) unavailable on the horn in F. Being a reed instrument, tonguing and articulations are more closely matched to the rest of the ensemble instruments and the blend between the saxophone and either/both the bassoon and clarinet can be quite effective. Saxophonists (generally) are more comfortable, adding stylistic interpretations to the part when required (i.e. bending notes, scooping into notes, etc.) than horn players. Though not the traditional approach, the inclusion of the saxophone in the wind quintet environment yields many creative opportunities.

Chamber Woodwinds

Like the string family, members of the woodwind family have well-established presence in chamber music. There is an abundance of both music and ensembles in this genre that employ woodwind instruments. The following is but a sampling of the possible ensemble combinations.

Ensemble Name:	*Instrumentation:*
Clarinet–viola–piano trio	clarinet, viola, piano
Clarinet–cello–piano trio	clarinet, violoncello, piano
Voice, clarinet and piano	voice, clarinet, piano
Flute, viola and harp	flute, viola, harp
Clarinet, violin, piano	clarinet, violin, piano
Violin, clarinet, cello and piano	violin, clarinet, violoncello, piano
Clarinet quartet	3 clarinets and bass clarinet
Saxophone quartet	soprano sax, alto sax, tenor sax, baritone sax (*or*) 2 alto saxes, tenor sax, baritone sax
Flute quartet	4 flutes (or) flute, violin, viola, and violoncello
Wind instrument and string trio	violin, viola, violoncello and flute, oboe, clarinet, bassoon
Piano and wind trio	piano, clarinet, horn, bassoon
Wind and strings quintet	oboe, clarinet, violin, viola, contrabass
Clarinet quintet	clarinet, 2 violins, 1 viola, 1 violoncello
Piano and wind quartet	piano, oboe, clarinet, horn, bassoon
Pierrot ensemble	flute, clarinet, violin, violoncello, piano
Wind sextet	2 oboes, 2 horns, 2 bassoons (or) 2 clarinet, 2 horns, 2 bassoons
Piano and wind quintet	flute, oboe, clarinet, horn, 2 bassoons, piano
Piano sextet	clarinet, 2 violins, viola, violoncello, piano

Wind and string septet	clarinet, horn, bassoon, violin, viola, violoncello, contrabass
Wind and string octet	clarinet, horn, bassoon, 2 violins, viola, violoncello, contrabass (*or*) clarinet, 2 horns, violin, 2 violas, violoncello, contrabass
Wind octet	2 oboes, 2 clarinets, 2 horns, 2 bassoons
Wind and string nonet	flute, oboe, clarinet, horn, bassoon, violin, viola, violoncello, and contrabass
Double wind quintet	2 oboes, 2 English horns, 2 clarinets, 2 horns, 2 bassoons (*or*) 2 flutes, oboe, English horn, 2 clarinets, 2 horns and 2 bassoons

Orchestral Woodwinds

The size of the woodwind section in the orchestral setting varies from ensemble to ensemble, but generally ranges from 8 to 12 instruments. The basic configuration is 2 flutes, 2 oboes, 2 clarinets and 2 bassoons. In contemporary music, including music for pops orchestra, it is not unusual to expand the orchestral woodwind section to include piccolo, English horn, E♭ clarinet, bass clarinet (occasionally contrabass clarinet) and contrabass bassoon. For certain selections, various members of the saxophone family may also be added.

Wind Ensemble and Concert Band Woodwinds

With more instruments at one's disposal than in the orchestral setting, one has more timbre and textures with which to work. All members of the woodwind section blend well with one another and, when scored as a full ensemble, produce a lush and homogeneous sound. When scoring woodwinds in a band environment, one can expect the availability of the following instruments:

Piccolo
Flutes (generally in two parts)
E♭ clarinet
B♭ clarinets (generally in three parts)
E♭ alto clarinet
B♭ bass clarinet (contrabass clarinet may be available as an auxiliary instrument)
Bassoons (generally in two parts; contrabass bassoon may be available as an auxiliary instrument)
Alto saxophone (generally in two parts)
Tenor saxophone
Baritone saxophone

If scoring for wind ensemble, one may expect either one or two players per part (depending upon if the director adheres to the original Frederick Fennell concept of the wind ensemble or not). If scoring for a concert band, one may expect multiple players per part (with the exception of piccolo, E♭ clarinet, bass and contrabass clarinet, and contrabass bassoon).

PRACTICAL CONSIDERATIONS

Practical Guidelines for Choosing a work to Orchestrate for Woodwinds

- Choose pieces that are stylistically applicable to your chosen instrumentation.
- Choose pieces that are applicable to the ranges and registers (and key signatures) of your chosen instrumentation (unless a selection specifically designates a key, such as "Sonata in A minor," one should feel free to alter the key to accommodate the instrumentation).
- Choose pieces that offer textural opportunities.
- Avoid pieces that are specifically idiomatic of piano.

Practical Guidelines when Writing for Woodwinds

- Avoid awkward intervals (both ascending or descending) in tonal voice-leading, i.e. aug. 2nd, dim 4th, aug. 4th, dim 5th, major 7th, minor 9th, etc. (*Note*: As intrinsic elements of contemporary, free chromatic, serialized, avant-garde and atonal music, use of "awkward intervals" may be required to maintain the stylistic intent of these genres.)
- In the case of the woodwind quintet, avoid large skips (in excess of an octave) in the horn.
- Always be cognizant of voice-leading in *all* parts.
- Remember that piano arpeggios (generally) do not translate well to ensemble instrumentation.
- Always attempt to remain true to the (perceived) intent of the composer.
- *Listen to and analyze* as many different examples of woodwind writing as possible.

IN THE PROFESSION

In the professional environment, an orchestrator who simply knows the ranges, registers and transposition of a given instrument is considered exceptionally ill prepared. Professional woodwind players expect their parts to read as if they were written by a woodwind player, with an intimate understanding of the idiosyncrasies of their particular instrument.

Unless needed for a very specific effect, one does not generally notate breath marks in a woodwind part. A skilled orchestrator implies an appropriate place to breathe through phrasing, slurs, rests and articulations (and immense attention should be devoted to these details). Based upon these implications, the players will determine the appropriate place to breathe. A woodwind part filled with breath marks would be considered offensive by advanced and professional players.

BUILDING THE SCORE

This example will demonstrate the process for creating a wind quintet orchestration from an existing piano selection. Once an appropriate work has been selected, one begins by performing a harmonic analysis to determine the harmonic content and context. These elements present vital considerations when determining the deletion or addition of harmonic elements. For the purposes of the exercise, the following selection will be used.

THE WOODWIND FAMILY

Edvard Grieg, *Spring Dance*, Op. 38 No. 5

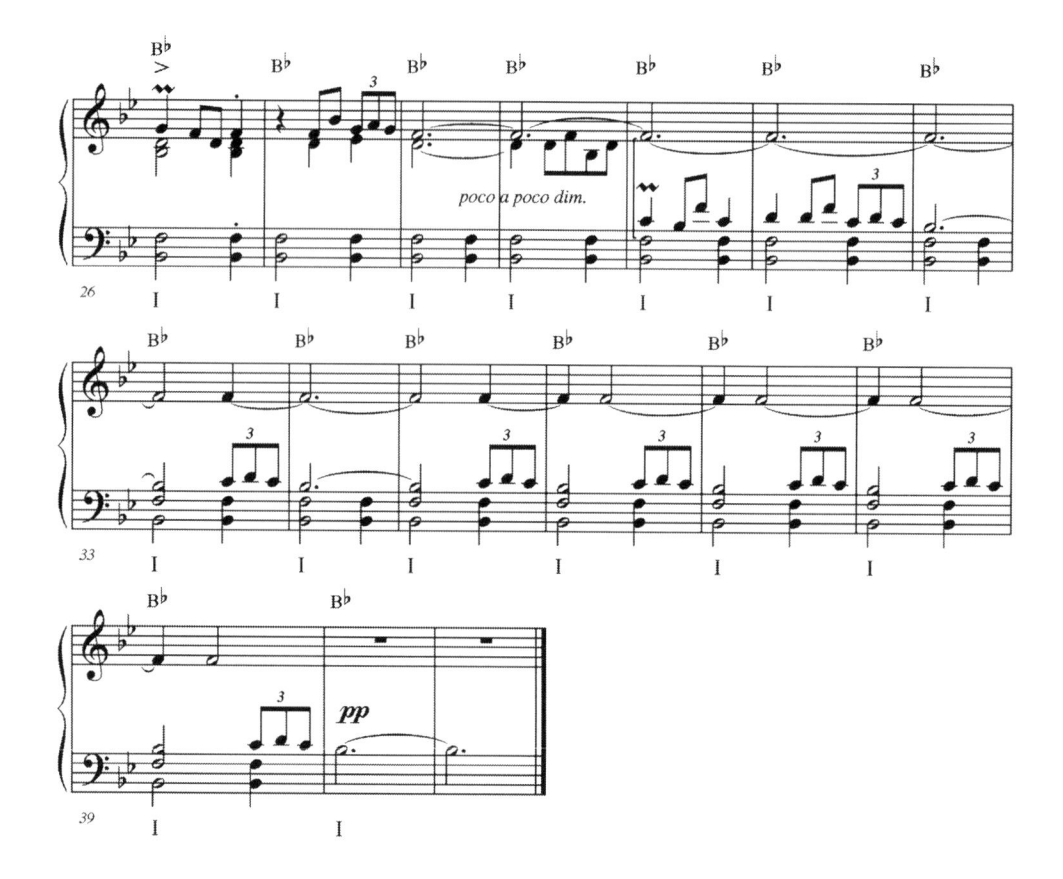

Upon completion of the analysis, one can delete the non-essential harmonic elements (or add appropriate harmonic elements, if needed). One then examines the selection for elements within the notation that must be addressed or altered to work for the instruments of the chosen ensemble. These elements may include pedal markings, crescendi and decrescendi of undefined dynamic scope, dynamics that may need to be modified to be appropriate for the chosen instrumentation, ornamentation, rhythmic subdivisions, arpeggios, etc.

In this particular example there is a lack of suitable dynamic variance. While one can rely upon the performer to interpret the solo piano selection, dynamic shaping in an ensemble is critical. The orchestrator must add these elements to achieve appropriate dynamic movement that is balance throughout the ensemble. One also uses the registers of the melodic and harmonic content to aid in the choices of featured instruments and harmonic textures.

THE WOODWIND FAMILY

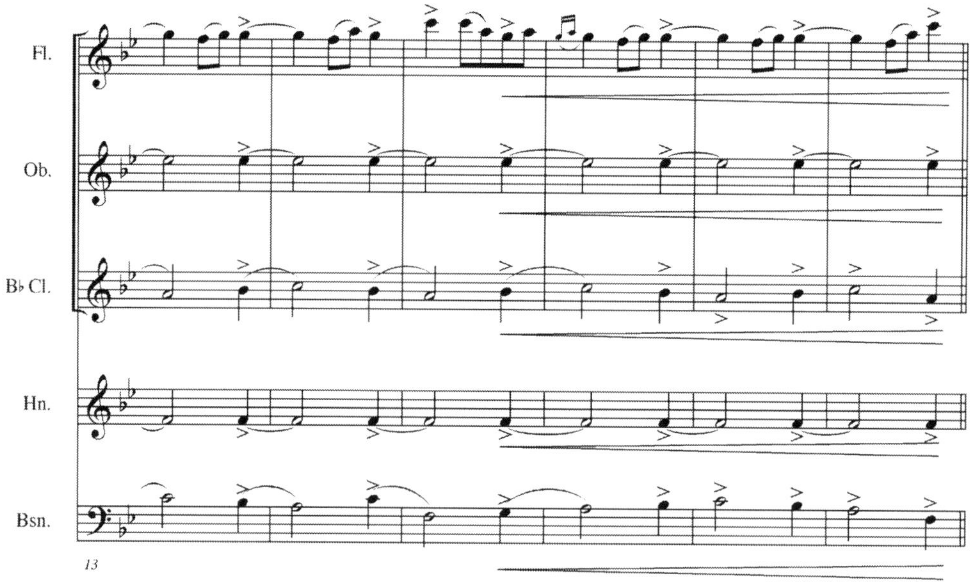
Fl.
Ob.
B♭ Cl.
Hn.
Bsn.
13

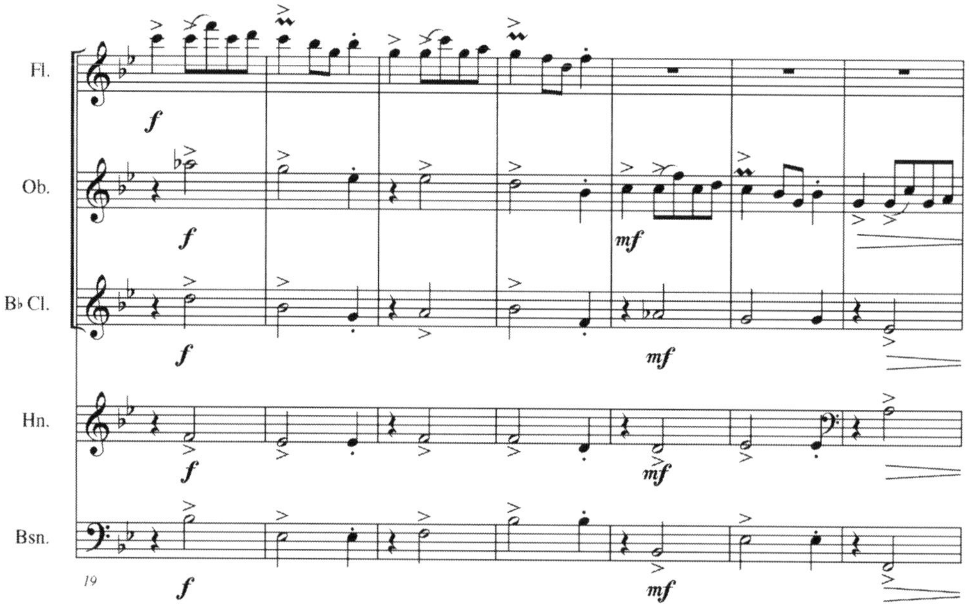
Fl.
Ob.
B♭ Cl.
Hn.
Bsn.
19
f
mf

THE WOODWIND FAMILY

This example will demonstrate the process for adapting an existing piano selection for orchestral woodwinds. As always, one should begin by performing a harmonic analysis to determine harmonic content and context. This enables one to competently add or delete appropriate harmonic elements. For the purposes of the exercise, the following selection will be used:

John Field, *Nocturne*

Upon completion of the harmonic analysis, one can add appropriate harmonic elements that are appropriate for the genre to accommodate the expanded instrumentation. One seeks opportunities for the expanded harmonic voicings appropriate for the ranges and registers of the chosen instruments, and to add intensity and texture to the selection.

In this particular example, the scope of the crescendi and decrescendi is undefined. One adds dynamic markings to the orchestration that provide appropriate dynamic shaping, and defines that shaping in each and every part. Another challenge is the continuous arpeggiated line in the left hand of the piano part. One must create a suitable substitute for this line that conveys the composer's original intent, but provides each instrument with a part that is more indicative of wind instruments.

Cantabile, assai lento
Flute 1
Flute 2
Oboe 1
Oboe 2
Clarinet in B♭ 1
Clarinet in B♭ 2
Bassoon 1
Bassoon 2
Fl. 1
Fl. 2
Ob. 1
Ob. 2
B♭ Cl. 1
B♭ Cl. 2
Bsn. 1
Bsn. 2

THE WOODWIND FAMILY

Fl. 1
Fl. 2
Ob. 1
Ob. 2
B♭ Cl. 1
B♭ Cl. 2
Bsn. 1
Bsn. 2
17
mp
mf
cresc.

Fl. 1
Fl. 2
Ob. 1
Ob. 2
B♭ Cl. 1
B♭ Cl. 2
Bsn. 1
Bsn. 2
21
fz

SCORING EXAMPLES

Scoring Example for Flute Choir

J. S. Bach, *Acknowledge me, my Keeper*, mm. 1–12, arranged and orchestrated by RJ Miller (flute quartet, transposed score)

Scoring Example for Flute Orchestra

Edvard Grieg, *Sylph*, Op. 62 No. 1, mm. 58–90, arranged and orchestrated by RJ Miller (transposed score)

THE WOODWIND FAMILY

209

77
Picc. 1
Picc. 2
Picc. 3
Fl. 1
Fl. 2
Fl. 3
Fl. 4
A. Fl. 1
A. Fl. 2
B. Fl. 1
B. Fl. 2
C.A. Fl.
C.B. Fl.
72
73
74
75
76
77
78

THE WOODWIND FAMILY

Picc. 1
Picc. 2
Picc. 3
Fl. 1
Fl. 2
Fl. 3
Fl. 4
A. Fl. 1
A. Fl. 2
B. Fl. 1
B. Fl. 2
C.A. Fl.
C.B. Fl.
mp
p
86
87
88
89
90

Scoring Examples for Clarinet Choir

Ludwig van Beethoven, *Prayer*, **Op. 48 No. 1 mm. 1–28, orchestrated by RJ Miller** (transposed score)

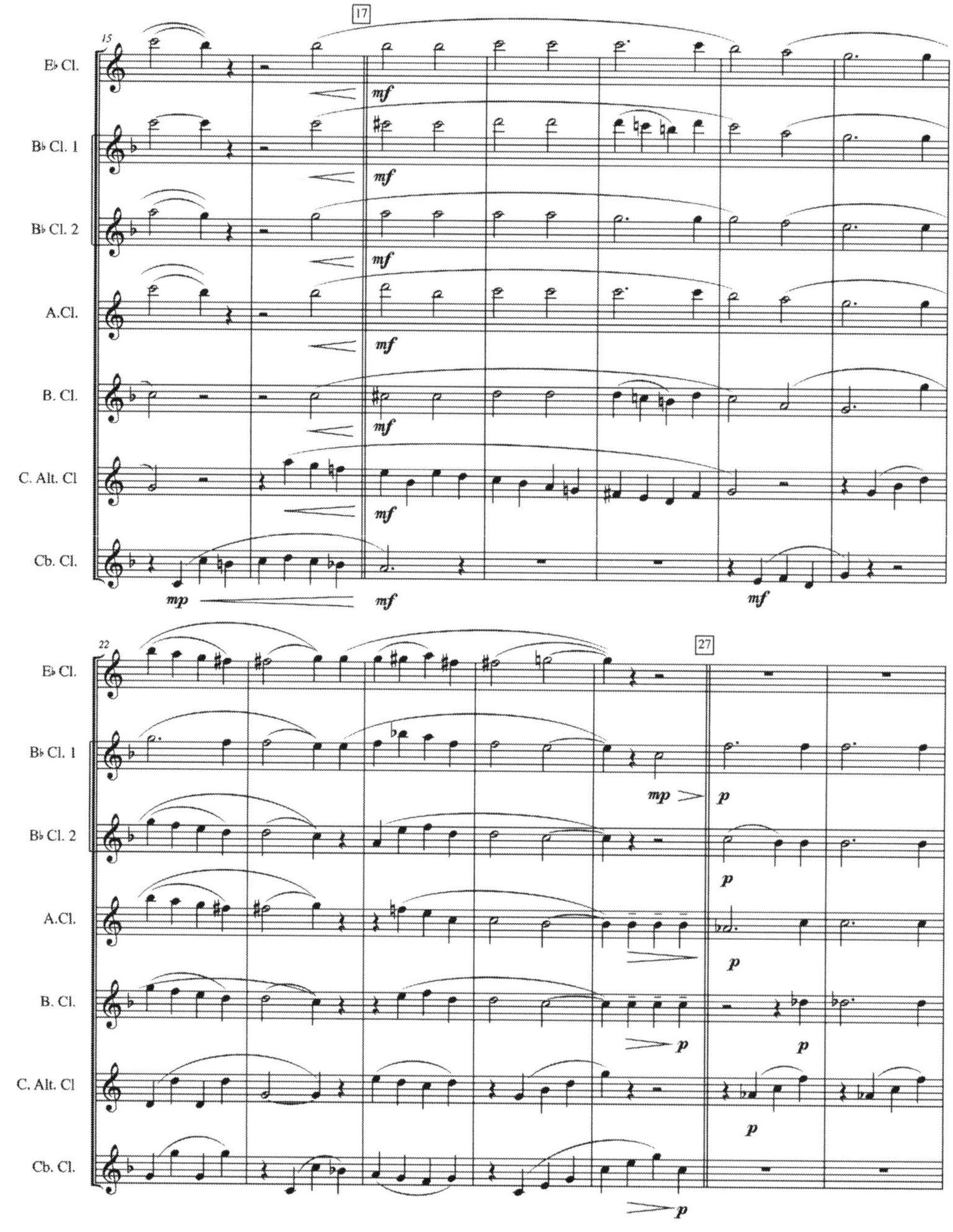
17
E♭ Cl.
B♭ Cl. 1
B♭ Cl. 2
A.Cl.
B. Cl.
C. Alt. Cl
Cb. Cl.
mp
mf
27
p

THE WOODWIND FAMILY

Scoring Examples for Wind Quintet

Fannie Blumenfeld Zeisler, *Près de L'Eau*, Op. 38 No. 3, mm 1–17, arranged and orchestrated by RJ Miller (transposed score)

216   THE WOODWIND FAMILY

Joseph Haydn, *Gipsy Rondo*, **mm. 1–18, arranged and orchestrated by RJ Miller (transposed score)**

Anton Reicha, Two Andantes and Adagio (*II. Andant pour le Cor Anglais*), mm. 1–22
(transposed score)

218 THE WOODWIND FAMILY

Antonio Rosetti, Quintet in E flat, mm. 17–35 (transposed score)

Scoring Examples for Orchestral Woodwinds

Joseph Haydn, Symphony No. 100 in G major, Movement I, mm. 24–31 (transposed score)

Franz Schubert, Symphony in B flat major, Movement I, mm. 118–134 (concert score)

Fl.
Ob.
Bsn. 1
Bsn. 2
Vln. I
Vln. II
Vla.
Vc.
Cb.
123
Fl.
Ob.
Bsn. 1
Bsn. 2
Vln. I
Vln. II
Vla.
Vc.
Cb.
129

Ludwig van Beethoven, Symphony No. 9, Op. 125 *(Finale)*, mm. 343–358 (transposed score)

Fl.
Picc.
Ob. 1
Ob. 2
B♭ Cl. 1
B♭ Cl. 2
Bsn. 1
Bsn. 2
Cbsn.
Hn.
Hn.
B♭ Tpt.
Trgl.
Cym.
B. Dr.
351

THE WOODWIND FAMILY 225

Pyotr Ilyich Tchaikovsky, *Nutcracker Suite* **(Dance of the Sugarplum Fairy), mm. 4–20 (transposed score)**

THE WOODWIND FAMILY

Scoring Examples for Woodwinds in Wind Ensemble/Concert Band Woodwinds

Alfred Reed, *A Sacred Suite*, mm. 1–22 (transposed score).

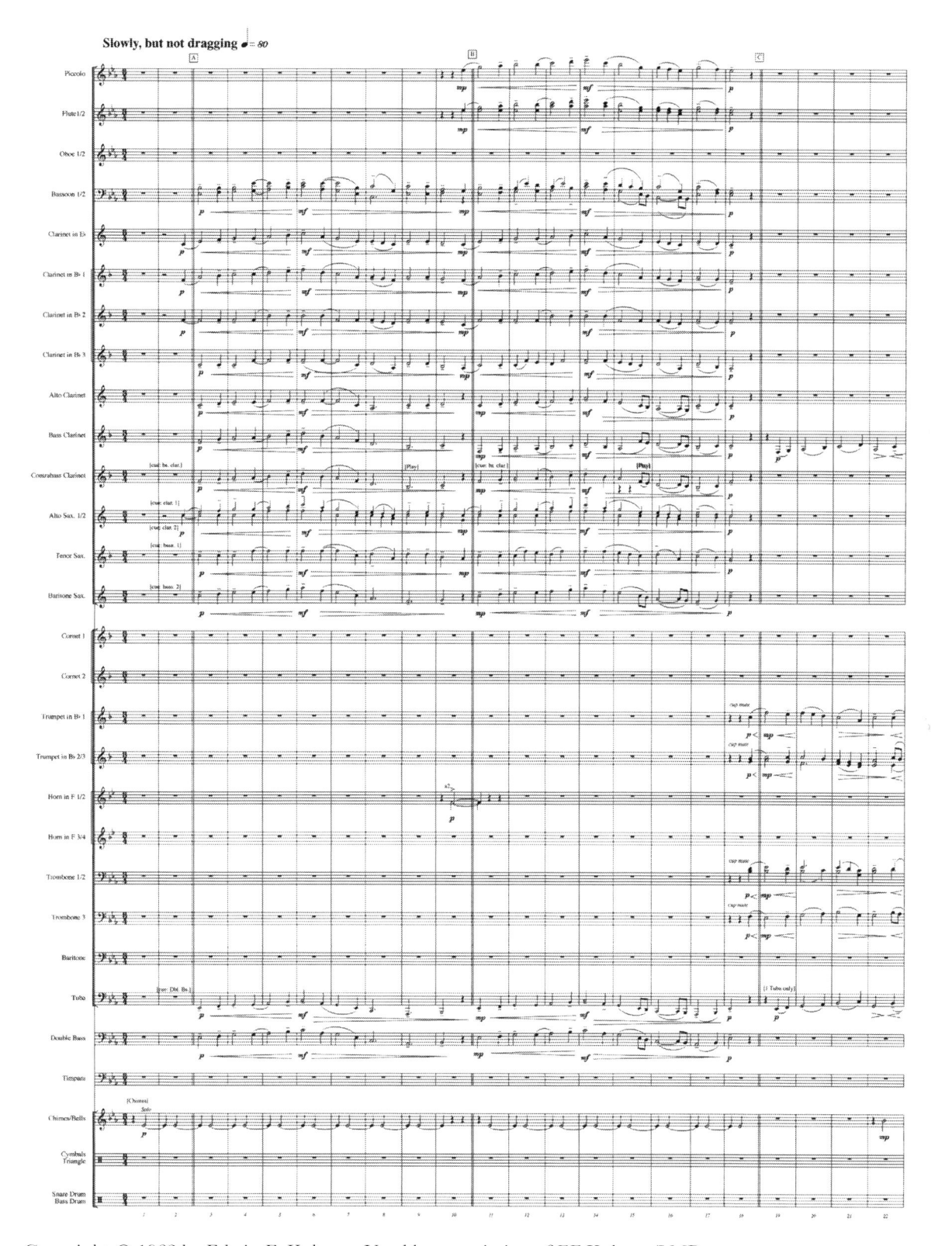

Copyright © 1962 by Edwin F. Kalmus. Used by permission of EF Kalmus/LMP.

Norman Dello Joio, *Fantasies on a Theme by Haydn,* **mm. 37–54.**

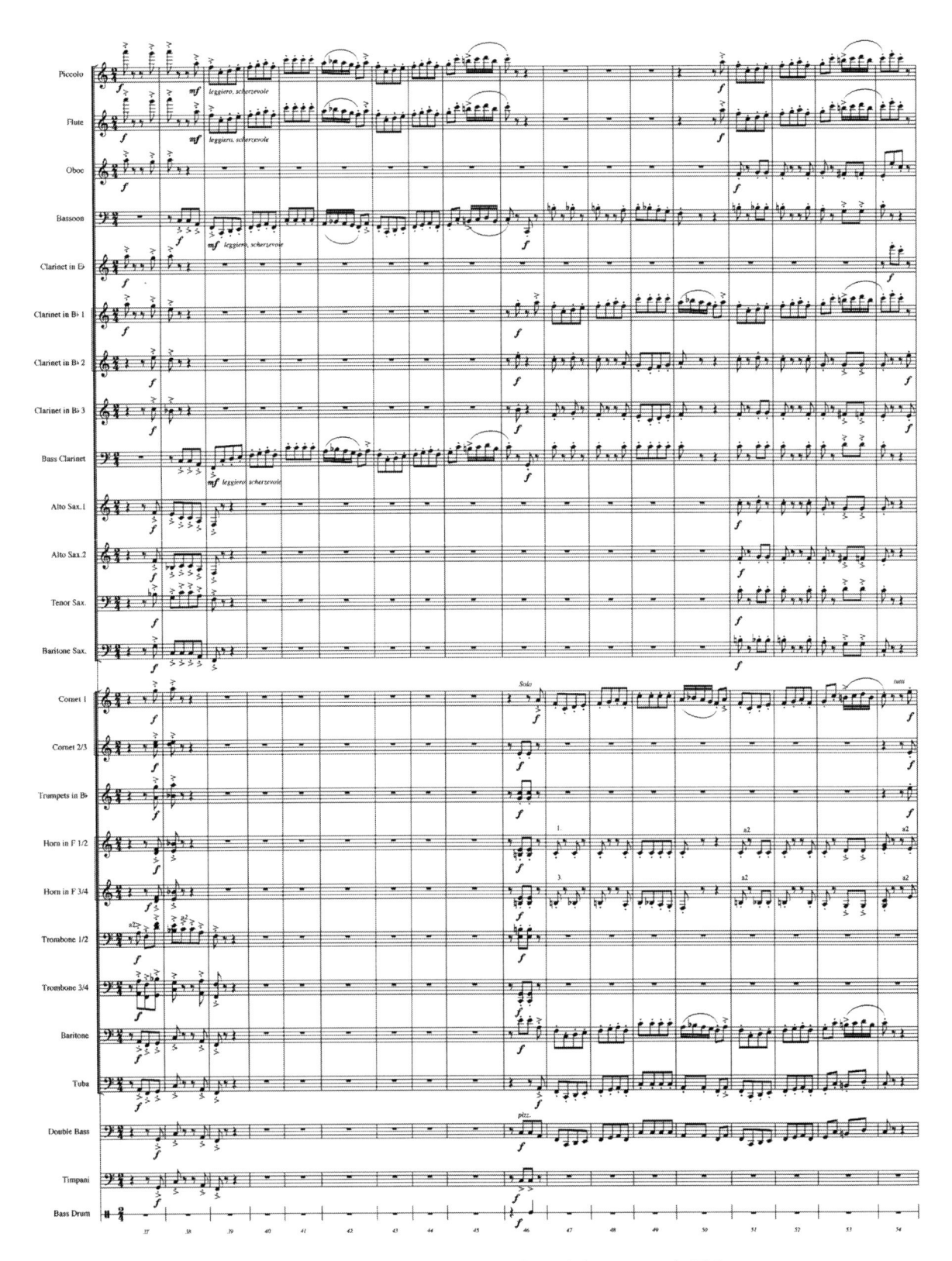

Copyright © 1968 by Edward B. Marks Music Company. Copyright renewed. This arrangement copyright © 2014 by Edward B. Marks Music Company. International copyright secured. All rights reserved. Used by permission. Reprinted by permission of Hal Leonard Corporation.

THE WOODWIND FAMILY

Vaclav Nelhybel, *Chorale*, mm. 72–86.

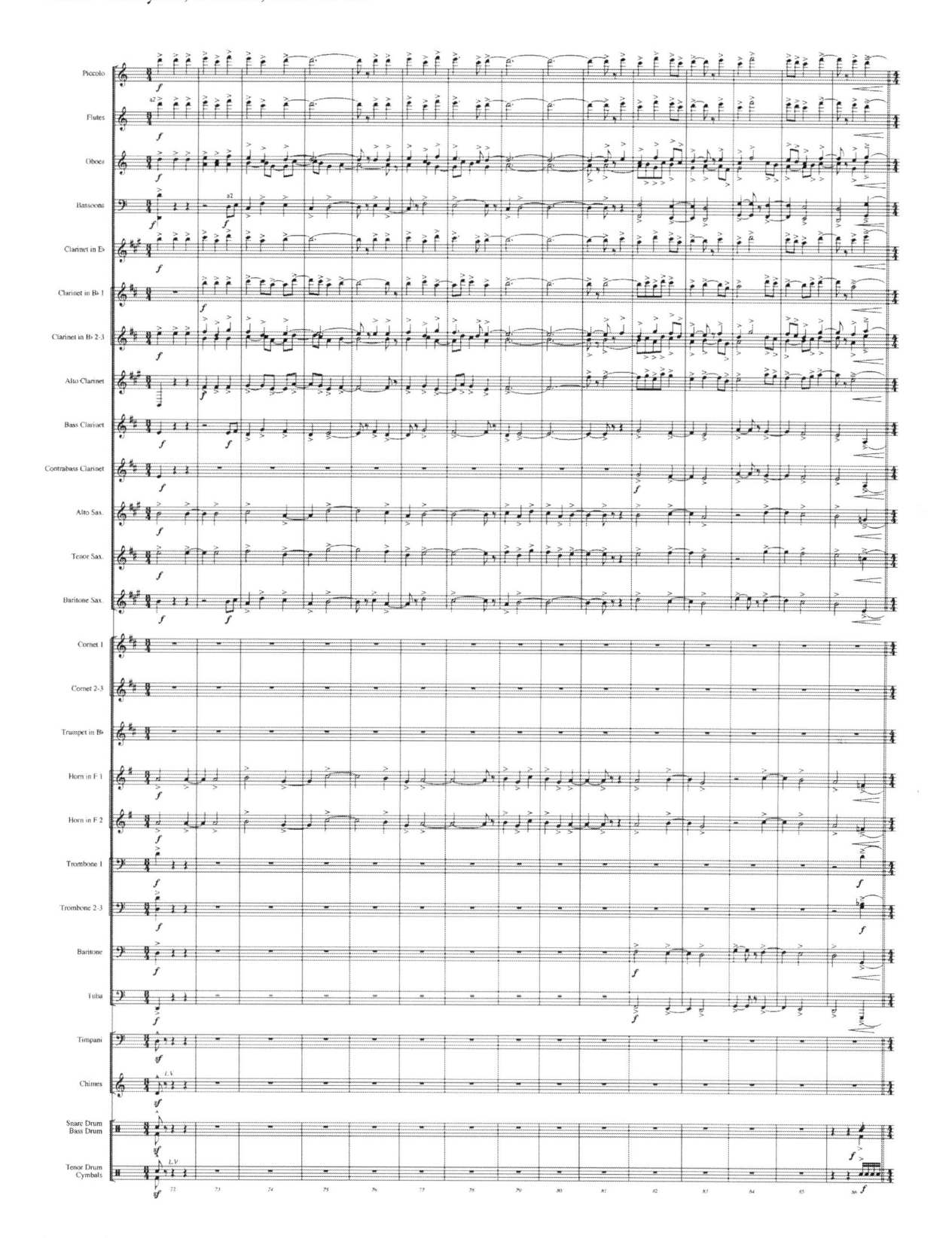

Copyright © 1965 Franco Columbo, Inc. Copyright assigned to and renewed by Belwin-Mills Publishing Corp. All rights controlled and administered by Alfred Music. All rights reserved. Used by permission of Alfred Music.

Vaclav Nelhybel, *Festivo***, mm. 43–63.**

THE WOODWIND FAMILY 231

Copyright © 1968 Franco Columbo, Inc. Copyright assigned to and renewed by Belwin-Mills Publishing Corp. All rights controlled and administered by Alfred Music. All rights reserved. Used by permission of Alfred Music.

SUGGESTED EXERCISES

Scoring Exercise for Wind Quintet

Using the information and guidelines presented in this chapter and in Chapter 3 (Practical Problem Solving), orchestrate the following example for wind quintet. Perform a harmonic analysis and seek ways to add textural interest.

Renaud de Vilac, *Adeste Fideles*

THE WOODWIND FAMILY   233

Scoring Exercise for Orchestral Woodwinds or Wind Ensemble Woodwinds

Using the information and guidelines presented in this chapter and in Chapter 3 (Practical Problem Solving), orchestrate the following example for orchestral woodwinds or wind ensemble woodwinds. Perform a harmonic analysis and seek ways to add textural interest.

Halfdan Kjerulf, *Berceuse*

THE WOODWIND FAMILY

235

7
THE PERCUSSION FAMILY

Instrument Classifications

All percussion instruments are divided into the following classifications:

- **Membranophones** produce their sound by the vibration of a membrane attached to a resonator. Striking the membrane with one's hand, a stick or a beater generates the vibration.
- **Idiophones** produce their sound by the vibration of either the entire body of the instrument, or several vibrating bodies combined into one instrument. Depending upon the specific instrument, vibrations are generated by striking, scraping, shaking or stroking the instrument (or bodies of the instrument).
- **Aerophones** generate sound by using an air column to produce vibrations within an enclosed body. While many aerophones are capable of generating specific pitches, these pitches are not generally specified in the orchestral score.
- **Chordaphones** produce their sound by the vibration of striking strings contained within a resonator that amplifies the sound. All chordaphones are tuned instruments, and those generally used in an orchestral setting are tuned in equal temperament.

Each of these categories is further divided into the following subsets:

- Instruments of definite pitch
- Instruments of indefinite pitch
- Instruments of approximate pitch

Synthetic and Sampled Sounds

Some orchestrators consider electronically generated or sampled sounds (either performed by computers, samplers, synthesizers or through the use of a prerecorded medium) to be part of the percussion section, placing these parts within the percussion area of the orchestral score. Others consider these elements to be auxiliary instruments and place them below the percussion section and above the string section in the orchestral score. Since there is no consensus on the appropriate practice, either method should be considered acceptable. One chooses the appropriate method for a specific score based upon personal preference, or by choosing the method that seems most logical (or least confusing).

Notation and Score Order

Over the years there have been numerous attempts to standardize percussion notation. Most have involved a system of symbolic or graphic notation and some have included symbolic designations for the instruments themselves. While many of these systems seem quite logical and even eloquent in theory, none have been adopted into standard practice. As such, one should use symbolic notation only if it seems the least confusing method to convey the desired performance. Since there is no standardization of symbolic notation, one must include a legend at the beginning of the part (and in the score) defining the symbols and describing their intent. From a practical perspective, using primarily standard notation for percussion parts yield the most concise, least confusing and most functional results.

Percussionists often will play more than one instrument during a piece. Since these instruments are from various categories, the concept of a percussion score order usually has little practical application. As first official member of the orchestra, the timpani are traditionally listed first in score order. Following the timpani, one places the parts in the most logical configuration. One should always provide a list of required instruments and beaters in one's score.

Ba-Da-Ka-Dup!
– for slightly warped percussionists –

Instrumentation:

Timpani
    29″/28″ tuned to G
    26″/25″ tuned to C
    24″/23″ ad lib tuning

Bass Drum
    Large Wool Beater

Snare Drum

Percussion 1
    Tam-Tam
    Hand Cymbals (Piatti)
    Suspended Cymbal (scraped with triangle beater)

Percussion 2
    VibraSlap
    Whip
    Flex-a-tone

Percussion 3
    Bell Tree
    Tambourine
    Coaches Whistle
    Ratchet

THE PERCUSSION FAMILY

239

Suggested configuration:

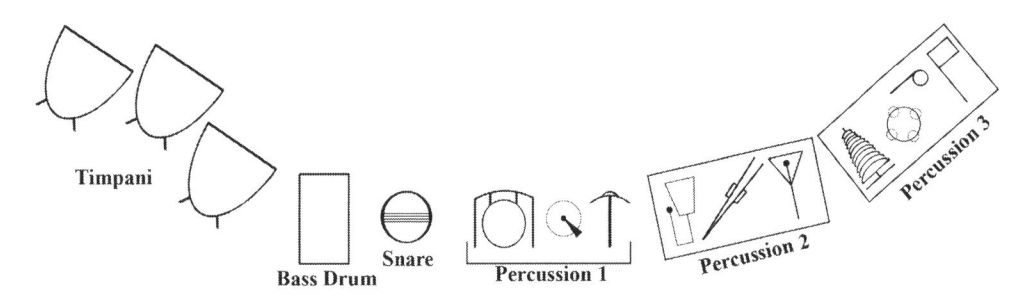

RJ Miller, *Ba-Da-Ka-Dup!*, mm. 1–17.

240   THE PERCUSSION FAMILY

- Ba-Da-Ka-Dup! - page 2 -

Copyright © 2004 by Appassionata Music. Used by permission.

Should one require a specific percussion score order for singular instruments in an orchestral or wind ensemble score, the following will serve for most purposes:

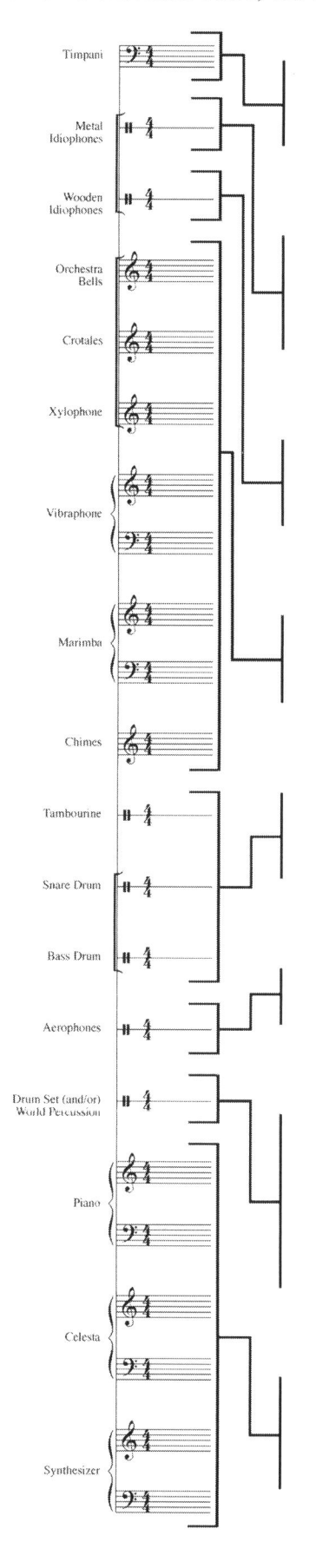

Timpani
As first official member of the orchestra, the timpani are traditionally listed first in score order.

Metal Idiophones (of indefinite pitch)
Wind Chimes, Mark Chimes, Bell Tree, Triangle, Finger Cymbals, Sleigh Bells, Cymbals, Cowbells, Agogo Bells, Flex-a-tone, Brake Drums, Gongs, Tam-Tam, Vibra-slap, Anvil, Shakers, Hanging Finger Cymbals, Ice Bells.

Wooden Idiophones (of indefinite pitch)
Slapstick, Sand Blocks, Ratchet, Wood Blocks, Tempo Blocks, Maracas, Castinets, Clavé, Wooden Clacker, Cricket, Guiro, Rain Sticks.

Pitched Idiophones
Orchestra Bells (Glockenspiel), Crotales, Crystal Glasses, Xylophone, Vibraphone, Marimba, Bass Marimba, Chimes (Tubular Bells).

Membranophones
Tambourine, Snare Drum, Tenor Drum, Tom-Toms, Roto-Toms, Bongos, Conga Drums, Bass Drum.

Aerophones
Whistles (coaches whistle, slide whistle, samba whistle), Sirens, Wind Machine.

Drum Set (or)
Additional Ethnic or World Percussion
(May be of definite pitch or indefinite pitch; use the appropriate clef and staff)
Steel Drums, Kalimba, Cajon, Caxixi, Afuche, Shekere, African Rattle, Timbale, Bodhran, Tabla, Ashiko, Darbuka, Djembe, Doumbek, Bata Drums, Monk Bell, Udu, Kokiriko.

Keyboards
Piano, Celesta, Carillon.
(If one subscribes to the premise that synthesizers, samplers, computerized music, etc., belong to the percussion section, they would be listed here.)

THE ESSENTIALS

Rudiments

Rudiments are the basic patterns used in rudimental drumming. Knowledge of these fundamental elements is vital to the orchestrator as they are the "building blocks" used to construct functional percussion parts. While the concept and performance of rudiments dates back centuries, it wasn't until the early 20th century that they were standardized in name, notation and execution. Initially, 13 "essential" rudiments were officially defined. Shortly thereafter the "essential" list was expanded to 26 rudiments and in 1984 the Percussive Arts Society expanded the list to 40 standardized rudiments. There are many additional rudiments (hybrid rudiments) that have yet to be officially accepted, but that serve useful purposes. One should endeavor to familiarize oneself with both the standard rudiments and the ever-expanding list of hybrid rudiments.

Rudiments are divided into four categories:

- Roll rudiments
- Diddle rudiments
- Flam rudiments
- Drag rudiments

The roll rudiments are further divided into the following subcategories:

- Single-stroke rudiments
- Multiple-bounce rudiments
- Double-stroke rudiments

Single-stroke Rudiments

1. Single-stroke Roll

The single-stroke roll consists of evenly spaced notes played with alternating sticking.

2. Single-stroke Four

The single-stroke four consists of four notes played with alternating sticking, usually with the first three notes written as triplets.

3. Single-stroke Seven

The single-stroke seven consists of seven notes played with alternating sticking, usually with the first six notes of the rudiment written as sextuplets.

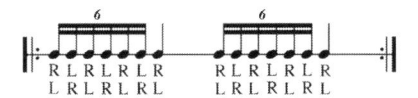

Multiple-bounce Rudiments

Performed with alternating sticking (RLRL, or LRLR), multiple-bounce rudiments allow the stick to bounce three or more times per stroke.

4. Multiple-bounce Roll (or Buzz Roll)

Played with alternating sticking, the player produces a consistent and sustained "buzz" by allowing each stick bounce an indeterminate number of times per stroke.

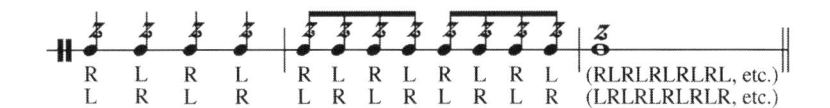

5. Triple-stroke Roll (or French Roll)

Played with alternating sticking, the triple-stroke roll is produced by allowing each stroke of the roll to bounce exactly three times.

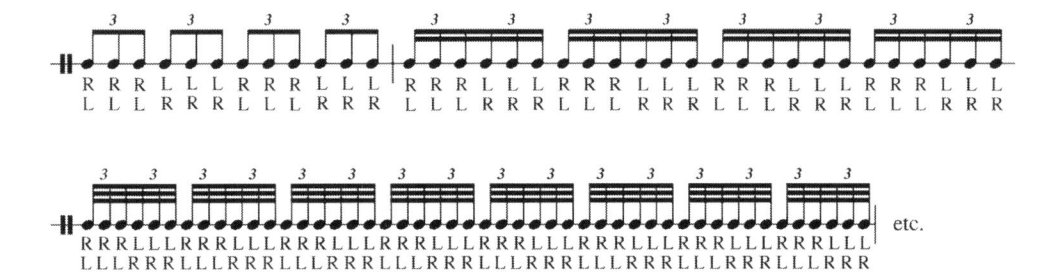

The triple-stroke roll in context is as follows.

Double-stroke Rudiments

In drum rudiment terminology, when a stick stroke is allowed to bounce twice (i.e. RR, LL, etc.) it is referred to as a "diddle." A double-stroke roll is produced with alternating diddles of indeterminate speed and duration. Currently, there are 10 official variations of the double-stroke roll.

6. Double-stroke Roll (Long Roll)

A double-stroke roll consists of evenly spaced, alternating diddles. It is performed in such a manner that each individual note is easily discernible.

```
R R L L R R L L   R R L L R R L L R R L L R R L L
L L R R L L R R   L L R R L L R R L L R R L L R R
```

7. Five-stroke Roll

A five-stroke roll consists of two diddles played with alternating sticking, followed by an accented note.

```
R R L L R   R R L L R
L L R R L   L L R R L
```

8. Six-stroke Roll

A six-stroke roll is slightly different from other double-stroke rudiments. It consists of a single stroke followed by two diddles of alternating sticking and a single, accented note. It may be notated as sextuplets, or as a single stroke, followed by two diddles (at half the duration of the single stroke), followed by a single stroke.

```
R L L R R L R L L R R L R L L R R L R L L R R L
L R R L L R L R R L L R L R R L L R L R R L L R
```

9. Seven-stroke Roll

A seven-stroke roll consists of three diddles played with alternating sticking, followed by an accented note. At slower tempos, it is usually notated as a sextuplet followed by a quarter note.

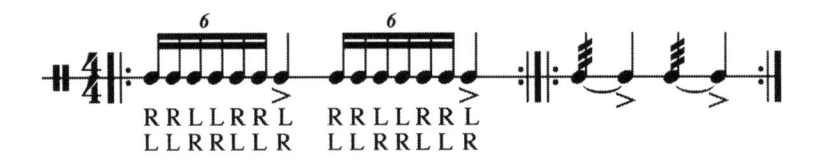

```
R R L L R R L   R R L L R R L
L L R R L L R   L L R R L L R
```

10. Nine-stroke Roll

A nine-stroke roll consists of four diddles played with alternating sticking, followed by an accented note.

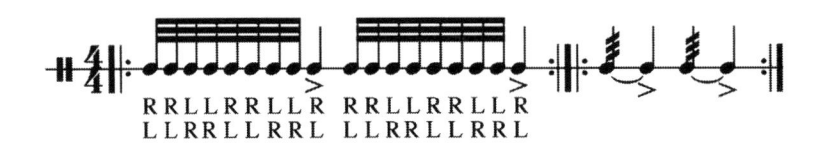

```
R R L L R R L L R   R R L L R R L L R
L L R R L L R R L   L L R R L L R R L
```

11. Ten-stroke Roll

A ten-stroke roll consists of four diddles played with alternating sticking, followed by two accented notes of alternating sticking.

RRLLRRLL RL RRLLRRLL RL
LLRRLLRR LR LLRRLLRR LR

12. Eleven-stroke Roll

An eleven-stroke roll consists of five diddles played with alternating sticking, followed by an accented note.

RRLLRRLLRRL RRLLRRLLRRL
LLRRLLRRLLR LLRRLLRRLLR

13. Thirteen-stroke Roll

A thirteen-stroke roll consists of six diddles played with alternating sticking, followed by an accented note.

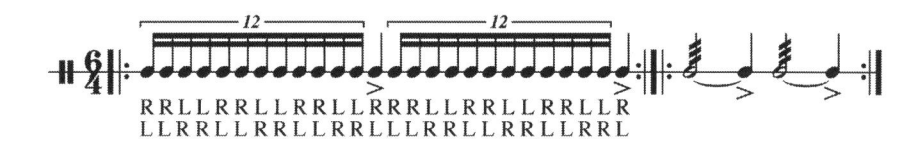

RRLLRRLLRRLLR RRLLRRLLRRLLR
LLRRLLRRLLRRL LLRRLLRRLLRRL

14. Fifteen-stroke Roll

A fifteen-stroke roll consists of seven diddles played with alternating sticking, followed by an accented note.

RRLLRRLLRRLLRRL RRLLRRLLRRLLRRL
LLRRLLRRLLRRLLR LLRRLLRRLLRRLLR

15. Seventeen-stroke Roll

A seventeen-stroke roll consists of eight diddles played with alternating sticking, followed by an accented note.

RRLLRRLLRRLLRRLLR RRLLRRLLRRLLRRLLR
LLRRLLRRLLRRLLRRL LLRRLLRRLLRRLLRRL

Diddle Rudiments

As previously mentioned, in drum rudiment terminology, when a stick stroke is allowed to bounce twice (i.e. RR, or LL) it is referred to as a diddle. A paradiddle is a rudiment consisting of four notes of equal duration, executed with two single strokes of alternating sticking, followed by a diddle (i.e. RLRR, or LRLL). There are nine official rudiments based upon the paradiddle. Four are classified simply as diddle rudiments. Two variations combine flams with paradiddles and are classified as "flam" rudiments. Three variations combine drags with paradiddles and are classified as drag rudiments.

16. Single Paradiddle

A single paradiddle consists of two single notes played with alternating sticking (the first of which is accented), followed by a diddle.

```
R L R R L R L L   R L R R L R L L R L R R L R L L
L R L L R L R R   L R L L R L R R L R L L R L R R
```

17. Double Paradiddle

A double paradiddle consists of four single notes played with alternating sticking (the first of which is accented), followed by a diddle.

```
R L R L R R L R L R L L   R L R L R R L R L R L L R L R L R R L R L R L L
L R L R L L R L R L R R   L R L R L L R L R L R R L R L R L L R L R L R R
```

18. Triple Paradiddle

A triple paradiddle consists of six single notes played with alternating sticking (the first of which is accented), followed by a diddle.

```
R L R L R L R R L R L R L L
L R L R L R L L R L R L R R
```

19. Paradiddle-diddle

The paradiddle-diddle consists of two single notes played with alternating sticking (the first of which is accented), followed by two alternating diddles.

```
R L R R L L R L R R L L   R L R R L L R L R R L L R L R R L L R L R R L L
L R L L R R L R L L R R   L R L L R R L R L L R R L R L L R R L R L L R R
```

Flam Rudiments

A flam is the combination of a principal note preceded by a grace note (with the grace note being played slightly softer than the principal note). These two notes are played almost simultaneously with alternating sticking. Since the resonance of the grace note overlaps the resonance of the principal note, the effect implies a singular broad and slightly emphasized note. Flam rudiments are those that contain flams, either in isolation or in combination with elements of other rudiments.

20. Flam

As previously stated, a flam consists of a principal note preceded by grace note. The rudiment is played with alternating sticking, with the grace note being played slightly softer than the principal note.

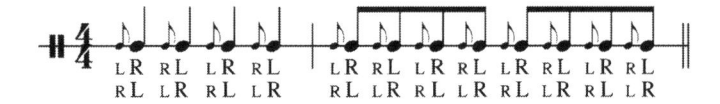

21. Flam Accent

A flam accent consists of a flam followed by two single notes played with alternating sticking. This rudiment is usually written as a triplet.

22. Flam Tap

A flam tap combines the flam with the diddle. It consists of alternating diddles with a flam on the first note of each diddle.

23. Flamacue

A flamacue consists of a five-note figure where the first note and the last note are flammed, and the second note is accented.

24. Flam Paradiddle (or Flamadiddle)

A flam paradiddle (or flamadiddle) consists of a single paradiddle with a flam on the first note.

25. Single-flammed Mill

A single-flammed mill consists of a diddle (with a flam on the first note of the diddle), followed by two strokes of alternating sticking.

26. Flam Paradiddle-diddle

The flam paradiddle-diddle consists of two single notes played with alternating sticking (the first of which is flammed and accented), followed by two alternating diddles.

27. Pataflafla

A pataflafla consists of a four-note figure where the first and fourth notes are flammed (and usually accented).

28. Swiss Army Triplet

Aurally identical to, and often used as a substitute for the flam accent, the Swiss Army triplet consists of a flam followed by a stroke using the same hand and a stroke using the other hand.

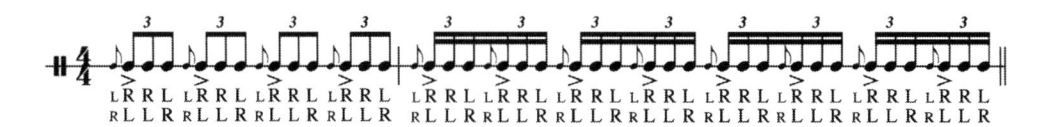

29. Inverted Flam Tap

The inverted flam tap consists of a flam followed by alternating diddles (with a flam on the second note of each diddle).

30. Flam Drag

A flam drag consists of an accented flam, followed by a drag (two consecutive notes played by the same hand), followed by a single stroke. (See below for the definition and description of a drag.)

Drag Rudiments

Technically, a drag is the combination of a principal note preceded by two notes of half the rhythmic value (or twice the speed) of the principal note. The notes preceding the principal note are played with the same hand and the principal note is played with the opposing hand (as demonstrated in the flam drag rudiment). The most practical and most commonly used configuration is that of two grace notes played with the same hand followed by a principal note played with the opposing hand. There are exceptions to this technique. When a drag is written for timpani, bass drum, or instruments of the idiophone family, the grace notes are always performed with alternating sticking. This rudiment was originally called a "ruff." However, the name has officially been changed to drag, and the term ruff currently has a different connotation. (See Supplemental and Hybrid Rudiments.)

31. Drag

As previously stated, the most practical application of the drag is that of two grace notes played with the same hand followed by a principal note played with the opposing hand.

32. Single-drag Tap

The single-drag tap consists of a grace note drag followed by an accented note.

33. Double-drag Tap

A double-drag tap consists of a grace note drag followed by a single-drag tap.

LLR LLR   L rrL rrL   R
rrL rrL   R llR llR   L

34. Lesson 25

The lesson 25 rudiment (also known as a "ratatap") consists of a three-note figure of alternating sticking with a grace note drag on the first note and an accent on the third note.

LLR L R LLR L R LLR L R LLR L R
rrL R L rrL R L rrL R L rrL R L

35. Single Dragadiddle

A single dragadiddle consists of a drag, followed by a diddle.

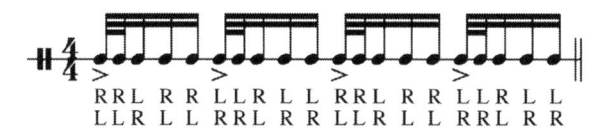

RRL R R LLR L L RRL R R LLR L L
LLR L L RRL R R LLR L L RRL R R

36. Drag Paradiddle No. 1

The drag paradiddle No. 1 consists of a single accented note, followed by a paradiddle with grace-note drag on the first note of the paradiddle.

RllR L R R LrrL R L L   RllR L R R LrrL R L L
LrrL R L L RllR L R R   LrrL R L L RllR L R R

37. Drag Paradiddle No. 2

The drag paradiddle No. 2 consists of a single accented note, followed by a grace-note drag, followed by a paradiddle with grace-note drag on the first note of the paradiddle.

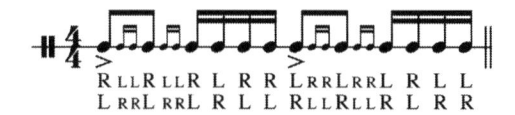

RllRllR L R R LrrLrrL R L L
LrrLrrL R L L RllRllR L R R

38. Single Ratamacue

A single ratamacue consists of four notes (the first three of which are usually triplets) where the first note is a grace-note drag and the fourth note is accented.

LLRLRL rrLRLR LLRLRL rrLRLR
RRLRLR LLRLRL RRLRLR LLRLRL

39. Double Ratamacue

A double ratamacue consists of a grace-note drag followed by a single ratamacue.

LLR LLRLRL rrL rrLRLR
RRL RRLRLR LLR LLRLRL

40. Triple Ratamacue

A triple ratamacue consists of two grace-note drags followed by a single ratamacue.

LLR LLR LLRLRL rrL rrL rrLRLR
RRL RRL RRLRLR LLR LLR LLRLRL

Supplemental Rudiments and Hybrid Rudiments

The preceding examples represent the *40 International Drum Rudiments* as defined by the Percussive Arts Society. These 40 rudiments will most likely constitute the majority of the rudiments used throughout one's orchestrating/arranging career. However, there are literally hundreds of additional rudiments at one's disposal, many of which can be quite useful not only in an orchestral setting, but also when writing for drum lines or drum corps.

Most of these additional rudiments are known as "hybrid rudiments." While there are exceptions, hybrid rudiments generally combine two or more of the 40 standardized rudiments to produce new rudimental patterns. Individual drummers create these hybrid rudiments to suit their needs or desires and as such there is no standardized list of these rudiments. There is neither standardization nor even agreement as to the (often creative) name of a given hybrid rudiment, as the rudiment may have been independently created and named by multiple percussionists. Hybrid rudiments are constantly evolving and it behoves the orchestrator to frequently peruse these new rudiments in an effort to expand one's creative palette. The following examples are but a sampling of the additional rudiments available.

Four-stroke Ruff

A ruff is a combination of grace notes and a principal note, all of which are played with alternating sticking. A four-stroke ruff consists of three grace notes followed by a principal note with all four notes played with alternating sticking. This rudiment is not practical if written in quick succession, but can be effective and quite emphatic singly.

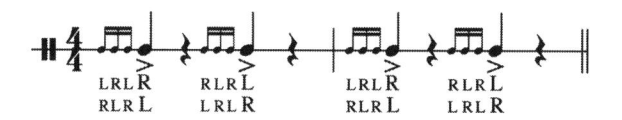

Double Flam Drag

A double flam drag consists of an accented flam, followed by two drags.

Double Flam Swiss Triplet

A variation of the Swiss Army triplet, the double flam Swiss triplet consists of an accented flam followed by a stroke using the same hand and an accented flam with the opposing hand.

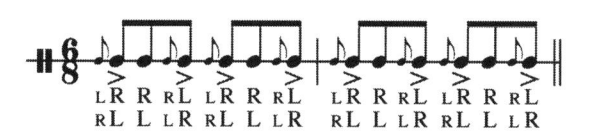

Eggbeater

An eggbeater is a quintuplet figure consisting of a triple stroke and a diddle.

Deviled Egg

A deviled egg is a septuplet figure consisting of an accented triple stroke and two diddles.

Choo-Choo

The choo-choo consists of a paradiddle with a flam on the diddle.

THE INSTRUMENTS

MEMBRANOPHONES

Timpani

Configurations

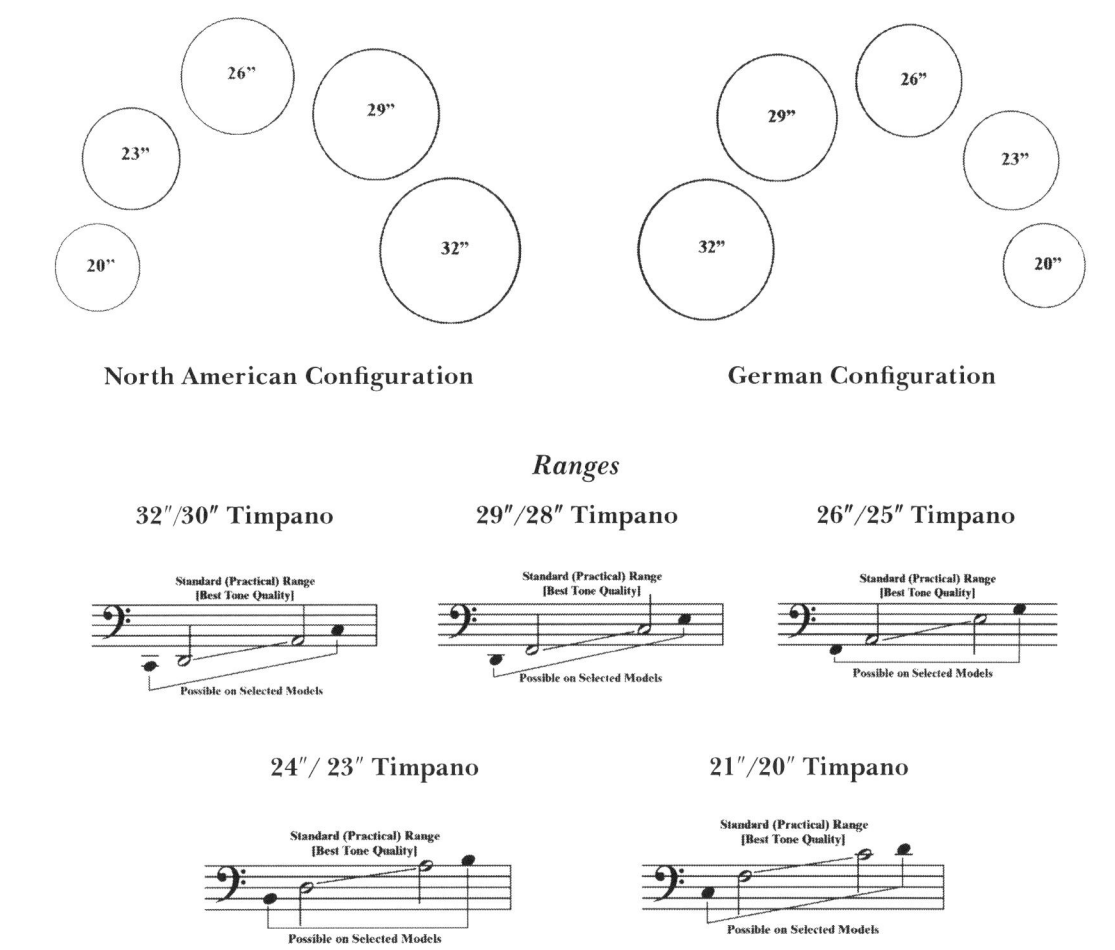

North American Configuration (20", 23", 26", 29", 32")

German Configuration (32", 29", 26", 23", 20")

Ranges

32″/30″ Timpano
Standard (Practical) Range [Best Tone Quality]
Possible on Selected Models

29″/28″ Timpano
Standard (Practical) Range [Best Tone Quality]
Possible on Selected Models

26″/25″ Timpano
Standard (Practical) Range [Best Tone Quality]
Possible on Selected Models

24″/23″ Timpano
Standard (Practical) Range [Best Tone Quality]
Possible on Selected Models

21″/20″ Timpano
Standard (Practical) Range [Best Tone Quality]
Possible on Selected Models

The most grievous error orchestrators make when scoring for timpani is to assume the entire range of a given timpano yields a full and characteristic sound. While many models of timpani have (or claim to have) a functional extended range both above and below the standard range, the resonance of the instrument suffers in both extremities. On notes below the standard range the head has less tension and can produce unfocused, inconsistent, and occasionally unpredictable results. Pitches in this lower extended range will often "drift" sharp. On notes above the standard range the head has greater tension and the tone quality and resonance of the instrument suffers. In the standard range the tension on the head is moderate and the instrument resonance is optimum. From a practical perspective, one should restrict one's writing to the standard range, spanning approximately a perfect 5th, for each timpano.

If one is scoring music intended for high schools or colleges, one can generally expect the availability of four timpani (32″/30″ to 24″/23″). At the professional level one may expect the additional availability of the smaller timpani (21″/20″), sometimes referred to as piccolo timpani.

Contemporary timpani are equipped with a foot pedal device that allows the pitch of the instrument to be changed. The timpano head is tuned to a predetermined low pitch with the pedal in its lowest (pitch) position. The pedal can then be used to tighten the head, thereby raising the pitch (spanning, in most cases, the interval of a perfect 5th). One should allow adequate time for pitch changes to avoid an unintended glissando between pitches. With the contemporary foot-pedal system, five seconds is usually sufficient for pitch changes.

Mallets

The hardness of the mallets can have a significant effect on the tone production of the instrument. One should always specify the type of mallet one deems appropriate for the desired articulation or tonal effect.

Wooden Mallets

Wooden mallets produce a rhythmically precise, but somewhat brittle sound and should be used sparingly.

Hard Mallets

Hard mallets produce a crisp sound with good tone production and are useful when an aggressive sound is desired.

Medium Mallets

Medium mallets are good for general usage and are the default mallets when the orchestrator does not designate a specific type of mallet in the part.

Soft Mallets

Soft mallets produce a somewhat less defined articulation than harder mallets and are excellent for sustained rolls in soft passages and on low pitches.

If desired, one can reduce any harshness produced by the use of harder mallets by placing a felt pad or soft cloth on the head of the timpano, resulting in a damped, more muted timbre.

In addition to the relative hardness of the mallet, the timbre of the instrument is determined by where the mallet strikes the timpano head. The best (and most characteristic) sound is produced by striking the head approximately one-third of the radius from the rim. Striking the center of the head produces a less resonant sound that can best be described as a "thud." Striking the edge of the head produces minimal useful resonance.

Timpani in the Orchestral Setting

Traditionally, timpani have been used with the brass section or tutti orchestra to accentuate climatic passages with rolls and singular strikes. While they are very effective on rolled pedal tones and on energetic rhythmic patterns, they can be equally functional in soft passages, providing a rhythmic pulse or ostinato bass.

As bass instruments, timpani are most effective when used in conjunction with the orchestral bass lines. Using timpani as a melodic instrument yields less than desirable, often comic results.

In the orchestral setting, they are best served in a supportive role, in pointillistic passages where they are in combination with other percussion instruments, or in brief solo roles.

One may designate two timpani to be played simultaneously. However, when doing so one should restrict oneself to using only perfect intervals. Perfect octaves, perfect 5ths and perfect 4ths yield the best results. Other intervals tend to sound harmonically convoluted and endanger the clarity of the harmonic content. In this context, notate the smaller timpano with stems up and the lower timpano with stems down.

A glissando effect can be achieved on timpani by moving the pedal after the head has been struck. Since a single strike on a timpano produces a tone of limited duration, the glissando effect seldom exceeds a few seconds in duration. An ascending glissando yields a slightly longer duration than a descending glissando (relaxing head tension tends to suppress the vibrations). Glissandi (both ascending and descending) can only be sustained by rolling as the position of the food-pedal is changed. One should restrict the range of a glissando to fit within the standard range of the timpano. While the glissando is an interesting effect, one should be aware of its overuse in cartoons and comic media. An audience's perception of the artistic intent of a timpani glissando will be biased by their exposure to this over-usage.

Snare Drum

The snare drum is a two-headed drum with strands of curled metal wire (called "snares") stretched firmly across the bottom drumhead. Sound is produced by striking the top drumhead (called the batter head), creating a vibration that causes the bottom drumhead (called the snare head) to vibrate against the snares producing the snare drum's characteristic rattling sound.

The drum is equipped with a lever (called the snare strainer control lever) which is used to engage or disengage the snares. With the snares disengaged, the drum produces a sound similar to a small tom-tom. The snare drum is played with the snares engaged unless otherwise specified. If one wishes a section to be played with the snare disengaged, place "snares off" at the beginning of the affected section. At the end of the section specify "snares on" to re-engage the snares. Be sure to allow adequate time for the lever to be quietly repositioned (two to three seconds should be sufficient).

Snare drums are available in a variety of sizes, with each offering a slightly different timbre (generally, the deeper the shell the more resonant the sound). The orchestrator should specify the approximate size of snare desired by generically stating "small," "medium," or "large" in the score. If a deeply resonant snare sound is desired, consider using a "field snare" (aka parade drum).

Sustained Durations

The resonance of singular notes on the snare drum has very little duration. There is no perceptible difference in the durations between of a singular eighth-note and a singular whole note (or any other singular note, for that matter). Sustained durations are created through the use of a "roll."

Drumsticks

Drumsticks are available in a variety of sizes and materials, from thin and lightweight to thick and heavy, and are constructed from wood, synthetics, or a combination of both. There is no need for the orchestrator to designate the type of sticks to be used. One should allow the drummer to choose the sticks appropriate for the demands of the music.

Wire Brushes

As wire brushes do not bounce off the batter head, only single stroke rudiments are viable. One can also "stir" the brush on the batter head, creating a sustainable "swishing" sound. If one wishes a section to be played with the wire brushes, place the term "brushes" at the beginning of the affected section. To return to drumsticks, place "sticks" at the beginning of the section where drumsticks are desired. Be sure to allow adequate time to change from bushes to sticks (three to four seconds should be sufficient).

Alternate Beaters

A variety of other methods may be used to initiate the sound on the snare drum. The drum may be played with the hands/fingers, with timpani or marimba mallets (a useful effect with the snares off), and one can even drop items such as marbles on the beater head for a unique result.

Rim Shots (and Stick Shots)

Rim shots and stick shots are two ways to generate an emphatic, "gunshot" type sound on the snare drum. A rim shot can be produced by placing the tip of the stick on the head while resting the shaft of the stick on the rim of the drum. The player then strikes this stick with the other stick. It can also be produced by striking the head and the rim simultaneously with one stick. A third method for creating this "gunshot" effect is sometimes called a "stick shot." The player places the tip of the stick on the head, then strikes the shaft of that stick with the other stick. It is not necessary for the orchestrator to designate which method to use. One should simply place "rim shot" over the note and allow the player to determine which method best serves the purpose.

Muting and Alternate Timbers

A less resonant, but still articulate sound can be produced by placing a piece of felt or soft cloth on the batter head. To designate this effect one should place "muted" at the beginning of the affected passage. To cancel the effect place "norm." at the beginning of the following unmuted passage.

A softer, more delicate sound can be produced by playing close edge of the beater head. This is designated by placing "near the edge" at the beginning of the affected passage. To cancel the effect place "norm." at the beginning of the next passage where the effect is not desired.

One may also designate passages to be played on the rim of the drum or on the shell of the drum. Note that the timbre of a shell strike varies with the size, depth and construction materials of the drum. One designates these effects by placing "on the rim" or "on the shell" at the beginning of the affected passage. To cancel the effect place "norm." at the beginning of the next passage where the effect is not desired.

Bass Drum

Bass drums are available in a variety of sizes and configurations. The tone varies from small to large drums; the larger the drum, the deeper and more resonant the tone. If the orchestrator desires different sizes of bass drums to be used in a score, sizes should be specified generically as "small," "medium," or "large."

Bass drums may have one or two heads and may be played in a horizontal or vertical position. The two-headed drum is the conventional instrument in use. However, most professional orchestras will also have a single-headed drum at their disposal and will use them interchangeably depending upon the context of the music. The orchestrator need not be concerned with designating a one- or two-headed drum.

Placing the bass drum in a horizontal position allows the percussionist to use two mallets or beaters on one head, facilitating the execution of more complex rhythmic patterns. There is no need for the orchestrator to specify horizontal or vertical, as the percussionist will position the bass drum as the music requires. However, one should be aware that the vertical position yields greater volume (and the sound is more directional) than the horizontal position.

Traditionally, the bass drum has been used to establish or reinforce a rhythmic pulse. It has also been used to emphasize climactic chords as well as rhythmic motives. It is capable of a wide dynamic range and can be used as a supportive element in wide variety of situations.

Thunder and Cannons

A bass drum roll (typically a two-beater roll) can be used to simulate rolling thunder. One can vary the perception of the proximity of the thunder with the dynamic level. A "cannon-shot" can be produced by forcibly striking the center of the drumhead (most effective with the drum in the vertical position).

Muting and Dampening

In the vertical position, the drum is muted with the left hand on the back head and the right knee on the front head. In the horizontal position, the drum is muted by placing a piece of cloth on the upper head or by placing a hand on the upper head. A note can be damped by placing the hand and/or knee on the head after the note is struck.

Large Wool Beater

Unless otherwise specified, the large wool beater is the default beater for the bass drum. It yields best results in passages where speed and/or sharply defined articulations are not required. It is also the best choice for the "thunder" and "cannon" effects.

Small Wool Beater

A small wool beater facilitates greater precision and more sharply defined articulations than the large wool beater. It yields slightly less depth of tone than that of the larger beater.

Marimba Mallets

Extremely precise articulations can be achieved through the use of marimba mallets. These mallets produce a clear, bright tone that lacks the depth of tone generated by the use of larger, softer mallets. They are quite useful in passages requiring rapid, complex rhythmic patterns.

Tambourine

Tambourines are available in an assortment of sizes and shapes, are constructed from a variety of materials, and may or may not have a head. In all cases the tambourine consists of small jingles suspended within openings in a shallow shell. Tambourines used in the orchestral setting have a calfskin (or synthetic) head on one side of the shell and are approximately 10 inches in diameter. Should the orchestrator desire different sizes of tambourines to be used in a score, the sizes should be generically specified as "small," "medium," or "large."

The tambourine is usually played with the hand, fingers, knuckles, or knee. It can also be placed on a table or mounted on a stand, and played with two hands, drumsticks, mallets, or brushes. The tambourine can be muted using either the fingers or a soft cloth. The orchestrator can indicate this effect generically by placing "mute" at the beginning of the passage, or specifically by designating "mute with fingers" or "mute with cloth."

The tambourine is capable of articulating intricate rhythmic patterns. When on a table or mounted on a stand, the instrument is capable of the same rhythmic complexity available on the timpani (including rolls). There are two methods of producing rolls on the tambourine. The "thumb roll" is produced by rubbing the thumb along the edge of the head. The thumb roll works well at lower dynamic levels, but has a limited sustainable duration of only 2–3 seconds. The "shake roll" is produced by shaking the tambourine. Shake rolls work well at higher dynamic levels and where a crescendo or decrescendo is required.

The tambourine should be used sparingly and only for specific effects. While its timbre is quite effective in many situations, extended usage can easily become tiresome to the ear.

Tenor Drum

Tenor drums are available in a variety of sizes and are similar in construction to the field snare (minus the snares). The larger tenor drums have a deep, resonant timbre approaching that of a small bass drum. When played with drumsticks, the drum is capable of executing intricate rudiments and rhythmic patterns. Since the sound is more resonant than that of the snare drum, extremely quick and complex patterns may have a tendency to sound less articulate. Many snare drum effects translate well to the tenor drum, including rim shots, near the edge and on the shell techniques. When played with felt mallets, the drum can produce a dark, dirge-like quality in lower dynamics. When played in higher dynamics, felt mallets produce a booming, forceful sound. The tenor drum may also be muted (by placing a soft cloth or felt pad on the head) or played with wire brushes.

Tom-toms

A tom-tom is available in two configurations, a two-headed tom-tom and the one-headed tom-tom. The one-headed tom-tom can generate greater volume than the two-headed drum as sound is unencumbered by the bottom head. On the other hand, the two-headed drum is capable of greater subtleties. Should one have a preference, one should specify that preference in the score.

Tom-toms can be used as singular drums or in sets. The orchestrator should specify the number of drums and their registers in the score. One need not designate specific drum dimensions, but rather generically state sizes as "high," "high-medium," "low medium," and/or "low." Confusion can be avoided by notating on a one-line (for singular drums), a three-line (for 2 and 3-drum sets), or a 5-line stave (for a 4-drum set) as follows:

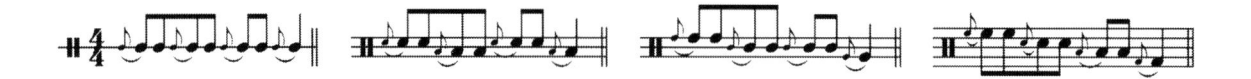

Tom-toms can be played with snare drumsticks or with mallets, depending upon the desired effect. One should specify "sticks" or "mallets" in the score. Playing "near the edge" produces a sound with less resonance, and playing "in the center" produces a booming, more forceful sound.

Bongos

Bongos consist of a pair of single-headed drums that are attached to one another. Traditionally, the drums are held between the knees and played by striking the edge of the drumheads with the fingers. In an orchestral setting the drums are usually mounted on a stand and played with either the hands or with drumsticks. They can be muted by placing the palm of one hand on the head while striking it with the other. A glissando (also called a "moose call") can be produced by rubbing the middle finger (usually supported by the thumb) across the head of either drum.

Though generally associated with Latin-style music and especially with Cuban music, the bongos have gained acceptance as a useful member of the orchestral percussion arsenal and are an established member of the percussion ensemble.

Conga

The conga is a tall, narrow, single-headed Cuban drum of African ancestry. The conga has a deeper, more resonant tone than that of the bongo. While a single conga may be used, they are usually played in sets of two (some players will even have sets of three or four drums). When scoring for conga, the orchestrator should assume access to two drums. The drums may be placed on the floor and played while seated, or mounted on a rack or in a stand and played while standing.

Occasionally in orchestra or percussion ensemble music, drumsticks will be used on congas. However, the most idiomatic sound is produced with the hands. There are a variety of hand strokes used on the conga to produce variations in tone. An experienced player can produce five types of sound from each drum, ranging from a crisp slap to a low-pitched bass note. In addition to these strokes, the player can produce glissandi and pitch bends. A player can bend the pitch of the drum by pressing the elbow into the head while striking with the opposing hand.

When scoring for bongos or conga in a traditional orchestral or percussion ensemble setting, one may use a 3-line or 5-line staff with standard notation.

When scoring for pops orchestra, one will often wish to use these instruments as part of a "rhythm section" accompaniment. The most practical method (and the method yielding the best results) is to notate only the sections that require specific rhythms. In the sections where the instruments are functioning as accompaniment, designate the style of accompaniment and notate with slashes and measure numbers. Allowing the percussionist freedom to work within a style will result in a flowing accompaniment that is far less rigid than a specifically notated accompaniment.

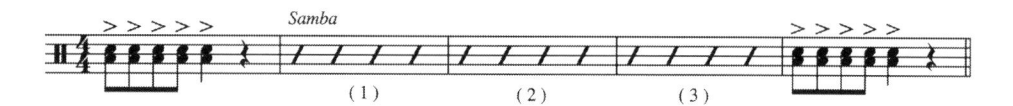

Timbales

Invented in Cuba, timbales are single-headed drums with metal shells. The instrument is played with a variety of stick strokes, stick shots, rim shots and shell strokes. Traditionally, a cowbell is mounted between the two drums and/or a suspended cymbal is placed next to the timbales. The cowbell, cymbal and even the shell are used to create a rhythmic pulse while using the drums for accents, rhythmic figures and fills.

As with bongos and conga, the most practical method of creating a timbale part is to notate only the sections that require specific rhythms. In the sections where the instrument is functioning as accompaniment, designate the style of accompaniment, notate with slashes and measure numbers, and specify the measure(s) where the player is to provide fills.

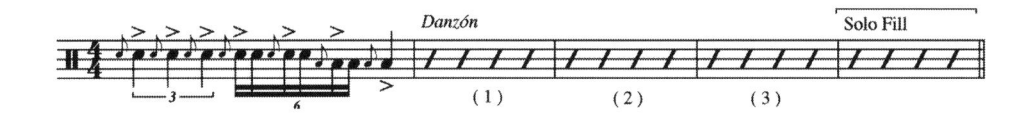

Exoticism is a long-accepted practice in orchestral music. Adding the flavor of a foreign land to a composition can add a level of excitement and interest not otherwise available. In today's global world, one easily has occasion to experience instruments and rhythmic patterns indigenous to other countries. When the situation is appropriate, incorporating these unique sounds into one's orchestrations is an opportunity not to be missed.

Most ethnic instruments were developed and evolved in environments not influenced by western European music. As such, rhythmic patterns (as well as tuning systems and melodic/harmonic content) rarely translate into standard western European notation practices. When incorporating ethnic instruments into an orchestral score, do not attempt to notate the part, as the notation will not be an accurate representation of the music. The best approach is to simply designate what type of rhythmic pattern is used and where it occurs. The areas where the player is the solo feature should also be designated. If using a native player, the form of the piece will most likely need to be learned by rote. This should never be viewed as an inconvenience but rather as an educational opportunity. The native player has intimate knowledge of the instrument, the ethnic rhythmic patterns, and regional traditions and beliefs that can be shared during this process.

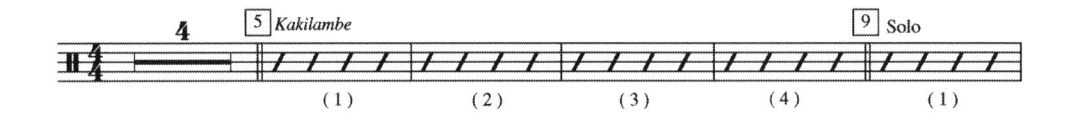

To add the essence of a particular country or region, incorporating an instrument and traditional rhythmic patterns indigenous to that area lends authenticity to the orchestration. (Using native players further adds to the authenticity.) One may wish to explore the following regions and instruments to add an international flair to one's orchestrations.

Drum Set

The drum set (or trap set) consists of a group of percussion instruments configured to be played by one drummer in a seated position. A basic set will contain a bass drum, snare drum, one or two rack-mount tom-toms, a floor tom-tom, a hi-hat, a ride cymbal and a crash cymbal. An expanded set may also contain an additional bass drum, several rack-mount tom-toms, and several floor tom-toms, additional cymbals of various sizes and thicknesses, cowbells, tambourine, mark tree, as well as an assortment of hand percussion instruments. Drumsticks are the most commonly employed beater. Timpani mallets and wire brushes may also be used for specific effects.

While not generally a member of the symphony orchestra, the drum set is an integral member of the rhythm section when scoring for pops orchestra, pit orchestra and jazz ensemble. Scoring rhythmic accompaniment for drum set yields more concise, coordinated and functional results than assigning the various components individually to multiple players. Never substitute a concert bass drum for the drum set bass drum part (or vice versa) as the two instruments are vastly different in both timbre and resonance.

Should one desire to precisely notate the drum set part, the following legend will cover most needs.

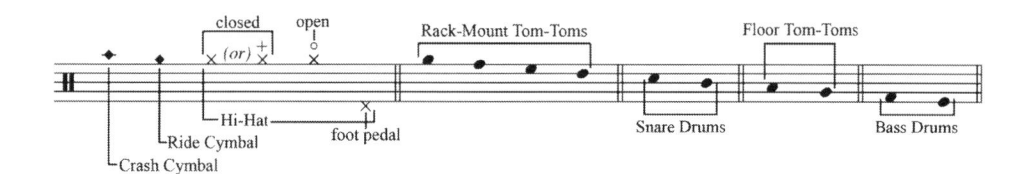

The following is an example of a drum set part notated using elements defined in the above legend.

While the above method of notation is precise and certainly functional, it is time-consuming to create, occasionally difficult to read and execute, and the resulting performance can sound rigid and mechanical.

The most practical method of creating a drum set part is to notate only the sections that require specific rhythms. In the sections where the instrument is functioning as accompaniment, designate the style of accompaniment, use slash notation and measure numbers, and specify the measure(s) where the player is to provide fills. Any areas where the player is the solo feature should also be designated. Adding "road map" elements, such as designing where certain instruments are added, where certain instruments are featured, where a specific instrument has the melody, etc. aids the player in creating a cohesive, supportive and stylistically appropriate accompaniment part.

Akumal

Trap Set

R.J. Miller

IDIOPHONES OF DEFINITE PITCH

Orchestra Bells

The orchestra bells (also called glockenspiel) consist of a set of tuned metal bars mounted on a frame. The frame of the 2½-octave model is usually attached to a portable case. The construction of the extended-range model is similar to that of the xylophone and may include resonators and a damper pedal. The orchestrator should not assume the availability of the extended-range model, restricting one's writing to the range of the standard instrument (unless writing for a specific ensemble in possession of the extended-range model). Orchestra bells are transposing instruments with the resultant pitch being two octaves above the written pitch. In both concert and transposed scores, they should always appear in their transposed form.

One should use restraint when scoring for orchestral bells in the orchestral setting. Use them for accentuating selected melodic lines and for "splashes" of color. Orchestra bells can easily be heard over an entire tutti orchestra. If not used conservatively, the timbre quickly becomes tiresome to the ear. One should be aware that the bars sustain for several seconds after impact and, as such, in fast passages the tones tend to run together. On the extended models with a damper pedal, this problem can be easily remedied. However, on standard models the percussionist must dampen the bars with the hand. This is difficult, if not impossible in quick passages.

Different mallets produce variances in timbre and one should specify the type of mallets to be used based upon the musical context. Brass mallets will yield a bright timbre and are the default mallets when other mallets are not specified. Hard rubber mallets will produce a less piercing sound that, while pleasant, does not project quite as well as with brass mallets. Medium rubber mallets will generate a mellower, more subdued sound. Softer mallets (i.e. soft rubber mallets, medium yarn mallets) produce a pleasing, but low-volume sound that must be unaccompanied or lightly accompanied to be heard.

When recording orchestra bells in the recording studio, brass mallets produce an undesirable, metal-on-metal "ping" when striking the bars. This "ping" is virtually imperceptible on stage, but becomes problematic with sensitive microphones. Hard rubber or medium rubber mallets are often preferable choices when recording orchestra bells in a recording studio.

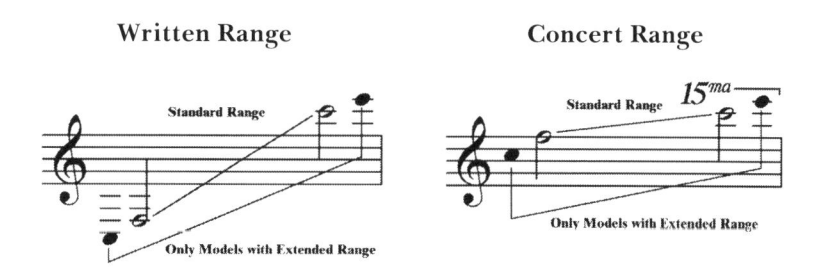

Written Range   **Concert Range**

Crotales

Crotales (or antique cymbals) are small, tuned bronze or brass disks, with a timbre less piercing and a resonance of longer duration than the orchestra bells. They are available as individual disks or as mounted chromatic sets. Sets are manufactured in one octave, two octave, and 2½-octave configurations, with the one octave set being the most commonly available. While they are generally played with hard mallets, they can also be played by striking two individual disks together (like finger cymbals) or bowed. Crotales are transposing instruments with the resultant pitch being two octaves above the written pitch. In both concert and transposed scores, they should always appear in their transposed form.

One should approach the use of crotales as one would the orchestra bells, using restraint when scoring in an orchestral setting. Though not as piercing as orchestra bells, the timbre of the crotales can quickly become tiresome if not scored conservatively. Because of their sustained resonance tones, notes in fast passages tend to run together. As with the orchestra bells, one should use crotales to accentuate selected melodic lines and as "splashes" of color. Crotales blend well with woodwinds and strings.

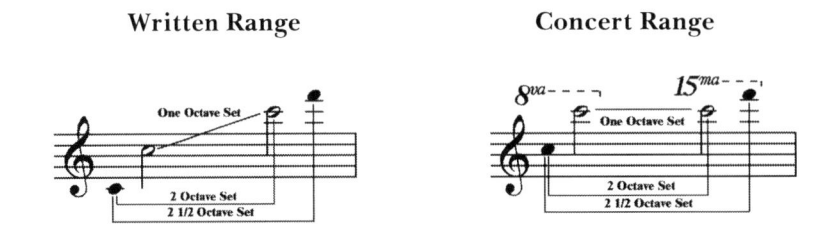

Written Range   **Concert Range**

Xylophone

The xylophone consists of chromatically tuned wooden bars (usually rosewood) mounted in a frame. Xylophones are manufactured in 3-octave, 3½-octave and 4-octave configurations, with the 4-octave instrument being the most commonly available instrument at the college and professional level. Most models are equipped with resonators. The xylophone is a transposing instrument with the resultant pitch being an octave above the written pitch. In both concert and transposed scores, it should always appear in its transposed form.

Typically played with hard plastic mallets, the idiomatic tone is extremely bright, clear and distinct. When struck, the tone dissipates quickly, having an approximate duration of only two seconds. If needed, tones may be sustained through the use of a roll (though this technique is more idiomatic of the marimba). The timbre of the instrument can be altered (moderately) using softer mallets. One should specify "hard mallets" for the idiomatic sound or "medium mallets" for a sound with slightly less bite. Soft mallets produce a subdued, atypical sound that has little use in an ensemble setting (but possibly useful in unaccompanied solo passages).

The xylophone adds an element of excitement when used to double rapid melodies (either in unison or at the octave). It is also quite effective in pointillistic writing and on melodic fragments. The xylophone glissando can be a useful effect, having a greater presence than that of the harp or piano. However, one should be aware that xylophone glissandi are only functional in certain keys. A glissando on the bars corresponding to the white keys of the piano (C–D–E–F–G–A–B) yields the best results. A glissando on the bars corresponding to the black keys of the piano (D♭, E♭, G♭, A♭, B♭, or enharmonic equivalents) is possible, but somewhat awkward due to the spacing gaps between bars (E♭ to G♭, and B♭ to D♭).

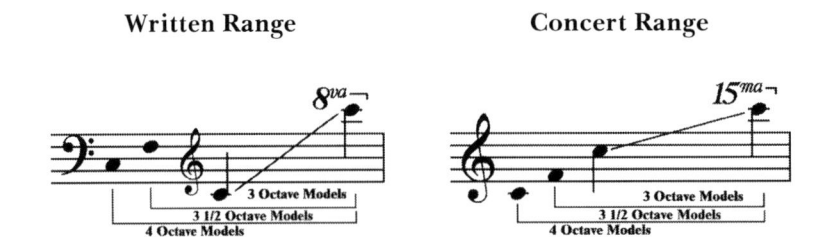

Written Range   **Concert Range**

Notate rolls and trills as follows. One should avoid using the antiquated percussion notation for a roll that employs the trill symbol.

Roll: **Obsolete Roll (avoid):** **Trill:**

A ripple roll (tremolo) is notated as follows:

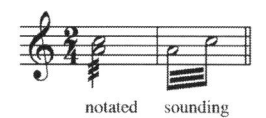

Marimba

The marimba consists of chromatically tuned wooden bars (usually rosewood) mounted in a frame that is equipped with resonators. Marimbas are manufactured in sizes ranging from 2½-octave to 5-octave configurations, with the 4-octave instrument being the generic default model for orchestrating purposes.

The ranges of the most commonly available sizes of marimbas are as follows:

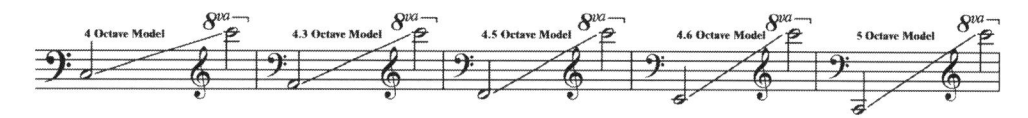

The marimba is a non-transposing instrument that can be written on a single staff or on a grand staff (depending upon the range and context of the music).

RJ Miller, *The Circus is in Town* **(Marimba part), mm. 72–80.**

Copyright © 2001 by Appassionata Music. Used by permission.

The instrument's timbre can vary from full and rich to clear and brilliant, depending upon the register and the choice of mallets. Medium yarn mallets are the default choice and yield a full, mellow tone throughout the entire range of instrument. Hard yarn mallets work well if one wishes to accentuate the note of the upper register, but produce a somewhat brittle timbre in lower register. Soft yarn mallets work best in the lower register, yielding a full, mellow tone, but are not advisable for the upper register. Mallets made of rubber and wound cord are also available and generate various alterations to the marimba's timbre. It is suggested that one spend adequate time with the instrument to research the sounds produced by each type of mallet, as the difference in tone from one type of mallet to another can be significant. The instrument can be played with two, three or four mallets at a time. However, the orchestrator should be aware that the more mallets are required for a selection/passage, the more practice/rehearsal time is required.

The marimba has limited projection in the higher dynamic range and will be difficult to hear in fortissimo or heavily scored passages. At a soft to medium dynamic level, the instrument projects well and its unique timbre will blend well with both woodwind and brass instruments.

Notate rolls and trills as follows. One should avoid using the antiquated notation for a roll that employs the trill symbol.

Roll: **Obsolete Roll (avoid):**   **Trill:**

A ripple roll (tremolo) is notated as follows:

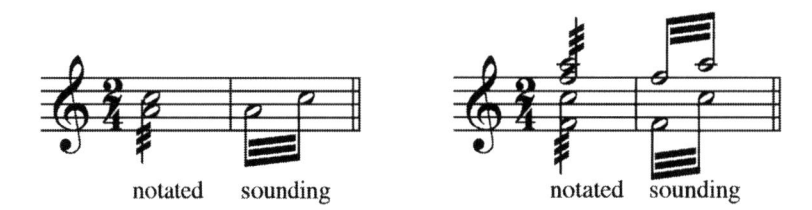

notated   sounding   notated   sounding

Vibraphone

Vibraphone (also called vibraharp or vibes) consists of a set of tuned metal bars mounted on a frame. The instrument is equipped with resonators and a damper pedal. The vibraphone is the only instrument equipped with a mechanism to create a tremolo (vibrato) effect. This tremolo is produced by motorized, rotating disks in the top of the resonator tubes. While some models offer a variable speed tremolo, most models offer three speeds of tremolo. The orchestrator should specify speed of desired tremolo by designating "no vib.," "slow vib.," "med. vib.," or "fast vib."

Vibraphones are manufactured in 3-octave and 4-octave configurations, with the 3-octave instrument being the standard and most readily available model. The orchestrator should not assume the availability of the 4-octave model, restricting one's writing to the range of the standard instrument (unless writing for a specific ensemble in possession of the extended range model). The vibraphone is a non-transposing instrument that can be written on a single staff or on a grand staff (depending upon the range and context of the music).

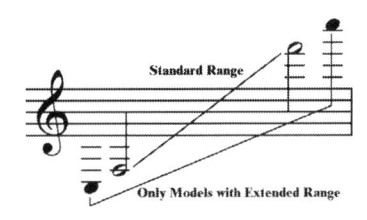

Unlike the xylophone and marimba, the tone of a vibraphone sustains for quite some time (when undampened). As such there is no need to use a roll to sustain the sound; the vibraphonist will not roll tones unless specifically indicated. Sustain is controlled by the damper pedal (or by dampening with the hand or tip of the mallet). One should notate the pedal usage in the same manner one would notate for piano.

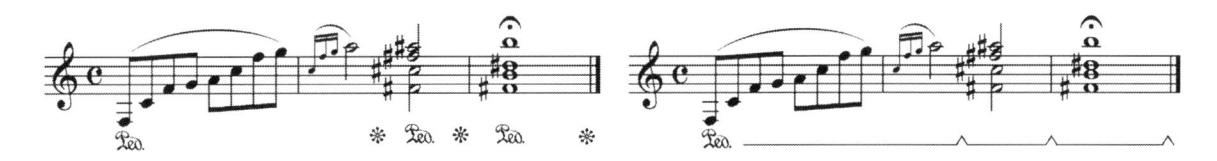

Cord mallets and yarn mallets yield the most practical results, with cord mallets having more edge to the sound and yarn mallets a somewhat more subdued sound. Medium mallets (either cord or yarn) are the default choice and are best for a consistent tone. Hard mallets generate a more percussive sound, while soft mallets produce a smooth, legato sound when played at lower dynamic levels. The tone produced with medium and soft mallets blends well with woodwinds and the tone produced with hard mallets bends well with brass. Single bars can also be bowed (with a cello bow) to create a haunting, eerie effect.

Chimes

The chimes (also called tubular bells) are chromatically tuned cylindrical brass tubes mounted in a rack that is equipped with a damper pedal. The instrument is played by striking the tubes with mallets and controlling its lengthy sustain capability with the damper mechanism. Traditionally, chimes have been used to imitate the sound of church bells and its tone easily projects over the orchestral tutti (even at the highest dynamic levels).

Chimes are commercially available in an extended range model (extending the ascending range by a major 2nd). However, it is rare for one to have access to this model. One should not assume its availability and restrict one's writing to the range of the standard instrument (unless writing for a specific ensemble in possession of the extended range model). The instrument is considered a non-transposing instrument and is written on a single (treble clef) staff.

The tubes generate the fundamental plus a very complex (and very audible) series of overtones that give the instrument a somewhat "out-of-tune" sound. For this reason, the instrument is neither a practical nor functional choice for melodic lines or two-part writing. Rawhide mallets (hammers) are the default choice, yielding the most idiomatic (church bell) sound. Wood or metal mallets can be used to produce a more vociferous tone that is effective in fortissimo tutti passages. Leather-covered (chamois) mallets produce softer attacks and are useful for passages at lower dynamic levels. Glissandi, while technically possible, are neither practical nor particularly useful in an orchestral setting.

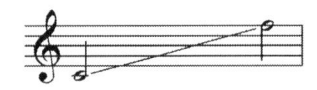

IDIOPHONES OF INDEFINITE PITCH

Triangle

The triangle is a round metal rod configured in the shape of a triangle and generally struck with a metal beater. It comes in a variety of sizes ranging from 4 inches to 12 inches, with the most commonly available being the 6 inches (small), 8 inches (medium) and 10 inches (large). The orchestrator should specify the number of triangles and their sizes in the score. One need not designate specific dimensions, but rather generically state sizes as "small," "medium" and/or "large."

At higher dynamics the triangle has a clear and brilliant percussive sound that can be heard over an entire tutti orchestra. When played at lower dynamic levels it produces a pleasant sonority that is useful when used in conjunction with the upper woodwinds or lightly scored strings.

Generally played with a single beater, two beaters may be employed in rapid passages. However, since the tone of the triangle is slow to decay, rapid passages scored for triangle can lack clarity. Triangle rolls can be quite effective and are notated in the same manner as other percussion. Muting the instrument with fingers produces a less penetrating sound that is quite effective when combined in patterns with non-muted strikes. The most practical method of notating this effect is to use "o" to designate the open strikes and "+" to designate the muted strikes.

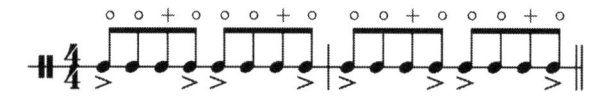

The thickness of the beater has an effect upon the tone and projection of the instrument. The thinner the beater, the more delicate the sound; the thicker the beater, the more brilliant the sound. If one has a preference, one should specify a "thin," "medium" or "thick" beater. If not specified, a medium beater is generally used by default.

Hand Cymbals (Piatti)

The hand cymbals (also called piatti or crash cymbals) consist of two cymbals that are struck against each other in a glancing manner. Piatti are manufactured in a variety of sizes with 18 in medium-weight cymbals most commonly available. One need not designate specific dimensions or weights, but rather generically state sizes as "small," "medium" and/or "large" should one have a preference.

Piatti are particularly effective for reinforcing accented, climatic events. The tone of the cymbals has a relatively long sustain (unless dampened against the body). The percussionist will dampen the cymbals at the end of the notated duration unless otherwise instructed. If one wishes the sound of the cymbal strike to sustain and decay naturally one should put *L.V.* (let vibrate, or *laissez-vibrer*) in the score. The orchestrator should exercise restraint when writing for piatti as the instrument can easily be over-used.

Suspended Cymbal

A cymbal suspended from a strap or mounted on a cymbal stand is referred to as a suspended cymbal. As with piatti, suspended cymbals are manufactured in a variety of sizes with 15 inches to 18 inches medium-weight cymbal being most commonly available. The thinner the cymbal, the quicker the response and decay; the heavier the cymbal, the slower the response and longer the decay. The orchestrator should generically state sizes as "small," "medium" and/or "large," should one have a preference. Striking the cymbals in different areas yields various sounds. Striking the bell area produces a tone that is described as bell-like or gong-like. Striking the edge produces a deep ping-like sound. Playing on the bow section of the cymbal produces the idiomatic sound and is the default technique if another locating is not specified. If one wishes the sound of the cymbal strike to sustain and decay naturally, one should put *L.V.* (let vibrate, or *laissez-vibrer*) in the score.

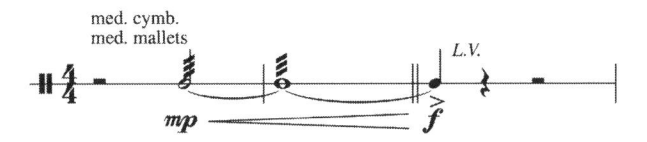

Suspended cymbals may be struck with a variety of beaters, with each type yielding different tones. Yarn mallets are the most practical in an orchestral setting, producing smooth, flowing rolls that mask the sounds of the individual strokes. They are useful for sustained rolls that vary in amplitude, for decrescendi and (especially) for crescendi. A drumstick may be used when a defined attack is desired. Wire brushes may be used when a "swishing" sound is desired. The cymbal may also be struck or scraped with a triangle beater for a more metallic sound. The sustain of the cymbal is dampened by the hand. It is suggested that one spend adequate time with the instrument to acquaint oneself with the tones produced by each type of beater, as the difference in tone from one type of mallet to another (as well as one striking location to another) can be significant. The instrument can also be bowed (with a cello or bass bow) to create an eerie, ominous effect.

Sizzle Cymbal

The sizzle cymbal is a variation of the suspended cymbal. It has metal rivets loosely installed in holes drilled approximately one-quarter the distance from the edge of the cymbal, and evenly spaced around its circumference. The "sizzle" is produced as the rivets bounce upon the cymbal as it vibrates. All of the considerations and all the techniques that apply to the suspended cymbal also apply to the sizzle cymbal.

An accented sizzle cymbal strike (preferably with a drumstick; *L.V.*) is quite effective when used to reinforce the beginning of a tremolo in the high strings, or the beginning of a trill in the upper woodwinds. The *L.V.* effect can be quite useful, as the vibrating rivets cause the tone to decay more slowly than that of a regular suspended cymbal.

Finger Cymbals

Finger cymbals are small, resonant, metal disks designed to work as a pair. While an individual finger cymbal may be played with a metal beater (a useful effect when paired in duet fashion with the triangle), the idiomatic sound is produced by striking two cymbals together. Each cymbal is "tuned" to an approximate pitch, with the pair being "tuned" approximately a quarter step apart. The result of this dissonance is a delicate, high-pitched sound of indefinite pitch that blends well with the higher orchestral sonorities. Finger cymbals are useful for adding a Middle Eastern or Asian flavor to one's orchestration.

Tam-tam

A tam-tam is a large disk of metal (usually with a flanged edge around its circumference) that is suspended from a frame. Tam-tams are considered instruments of indefinite pitch, as opposed to gongs, that are instruments of definite pitch. One should never confuse the two in one's orchestrations. They are available in a variety of non-standardized sizes ranging from very small (14 inches to 18 inches) to very large (48 inches to 60 inches or larger). Due to the expense of the large models, one should not assume access to a tam-tam larger than 36 inches. One should generically state the desired size as "small," "medium" and/or "large," should one have a preference.

Before a forceful strike on a tam-tam, one should "warm-up" the instrument by lightly tapping or stroking the disk with the beater. While this "warm-up" process does produce a quiet tone, it will be imperceptible to the audience. One should allow for adequate warm-up time (approximately 10 seconds) to avoid disappointment in the timbre and presence on a forceful strike. Tam-tams are usually struck with a special tam-tam beater. This beater will be the default choice of the percussionist if no other choice is designated. Other unique tones can be generated on the instrument by striking (or scraping) the instrument with a triangle beater, drumstick, marimba or timpani mallet, or wire brushes. As with other instruments, it is suggested that one spend adequate time with the tam-tam to acquaint oneself with the tones produced by each type of beater, as the difference in tone from one type of beater to another can be significant. The instrument can also be bowed (with a cello or bass bow) to create an eerie, almost menacing effect (similar to the same effect on suspended cymbal, but with a deeper resonance).

Tam-tams are most idiomatic when used to reinforce fortissimo climactic events. However, one should not shy from using the instrument at other dynamic levels. A soft, sustained roll can provide a haunted, almost foreboding ostinato that can be most useful. One should be aware that the tone sustains for an exceptionally long time, and dampening the instrument with the hand, body, or mallet produces a less than subtle (choked) sound. For best results, one should score the tam-tam in a manner that allows the tone to sustain and decay naturally. One should designate this by placing *L.V.* (let vibrate, or *laissez-vibrer*) in the score.

Woodblocks

In essence, a woodblock is simply a small, rectangular block of wood (usually teak or similar hardwood) containing a craved chamber, or slit, that functions as a resonator. Striking the woodblock with a drumstick or similar beater produces the sound. Woodblocks are available in a variety of sizes, generally ranging from approximately 8 inches to 12 inches in length. Piccolo woodblocks (approximately 4 inches to 6 inches in length and of lesser proportional girth) are also available. If one desires multiple sizes of woodblocks, one should state the desired sizes in the most generic of terms, "small," "medium" and/or "large," rather than designating specific dimensions. The tone of the woodblock decays immediately, with no perceptible sustain.

Temple Blocks (Tempo Blocks)

With a slightly darker and more resonant sound than the woodblock, temple blocks are also wooden blocks with carved resonating chambers. Traditional temple blocks were carved in the shape of a fish or dragon (with the mouth of the animal being the resonator) and available in sets of five different sized blocks. Contemporary instruments consist of rectangular blocks (of either wood or plastic), usually in sets of five or eight blocks. Five-block sets should be notated on a five-line percussion staff with each line representing the five approximate pitches. Eight-block sets are notated on a five-line percussion staff with each line and space representing the approximate pitches.

Ratchet

The ratchet consists of a cogwheel and two wooden flanges mounted in a handle. When the cogwheel is rotated (by use of a crank) the wooden flanges hit the teeth of the cog, producing a loud rapid clicking sound. Short bursts should be notated with singular notes (even though multiple clicks will most likely sound). Sustained durations should be notated as rolls.

Shakers

A shaker consists of a container (usually a tube or an egg-shaped vessel) that is partly filled with loose objects. When shaken, the objects impact the side of the container, producing a rhythmic sound. Repeating rhythmic figures are usually used as accompany elements and should be notated with singular notes. Sustained durations should be notated as rolls and are produced by swirling the container.

Sleigh Bells

The commercially available sleigh bells are a set of multiple individual bells attached to a handle. Some organizations may have authentic sleigh bells with fewer bells attached to a strap. Since sleigh bells principally are used in descriptive music, such as Leroy Anderson's *Sleigh Ride*, they are generally used for simple repetitive rhythms (representing the gait of an animal). One can also produce a roll effect by shaking the instrument.

Though many sizes of sleigh bells exist (small, medium, large and even "tuned" sets), one should not assume access to anything other than the most generic sounding (medium) set. Sleigh bells have little practical dynamic range. The idiomatic sleigh-bell sound is best achieved at the *mf* and *mp* dynamic levels. The sound lacks consistency at lower dynamics and an attempt at higher dynamics does not yield a variance in sound or amplitude sufficient enough to be useful. Notate sleigh bells on a one-line staff.

Mark Tree

The mark tree is also called mark chimes or bar chimes by various manufacturers. However, since the inventor of the instrument called it a mark tree, it is prudent for the orchestrator to use that term. A mark tree consists of a series of brass, aluminum or glass tubes suspended from a long wooden bar in the order of their respective lengths. The instrument may contain as few as 20 or as many as 40 tubes, and may be configured in single or double rows. Its idiomatic sound is produced by brushing tubes, in an ascending or descending glissandi style, with either the hand or with a stick, causing the tubes to strike one another. The mark tree does not create a definite pitch, but rather produces a shimmering, ethereal effect.

The majority of mark trees are not equipped with a dampening mechanism and, as such, the sound cannot be silenced quickly. The most practical approach is to score the part in such a manner as to allow the sound to decay naturally, placing *L.V.* (let vibrate, or *laissez- vibrer*) in the score. If it is absolutely necessary to dampen the instrument, place *dampen* in the score and the percussionist will silence the tubes with the forearm.

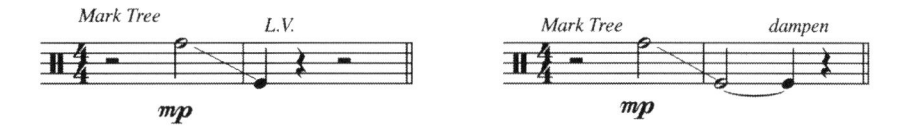

Wind Chimes

Wind chimes consist of glass, metal or wooden tubes suspended from a (usually circular) disk. They are available in an array of shapes and sizes, with no one configuration considered standard. If one does not have a preference or does not specify the type and size of wind chimes to be used, the percussionist will use whatever set is at hand. Should one have a preference as to size, one should state generic sizes, "small," "medium," or "large." Should one have a preference as to the material of the tubes, one should state generic materials, "glass," "metallic," or "wooden." The most practical approach is to score the part in such a manner as to allow the sound to decay naturally, placing *L.V.* (let vibrate, or *laissez-vibrer*) in the score. If it is absolutely necessary to dampen the instrument, place *dampen* in the score and the percussionist will silence the chimes with the hand.

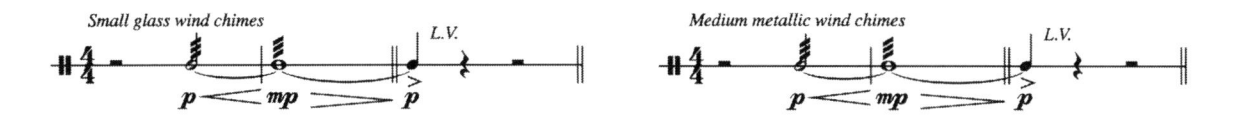

Bell Tree

A bell tree consists of a series of vertically nested metal bells, arranged in order of size and connected by a long rod. The bells resemble inverted bowls that produce a "mysterious" sound when played as a glissando. There is no standardized number of bells and the actual number of bells has little consequence on the overall effect. Sliding a beater across the bells in a descending or ascending manner produces the idiomatic glissando effect. Triangle beaters, glockenspiel mallets or hard xylophone mallets yield the best results. The bells may also be played individually and are notated with an approximation of the desired pitch.

As with the bell tree and wind chimes, the most practical approach is to score the part in such a manner as to allow the sound to decay naturally, placing *L.V.* (let vibrate, or *laissez-vibrer*) in the score. If it is absolutely necessary to dampen the instrument, place *dampen* in the score and the percussionist will silence the bells with the hand. If notating a glissando, one should designate the direction (ascending or descending) of the glissando.

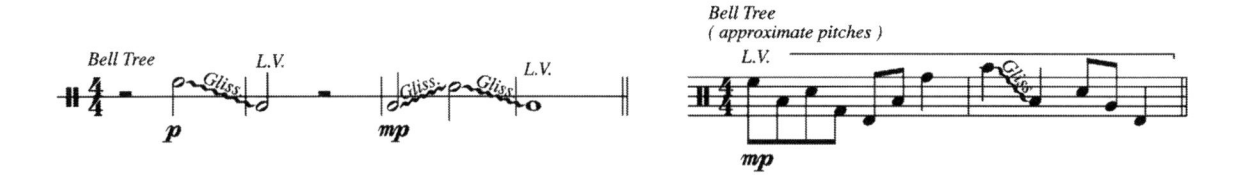

Flexatone

A flexatone consists of one or two wooden balls on a spring attached to a flexible metal sheet within a wire frame. The instrument has traditionally been used to create a comic glissando effect. The percussionist holds the frame with the thumb on the end of the metal sheet. The instrument is shaken, causing the wooden balls to impact the metal sheet. As the thumb depresses the vibrating metal sheet, the relative pitch of the instrument ascends; as the thumb pressure is released, the relative pitch of the instrument descends. Percussionists will often remove the wooden balls and strike the metal sheet with a beater (a triangle beater, glockenspiel mallet, or hard xylophone mallet will yield the best results). This method gives the player greater control of the sound of the flexatone as it eliminates the need to shake the instrument. To notate the desired effect one should use visual indicators. Use a roll symbol to designate shaking the instrument with lines indicating the direction of the desired glissando. Use a wavy line in conjunction with roll symbols to designate shaking the instrument while alternating the thumb pressure on the metal sheet. If using a flexatone without attached wooden balls, designate singular strikes with a symbol showing the desire direction of the pitch bend. The designation of desired pitches should be approximate.

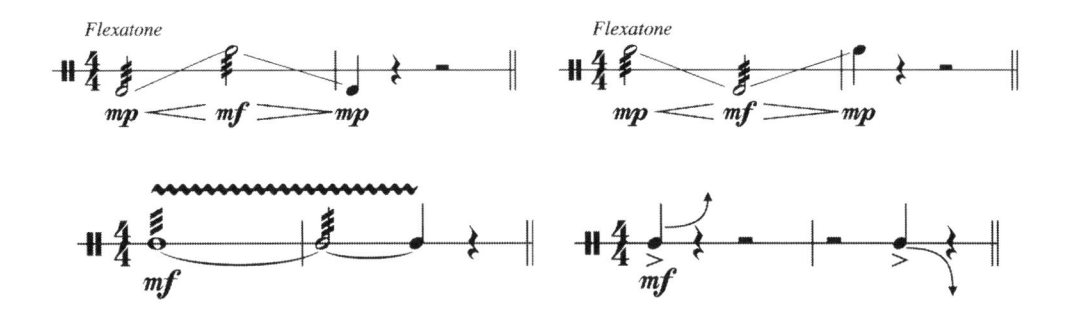

Vibraslap

A vibraslap consists of a rigid (shaped) rod with a hollow box containing metal pegs (or teeth) mounted on one end and a wooden ball on the opposing end. The vibraslap is the modern version of the "jawbone." The sound is initiated by striking the wooden ball against the palm of the hand, or against the knee. Vibrations are transmitted through the rod to the box containing the teeth, causing them to rattle. The hollow box functions as a resonator, amplifying the sound. The instrument is available in a three basic sizes and, should one have a preference, one should designate that preference in the most generic sense, stating "small," "medium" or "large" in the score. To achieve the idiomatic (and most practical) sound, the sustain of the instrument should be allowed to decay naturally.

Anvil

An anvil is a length of metal that is struck with a hammer or metal mallet and approximates the sound of a blacksmith's anvil. While traditionally used for simplistic, repetitive rhythmic patterns, generally performed at higher dynamic levels, playing the instrument at lower dynamic levels (with wooden mallets) can yield a useful, somewhat muted metallic pulse. The instrument is available is several sizes, though most ensembles will have only one size in their percussion arsenal. If one desires, and has confirmed that a given ensemble has access to multiple sizes of anvils, one should designate one's preference by stating "small," "medium" and/or "large" in the score.

Brake Drum

The brake drum is literally a brake drum from a vehicle. When struck with a metal hammer or a metal glockenspiel mallet it produces a clear, almost bell-like sound. Wooden mallets or marimba mallets may be used to achieve a more muted, less resonant sound. One should state the desired type of beater in the score.

Most ensembles will have two or three sizes of brake drums at their disposal. Some ensembles may have access to as many as four or five drums. Unless one has confirmed the availability of multiple brakes drums, one should err on the conservative side, restricting oneself to two or (a maximum of) three brake drums. Generally, one should use the same approach in scoring for brake drums that one does when scoring for anvil.

Thunder Sheet

Usually suspended from a frame, a thunder sheet is a thin sheet of metal that is used to approximate the sound of thunder. Large, thin metal sheets yield the most thunder-like timbre. Shaking the metal sheet with various intensities produces the idiomatic thunder-like sound. The instrument can also be played with a mallet to produce a resonant, metallic strike. As with the tam-tam, one should "warm up" the instrument by lightly tapping or shaking the sheet before the effect is to begin in earnest. This "warm-up" process does produce a quiet tone, but it will be imperceptible to the audience. One should allow approximately five seconds to adequately warm up the instrument. Use the roll symbol to designate the duration of the effect, specify the dynamic level and contour, and, whenever possible, allow the resonance of the instrument to decay naturally.

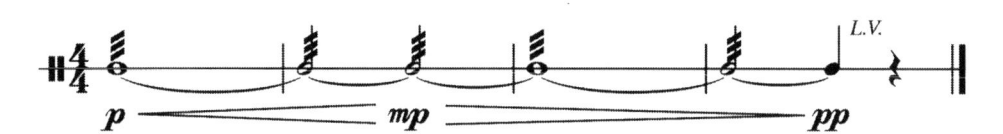

Cowbells and Agogo Bells

The cowbell used in musical contexts is a (clapper-less) descendant of the bells used by herdsmen to track the location of livestock. Cowbells are available in a multitude of sizes and most ensembles will have at least three at their disposal. If one has need for multiple cowbells in a score, one should restrict oneself to no more than three, designating them as "small," "medium" and/or "large."

Cowbells are usually played with a cowbell beater or the butt end of a drumstick. Other mallets made of metal, wood, plastic, or rubber may be used to alter the sound of the bell. A cowbell may be held in the hand and played with one beater. This technique allows the player to use the hand to alter the tone by muting (or partially muting) the bell. Cowbells can also be mounted on a stand, allowing the player to use two sticks. This technique allows the percussionist to play multiple cowbells and more intricate figures, but it also makes the process of muting difficult. There exists no standardized method for notating strikes on various parts of the cowbell. One should use whatever notation seems most logical and requires the least explanation (i.e. using x-noteheads for a particular type of strike). The most practical method of notating the muted effect is to use "o" to designate the open strikes and "+" to designate the muted strikes.

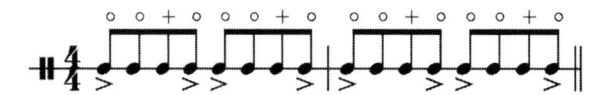

The agogo bells usually consist of two (approximately) tuned conical bells attached to a bent rod which functions as a handle. Typically the instrument is held in one hand and struck with the butt end of a drumstick (or cowbell beater) that is held in the opposing hand.

One may occasionally encounter a set of agogo bells consisting of three bells, but these are not the standard and one should not assume access to three different pitches in one's orchestration.

The resonance of both cowbell and agogo bells has little sustain, decaying almost immediately. As such, there is no need to specify durations in the notation. One should simply notate the strikes. Rolls on the instrument are harsh and serve no functional purpose in the orchestral setting. Cowbells and agogo bells are best used as a rhythm accompaniment in orchestrations with a Latin or African flavor. In this context, best results are achieved by using traditional rhythmic patterns associated with Latin (primarily Cuban) or African dances and by using the instrument to reinforce accented figures.

Claves

Claves are a pair of short, thick hardwood sticks which, when struck together, produce a vivid clicking sound. (Contemporary models may alternately be made of synthetic or composite materials.) A clave is held in one hand (the hand is cupped to create a resonating chamber) and struck by the clave in the opposing hand. Traditionally, in African- and Brazilian-influenced music, claves play a repeating pattern (also known as clave) that is the foundation of the rhythmic accompaniment.

One should restrict one's writing for clave to basic, repetitive rhythmic patterns, staying within the context of Latin-American, Brazilian or African rhythmic traditions. Rolls and rudiments are not applicable to the clave and medium dynamic levels yield the best results.

Maracas

A maraca consists of a gourd shell filled with seeds or dried beans that is attached to a handle. Commercially available models are often made from wood, leather, or plastic, and filled with beads or shot. Maracas are generally played in pairs and come in a variety of sizes. The smaller the maraca, the more delicate the sound; the larger the maraca, the more penetrating the sound. Most ensembles will have two sizes of maracas at their disposal. If one has need for contrasting timbres, one should restrict oneself to two sizes of maracas, designating them as "small" and "large" in the score.

Though similar in sound and usage to the shaker, maracas (when played in pairs, with one in each hand) are capable of more intricate and complex rhythms. Native to Latin America, and both a traditional and idiomatic component of Latin-influenced music, the maracas are also quite useful in other genres. Rolls are quite effective and varied on the instrument. One type of roll involves shaking the maracas as one would for a single-stroke roll. This style of roll is simply notated with the roll symbol. Holding the gourd part (or ball) of the maraca in a downward position and swirling produces the second type of roll. Placing the word "swirl" directly above the note containing the roll symbol best notates this style of roll.

Cabasa and Afuche-Cabasa

Traditionally, the cabasa (cabaza) is a large, serrated gourd covered with multiple loose strands of beads. A shaker-like sound is produced when the beads skim across the serrated surface. Commercially available cabasas are equipped with a handle, allowing the percussionist to rest the instrument in the palm of one hand, while rotating the handle back-and-forth, causing the beads to scrape against the serrated surface. The gourd can be struck with the hand, causing a short, rattle-like sound. It is also capable of the same type of rolls available on the maracas (produced using the same techniques).

The afuche-cabasa consists of loose strands of steel-ball chain loops around a wide cylinder (with a serrated metal surface) that is attached to a handle. Its metallic timbre is a more penetrating, but less organic sounding than that of the cabasa. All the playing techniques available on the cabasa are available on the afuche-cabasa. When scoring for either instrument, one should employ the same approach one would when scoring for maracas.

Guiro

The guiro (also known as a reco-reco) is a hollow, serrated tube. A ratchet-like sound is produced when the serrated surface is scraped with a stick (or pua). Traditionally made from a gourd, commercially manufactured models are made of wood, metal or plastic. The pua may be a wooden, plastic or metal stick, or a long-toothed wire comb.

The instrument commonly supplies rhythmic accompaniment in Latin-influenced music. Patterns consist of a combination of long and short strokes, with the duration of the long stroke limited to the time needed to scrape the entire length of the serrations. The functional dynamic range of the guiro is limited, yielding best results at ***mp*** or ***mf***.

Castanets

Castanets consist of a pair of concave (usually) hardwood shells that produce a clicking sound when struck together. The instrument is commercially available in three different configurations – namely, hand castanets, machine castanets and paddle castanets. With hand castanets, a pair is held in each hand and struck together using the fingers. With machine castanets the shells are mounted to a hardwood board and struck against the board with the fingers (machine castanets can also be struck with mallets, yielding a less than idiomatic timbre). With paddle castanets, the shells are mounted on a paddle (handle) and the sound is produced by striking the paddle against the knee, or by shaking it as one would with a set of maracas (least effective method). The orchestrator is to simply designate "castanets" in the score; the percussionist will determine which specific model and playing technique best suits the musical context.

Rolls and single-stroke rudiments are possible and are notated as one would notate for membranophones. Castanets are best used when one wishes to imply a Spanish-style ambiance. They are also useful for rhythmically reinforcing accented staccato chords.

Rainstick

In essence, a rainstick is a hollow tube with needles protruding (in a spiral manner) from the inner surface, which is partially filled with small, round objects (beads, pebbles, or beans). When the tube is slowly inverted, the objects flow through the needles, producing a sound reminiscent of rainfall or a delicate waterfall. Indigenous to South America, the rainstick was once part of native mythology and believed to have magical, rainmaking powers. Traditional rainsticks are constructed from cacti. Commercially manufactured instruments are generally constructed from wood or plastic, and filled with plastic beads. The sound of a rainstick is very delicate and only effective at the lowest dynamic levels. Since the instrument is only capable of one functional sound, at one functional dynamic level, the orchestrator need only notate the desired duration of the effect.

AEROPHONES

Slide Whistle

A slide whistle consists of a tube with a fipple (a chamber that directs the air-stream towards the sound-producing edge of an opening) on one end, closed on the other end, and containing an internal piston which is used to alter the length of the tube (and therefore, the resultant pitch). The commonly available instruments are generally made of metal or plastic. Though it is technically possible to play melodies on the instrument, the most practical use is as a sound-effect device. The idiomatic ascending and descending glissandi remain a staple when depicting comic situations. The actual range of a given instrument is dependent upon the dimensions of the tube, and there is no standardized size. If using the slide whistle as a sound-effect device, notate as one would notate an instrument of indefinite pitch (a one-line staff will suffice).

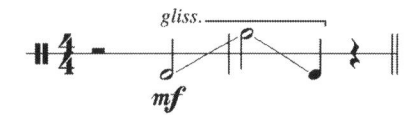

Coach's Whistle

A coach's whistle (sports whistle, police whistle, or pea whistle) consists of fipple and an enclosed chamber containing a loose pea (or bead). It is capable of one basic sound and best results are achieved at higher dynamic levels (*mf* to *ff*). Since this type of whistle is incapable of melodic contour, it should be notated as an instrument of indefinite pitch on a one-line staff. One idiomatic use of the instrument is as a signal to the drum corps to end a cadence and execute the introductory pattern that leads into the featured ensemble selection.

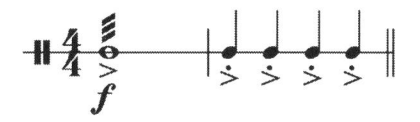

Samba Whistle

Native to Brazil, the samba whistle is a pea whistle capable of producing three distinct tones. These tones are generated by covering (or uncovering) holes in the side chambers. The traditional whistle is constructed of wood, and commercial manufactured models are made of metal. The instrument's idiomatic sound is produced at higher dynamic levels (*mf* to *ff*). The sound is somewhat shrill and piercing, capable of being heard over an entire ensemble. Even though the samba whistle is capable of three tones, it should be treated as an instrument of indefinite pitch. It can be notated rhythmically, with non-specific pitches, on a three-line staff or a five-line staff.

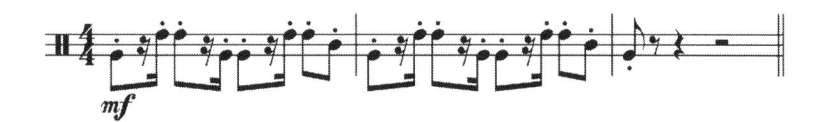

Siren

The siren is a device that replicates the sound of fire truck, ambulance, police, or civil defense sirens. They may be pneumatic (hand-cranked) and electronic. Certain devices can simulate the alternating tri-tone pitches of a British police siren. This instrument is used only for special effects. Electronic sirens will reach their full dynamic level almost immediately. Pneumatic models crescendo into the sustained pitch and are notated as such (specifying when the instrument is to reach its full dynamic level). One should specify the type of siren desired and notate the duration of the effect on a one-line staff.

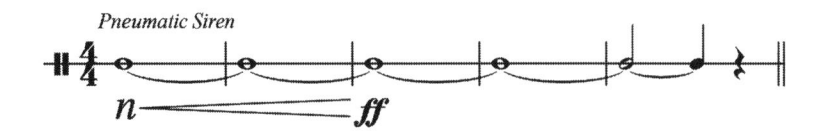

CHORDAPHONES

Celesta

The celesta (celeste) is a keyboard instrument that superficially resembles a small upright piano. It is manufactured in 3-, 4- and 5-octave configurations, with the 4-octave model being the current standard. The celesta consists of a series of small metal bars (with resonators) that are struck by felt hammers, producing a sound similar to, but more delicate than the orchestra bells. The 4- and 5-octave models are equipped with a damper pedal that can either allow the bars to sustain, or be dampened in a staccato fashion. The instrument is capable of executing rapid and intricate passages. The celesta is a transposing instrument, sounding an octave higher than written. It is always placed on a grand staff, and appears in the score in the transposed form (in both concert scores and transposed scores).

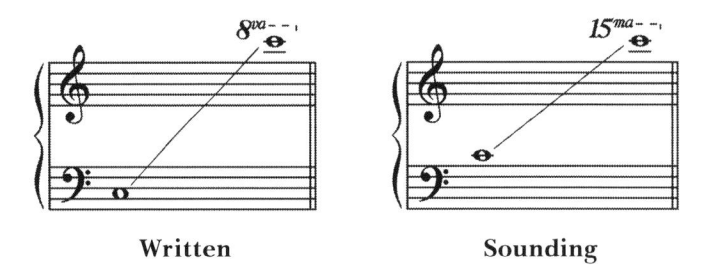

Written   Sounding

Piano

In an orchestral setting the piano is best known and most widely used as a solo instrument. However, the instrument can add a wide variety of textual and percussive elements to one's orchestral scoring when used as part of the ensemble. It has the widest range of any instrument in the orchestral palette, blends with virtually every instrument and section in the orchestra, adds texture and reinforcement when used for doubling other instruments, and adds a percussive edge to the beginning of sustained chords.

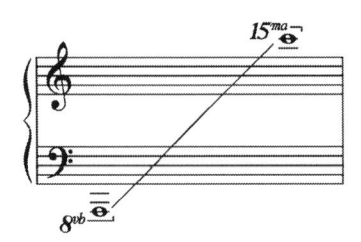

The three pedals of the grand piano offer unique opportunities for the orchestrator. The damper pedal, when depressed, lifts the dampers, allowing the strings to continue vibrating after the keys have been released. It is acceptable to notate the effect in either the traditional or contemporary manner.

Traditional method:

Contemporary method:

The una corde pedal, when depressed, allows the hammers to strike only one (in some cases two) of the strings per pitch, resulting in a softer, more delicate sound. One notates the effect by placing *u.c.* at the position where the effect begins and designating the duration of the effect.

The sostenuto pedal affects only those pitches that are depressed at the time the pedal is depressed. Notes not struck at the time the pedal is depressed are unaffected. One notates the effect by placing *sos.* or *sost.* at the position where the effect begins and designating the duration of the effect.

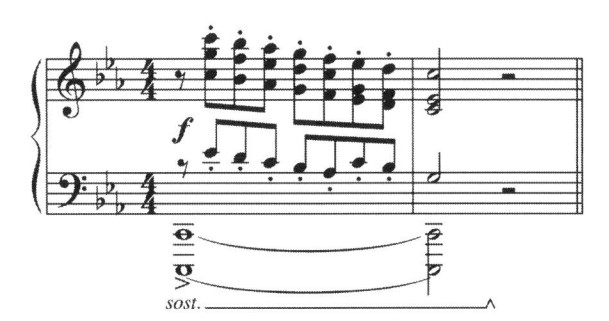

The piano works nicely as doubling, complementary or contrasting elements for the harp, orchestra bells, xylophone, marimba or vibraphone. It blends well with woodwinds and strings, and its percussive attacks can add emphasis to brass notes or chords. The piano is a non-transposing instrument that is usually written on a grand staff. It is acceptable under certain circumstances to notate the instrument on three staves if the process eliminates confusion and adds clarity to the part.

Contemporary techniques such as prepared piano or plucking/striking strings inside the piano normally do not render well in the orchestral environment. These effects are not practical with a large ensemble and should be avoided unless completely exposed in isolated or soloistic passages.

THE ENSEMBLES

Percussion Ensemble

The percussion ensemble consists of multiple, classically trained and versatile percussionists. There is no standardized number of players and no consistent instrumentation in a percussion ensemble. While there are a few professional ensembles, these ensembles generally exist within the academic environment, or are attached to professional organizations, i.e. the percussion section of a symphony orchestra. The instrumentation may include traditional percussion instruments, ethnic instruments, drum set, and even items found in the kitchen, the toy chest, or the junkyard. The music can vary from loud and rambunctious, to soft and subtle, and anything in between.

Orchestral (and Wind Ensemble/Concert Band) Percussion

The percussion section of the orchestra (and wind ensemble/concert band) may vary from the traditional instruments of the classical orchestra to the avant-garde. Though the percussion complement available varies from ensemble to ensemble, a full battery of instruments would likely include the following:

Snare Drum	Tam-tam	Temple Blocks
Field snare	Triangle	Anvil
Tom-toms	Tambourine	Brake drums
Bass drum	Wind chimes	Bongos
Hand cymbals (piatti)	Mark tree	Congas
Suspended cymbals	Bell tree	Claves
Finger cymbals	Wood Blocks	Guiro

Maracas	Timbales	Marimba
Shakers	Drum set	Crotales
Castanets	Timpani (4 drums)	Vibraphone
Whip	Glockenspiel	Chimes
Sleigh bells	Xylophone	

PRACTICAL CONSIDERATIONS

Practical Guidelines for Choosing a Work to Orchestrate for Percussion

- If working with mallet instruments, choose pieces that stylistically apply to your chosen instrumentation.
- Choose pieces that are applicable to the ranges your chosen instrumentation.
- Choose pieces that offer textural opportunities.
- Avoid pieces that are specifically idiomatic of piano.

Practical Guidelines when Scoring for Percussion

- When scoring mallet instrument, avoid three- and four-mallet techniques unless adequate rehearsal/practice time is available.
- When scoring multiple instruments for a singular player, allow adequate time for the player to switch from instrument to instrument.
- Define the type(s) of mallets/beaters desired.
- Use clear and precise notation.
- Don't hesitate to use text to describe the desired playing technique/effect.
- Always attempt to remain true to the (perceived) intent of the composer.
- Learn from the *masters*! *Listen to and analyze* as many different examples of percussion writing as possible.

Practical Solutions when Scoring for Percussion

The options when scoring percussion are virtually endless, limited only by the orchestrator's creativity and knowledge of the percussion instruments. Among many other possible applications, percussion instruments may be used as an ensemble unto itself, as solo instruments, as featured instruments or sections, as rhythmic and/or chordal reinforcement for other instruments, or supportive elements in transitions from passage to passage. The following examples are but a few of the possible approaches one might choose, and are applicable to the orchestral, wind ensemble/concert band, brass band and percussion ensemble settings.

IN THE PROFESSION

Most percussionists prefer to read standard notation, rather than being required to refer to a legend to determine what symbolic or graphic notation represents. The use of a singular symbolic element, such as the use of "x" noteheads or slashes in a part, is generally not problematic. However, a part filled with triangle noteheads, square noteheads and other symbol designations can be confusing and time-consuming to decode. If an unusual technique is required, use clear and precise text that describes a desired effect. Percussionists are versatile and accommodating musicians who often provide the spark that brings an orchestration to life. It is the responsibility of the orchestrator to provide them with parts that are easy to understand and execute.

BUILDING THE SCORE

This example will demonstrate the process for creating a percussion ensemble orchestration from an existing piano selection. Once an appropriate work has been selected, one should begin by performing a harmonic analysis. This analysis will determine the harmonic content and context. These elements are decisive factors when determining the deletion or addition of harmonic elements.

For the purposes of the exercise the following selection will be used:

RJ Miller, *Zounds* **(from the** *Ragtime Collection***).**

Copyright © 2009 by Appassionata Music. Used by permission.

Upon completion of the analysis, one can delete the non-essential harmonic elements (or add appropriate harmonic elements, if needed). One then examines the selection for elements within the notation that must be addressed or altered to work for the instruments of the chosen ensemble.

This example lends itself particularly well to scoring for a xylophone and marimba ensemble consisting of one xylophone (lead instrument) and four marimbas (accompaniment instruments). Since the original piano part was scored to accommodate the span of the human hand, genre-appropriate elements have been added to suit the chosen instrumentation.

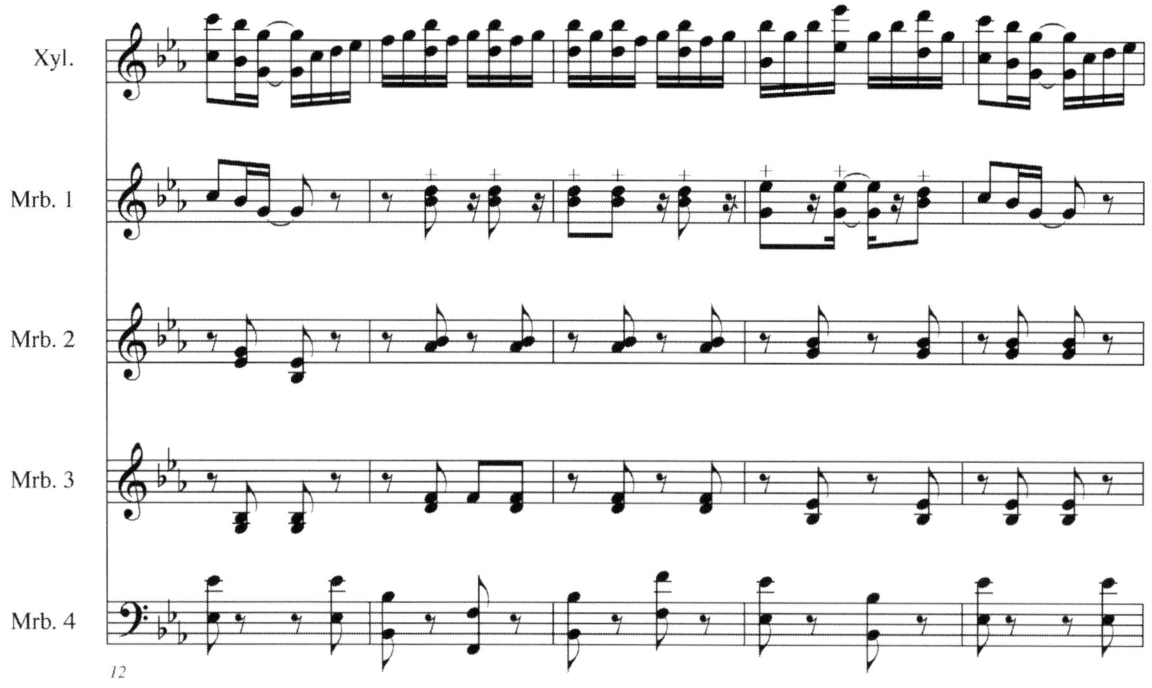
Xyl.
Mrb. 1
Mrb. 2
Mrb. 3
Mrb. 4
12

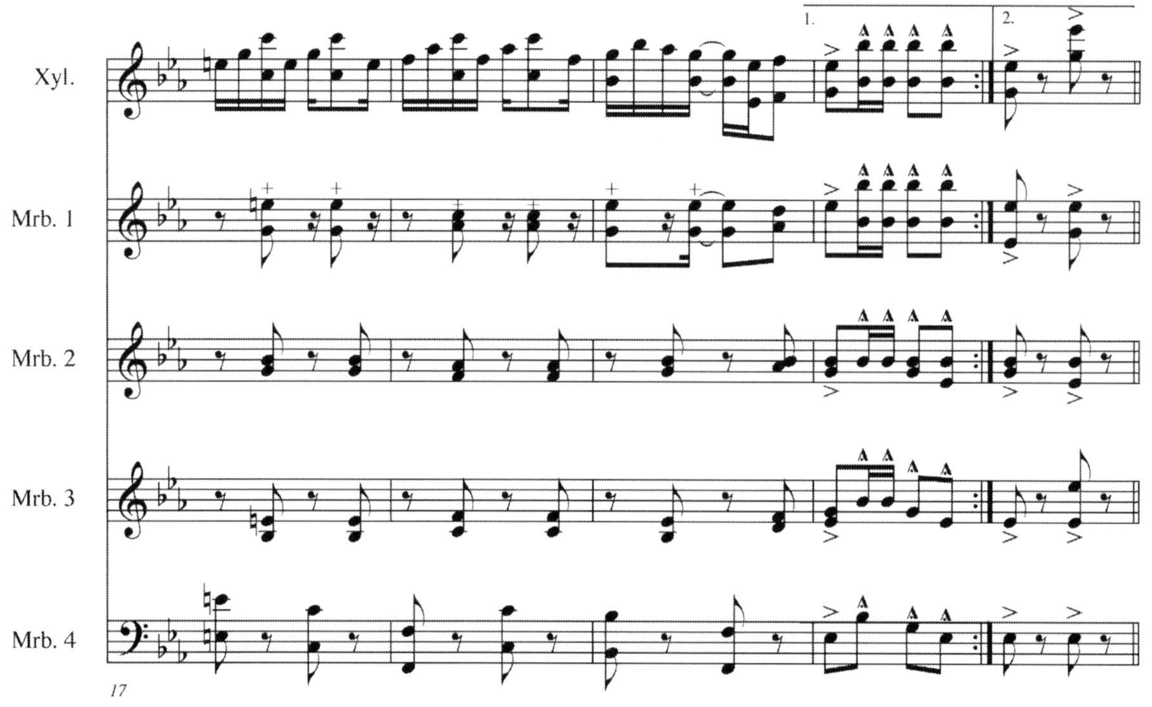
1.
2.
Xyl.
Mrb. 1
Mrb. 2
Mrb. 3
Mrb. 4
17

SCORING EXAMPLES

Alan Hovhaness, *October Mountain*, **Op. 135. Movement I, mm. 1–80.**

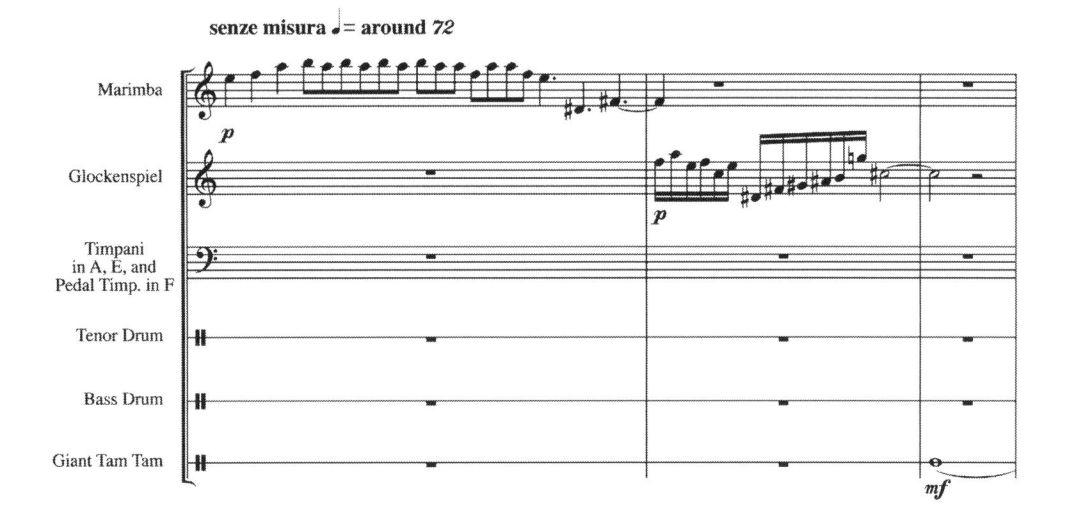

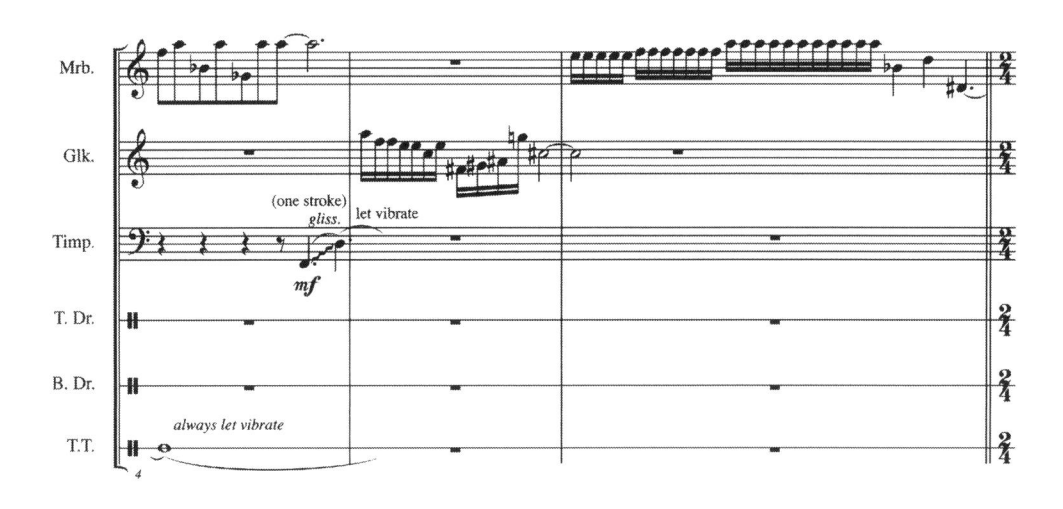

286 THE PERCUSSION FAMILY

Copyright © 1957 by C.F. Peters. Used by permission of C.F. Peters Corporation.

RJ Miller, *Yellowstone*, mm. 165–181.

288 THE PERCUSSION FAMILY

THE PERCUSSION FAMILY

Copyright © 2001 by Appassionata Music. Used by permission.

SUGGESTED EXERCISES

Scoring Exercise for Membranophones and Idiophones

Using the information and guidelines presented in this chapter and in Chapter 3 (Practical Problem Solving), create a work for percussion ensemble (consisting of membranophones and idiophones), using the following sequence of rudiments.

RJ Miller, *Cadence #1*, mm. 1–12.

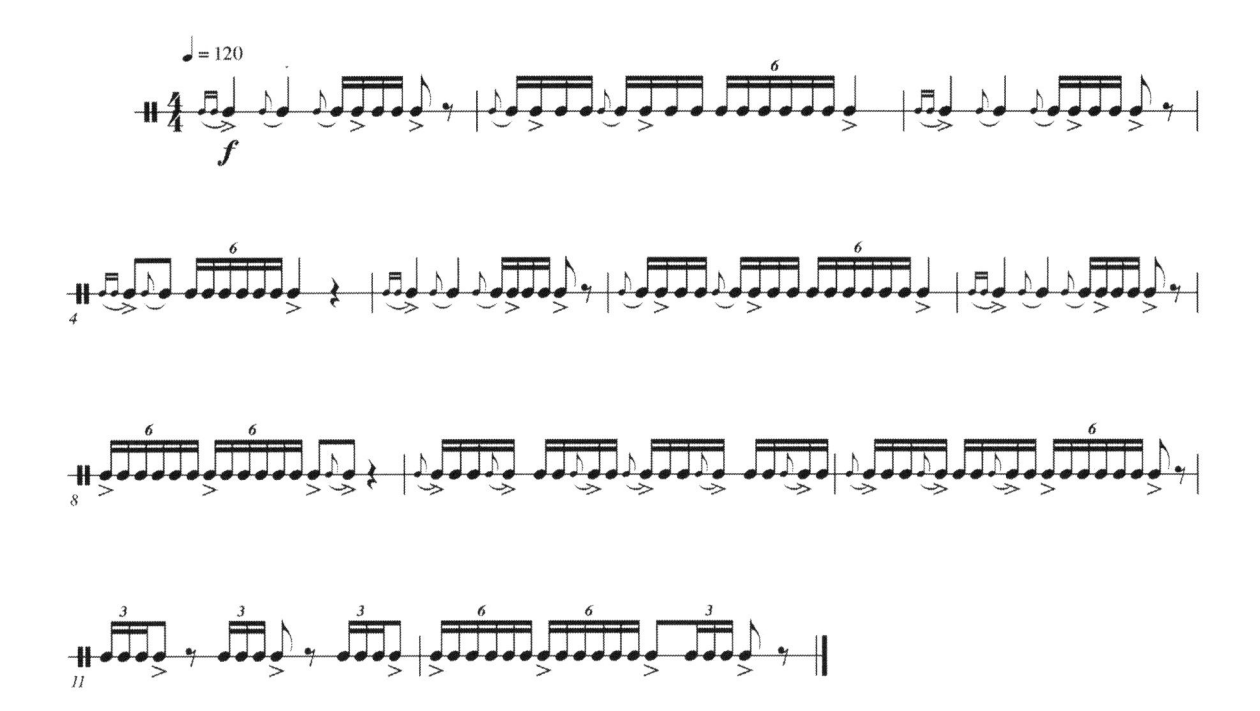

Copyright © 2008 by Appassionata Music. Used by permission.

Scoring Exercise for Mallet Instruments

Using the information and guidelines presented in this chapter and in Chapter 3 (Practical Problem Solving), orchestrate the following example for any combination of mallet instruments. Perform a harmonic analysis and seek ways to add textural interest.

RJ Miller, *Your Heart's Desire*, mm. 1–69.

292 THE PERCUSSION FAMILY

Copyright © 2001 by Appassionata Music. Used by permission.

8
VOICES

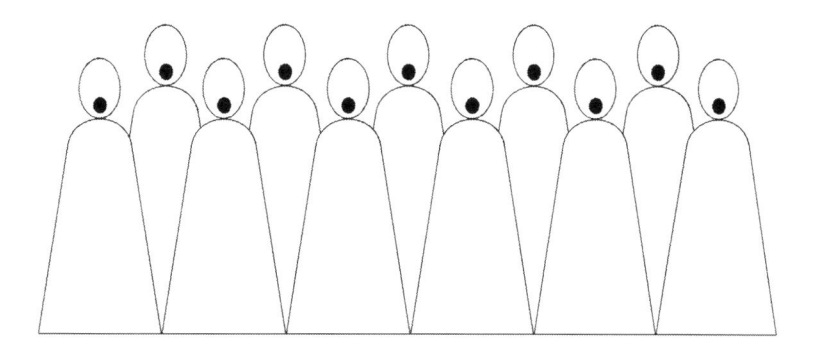

The human voice is an intensely personal instrument. Range, register and timbre vary significantly from person to person, even between singers of the same vocal classification. One must also exercise caution with young voices as the vocal chords can be damaged by over-exertion and the use of heavy mechanisms too high in the range.

THE ESSENTIALS

Vocal Notation

Notating vocal music is slightly different from notating instrumental music. In vocal parts all expression marks (dynamics, *rit.*, *accel.*, *cresc.*, *decresc.*, etc.) go above the staff to accommodate the placement of the lyrics below the staff. Traditionally, if a syllable is sung on a singular note, that note is not beamed. If a syllable is sustained through notes of different pitches (as in a melisma), the notes are beamed as in instrumental music. The contemporary practice is to beam all notes in the same manner as instrumental music. Either practice is acceptable in the professional world.

Horizontal note spacing in instrumental music is determined by the rhythmic content. Horizontal note spacing in vocal music is determined by the lyrics. Notes are spaced in such a manner as to avoid collision, crowding or confusion in the lyrics.

Robert Franz, Wolfgang Müller, *Widmung*, mm. 1–8.

Traditional Notation

Contemporary Notation

Vocal Ranges

Adult Vocal Ranges and Registers

When scoring for a specific (known) vocalist, one may write in extended registers as determined by the vocalist's capabilities. However, when scoring for a chorus, use of generic ranges for the respective vocal classifications will yield the most pleasing and performable result.

The extended ranges should be used in moderation (even under the most favorable circumstances). Use of these registers must be of limited duration and should be reserved only for climactic selections. Prolonged singing in extremely high or low tessitura will overtax the voices and can be damaging to younger voices.

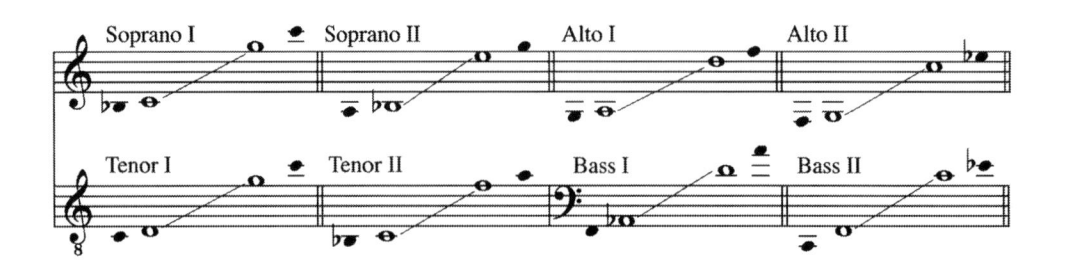

When writing unison sections, limited use of the extended ranges is acceptable in the downward direction for Soprano and Tenor, and the upward direction for Alto and Bass. However, one should rely upon the voices that are still in their comfortable ranges to maintain the volume of these sections and these sections should not be prolonged.

Adolescent Voices

Adolescent voices present unique problems. During these formative years young voices change significantly, sometimes from day to day. Ranges, tone quality and tessitura are often unreliable and frequently inconsistent. The ability to transition from chest voice to head voice is in its developmental phase, and unreliable at best. When scoring for an ensemble of adolescent voices it is wise to avoid the extremes of the ranges (especially on the high end of the range). Being conservative with one scoring is the best approach.

Children's Vocal Ranges

Most child vocalists, both male and female, under the age of 11 years old are sopranos (with a limited useful range, tessitura, and dynamic contrast). At approximately age 11 some children will be able to sing in the alto range. A specific child may be able to exceed the ranges/tessitura listed below, but one should not expect a group of children to do so. One should write simplistically for a children's choir. As a general rule, one should avoid writing more than one or two vocal lines. Keep the accompaniment simple and make it easy for the children to find reference pitches in the accompaniment (it is often advisable to place the melody in the accompaniment part to aid this process).

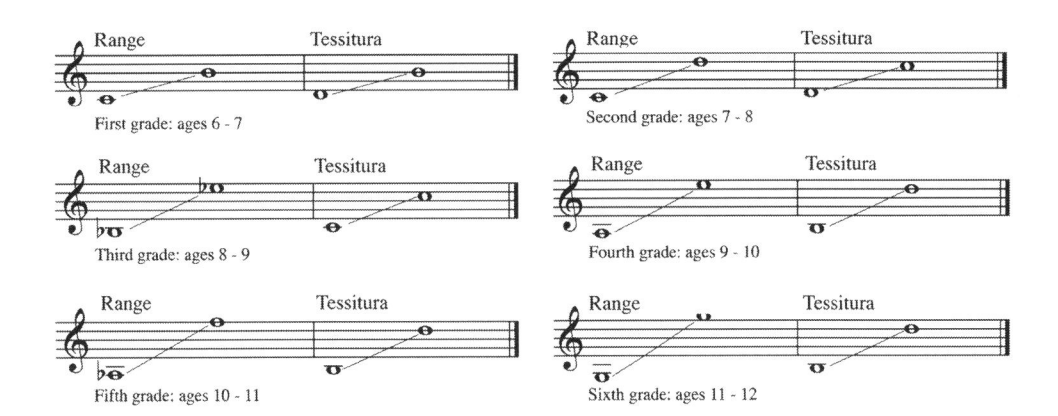

Vowel Considerations

Certain vowels are quite difficult to sing (without modifying the vowel sound). In female voices (and children's voices the following "closed" vowel sounds are problematic in the higher range:

ee as in bee
e as in red
i as in ring
ay as in may

With the exception of *ee* (as in bee) male voices do not have difficulty with "closed" vowels in the upper register. However, male voices have difficulty with "open" vowel sounds in the higher range. The following vowel sounds will require modification in the upper register:

a as is psalm
o as in bow
oo as in soon
aw as in law

Difficult Intervals

Certain intervals are quite difficult to sing and should be avoided (if possible), particularly when writing for young or inexperienced groups. The most perilous intervals are augmented seconds (both ascending and descending), ascending augmented fourths, descending diminished fifths, and any interval in excess of an octave.

Voicings

Since, in classical music, continued use of either closed or open voicing tends to result in stylist monotony, the free interchange between the two (mixed voicings) is highly recommended, except when a monochromatic effect is desired.

Close Voicing

Close voicing is the spacing of the three upper voices within an octave:

Open Voicing

Open voicing is spacing of the three upper voices so that they span an interval greater than an octave:

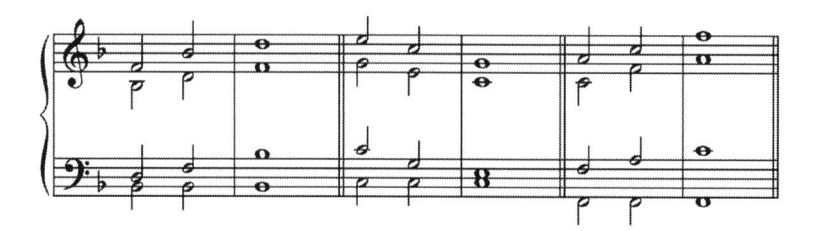

Mixed Voicing

Mixed voicing is the technique of spacing the upper three voices so that they contain an interchange between closed voicing and open voicing.

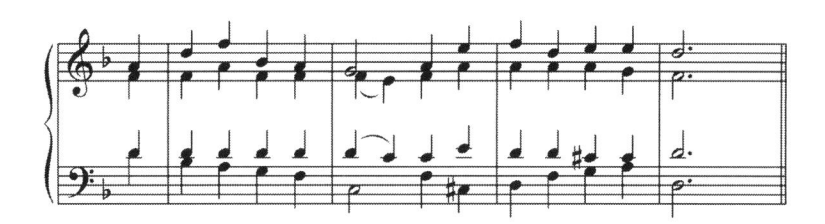

PRACTICAL CONSIDERATIONS

Practical Guidelines when Scoring for Adult Voices

- Range and tessitura
- Phrases—(length/shape)
- Level of difficulty
- Vowels (vocal formants—male and female being treated differently)
- Durations

Practical Guidelines when Scoring for Adolescent Voices

- Unusual useful range and tessitura
- Vocal quality
- Problems with register transition
- Avoid use of heavy mechanism too high in the range

Practical Guidelines when Scoring for Children's Voices

- Limited useful range
- Use stepwise melodic lines
- Limited breathing capacity
- Limited length of note duration
- Limited dynamic contrast
- Write clearly and simplistically for the voices
- Keep the accompaniment simple

THE ENSEMBLES

Unaccompanied Choir

When scoring for unaccompanied choir, careful attention must be paid to the harmonic balance and voice-leading on every note on every chord. One should strive for a homogeneous blend within the ensemble by scoring voices in comfortable ranges. Reserve scoring extreme registers for climatic sections or section where specific effect is desired. An interchange between open and closed voicings, and the use of passing tones and counterpoint add interest to the orchestration. Dynamic variation and melodic interplay between sections are useful tools to create variances in texture.

Choir with Keyboard Accompaniment

Scoring a choir with keyboard accompaniment (or small ensemble accompaniment, such as string quartet, brass quintet, etc.) offers greater flexibility in scoring techniques than choir alone. When combined with other instruments, the choir is no longer the sole source of harmonic content. This allows for a variety of possible scoring approaches. The accompaniment can serve a supportive role, function as an independent element, alternate between supportive and independent, or combine supportive and independent elements.

Choir with Orchestra (or Wind Ensemble)

When scoring for choir and orchestra (or wind ensemble) the options are extensive. However, in every instance one must strive to maintain a functional balance between the choir and instrumental ensemble. Large brass sections (as well as large percussion sections) are capable of very powerful dynamics that can easily overpower the choir. Though the choir may still be heard in combination with loud brass and percussion passages, it becomes an added texture rather than the featured timbre. Lyrics often become unintelligible in this context. A choir needs to contain two to three times the personnel of the orchestra to maintain balance with the orchestra in fortissimo passages.

The use of colla voce can be very useful in the combined choral/instrumental ensemble. Doubling the vocal lines in the string section or woodwind section (or both), in unison or at the octave, is a long accepted practice. This type of colla voce not only supports and reinforces the vocal lines, but also may give the illusion of a larger, more homogeneous choir. Brass can certainly be used for this purpose as well. However, a combination of brass and woodwinds, or brass, woodwind, and strings yield a more desirable result. Again, one must exercise caution with dynamics when using brass as colla voce parts.

The choir may also be used as a self-contained orchestral section (sans colla voce). One may alternate choral passages with instrumental passages. One may use the choir to accompany instrumental soloists (usually oos, ahs, or humming).

Special vocal effects, such as whispering, Sprechstimme, laughing, whistling, glissandi, sighing, scat syllables, etc., are all useful additions to the textural palette. One should not shy from using any functional (non-damaging) vocal effect if it serves the desired result.

IN THE PROFESSION

Professional vocalists will attempt to sing what is written, and generally this is not a problem with the outer voices (soprano and bass). However, inappropriate and illogical voice-leading within the inner parts often complicates their efforts. Scoring in a comfortable tessitura for all parts, with well-written voice-leading, aids greatly in the rehearsal (and performance) process. While professional vocalists will quickly become frustrated with ineptly penned vocal lines, they will appreciate competently written parts. When the vocalist is not concerned about the parts, they are free to devote more effort to interpretation.

BUILDING THE SCORE

This example will demonstrate the process for creating a vocal ensemble work from a traditional song. As always, one begins the process by performing a harmonic analysis. This analysis will determine the harmonic content and context. These elements are decisive factors when determining the deletion or addition of harmonic elements.

For the purposes of the exercise the following selection will be used:

Traditional, *Auld Lang Syne*.

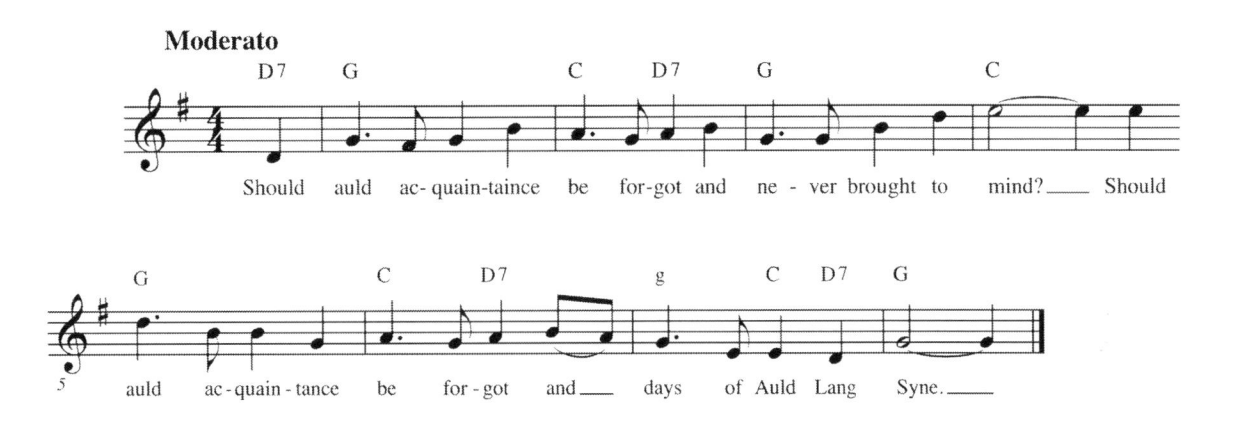

Upon completion of the analysis, one decides the manner in which the selection is to be scored. Since classical-style scoring is appropriate in a variety of situations, one occasionally wishes to create a less traditional rendition by borrowing techniques from other genres. For this particular example, the vocals (scored in five parts) will be voiced in a manner often used in jazz and contemporary arrangements. This technique is referred to as "drop 2" scoring. Every chord has an additional "color tone" to add dissonance, and every passing tone becomes a passing chord. The original chord progress is often modified and parallel intervals are not only acceptable, but required in this style. The melody is placed in the soprano and doubled (parallel octaves) in the baritone. The chord member that would traditionally appear next below the soprano is placed octavo basso in the bass part. The remaining two chord members are placed between the soprano and the baritone. There are no triads in this style, and at no time do the voices cross.

Moderato
D7 G6 Em7 C6 D7 D6 G6 C6
Soprano
Alto
Tenor 1
Baritone
Bass
Should auld ac-quain-taince be for-got and ne - ver brought to mind? Should
G6 Em7 C6 D7 B6 Em7 C6 D7 G6
S
A
T 1
Bar
Bs
auld ac-quain-tance be for-got and days of Auld Lang Syne.

SCORING EXAMPLES

Scoring Examples for Adult Choir

Dimitri Bortnianski, *Cherubic Hymn*, mm. 1–38.

Copyright © 1977 by Hinshaw Music, Inc., edited by Ray Robinson and available from Hinshaw Music, Inc. (www.hinshawmusic.com) as HMC323. Used by permission of Hinshaw Music, Inc.

Scoring Examples for Choir and Orchestra

Ludwig van Beethoven, *Gloria*, **from Mass in C, Op. 86, mm. 1–28.**

VOICES

16
Fl.
Ob.
C Cl.
Bsn.
Hn.
C Tpt.
Timp.
S
A
T
B
De - - - - - - o,
Et in ter - ra pax, pax ho -
Vln. I
Vln. II
Vla.
Vc.
Cb.
p
pizz.
6

24
Fl.
Ob.
C Cl.
Bsn.
24
Hn.
C Tpt.
24
Timp.
24
S
mi - ni-bus bo - næ vo - lun - ta - - - tis, bo - næ
A
mi - ni-bus bo - næ vo - lun - ta - - - tis,
T
mi - ni-bus bo - næ vo - lun - ta - - - tis,
B
mi - ni-bus bo - næ vo - lun - ta - - - tis,
24
arco
Vln. I
f
arco
Vln. II
arco
Vla.
arco
Vc.
arco
Cb.

Scoring Example for Children's Choir

RJ Miller, *Good Tidings.*

Copyright © 2008 by Appassionata Music. Used by permission.

SUGGESTED EXERCISE

Using the information and guidelines presented in this chapter and in Chapter 3 (Practical Problem Solving), adapt and enhance the following selection for an SSAATTBB choir. Since there are multiple layers suggested in the score, one may wish to approach the work by scoring it for two antiphonal choirs.

Edward MacDowell, *The Brook*

15
on, runs on, runs on, runs
14 on,
runs on, runs on, runs
lost in the
rit. on, 20
on From steam - let to riv - er Till lost in the
rit.
19 on
o - cean, Dream-ing of love, of strife, of de-vo-tion. So runs our life,
o - cean. So runs our life, runs our life,
24
ends our life of e - mo - tion.
Ends our life of e - mo - tion, so ends our life of e - mo - tion.
Ends our life,
29
Ends our life of e - mo - tion.

Ah! Ah! Ah!
So runs our life, Ends our life of e-mo-tion,
Ah! Ah!
34
Ah! Ah!
So ends our life.
Ah!
40
Ah!

9
PEDAL HARP

The standard harp used in the orchestral setting is the double-action pedal harp (also known as the concert grand pedal harp, pedal harp, or concert harp). In an orchestral score, in discussions of orchestration, and in practical application, the instrument is simply designated as the harp.

THE ESSENTIALS

Standard concert harps have 47 strings (though a 46-string version is also produced) spanning a range from C_1 (D_1 on the 46-string harp) to g''''.

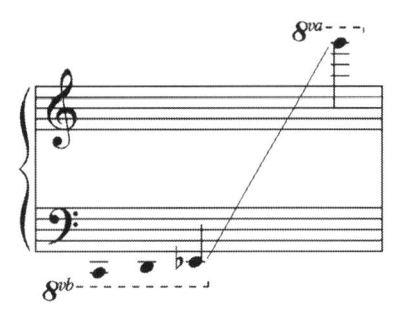

Harps are tuned diatonically in C major. To provide visual references for the harpist, the C-strings are red and the F-strings are dark blue or black. The lowest strings (C1 to G) are wire-wrapped strings; the middle strings (A to e''') are gut strings or an appropriate synthetic equivalent and highest strings (f'''' to g'''') are nylon. Each of these materials provides a unique timbre to the register in which it is used.

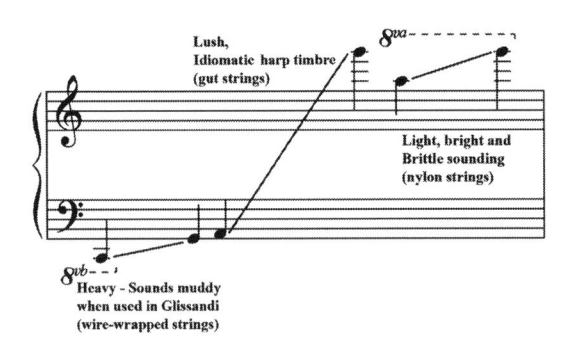

The Grand Staff

Harp parts are written on a grand staff with (generally) the upper staff designating the part to be played by the right hand and the lower staff designating the part to be played by the left hand.

Jules Massenet, *Last Dream of the Virgin*, Prelude, mm. 59–64 (adapted for harp by RJ Miller).

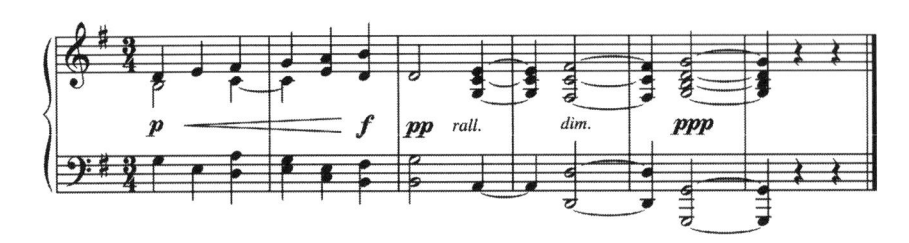

On occasions, when all notes are placed upon the same staff, one should indicate those played by the left hand with stems down, and those played by the right hand with stems up.

Playing Position and Range of Hands

In the proper playing position the harpist is seated with the instrument resting against the right shoulder. One must be aware that in this position (with the right arm wrapped around the instrument) the harpist's right hand cannot reach the lower strings of the instrument. While the exact reach of the right hand is dependent upon the physique of the player, the left hand is capable of reaching the entire range of the instrument.

Only four fingers on each hand are used when playing the harp. The thumb is designated as "1," the index finger as "2," the middle finger as "3," and the ring finger as "4." Because the little finger is shorter than the fourth finger and has movement coupled to that of the fourth finger, it is not used to pluck the strings. For notes plucked simultaneously with one hand, a 10th is the maximum acceptable interval between thumb and fourth finger (this may be a major or minor 10th depending upon the pedal positions).

One must not write for the harp as one would for the piano, as they are vastly different instruments. The "eight-finger" technique of the harp is quite dissimilar to the "ten-finger" technique of the piano, and when combined with the fact that on the harp the hands play on opposing sides of the strings, versus the horizontal plane of the piano keys, one must approach each instrument with scoring techniques independent of the other.

Since harpists employ a "four-finger" technique in each hand, passages easily performed with the "five-finger" technique of pianists become problematic, especially at faster tempi.

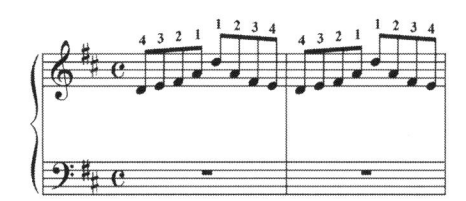

Awkward and impractical at fast tempi

One may often find a suitable solution by incorporating the left hand into the passage, as follows:

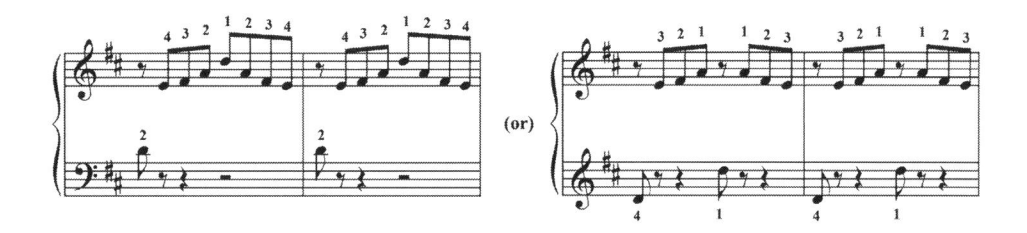

Additionally, one must often take vastly different approaches in notation to accomplish similar results.

Pedals

Concert harps have seven pedals, one for each note of the C diatonic scale. These pedals are attached mechanically to discs at the top of the strings that are used to chromatically alter the pitch of the strings. By changing the position of a given pedal, tension on the string is either increased or decreased, thereby altering the pitch of the string. Changing the position of a pedal affects all octaves of the note controlled by the pedal (i.e. changing the position of the F-pedal alters the pitch of all the F-strings on the instrument).

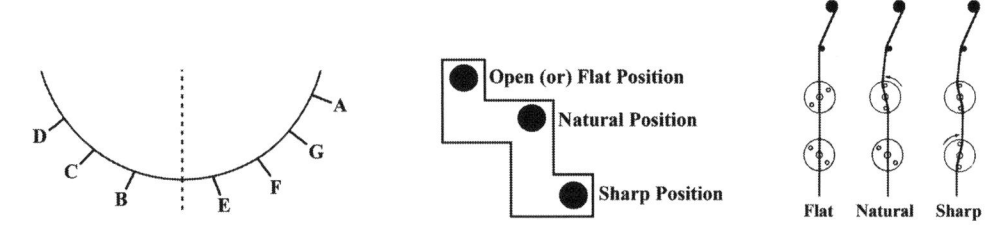

Pedals in flat (open) position   **Pedals in natural position**   **Pedals in sharp position**

Note: The C_1, D_1, and g'''' strings are not connected to the pedals, have no mechanism, and therefore cannot be chromatically altered during a performance. If desired, one may designate these strings to be pre-tuned to alternate pitches (one should restrict oneself to only a semitone deviation from the standard tuning).

Pedal Diagrams

Pedal diagrams are visual representations of the pedal positions and are very useful tools for composers and orchestrators. One should use pedal diagrams as a guide to ensure one is adhering to the enharmonic nature of the instrument, and to track necessary pedal changes needed to accommodate the part.

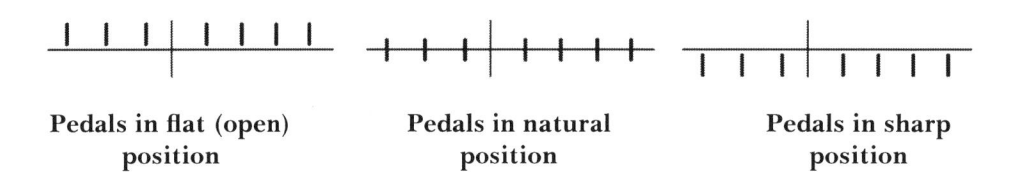

Pedals in flat (open) position   **Pedals in natural position**   **Pedals in sharp position**

While not required and not even necessary, it is acceptable to place pedal markings or diagrams in one's score. However, *do not place pedal diagrams in the harp part*. If one is utilizing music notation software to create the score, one should delete all pedal diagrams from the harp part, once the part has been extracted from the score. Most professional harpists find the placement of pedal diagrams in their part *offensive* and akin to writing fingerings under the notes in a clarinet part. It is simply not done.

Pedal Changes

One must allow a sufficient amount of time to execute a pedal change. Failure to do so can result in extraneous sounds, such as an undesirable portamento between notes. Pedal changes where the pedal is being depressed (from flat to natural to sharp) can be executed quicker than pedal changes where the pedal is being released (sharp to natural to flat). In general, it takes approximately one second to execute a pedal change (two pedals can be changed simultaneously if one is controlled by the left foot and one by the right). Therefore, the number of beats required to make a pedal change is dependent upon the tempo of the work. For example, one should allow a minimum of two seconds to execute the following pedal change.

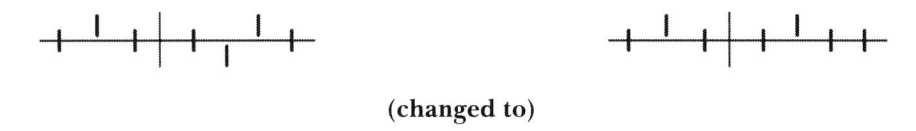

(changed to)

Enharmonics

Since the harp does not function like other chromatic instruments (never having all chromatic possibilities available at any given time), the composer and orchestrator must become accustomed to writing pitches enharmonically for the harp. As an equal temperament instrument, it matters little to the harpist if a pitch is notated as E♭ or as D♯. However, such a designation may be critical to accommodate the pedal configuration necessary to execute a passage.

By appropriately configuring the pedals, the harp is capable of producing most pitches enharmonically (the exceptions being D♮, G♮ and A♮). By "re-spelling" (harpist's term) enharmonically, one can transform a seemly unplayable or impractical passage into one that is easily performed.

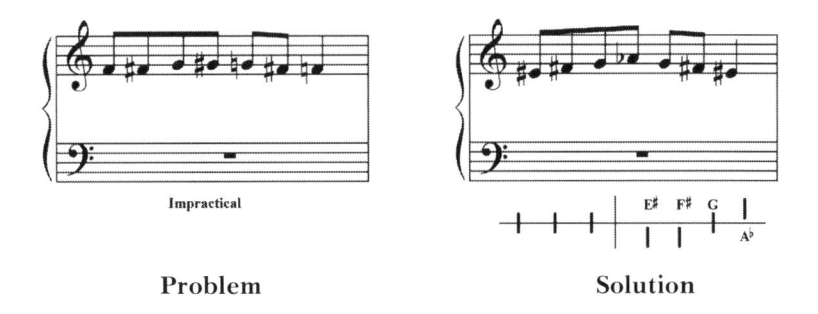

Problem   **Solution**

Arpeggios

Chords of three or more notes are typically arpeggiated on the harp. As such, it is not necessary to write the arpeggio marking in the part for chords. Harpists will arpeggiate the chord by default. The traditional method for playing chords is to slightly anticipate the beat upon which the chord is written, quickly arpeggiating the chord from its lowest note to its highest, with the highest note occurring on the designated beat. Since a chord will be arpeggiated by default, one must designate a non-arpeggiated chord by bracketing the chord.

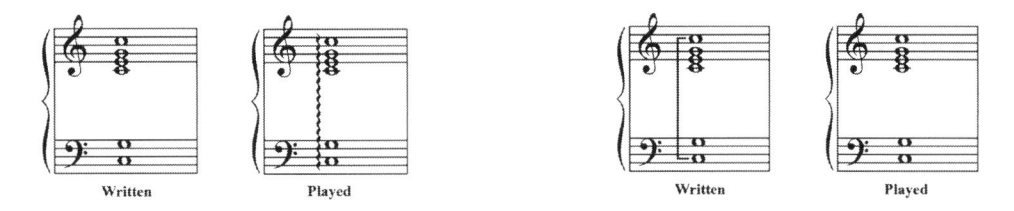

Arpeggios can also be designated as ascending arpeggios or descending arpeggios by adding a directional arrow to the appropriate end of an arpeggio mark.

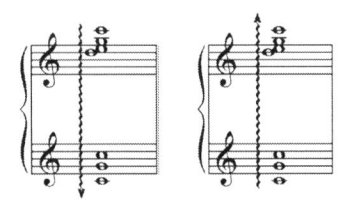

To indicate a passage of continuous arpeggiation, place *sempre arp.* where the continuous arpeggiation begins. To terminate the continuous apreggiation, place *non arp.* in the part, or bracket the non-arpeggiated chord.

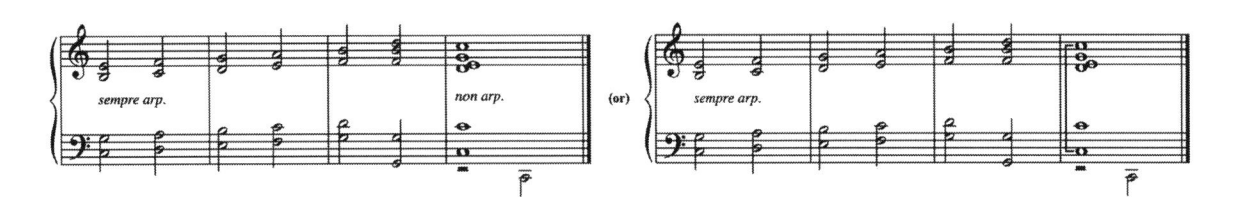

Arpeggios can be executed quite quickly when both hands are utilized (in an alternating manner). However, in the case where one has scored an arpeggio in one hand and a written line in the other, the arpeggio will be executed considerably more slowly.

Sustain

Harps are not equipped with dampening devices. Therefore, once plucked, a string will continue to vibrate for durations proportional to its length. Strings of the lowest octave will continue to vibrate for 20 seconds or more. Strings in the highest octave will have virtually no useful sustain.

The harpist must dampen the strings manually. This is accomplished by placing the open hand (and sometimes forearm) against the vibrating strings. A string will also cease to vibrate when the harpist places a finger on it to initiate another note. One must be cognizant of this sustain, especially with calculating pedal changes within a passage. An undampened, sustaining string that is affected by a pedal change will result in an undesired portamento.

Glissandi

The harp glissando is one of the most useful, idiomatic and iconic effects available to the orchestrator. While glissandi can certainly be constructed from scales, the most effective glissandi are built from chords. Using a glissando as a lead-in to the climatic point in an orchestration adds a sense of arrival not achievable by other instruments. A glissando on the penultimate chord, leading in the final cadence, provides a sense of finality. Passages of continuous glissandi, such as in Tchaikovsky's *Nutcracker*, create an ethereal effect possible only on the harp.

There are a number of ways to notate glissandi. For a single glissando, in an orchestral setting, one should notate the first octave of the glissando, followed by a line leading to the note ending the glissando, and abbreviation, *gliss.* should be included. Another (but somewhat less favorable) option is to provide the beginning and ending notes of the glissando, a line leading from one to the other, the abbreviation, *gliss.* and the appropriate pedal diagram. For recording-studio applications, provide the beginning and ending notes of the glissando, a line leading from one to the other, the abbreviation *gliss.* and the applicable chord symbol (the harpist will determine the most appropriate pedal configuration).

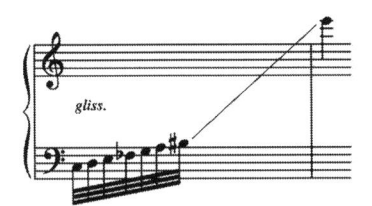

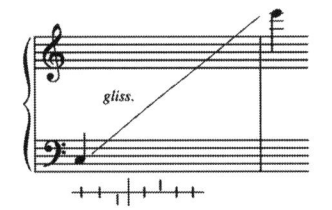

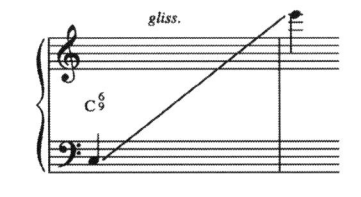

Using similar techniques, one can designate specific glissandi for each hand.

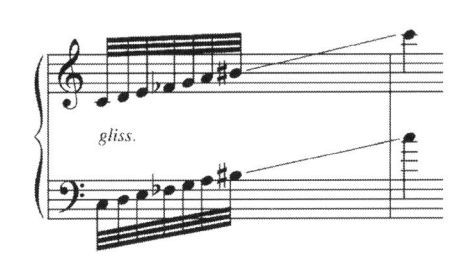

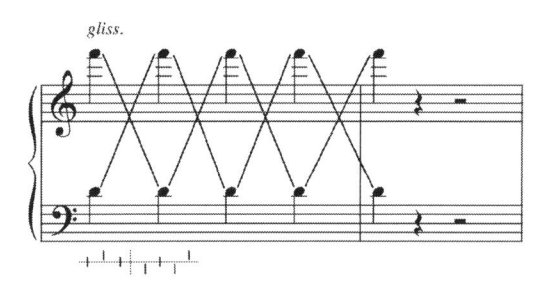

Ad lib. glissandi are lush, full, two-handed glissandi, usually designated by the use of a graphic representation and the abbreviation *gliss. ad lib.*

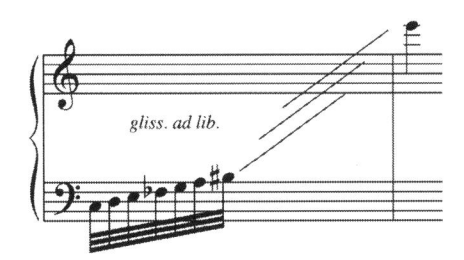

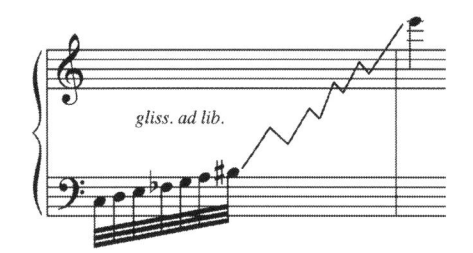

Repeated Notes

Rapidly repeating notes on a single string are difficult to execute, and result in a less than optimum sound. One can improve the effect by utilizing an enharmonic equivalent and alternately plucking those strings with fingers on opposing hands.

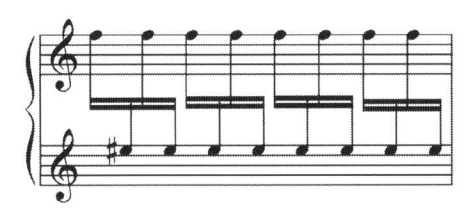

Harmonics

Harmonics of a 2:1 ratio (at the octave) are the most resonant and the easiest to produce on the harp, resulting in a clear and bell-like tone. While other natural harmonics are technically possible, they are more difficult to achieve and lack useful resonance. As such, the octave harmonic (2:1) is the default harmonic.

Harp harmonics are notated on the string upon which they are played (not at the resultant pitch).

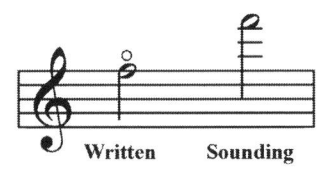

Pedal Diagrams: C

Standard Scales:

C Major

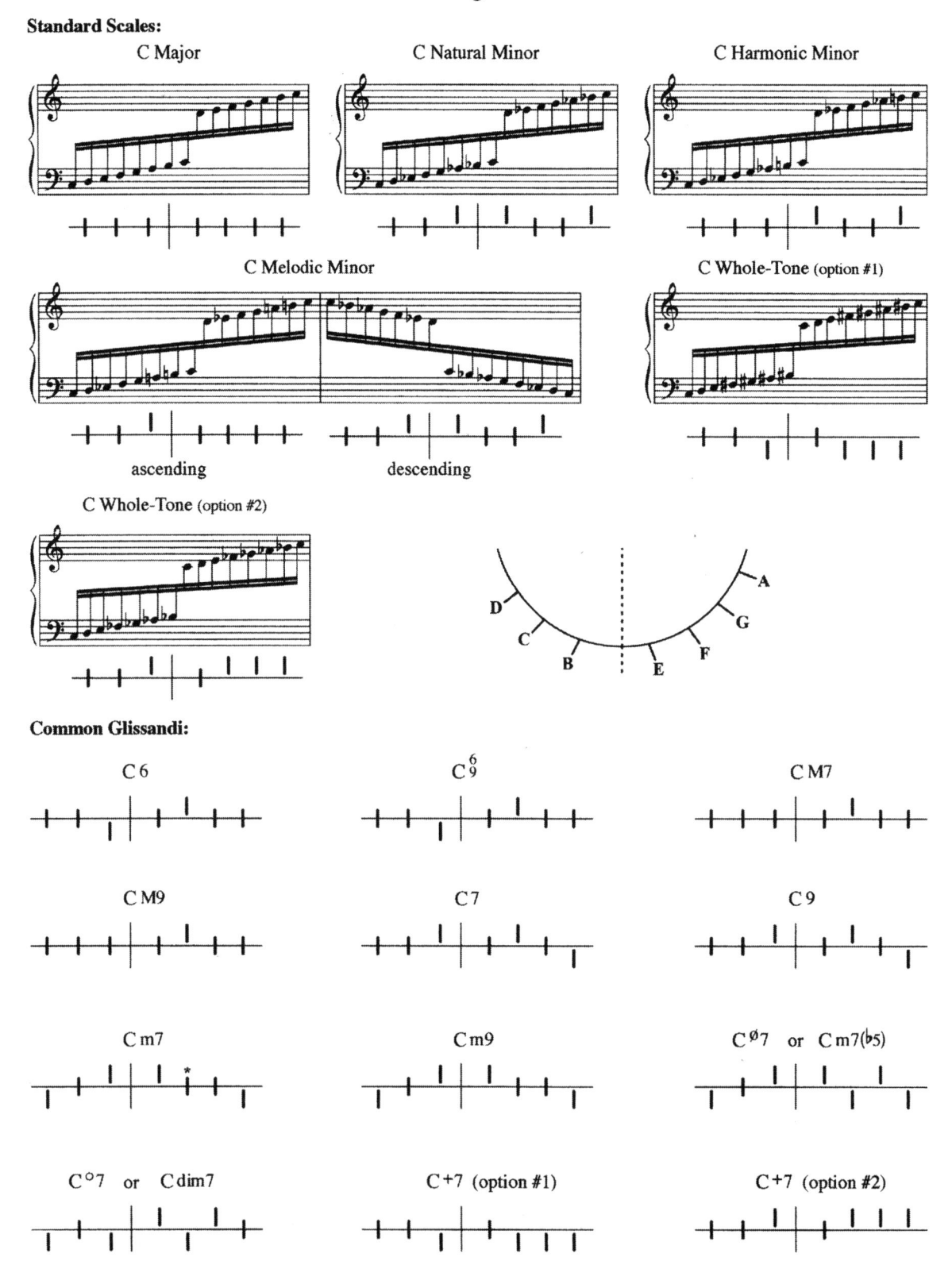

C Natural Minor

C Harmonic Minor

C Melodic Minor (ascending / descending)

C Whole-Tone (option #1)

C Whole-Tone (option #2)

Common Glissandi:

C 6

C $^6_9$

C M7

C M9

C 7

C 9

C m7

C m9

C ^{ø}7 or C m7($\flat$5)

C $^{°}$7 or C dim7

C +7 (option #1)

C +7 (option #2)

Pedal Diagrams: C-sharp/D-flat

Standard Scales:

D-flat Major

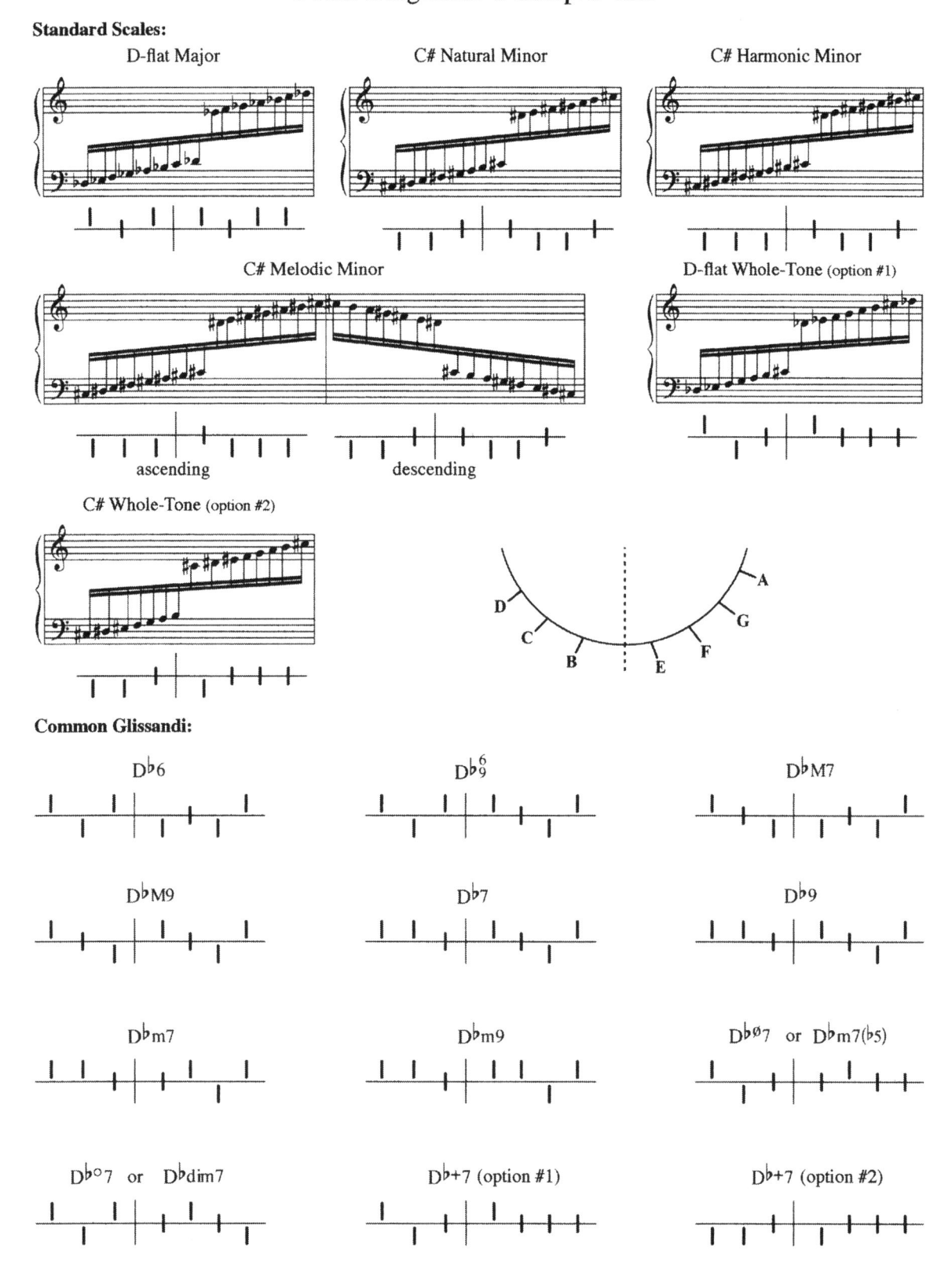

C# Natural Minor

C# Harmonic Minor

C# Melodic Minor

D-flat Whole-Tone (option #1)

ascending   descending

C# Whole-Tone (option #2)

Common Glissandi:

$D\flat 6$

$D\flat{}^6_9$

$D\flat M7$

$D\flat M9$

$D\flat 7$

$D\flat 9$

$D\flat m7$

$D\flat m9$

$D\flat \o 7$ or $D\flat m7(\flat 5)$

$D\flat {}^\circ 7$ or $D\flat \text{dim}7$

$D\flat +7$ (option #1)

$D\flat +7$ (option #2)

Pedal Diagrams: D

Standard Scales:

D Major

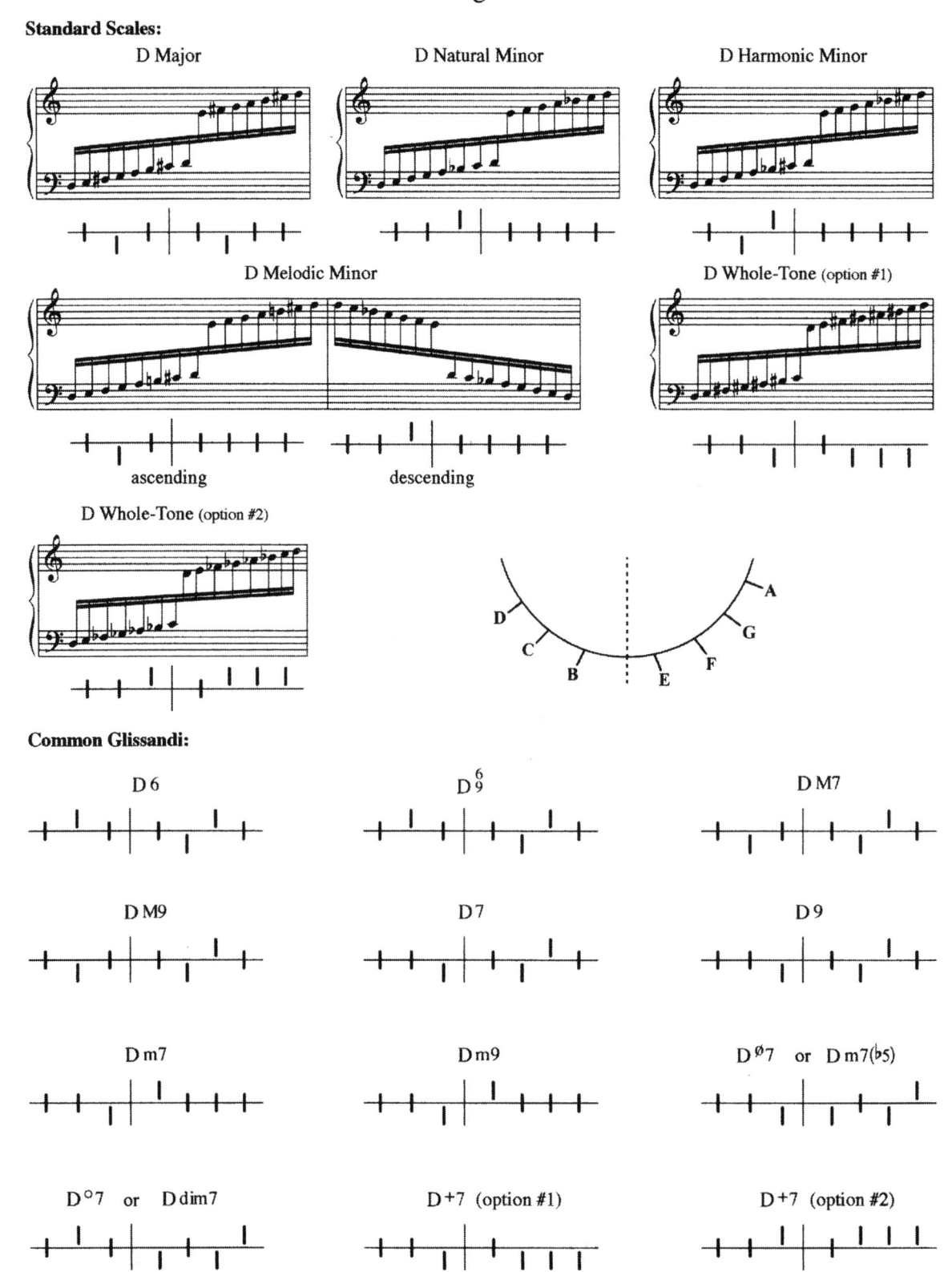

D Natural Minor

D Harmonic Minor

D Melodic Minor (ascending / descending)

D Whole-Tone (option #1)

D Whole-Tone (option #2)

Common Glissandi:

D 6

D 6/9

D M7

D M9

D 7

D 9

D m7

D m9

D ø7 or D m7(♭5)

D °7 or D dim7

D +7 (option #1)

D +7 (option #2)

Pedal Diagrams: D-sharp/E-flat

Standard Scales:

E-flat Major

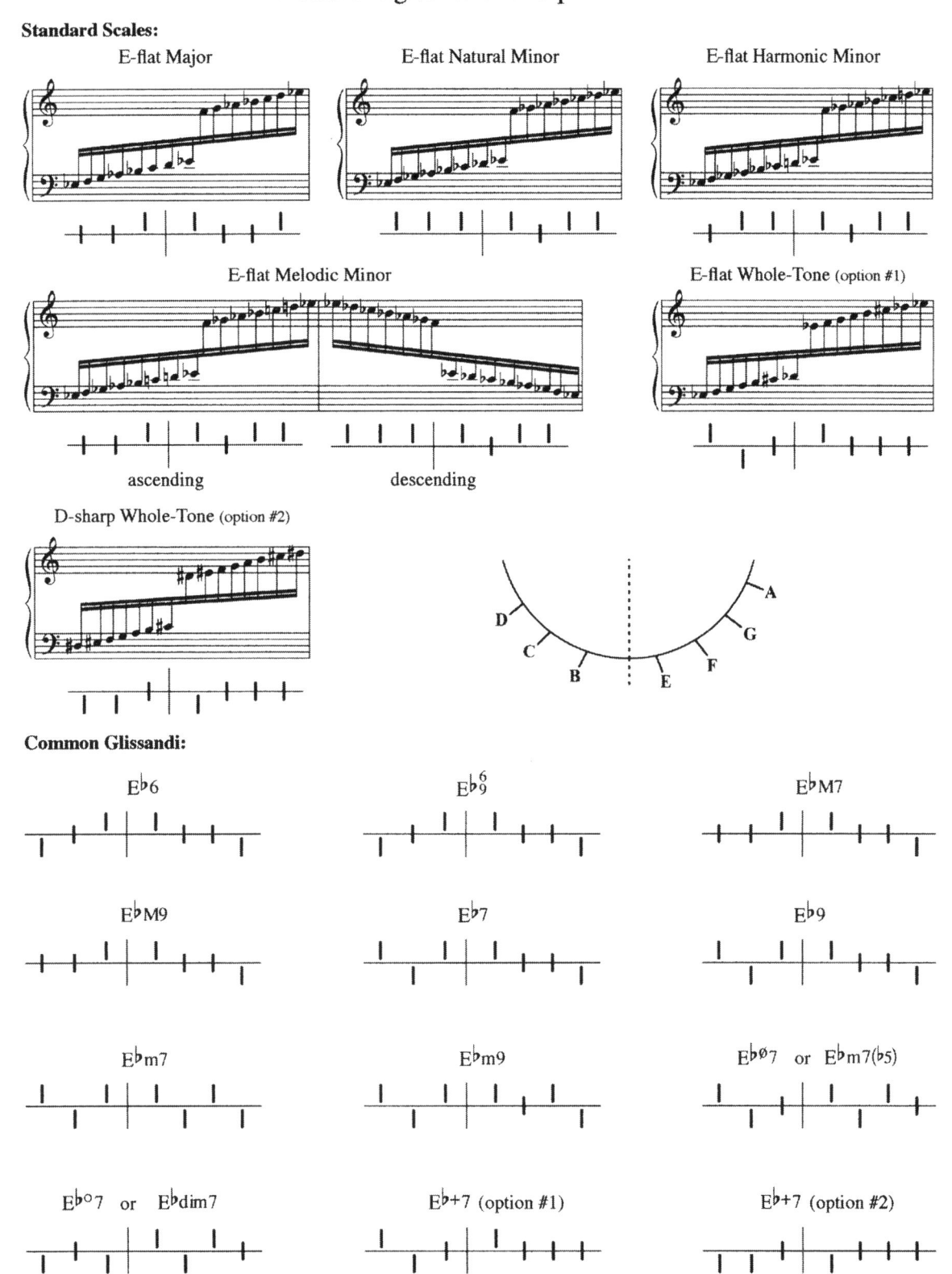

E-flat Natural Minor

E-flat Harmonic Minor

E-flat Melodic Minor

ascending   descending

E-flat Whole-Tone (option #1)

D-sharp Whole-Tone (option #2)

Common Glissandi:

$E\flat 6$

$E\flat {}^6_9$

$E\flat M7$

$E\flat M9$

$E\flat 7$

$E\flat 9$

$E\flat m7$

$E\flat m9$

$E\flat \varnothing 7$ or $E\flat m7(\flat 5)$

$E\flat °7$ or $E\flat dim7$

$E\flat +7$ (option #1)

$E\flat +7$ (option #2)

Pedal Diagrams: E

Standard Scales:

E Major

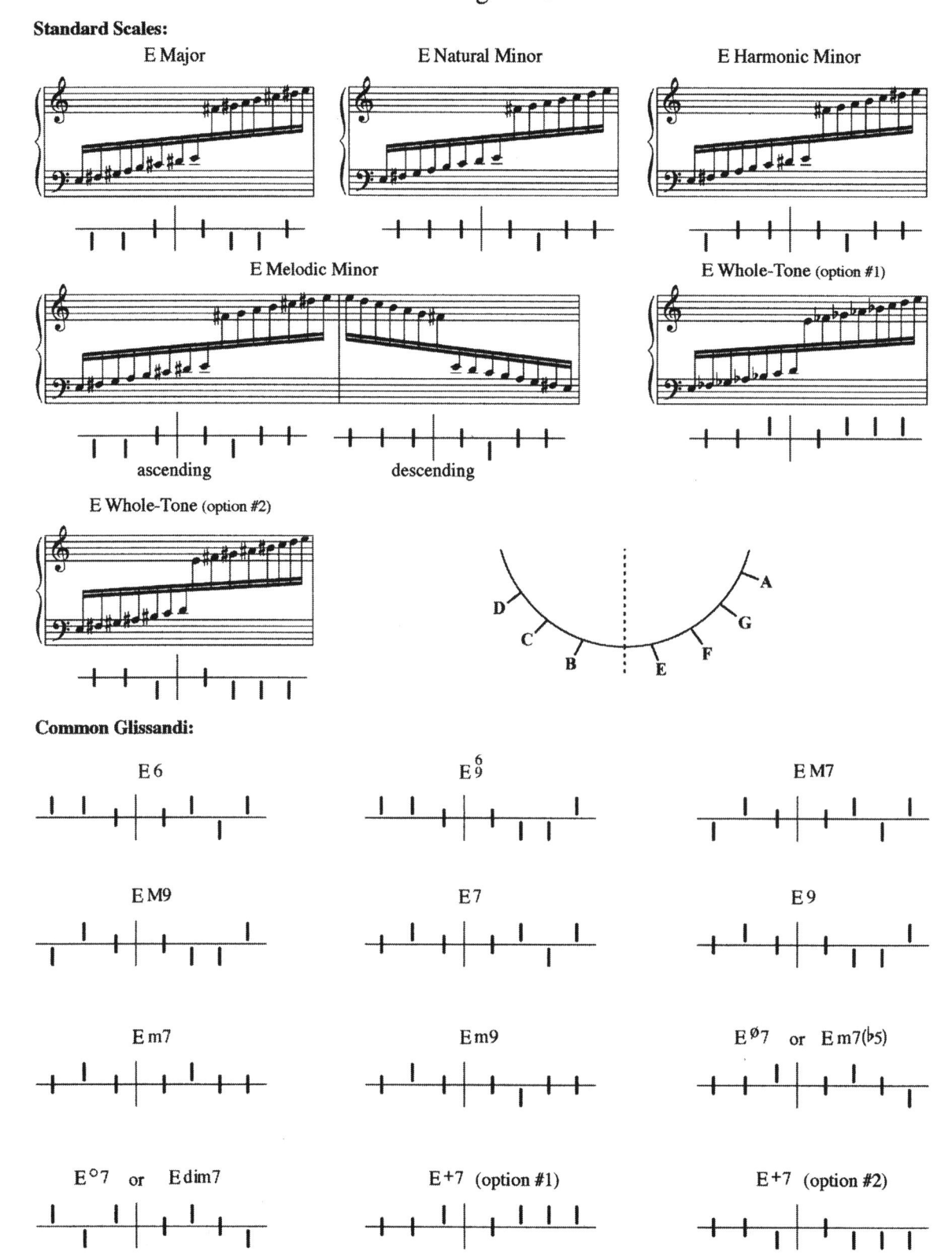

E Natural Minor

E Harmonic Minor

E Melodic Minor (ascending / descending)

E Whole-Tone (option #1)

E Whole-Tone (option #2)

Common Glissandi:

E6

E 6/9

E M7

E M9

E7

E9

E m7

E m9

E ø7 or E m7(♭5)

E °7 or E dim7

E +7 (option #1)

E +7 (option #2)

Pedal Diagrams: F

Standard Scales:

F Major

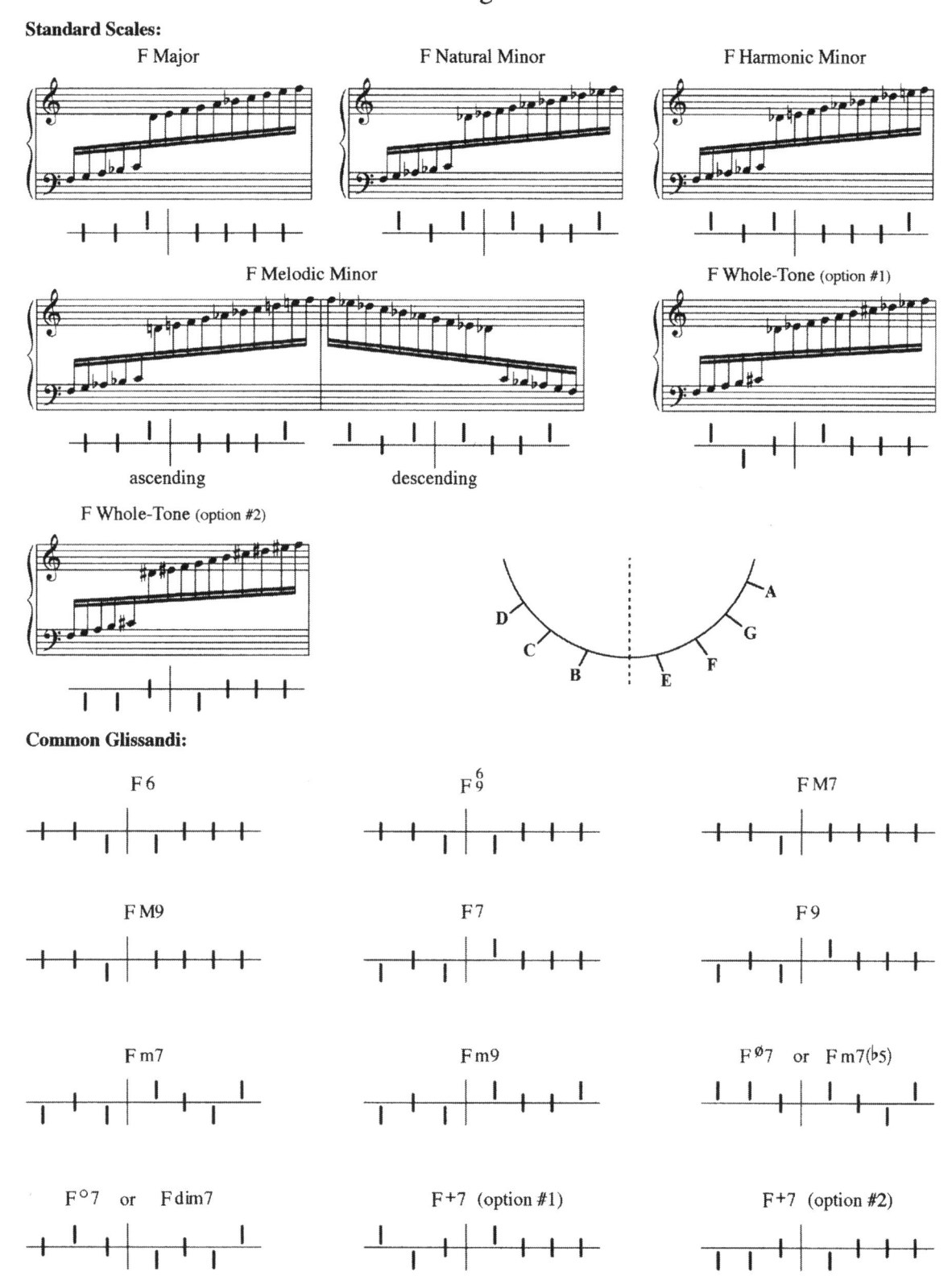

F Natural Minor

F Harmonic Minor

F Melodic Minor

F Whole-Tone (option #1)

F Whole-Tone (option #2)

Common Glissandi:

F 6

F $^6_9$

F M7

F M9

F 7

F 9

F m7

F m9

F ø7 or F m7(♭5)

F °7 or F dim7

F +7 (option #1)

F +7 (option #2)

Pedal Diagrams: F-sharp/G-flat

Standard Scales:

F-sharp Major

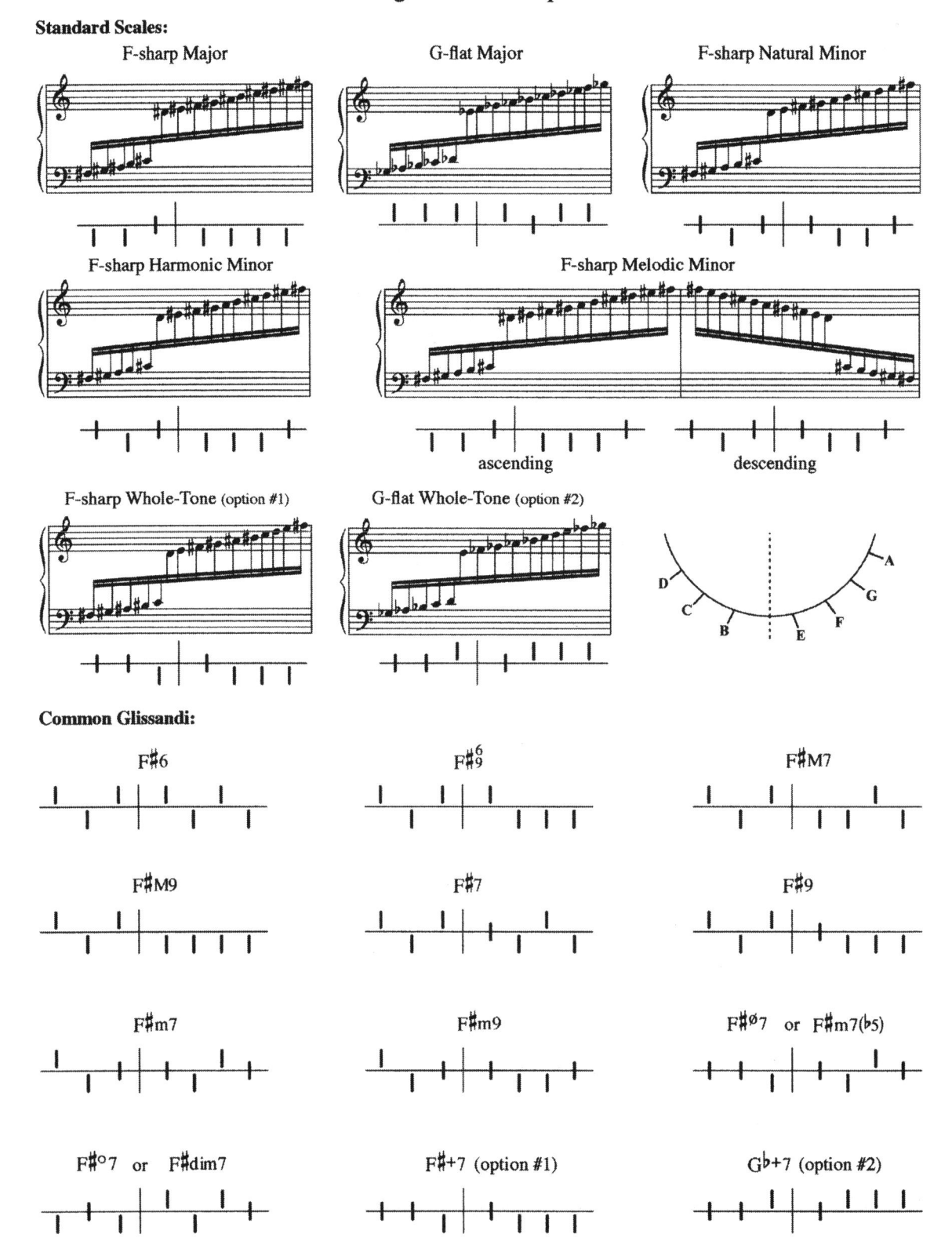

G-flat Major

F-sharp Natural Minor

F-sharp Harmonic Minor

F-sharp Melodic Minor (ascending / descending)

F-sharp Whole-Tone (option #1)

G-flat Whole-Tone (option #2)

Common Glissandi:

F#6

F#6/9 (#)

F#M7

F#M9

F#7

F#9

F#m7

F#m9

F#ø7 or F#m7(♭5)

F#°7 or F#dim7

F#+7 (option #1)

G♭+7 (option #2)

Pedal Diagrams: G

Standard Scales:

G Major   G Natural Minor   G Harmonic Minor

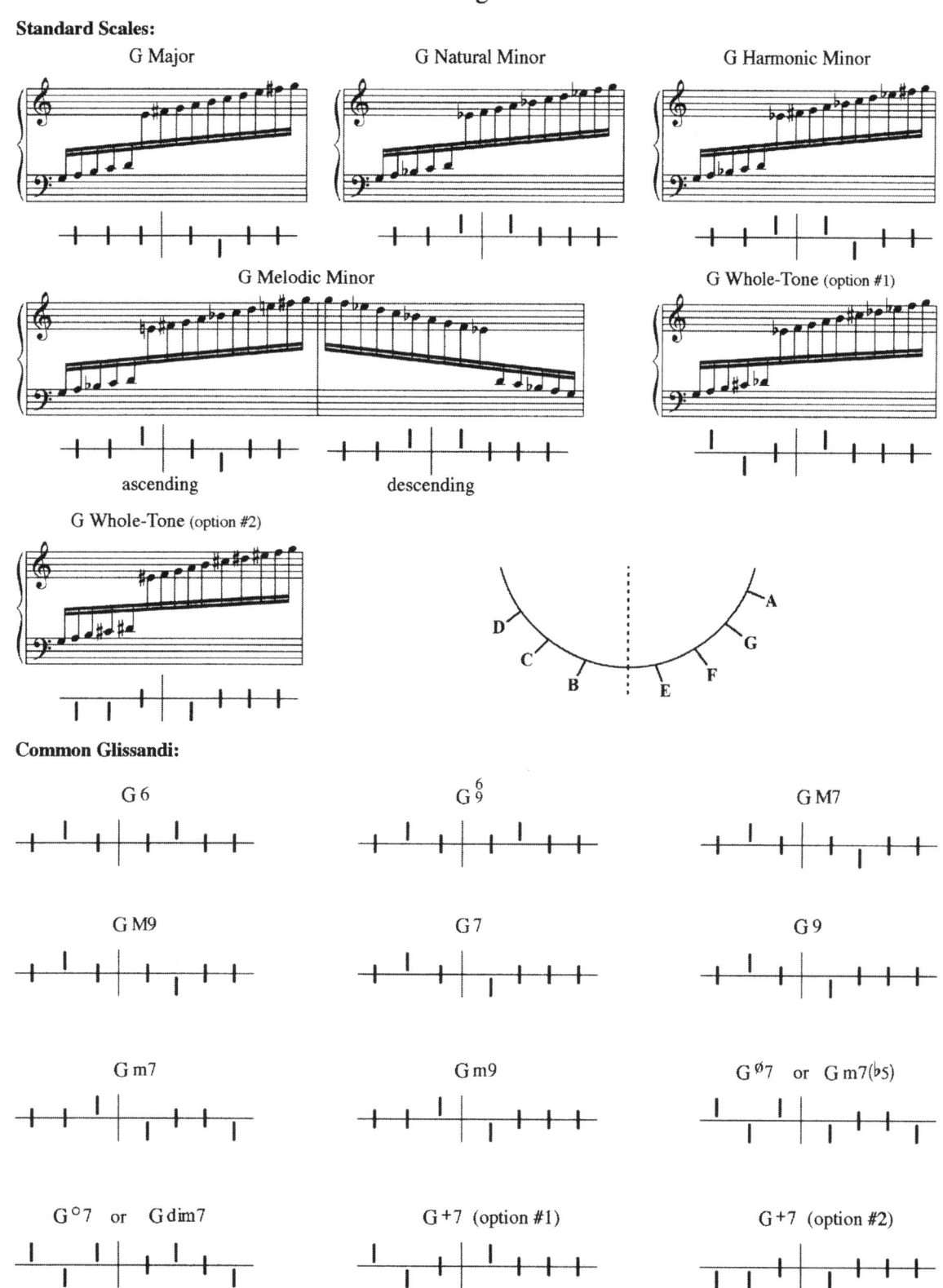

G Melodic Minor (ascending / descending)   G Whole-Tone (option #1)

G Whole-Tone (option #2)

Common Glissandi:

G 6   G $^6_9$ G M7

G M9   G 7   G 9

G m7   G m9   G ^{ø}7 or G m7($\flat$5)

G °7 or G dim7   G +7 (option #1)   G +7 (option #2)

Pedal Diagrams: G-sharp/A-flat

Standard Scales:

A-flat Major

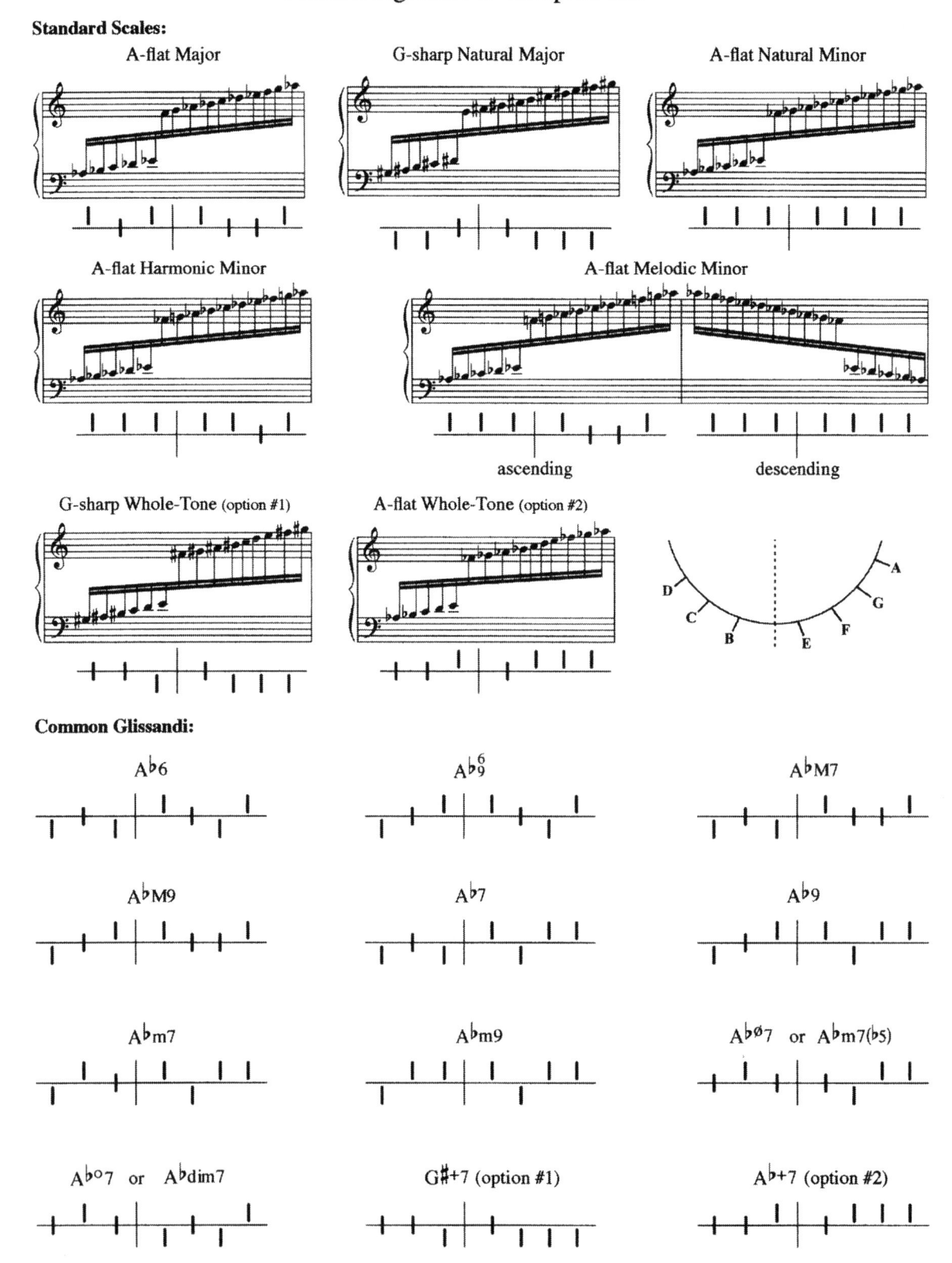

G-sharp Natural Major

A-flat Natural Minor

A-flat Harmonic Minor

A-flat Melodic Minor

ascending   *descending*

G-sharp Whole-Tone (option #1)

A-flat Whole-Tone (option #2)

Common Glissandi:

A♭6

A♭6/9

A♭M7

A♭M9

A♭7

A♭9

A♭m7

A♭m9

A♭ø7 or A♭m7(♭5)

A♭°7 or A♭dim7

G♯+7 (option #1)

A♭+7 (option #2)

Pedal Diagrams: A

Standard Scales:

A Major

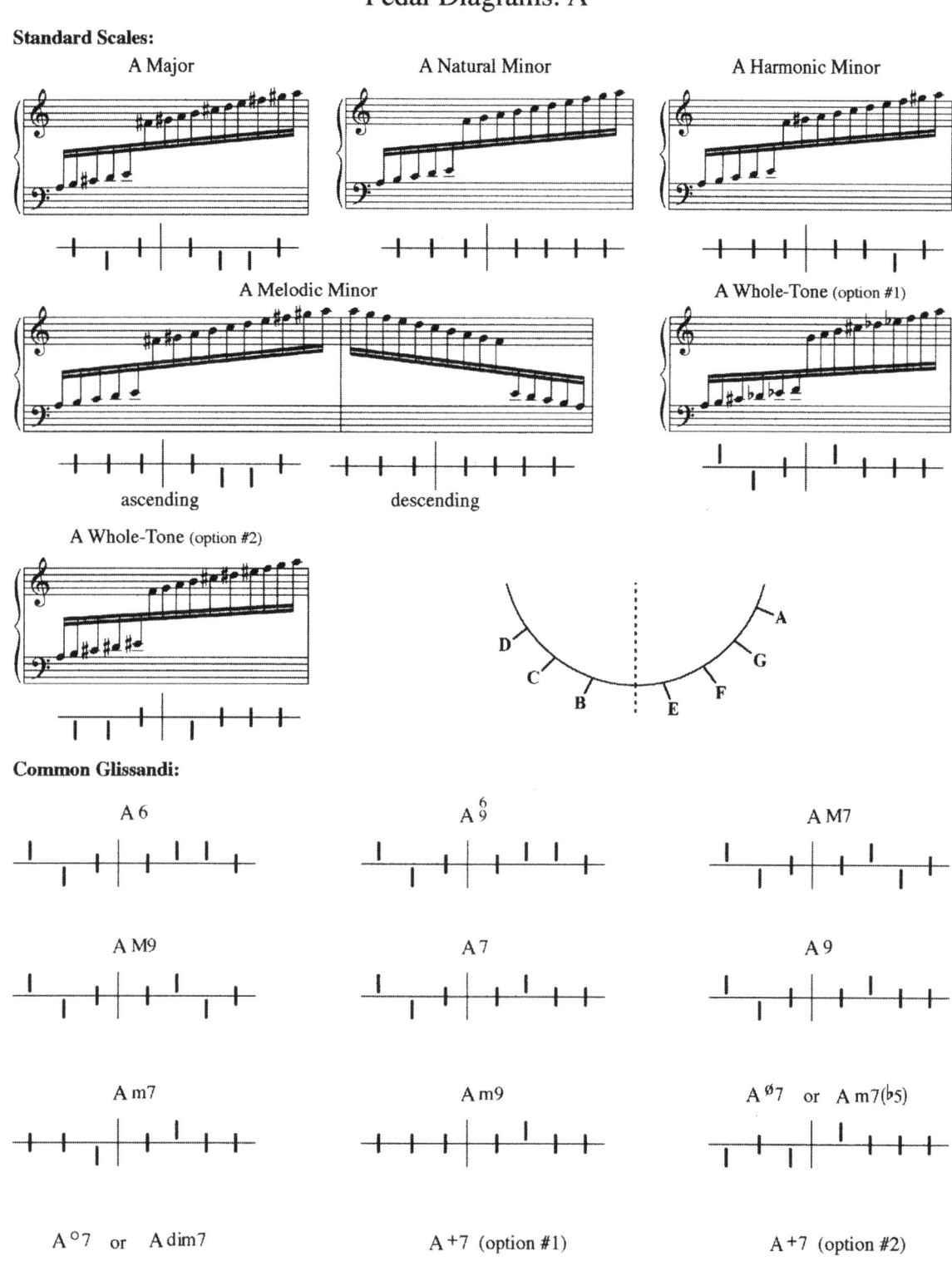

A Natural Minor

A Harmonic Minor

A Melodic Minor (ascending / descending)

A Whole-Tone (option #1)

A Whole-Tone (option #2)

Common Glissandi:

A 6

A $^6_9$

A M7

A M9

A 7

A 9

A m7

A m9

A ø7 or A m7(♭5)

A °7 or A dim7

A +7 (option #1)

A +7 (option #2)

Pedal Diagrams: A-sharp/B-flat

Standard Scales:

B-flat Major • B-flat Natural Minor • B-flat Harmonic Minor

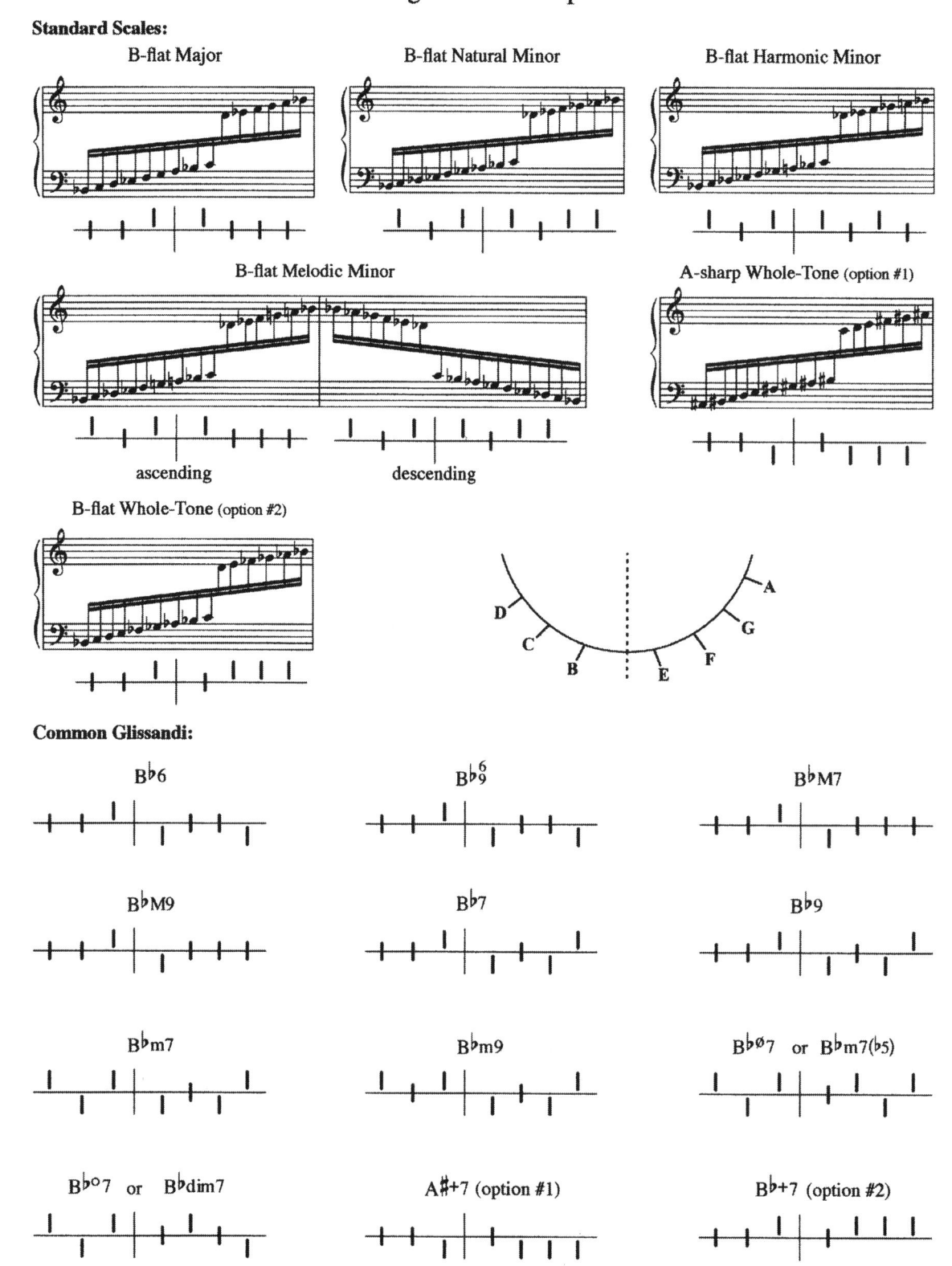

B-flat Melodic Minor (ascending / descending) • A-sharp Whole-Tone (option #1)

B-flat Whole-Tone (option #2)

Common Glissandi:

$B{\flat}6$ • $B{\flat}{}^6_9$ • $B{\flat}M7$

$B{\flat}M9$ • $B{\flat}7$ • $B{\flat}9$

$B{\flat}m7$ • $B{\flat}m9$ • $B{\flat}{}^{\varnothing}7$ or $B{\flat}m7({\flat}5)$

$B{\flat}{}^{\circ}7$ or $B{\flat}dim7$ • $A{\sharp}+7$ (option #1) • $B{\flat}+7$ (option #2)

Pedal Diagrams: B

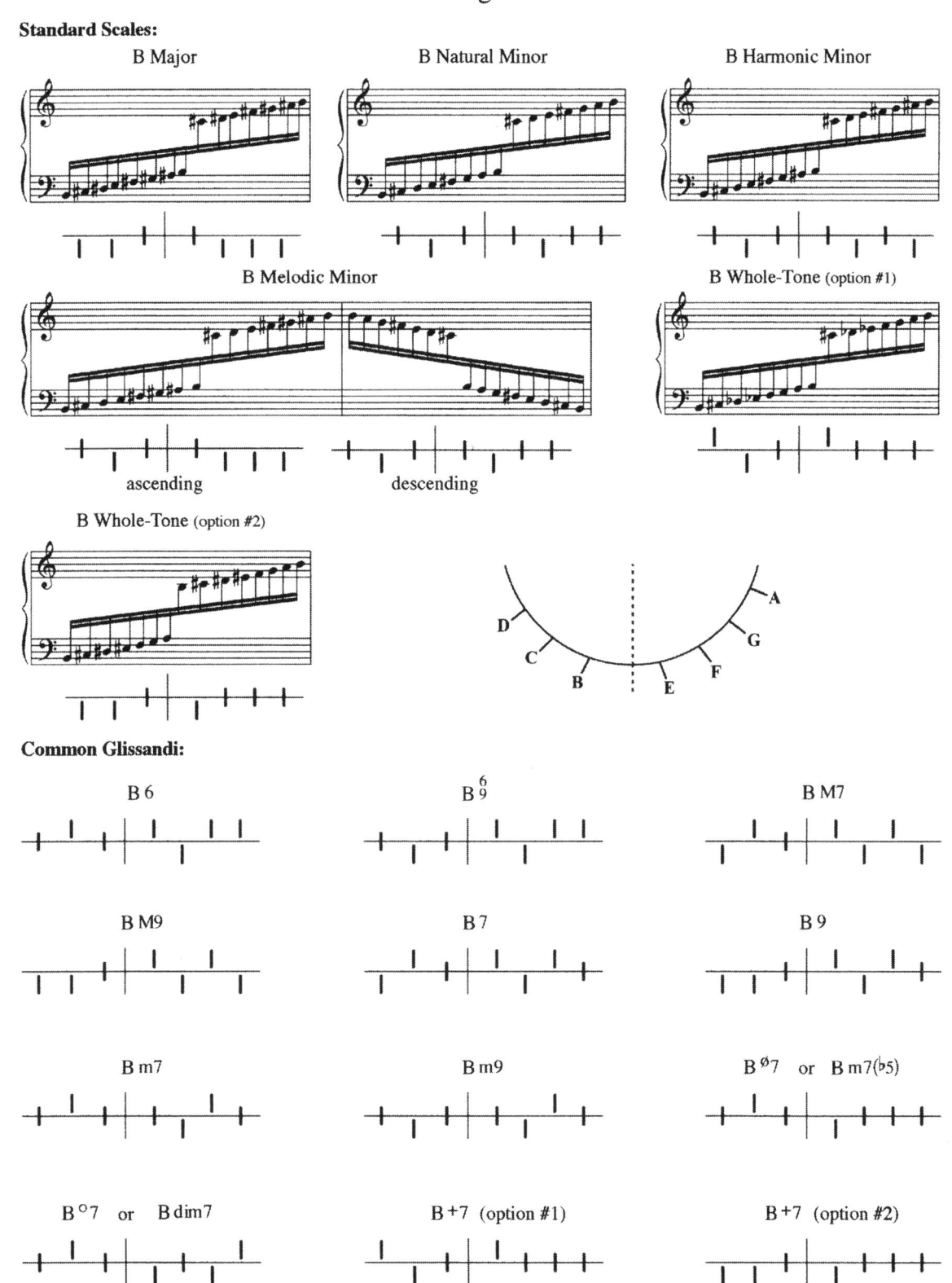

Standard Scales:

B Major

B Natural Minor

B Harmonic Minor

B Melodic Minor (ascending / descending)

B Whole-Tone (option #1)

B Whole-Tone (option #2)

Common Glissandi:

B 6

B $^6_9$

B M7

B M9

B 7

B 9

B m7

B m9

B ⌀7 or B m7(♭5)

B °7 or B dim7

B +7 (option #1)

B +7 (option #2)

PRACTICAL CONSIDERATIONS

Practical Guidelines when Scoring for Harp

Elements to Use

- Glissandi
- Arpeggios
- Melodies, with simplistic harmonic accompaniment or counterpoint (parts that would sound overly simplistic on other instruments sound full and lush on harp)
- Enharmonic writing
- Exposed harmonics (simplistic in nature)
- Melodic or harmonic writing that incorporates two-handed techniques

Elements to Avoid

- Chromaticism (unless enharmonic solutions exist)
- Adaptations of idiomatically pianistic material
- "Ten-finger" piano-derivative material
- Quickly changing notes and chordal harmonies requiring impractical pedal changes
- Rapidly repeating chords

IN THE PROFESSION

Professional harpists prefer that the orchestrator does *not* place pedal diagrams in the harp part. The practice is considered offensive and akin to writing the fingerings under the notes in the trumpet part. Harpists would rather be responsible for calculating the pedal changes themselves.

One never asks a harpist to employ a technique that could (even slightly) damage the instrument. Techniques such as weaving aluminum fold through the strings can produce an interesting, percussive effect. However, unless this only involves the metal strings, damage can result. The instrument represents a significant financial investment and, as such, professional players simply will not use their instruments in a manner for which they were not designed.

BUILDING THE SCORE

This example will demonstrate the process for creating a harp adaptation from an existing piano piece. As always, one begins the process by performing a harmonic analysis. This analysis will determine the harmonic content and context. These elements are decisive factors when determining the deletion or addition of harmonic elements. In most cases, one will need to alter the work to accommodate the instrument. Since harpists play using only four fingers, this often requires deleting non-essential harmonic elements (as is the case with the provided example).

Even if one is quite familiar with the pedal harp, it is wise to calculate pedal changes to insure the part is easily playable. One should attempt to accomplish the performance with as few pedal changes as possible, using enharmonic equivalents as needed. When writing multiple simultaneous pedal changes, always attempt to write changes using opposing feet. Remember to remove the pedal diagrams from the part prior to printing the part for the harpist.

For the purposes of the exercise the following selection will be used:

Carlos de Mesquita, *Esmeralda* **(excerpt)**

334 PEDAL HARP

SUGGESTED EXERCISE

Using the information and guidelines presented in this chapter and in Chapter 3 (Practical Problem Solving), modify and adapt the following example for harp. Perform a harmonic analysis to determine the non-essential harmonic elements and adjust the pitches to enharmonic spellings as needed to accommodate pedal changes.

Eduard Schütt, *En Berçant*

10
GUITAR

The classical guitar used in the orchestral setting is the *modern* classical guitar. The term is used to differentiate the instrument from *early* guitars that are occasionally (and generally only in specific settings) used in a classical setting. In an orchestral score and in discussions of orchestration the instrument is simply designated as the guitar.

THE ESSENTIALS

Tuning

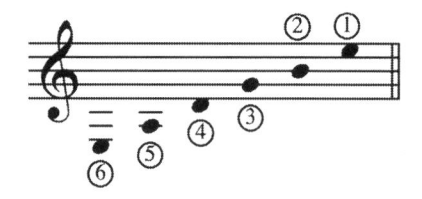

Guitar Range and Transposition

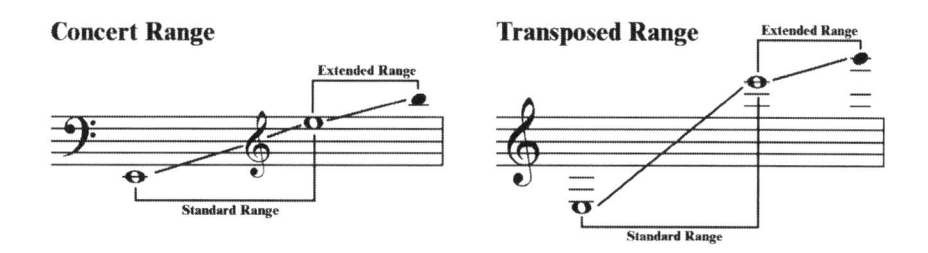

In its transposed form, guitar is always notated in the treble clef. It appears in its transposed form in both concert and transposed scores.

Guitar Notation

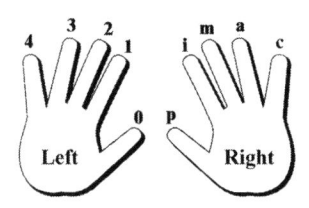

In guitar notation, the fingers of the left hand are numbered (from the index finger to the little finger) with the digitals 1 through 4. The thumb, though rarely used, is designated with the number 0. The fingers of the right hand are designated (from the thumb to the ring finger) with the letters p, i, m, and a. The little finger, though rarely used, is designated with the letter d.

Numbers

Use of a specific finger of the left hand is designated with the number (relating to the appropriate finger).

Letters

Use of a specific finger of the right hand to pluck the string is designated with the letter (relating to the appropriate finger).

Circled Numbers

Use of a specific string is designated with a number (referring to the string) placed within a circle.

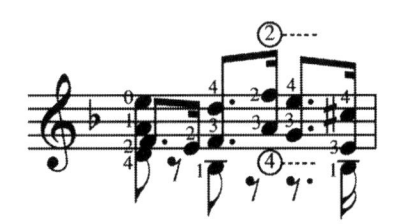

Circled Numbers followed by a Dashed Line

As stated above, the use of a specific string is designated with a number (referring to the string) placed within a circle. The dashed line specifies that the notes encompassed by the line are to be played upon the string designated by the number within the circle.

Roman Numerals

Roman numerals (sometimes preceded by the letter C and occasionally followed by a subscript number) designate the fret upon which the notes are to be played.

Solid Dash

A solid dash in front of a fingering number or extending from one note to the next (played with the same finger) specifies that the finger remains upon the string and "slides" from one note to the next.

Combined Notation

When the performance designations described above are incorporated into the notation of a selection, one must exercise both precision and patience. With more detail contained in the notation, the greater the need for the precise placement of notational elements. This detailed process naturally increases the amount of time needed to produce clear and concise notation. One should be aware that heavily detailed selections (such as that below) will require adequate preparation, practice and rehearsal to yield acceptable results.

Non-classical Notation

When guitar is incorporated into a "pops orchestra" environment, or when writing selections for popular genres (rock, pop, R&B, etc.), the most practical approach is to write a chord chart. This type of notation allows the player the freedom to interpret the performance (within the accepted parameters of the genre). A genre-stylistic accompaniment is designated by placing the chord symbol above the measure and placing slash marks (one for each beat) in the measure. Specific rhythmic content is designated by notes with slashes for noteheads.

Sample Chords in C
(transposed)

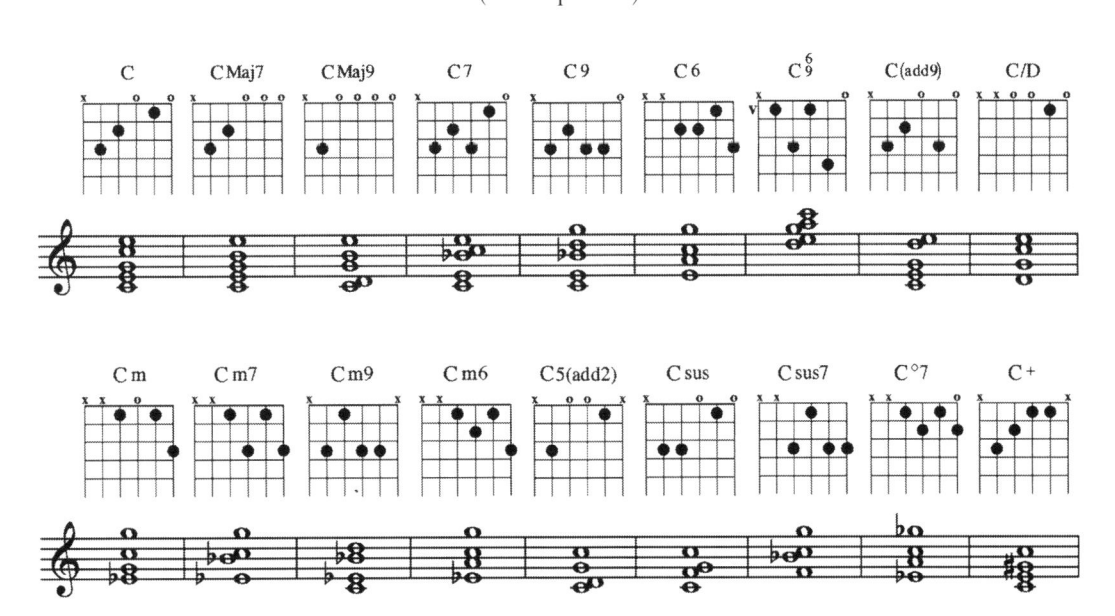

Sample Chords in C♯
(transposed)

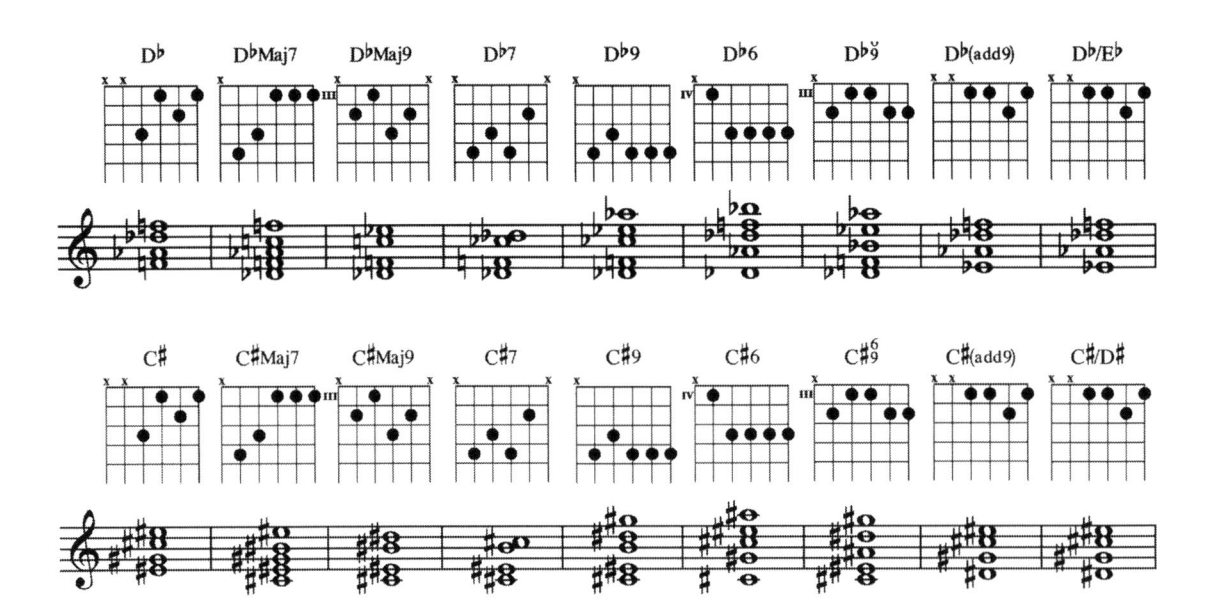

Sample Chords in D♭
(transposed)

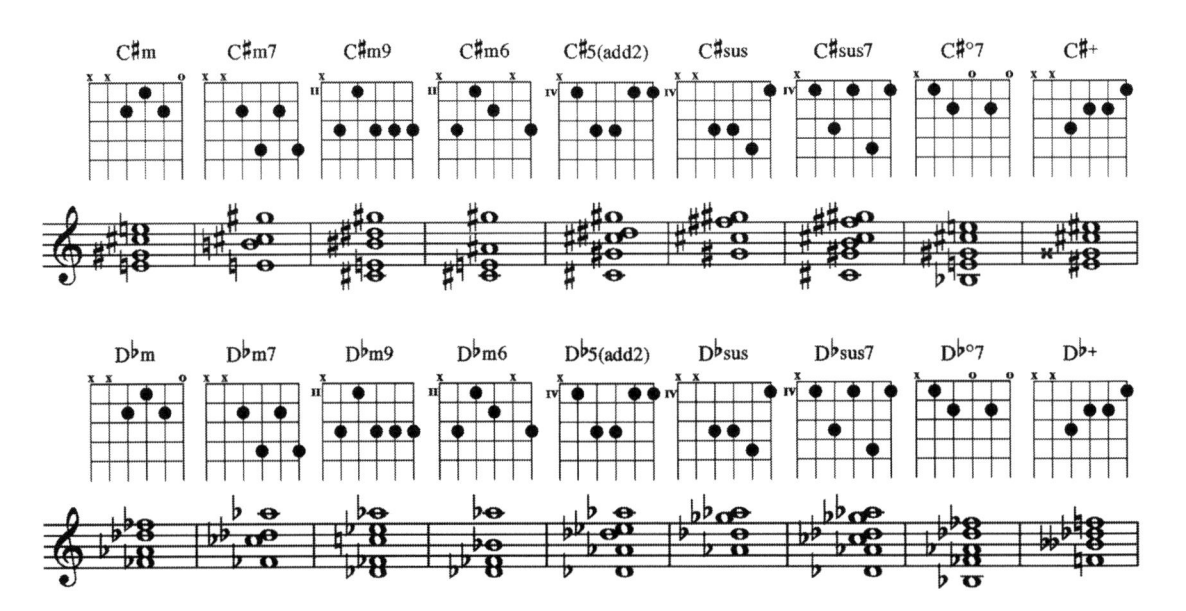

GUITAR

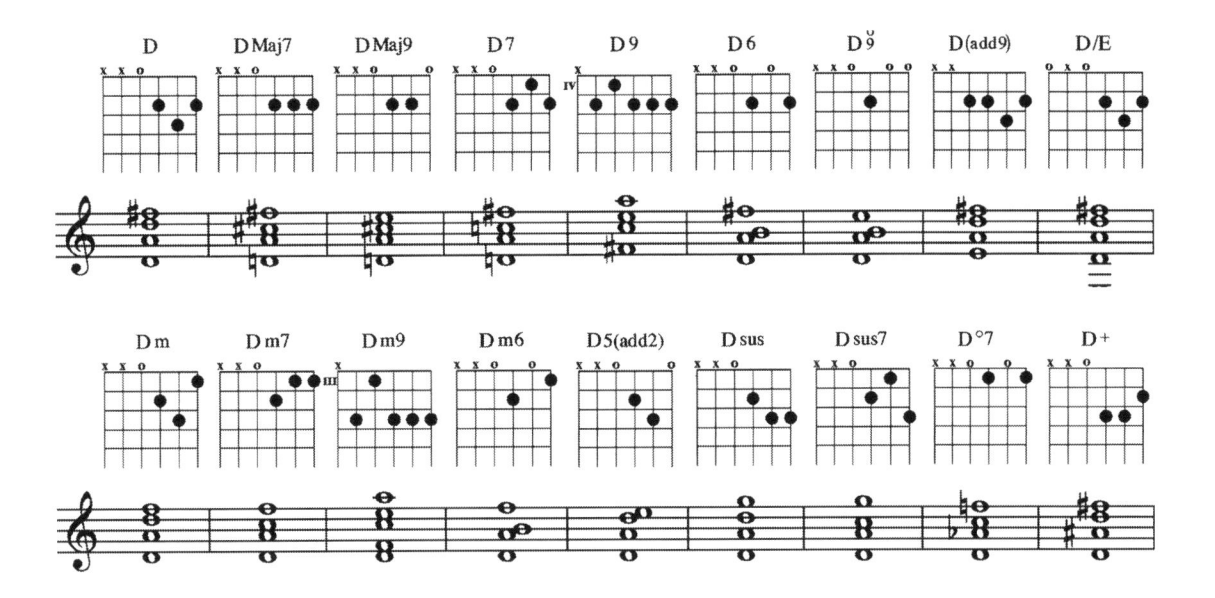

Sample Chords in D
(transposed)

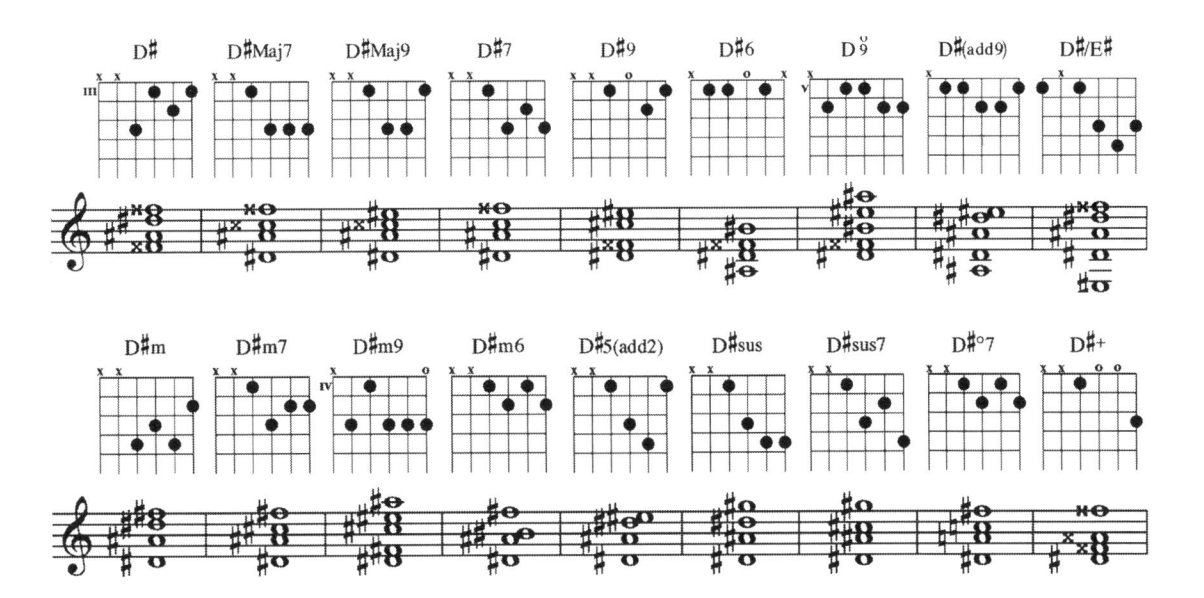

Sample Chords in E♭
(transposed)

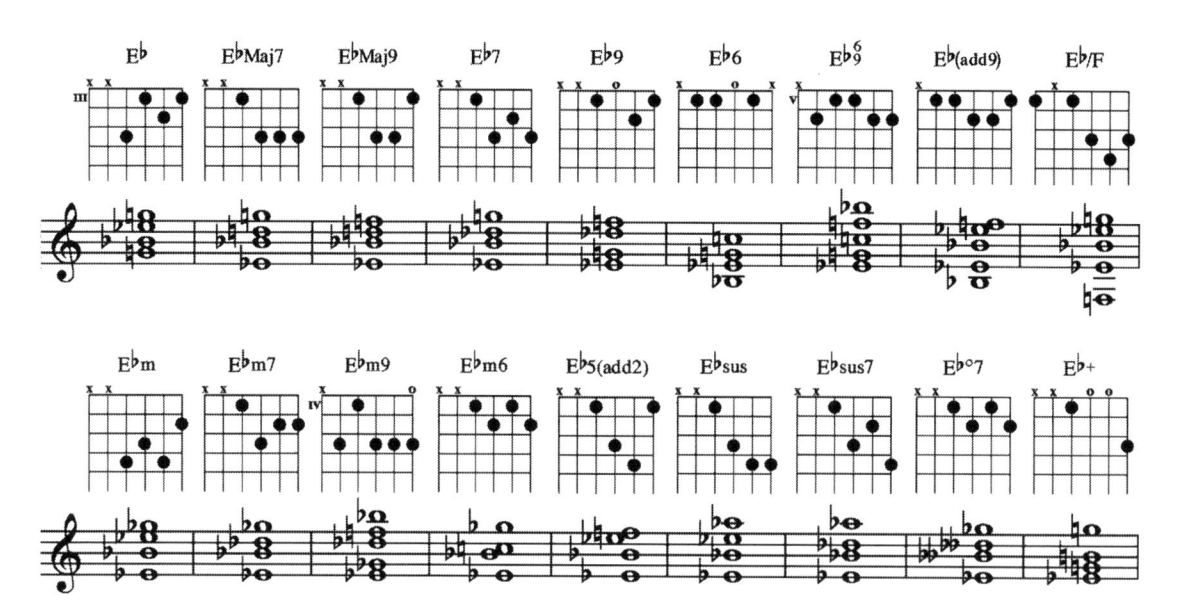

Sample Chords in E
(transposed)

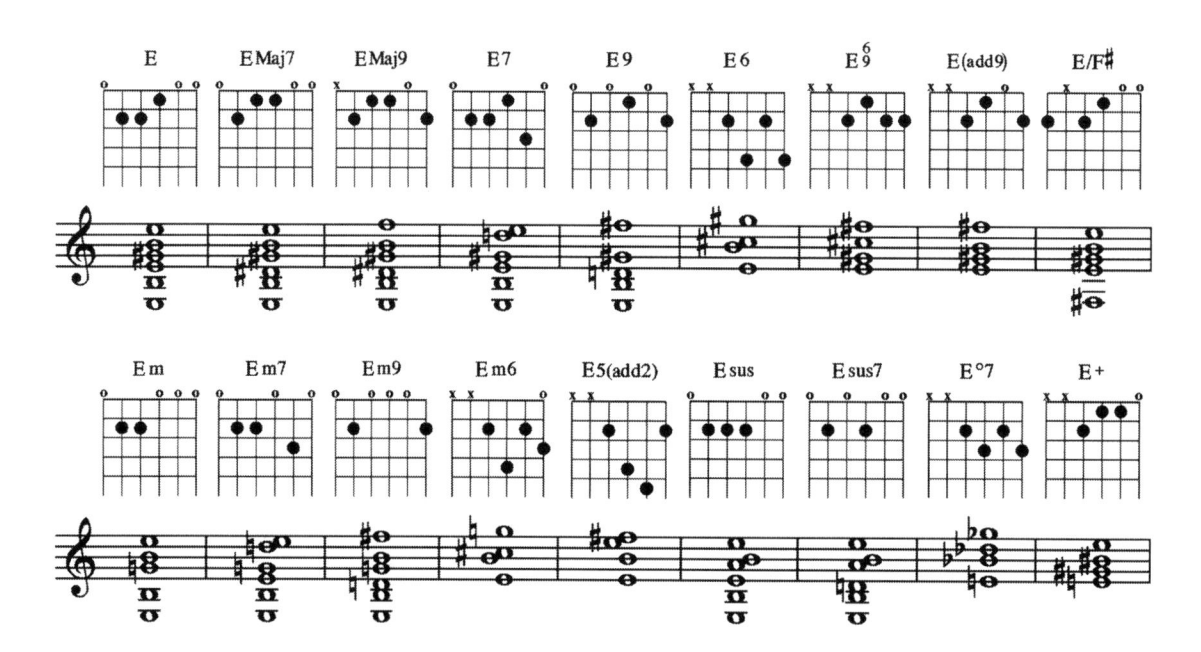

Sample Chords in F
(transposed)

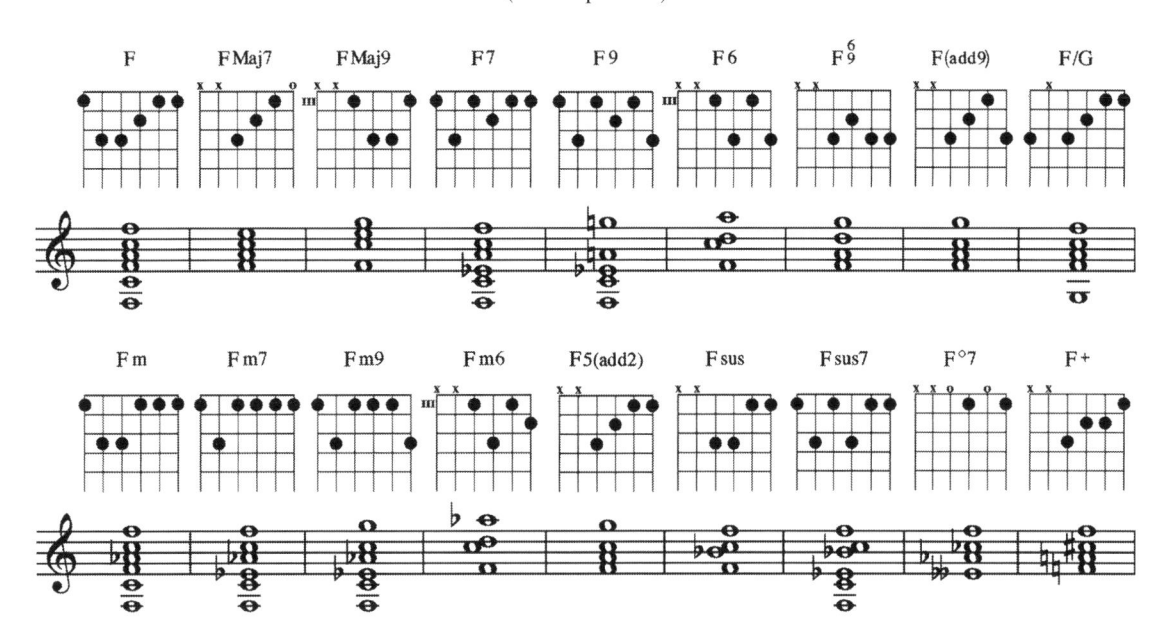

Sample Chords in F♯
(transposed)

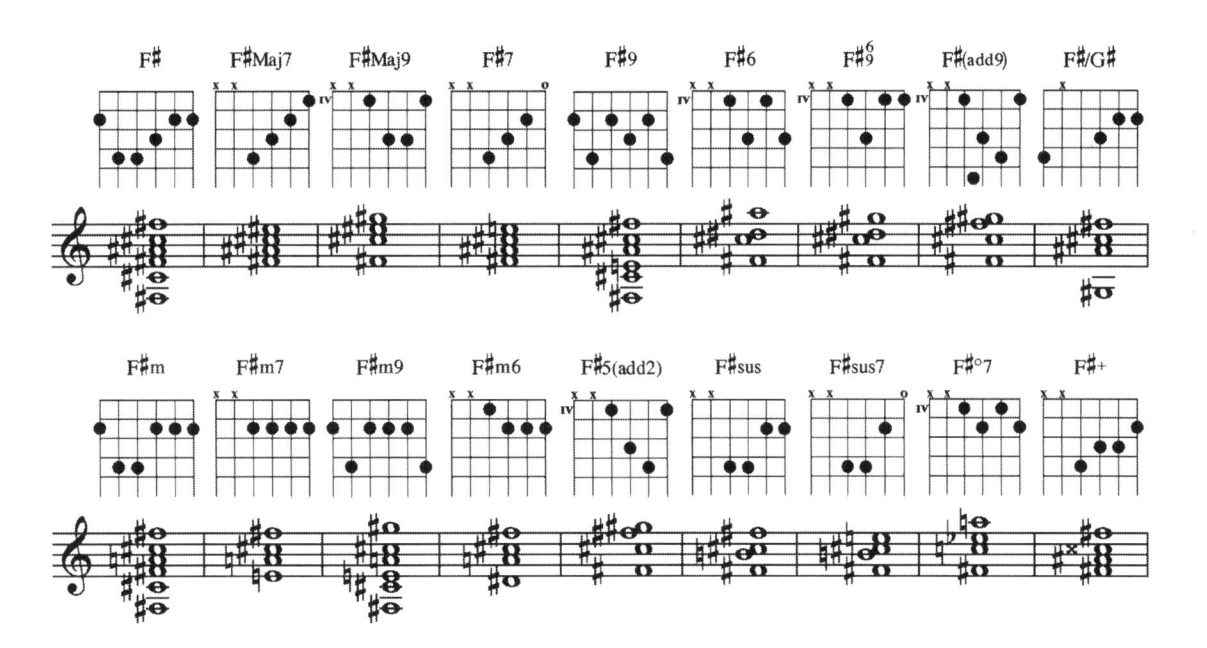

Sample Chords in G♭
(transposed)

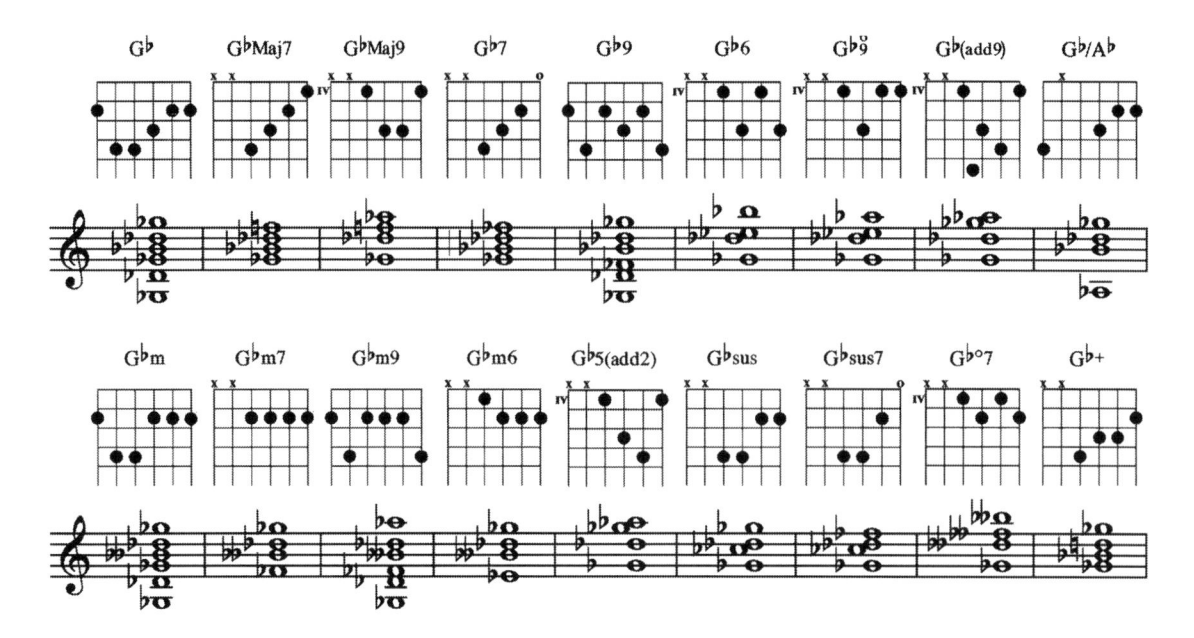

Sample Chords in G
(transposed)

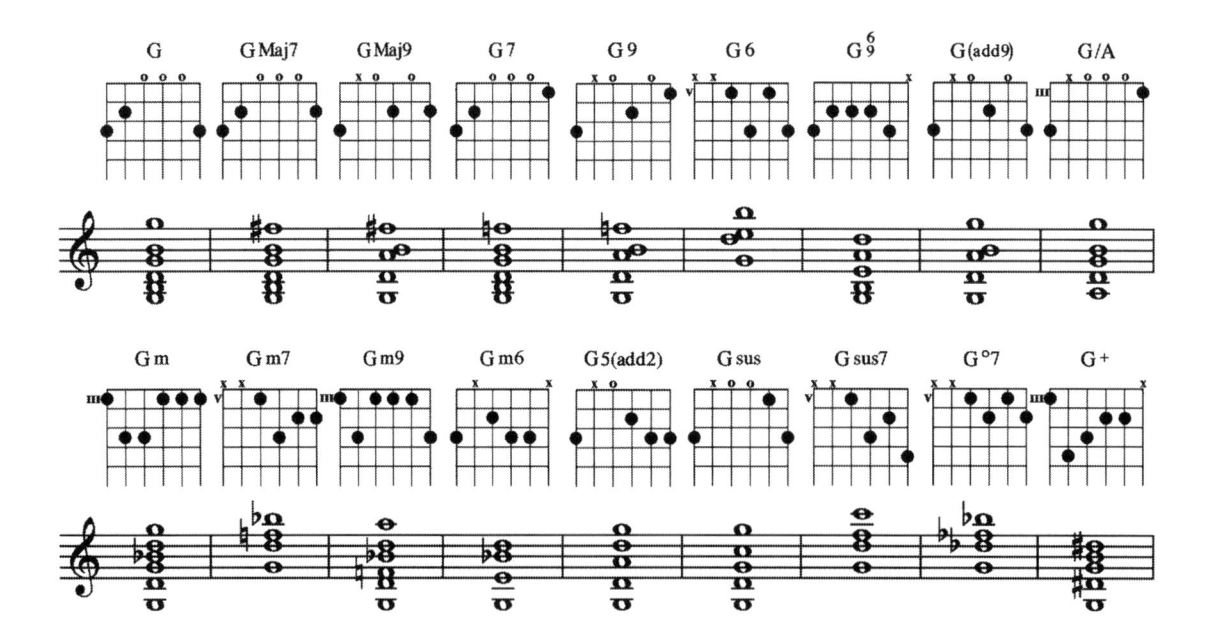

Sample Chords in G♯
(transposed)

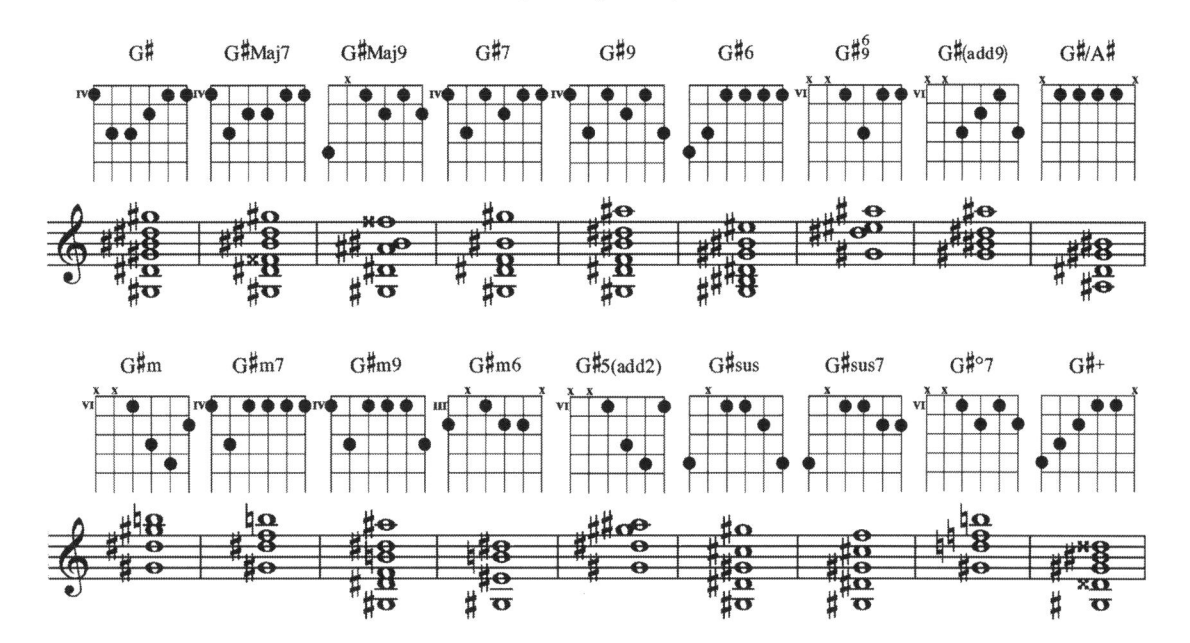

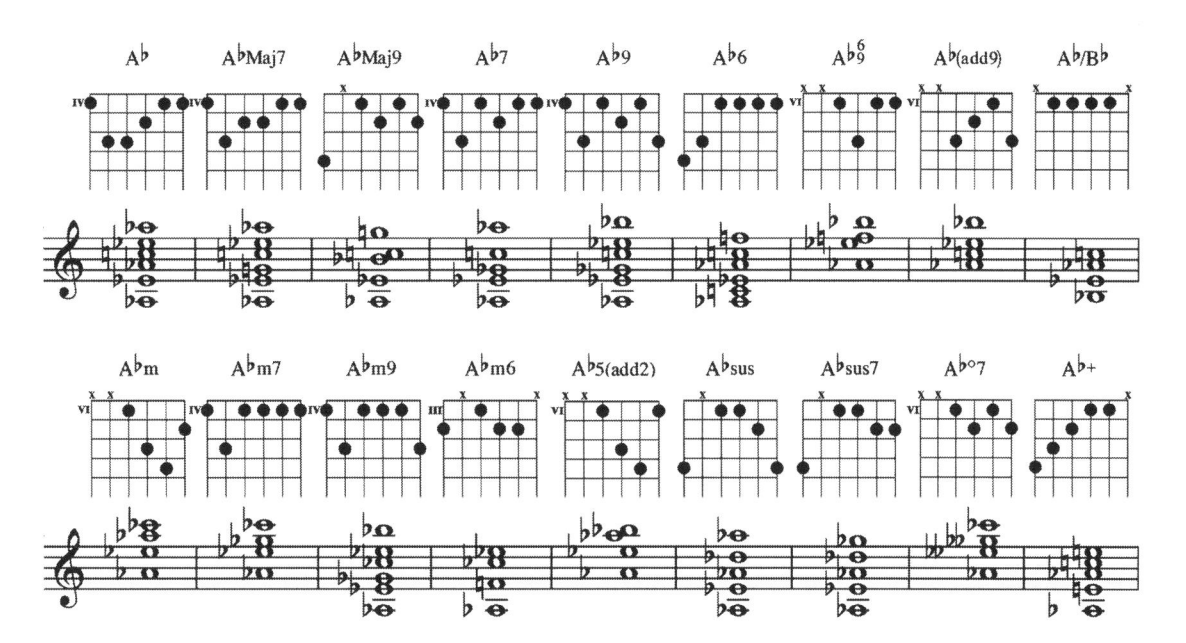

Sample Chords in A
(transposed)

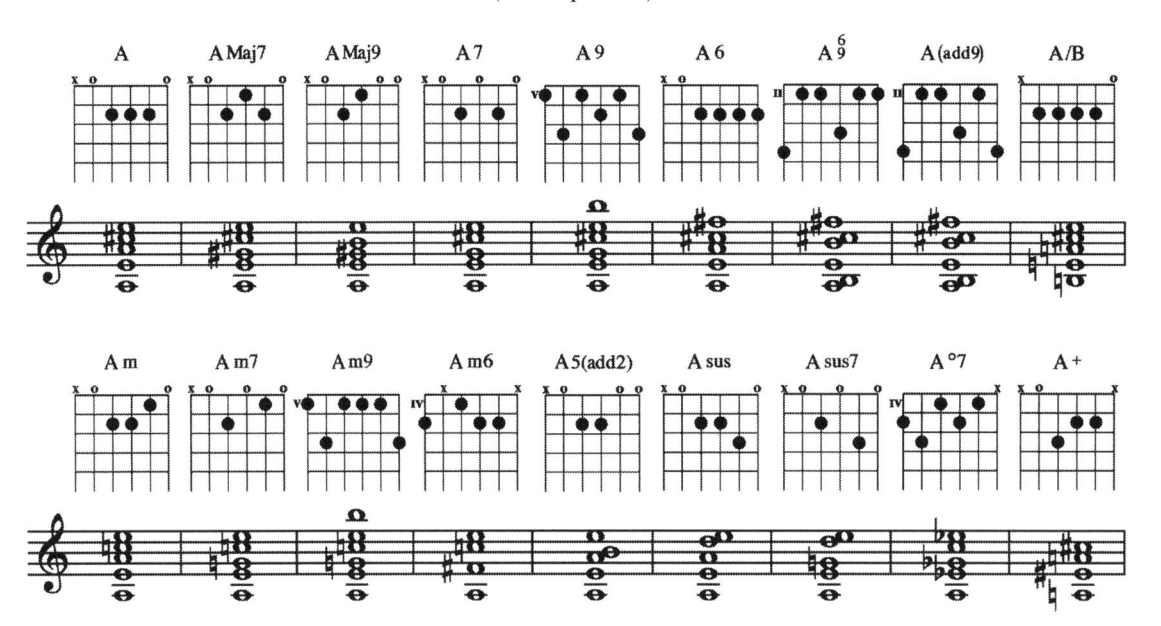

Sample Chords in B♭
(transposed)

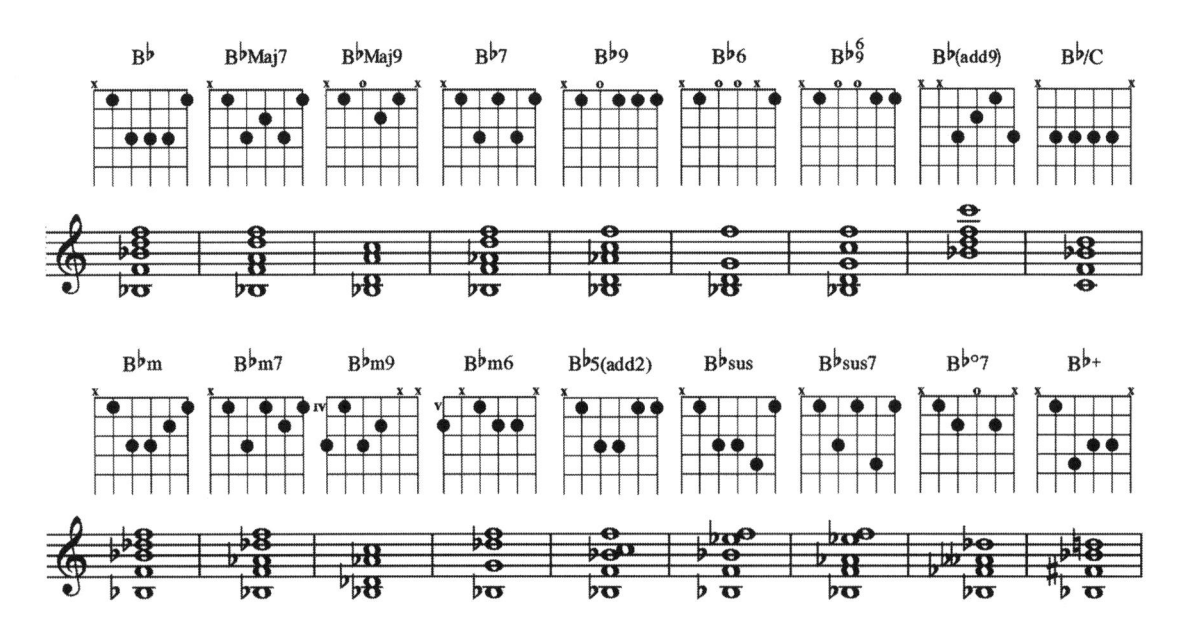

Sample Chords in B
(transposed)

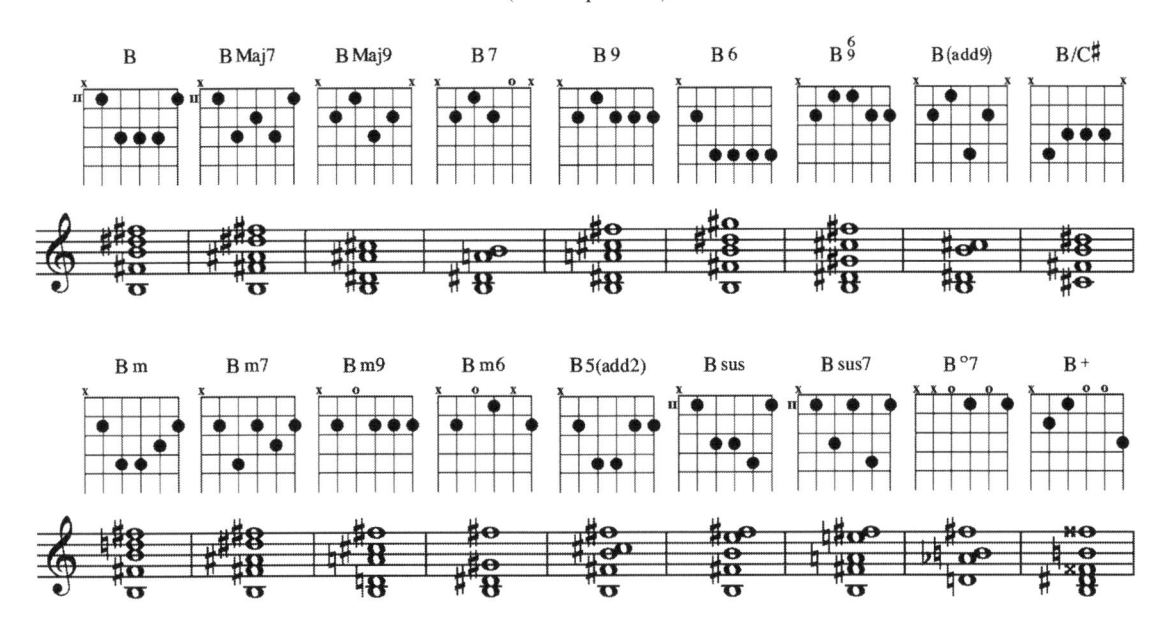

Harmonics

As with other string instruments, the guitar is capable of both natural and artificial harmonics. As previously stated, *natural harmonics* are where the resultant pitch is produced by lightly touching an open, vibrating string (the fundamental pitch) at one to the nodal points; *artificial harmonics* are where the fundament is artificially created by fingering the desired fundament and lightly touching the nodal point with another finger.

Professional guitarists are capable of competently performing most, if not all of the harmonics possible on the instrument; however, from a practical standpoint, harmonics generated from partial 2 through partial 6 yield the most stable and reliable results. Artificial harmonics yield the best results when spanning a distance of four frets from the fingered fundamental to the node point. One should note that harmonics function best at lower dynamic levels (mezzo piano, or lower), with a maximum functional dynamic level of mezzo forte.

Practical Natural Harmonics

Overtone Partial	Resultant Pitch (above fundamental)
1	fundamental pitch
2	1 octave above the fundamental
3	1 octave, plus a perfect 5th above the fundamental
4	2 octaves above the fundamental
5	2 octaves, plus a major 3rd above the fundamental
6	2 octaves, plus a perfect 5th above the fundamental
7	2 octaves, plus a minor 7th above the fundamental
8	3 octaves above the fundamental

Notation of Guitar Harmonics

There are a variety of accepted methods for notating harmonics for guitar, all of which can be found in published selections. One should be familiar with all of the following methods, as one will undoubtedly encounter a variety of notation (sometimes within the same selection) when orchestrating works for guitar.

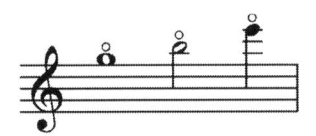

The most practical (and recommended) method of designating harmonics is to notate the desired pitch, placing the harmonic symbol (°) directly above the note. This method may be used for both natural and artificial harmonics.

Other accepted methods include notating the pitch one octave below the desired pitch, with the harmonic symbol (°) directly above the note and the abbreviation *harm.* placed above the affected notes.

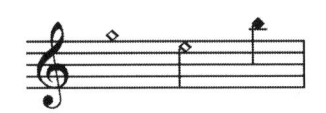

Notating the pitch one octave below the desired pitch and designating harmonics through the use of diamond-shaped noteheads.

Notating the desired pitch and placing the letter "o" above the notehead, indicating an open string (for second partial natural harmonics only).

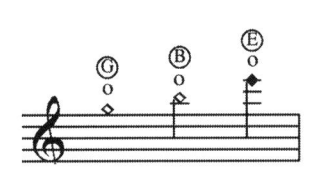

Placing the note (with a diamond-shaped notehead) on the desired fret (node point), designating the string with the letter name of the string contained within a circle, and placing the letter "o" above the notehead, indicating an open string (for natural harmonics only).

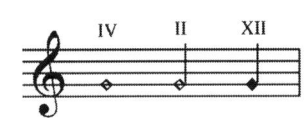

Placing the note (with a diamond-shaped notehead) on the desired string, designating the fret (node point) with a Roman numeral place above the notehead (for natural harmonics only).

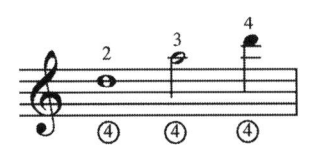

Notating the pitch one octave below the desired pitch, designating the fret (node point) with numbers placed above the notehead, and designating the string with a circled number placed below the note (for natural harmonics only).

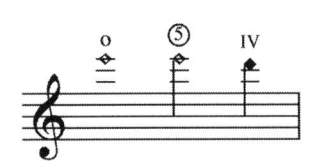

Placing the note (with a diamond-shaped notehead) on the desired pitch. One may also designate use of an open string by placing the letter "o" above the notehead, or designate the string by using a circled number, or designate the fret (node point) with a Roman numeral. This method may be used for both natural and artificial harmonics.

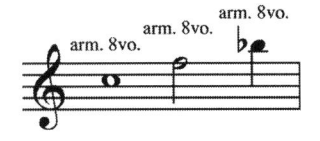

Notating the pitch one octave below the desired pitch, designating a harmonic at the octave with the Italian abbreviation "arm. 8vo." This method may be used for both natural and artificial harmonics.

Placing the note on the desired string, designating the node point with the abbreviation *harm.*, followed by a number designating the desire partial (for natural harmonics only).

Artificial harmonics may be notated by designating the fingered note (fundamental) with a standard notehead and designating the node point with a diamond-shaped notehead.

THE ENSEMBLES

Guitar Ensemble

A guitar ensemble is a collection of standard classical guitars. The music for this ensemble is normally written to be played with one guitar per part. A guitar ensemble may consist of as few as three (guitar trio) to four (guitar quartet) instruments, or as many as eight (double quartet) to nine (guitar nonet) instruments. The trio and quartet are the most common configurations, with the guitar quartet being the standard.

Guitar Orchestra

A guitar orchestra is an ensemble of guitars of different sizes, with multiple players per part. There is no standard instrumentation for the ensemble, but generally it will include standard classical guitars, plus guitars tuned higher (alto guitars) and lower (bass and contrabass guitars) than the standard classical guitar. While the overall sound of the ensemble is decidedly unique, worldwide there are relatively few guitar orchestras and most orchestrations are customized to a specific ensemble.

IN THE PROFESSION

Few instances frustrate classical guitarists more than trying to perform against an orchestration that is weightily scored. Though classical guitar can be strummed loudly, most of the playing is subtle, delicate and sophisticated in nature. One must understand that the instrument cannot project over a heavily scored orchestra, and adjust one's writing appropriately. Lightly scored strings or woodwinds should be used, and brass scoring should be avoided when the classical guitar is featured. The best results are often achieved when the orchestra tacets during solo (non-strumming) sections.

BUILDING THE SCORE

This example will demonstrate the process for creating a guitar quartet orchestration from an existing piano selection. Once an appropriate work has been selected and the harmonic analysis is completed, one examines the selection for elements within the notation that must be addressed or altered to work for the instruments of the chosen ensemble. These elements may include crescendi and decrescendi of undefined dynamic scope, dynamics that may need to be modified to be appropriate for the chosen instrumentation, ornamentation, rhythmic subdivisions, arpeggios, etc.

For the purposes of the exercise, the following selection will be used:

Traditional, *Greensleeves* **(arrangement by RJ Miller)**

In this particular example there is a lack of dynamic designations. While one can rely upon the performer to interpret the solo piano selection, dynamic shaping in an ensemble is critical. The orchestrator must add these elements to achieve appropriate dynamic movement that is balanced throughout the ensemble. One would also wish to address registers and decide the appropriate method for handling designated argeggios.

GUITAR

GUITAR

353

354 GUITAR

SCORING EXAMPLES

Scoring Example for Solo Guitar

Ferninando Sor, *Sonata in C Major for Guitar*, Op. 15b, transcribed and edited by Alex Komodore.

Copyright © MMXIV by Alex Komodore. Used by permission.

Scoring Examples for Guitar in an Orchestral Setting

Note that since the acoustic guitar can easily be overpowered in an orchestral setting, the orchestral accompaniment is scored very lightly, and great care is taken to insure the guitar is not subjugated.

Antonio Vivaldi, *Concerto in D major*, **Movement I, transcribed and edited by Alex Komodore.**

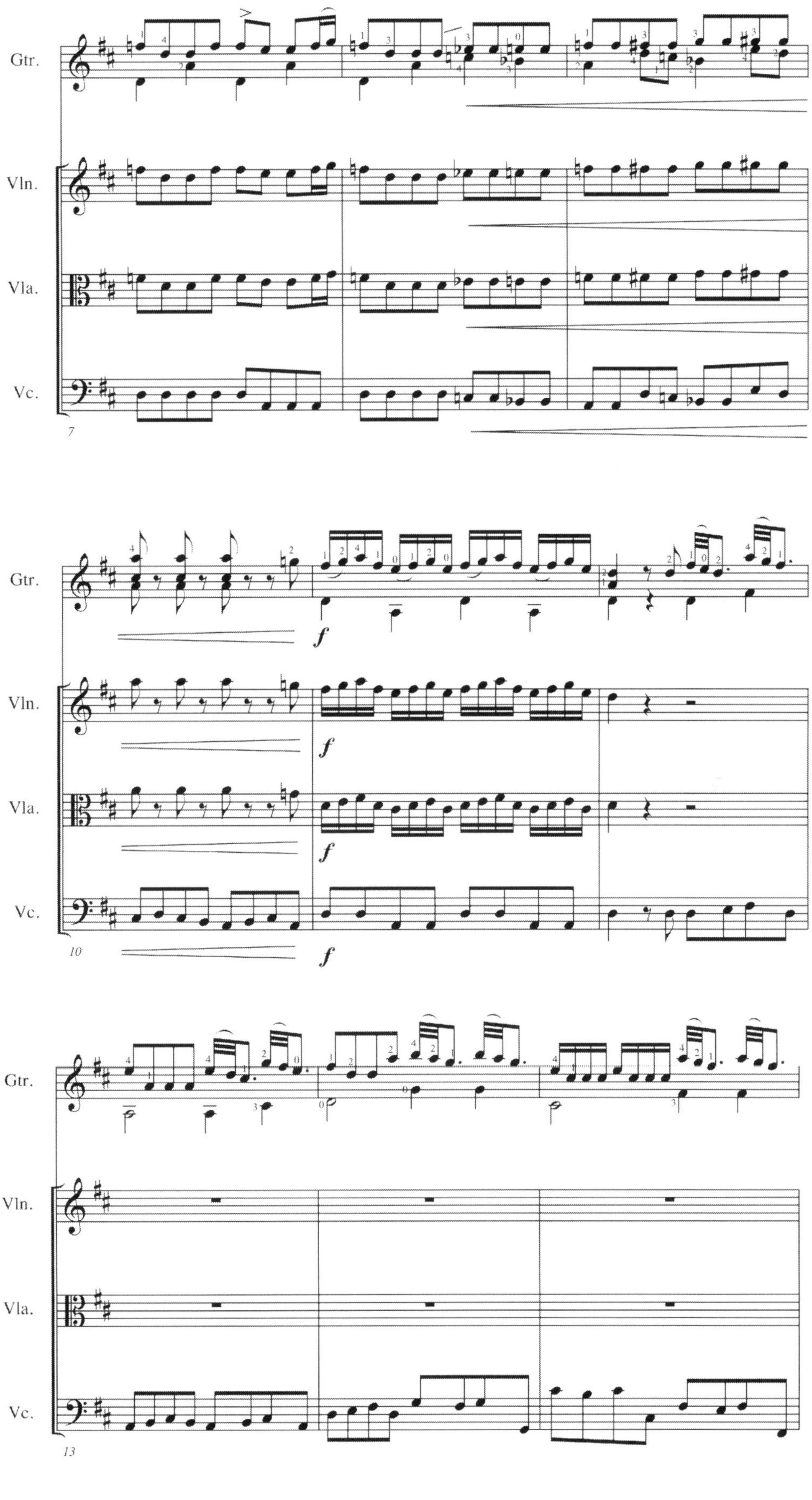
Gtr.
Vln.
Vla.
Vc.
7
10
13
f

Copyright © MMXIV by Alex Komodore. Used by permission.

RJ Miller, *Zoot Suit* **(for Pops Orchestra), guitar part.**

Copyright © 2004 by Appassionata Music. Used by permission.

SUGGESTED EXERCISE

Using the information and guidelines presented in this chapter and in Chapter 3 (Practical Problem Solving), orchestrate the following example for guitar quartet. Perform a harmonic analysis and seek ways to add textural interest.

Victor Hollaender, *Canzonetta*

GUITAR 361

11
SCORING FOR ORCHESTRAL TUTTI

Since scoring for the various individual instruments and orchestral sections has been previously addressed in this text, writing for the full orchestral tutti will be the focus of this chapter. There are many viable approaches to writing for the entire ensemble and the method one chooses is based upon factors such as the register of the selection, the style and type of accompaniment, the inclusion (or lack of) a countermelody and the overall texture one might wish to create. In all cases, one should strive to ensure that each orchestral family (strings, woodwinds, brass) sounds full and complete as an individual section. Doing so yields a thick, rich and homogeneous ensemble sound when all sections are combined. Since the melody should always be the predominant element, it should be doubled throughout the instrumental families and, when possible, reinforced by additionally doubling it at the octave (either above, below or, in some circumstances, both).

PRACTICAL CONSIDERATIONS

Practical Guidelines when Scoring for Orchestral Tutti

- Instrumental and harmonic balances are critical.
- Score all instruments in comfortable registers.
- Avoid altissimo registers, especially in brass.
- Score each instrumental family is such a manner that they sound rich and full independently.
- Also be aware of the implied fundamental generated by each and every voicing.
- Learn from the *masters*! *Listen to and analyze* as many different examples of orchestral tutti scoring as possible.

BUILDING THE SCORE

When scoring a simple SATB selection for orchestral tutti, one generally attempts to expand the presence of the elements into a sonic palette encompassing several octaves (much as when one expands the sound of a pipe organ by adding stops). Even though an SATB selection would appear to be one of the simplest compositions with which to work, the orchestrator still has multiple scoring opportunities. The option one chooses depends upon the overall effect one wishes to create.

When scoring a simple SATB selection for orchestral tutti, one generally attempts to expand the presence of the elements into a sonic palette encompassing several octaves (much as when one expands the sound of a pipe organ by adding stops). Even though an SATB selection would appear to be one of the simplest compositions with which to work, the orchestrator still has multiple scoring opportunities. The option one chooses depends upon the overall affect one wishes to create.

John Antes, Christ the Lord, the Lord Most Glorious, mm. 1–9.

Public Domain

Even with a simplistic work such as this, one should always perform a harmonic analysis prior to orchestrating the selection to assure a thorough understanding of the harmonic content and balance.

Since the strings constitute the largest section in the orchestral tutti, one generally begins the orchestration process with this family. If one wishes to create an orchestration with registers and fullness similar to that of a full vocal choir, one may place the soprano part in the 1st violins, the alto part in the 2nd violins, the tenor part in the viols, the bass part in the cellos and the bass part (sounding octavo basso) in the contrabasses.

One can expand the overall texture by placing some of the upper woodwinds an octave above that of the original content (the "added stop" effect), with the remainder of the section reinforcing and adding texture to the string parts. However one chooses to distribute the content within the section, each individual instrument should be written in a practical and comfortable register. Scoring any instrument in an extreme register will draw attention to that particular element, thereby degrading the homogeneous blend of the tutti. For this particular example, one could place the soprano part (8va) in the flutes, the alto part (8va) in the 1st oboe, the tenor part (8va) in the 2nd oboe, the soprano part (as is) in the 1st clarinet, the alto part (as is) in the 2nd clarinet, the tenor part (as is) in the 1st bassoon and the bass part (as is) in the 2nd bassoon (or contrabassoon, if applicable). In this particular case, doubling the flutes will add a slight emphasis to the melody line. If this example were in a higher register where the flutes would be approaching the altissimo register, doubling the flutes would not be advisable.

When scored in this manner and combined with the string section, the lower woodwinds reinforce and add texture to the string timbre, while the octave doublings in the upper woodwinds enrich the texture of the content, much as a 4′ stop would add texture to an 8′ stop of a pipe organ.

The brass section is used to reinforce the strings and lower woodwinds, while adding a full and powerful texture to the orchestration. Though several options exist, a practical tactic is to place the soprano part in the trumpets, the alto part in the upper horns, the tenor part in the lower horns and 1st trombone, the bass part in the 2nd trombone and the bass part (octavo basso) in the tuba. This technique results in a balanced brass choir sound with a firm foundation provided by the octave doubling of the bass line.

Scoring the ensemble as described above results in the following orchestration:

John Antes, *Christ the Lord, the Lord Most Glorious*, mm. 1–9 (orchestrated by RJ Miller, concert score)

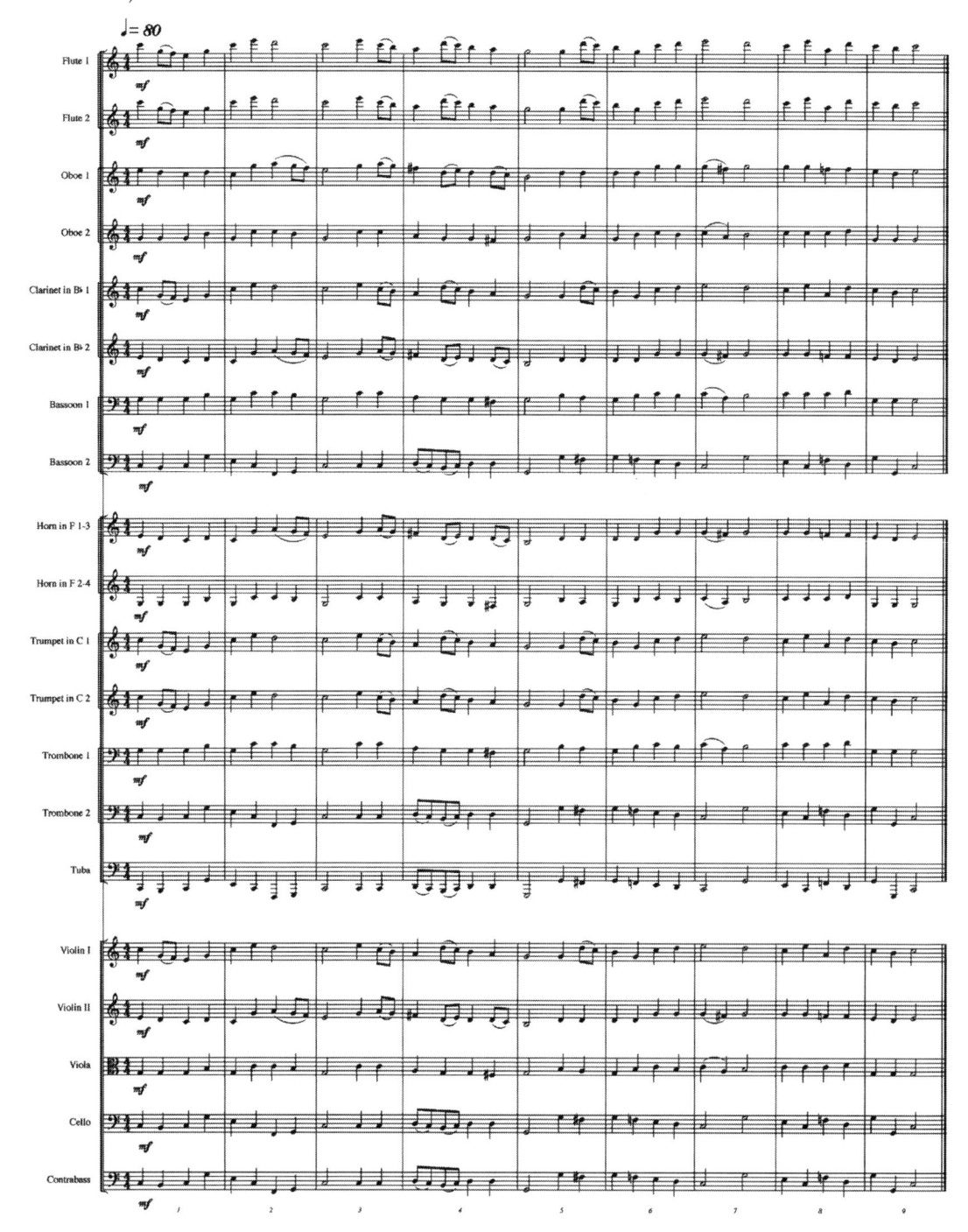

One can alter the overall richness of the orchestration by simply modifying the scoring of the string section (leaving the woodwinds and brass as previously described).

By placing the soprano part (8va) in the 1st violins, the soprano part (in its original octave) in the 2nd violins, the alto part in the viols, the tenor part in the cellos and the bass part (sounding octavo basso) in the contrabasses, one adds emphasis to the melodic content while leaving the harmonic elements intact. Texture is added to the 1st violin part with the flutes, and the space between the 1st and 2nd violins is filled by the 1st oboe (and occasionally the 2nd oboe). One need not be concerned that the bass line appears only in its octavo basso form in the string section as it appears in its original octave in both the 2nd bassoon and 2nd trombone parts.

String scoring (variation #1):

Another possible scoring variation that provides even more richness and power to the overall texture can be achieved by further altering the string scoring (leaving the woodwinds and brass as previously described). One may place the soprano part (8va) in the 1st violins, the alto part (8va) in the 2nd violins, the soprano part (in its original octave) in the viols, the tenor part in the cellos and the bass part (sounding octavo basso) in the contrabasses.

String scoring (variation #2):

In this configuration, texture is added to the 1st violin part with the flutes and to the 2nd violins with the 1st oboe and the upper horns (octavo basso). The melody in its original octave appears in the viols and is reinforced by the 1st clarinet and trumpets. The tenor part appears in the celli, and is reinforced in the 2nd oboe (8va), the lower horns and the 1st bassoon. The bass line (in its original octave) appears in the 2nd bassoon and the 2nd trombone, and the bass line (octavo basso) appears in the tuba and contrabasses. This scoring technique distributes the melodic and harmonic content over several octaves and creates a rich, almost pipe organ-like texture (the previously described "added stop" effect). It also works quite well for passages at higher dynamic levels, and is extremely useful for climatic segments.

John Antes, *Christ the Lord, the Lord Most Glorious,* **mm. 1–9 (orchestrated by RJ Miller, concert score, string scoring variation #1):**

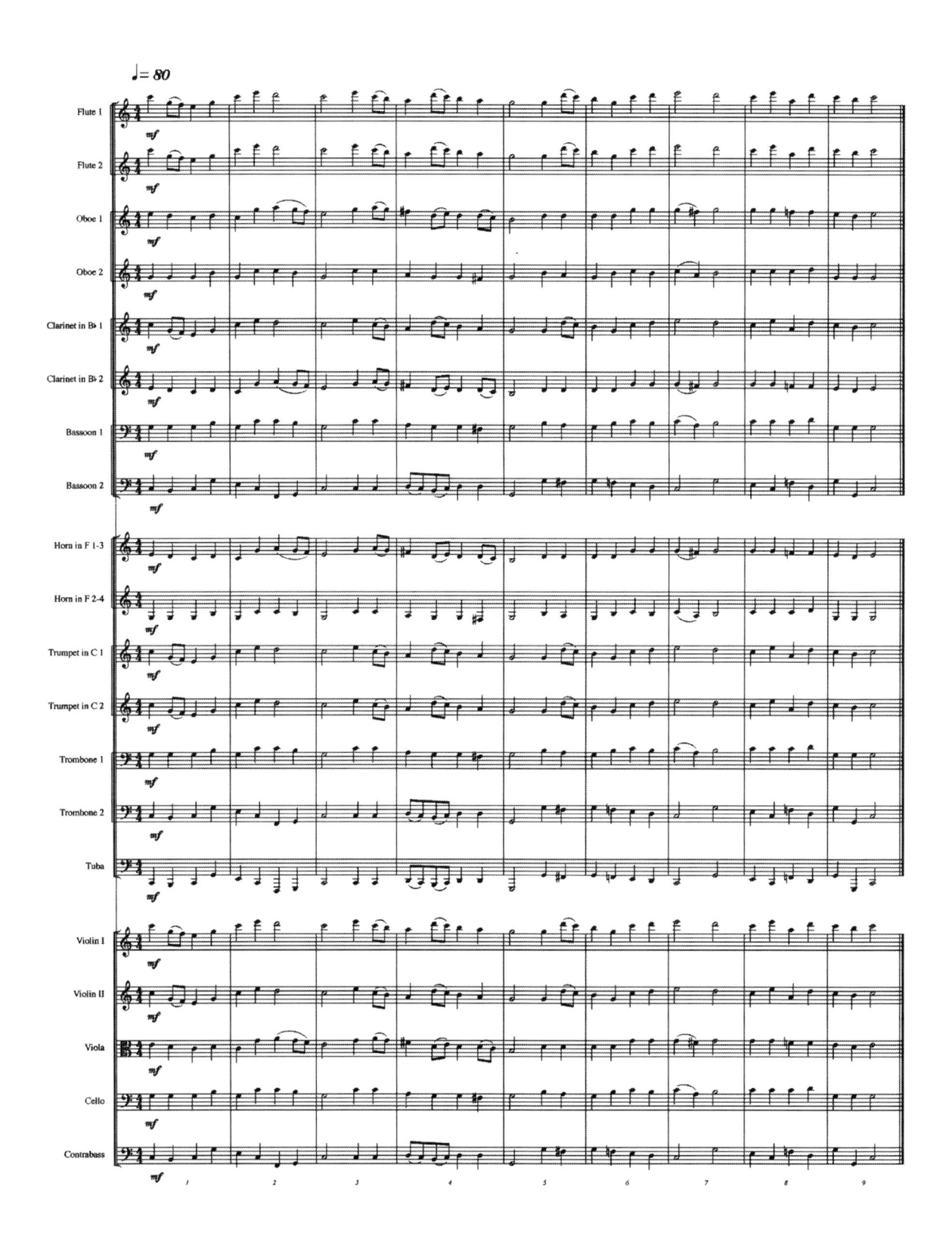

John Antes, *Christ the Lord, the Lord Most Glorious*, mm. 1–9 (orchestrated by RJ Miller, concert score, string scoring variation #2):

The following example consists of a melody line (doubled octavo basso), a harmony line, a fragmented countermelody and a bass line. While any one of several approaches would yield adequate results, the following method is a practical approach that generates a lush texture, with melodic content that remains clearly defined.

RJ Miller, *Promises*, mm. 98–105.

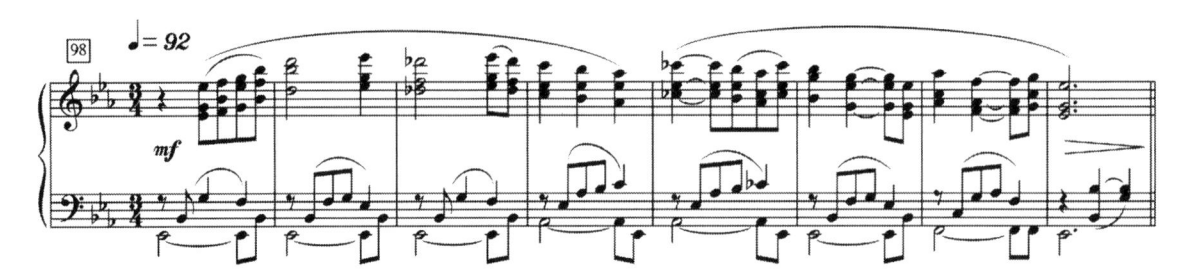

Copyright © 2010 by Appassionata Music. Used by permission.

As with any orchestration, one begins by performing a harmonic analysis, followed by an examination of the various components of the content (i.e. melody, harmony, counterpoint, bass line, etc.).

Once all the above elements have been identified and analyzed, one may address the string section by placing the melody in the 1st violins, the harmony in the 2nd violins, the melody (octavo basso) in the viols, the countermelody in the cellos and the bass line in the contrabasses.

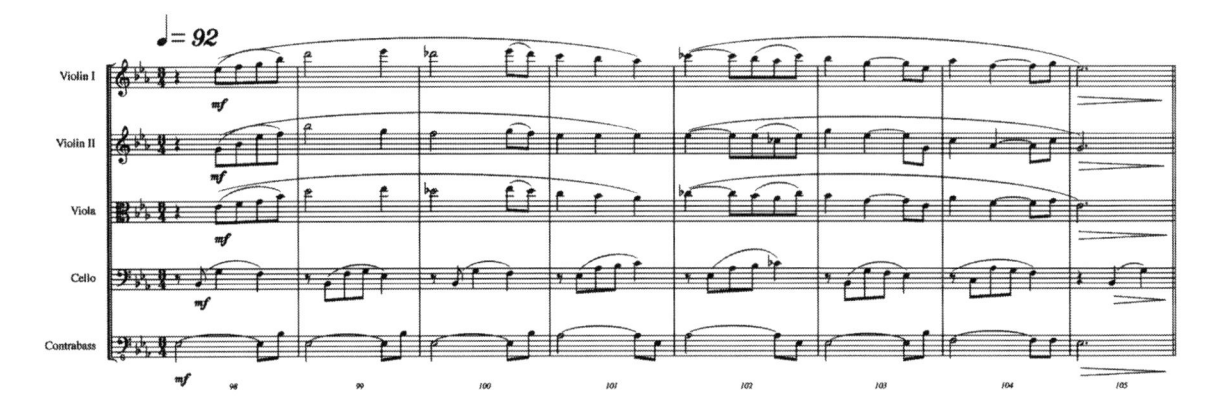

In circumstances where the octavo basso melody would force the viols into an uncharacteristic register, it is perfectly acceptable to score the 1st violins on the melody, the 2nd violins on the melody (octavo basso) and the viols on the harmony line, scored below the second violin line.

To create a similar blend in the woodwinds, place the melody in the flutes, the harmony in the 1st oboe, the melody (octavo basso) in the 2nd oboe and 1st clarinet, the harmony (octavo basso) in the 2nd clarinet, the countermelody in the 1st bassoon and the bass line in the 2nd bassoon (or contrabassoon, if applicable). *Note*: In circumstances where the flutes would be approaching the altissimo register, doubling the 2nd flute with the 1st oboe would be a more advisable solution.

The combination of these two families is a well-blended, merged texture that is full, yet still somewhat transparent.

The brass section will add weight and power to the overall texture. Even in this basic approach, there are several options, depending upon the desired result. The most simplistic tactic is to place the melody (octavo basso) in the trumpets, the harmony (octavo basso) in the horns, the countermelody in the trombones and the bass line in the tuba.

The resultant orchestral texture is robust, while retaining melodic clarity.

The following example consists of a melody (doubled octavo basso), a harmony line, a fragmented countermelody, accompaniment chords and a bass line. Though this example offers a variety of plausible approaches, a sumptuous texture and clearly defined melody should remain the goal of the orchestrator.

RJ Miller, *Celebration Waltz*, mm. 73–105.

Copyright © 2010 by Appassionata Music. Used by permission.

Once again, one begins by performing a harmonic analysis, followed by an examination of the various components of the content (i.e. melody, harmony, counterpoint, bass line, etc.).

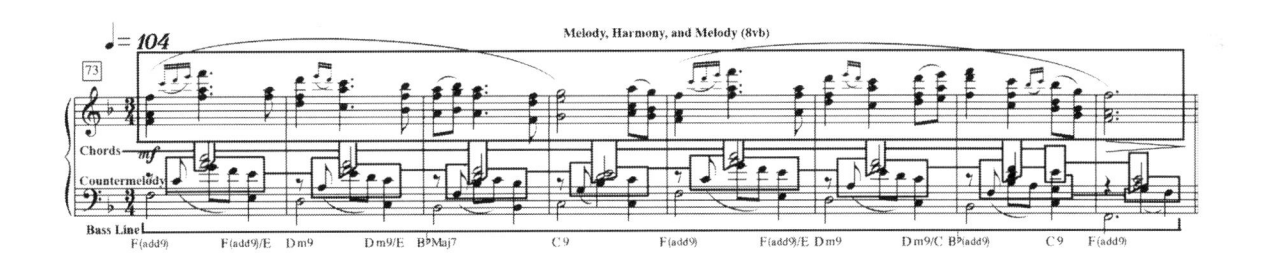

Once the harmonic progression and content elements have been analyzed and identified, the strings may be orchestrated by placing the melody in the 1st violins, the harmony in the 2nd violins, the melody (octavo basso) in the viols, the countermelody in the cellos and the bass line in the contrabasses.

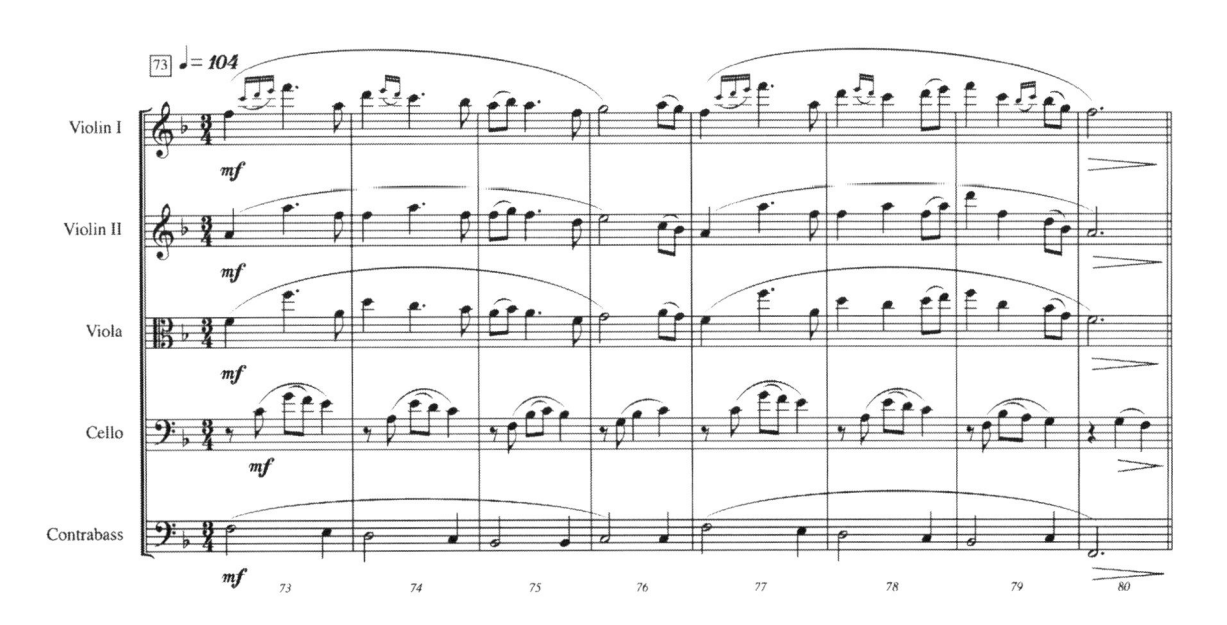

As previously stated, circumstances may exist where scoring the viols on the octavo basso melody becomes problematic. In those situations, one would score the 1st violins on the melody, the 2nd violins on the melody (octavo basso) and the viols on the harmony line, scored below the second violin line.

Since the accompaniment chords are not contained within the string section, one must orchestrate the woodwind section in a manner that accommodates this content. One would place the melody in the 1st flute, the harmony in the 2nd flute, the melody (octavo basso) in the 1st oboe, the accompaniment chords voiced in the 2nd oboe and clarinets, the countermelody in the 1st bassoon and the bass line in the 2nd bassoon (or contrabassoon, if applicable).

As with the previous technique, the combination of these two families is a merged texture that is rich and somewhat translucent.

There are several options available when scoring the brass section, with each yielding a slightly different overall texture. One method would be to place the melody in the trumpets, the harmony in the horns, the countermelody in the 1st trombone, part of the accompaniment chords in the 2nd trombone and the bass line in the tuba.

Another method would be to place the melody in the 1st trumpet, the harmony in the 2nd trumpet, the melody (octavo basso) in the horns, the accompaniment chords in the trombones and the bass line in the tuba. The resultant overall texture is adequate with this technique, though the countermelody would lack presence.

A third, and probably most viable method, would be to place the melody in the 1st trumpet, the harmony in the 2nd trumpet, the countermelody in the horns, the accompaniment chords in the trombones and the bass line in the tuba.

The following is the resultant orchestration when using the first brass section scoring technique listed above.

The following is the resultant orchestration when using the second brass section scoring technique listed above.

The following is the resultant orchestration when using the third brass section scoring technique listed above.

SCORING EXAMPLES

Franz Schubert, Symphony in C Major, Movement IV, Op. posth., mm. 15–25.

RJ Miller, *Processional*, mm. 5–11.

Copyright © 1997 by Appassionata Music. Used by permission.

SUGGESTED EXERCISE

Using the information and guidelines presented in this chapter and in Chapter 3 (Practical Problem Solving), orchestrate the following example for string orchestral tutti. Start by performing a harmonic analysis and ensure harmonic balance in each instrumental family.

Moritz Moszkowski, *Spanish Dance*, **Op. 12 No. 1**

12

SCORING FOR WIND ENSEMBLE/ CONCERT BAND TUTTI

A large ensemble consisting of wind and percussion instruments may be known by one of several names, including concert band, symphonic band, wind symphony, wind ensemble and wind band. Since there is no internationally standardized instrumentation for these ensembles, and though certain ensemble directors may site personal distinctions, all (with the exception of the wind ensemble) may be classified as concert bands.

Wind Ensemble

As previously mentioned, the wind ensemble is, in essence, a diminutive version of the concert band. One popular disposition of wind ensemble instrumentation is the Eastman Wind Ensemble configuration (established in 1952 by Frederick Fennell). In this method, instrumentation is limited to one player per part, resulting in a transparent quality that is unencumbered by excessive doubling. While some wind ensembles adhere to the "Eastman" approach, many contemporary ensembles tend to favor the fuller, more powerful sound produced by two players per part. In either case, one can assume a balanced distribution of parts within the ensemble and the availability of all of the standard wind and percussion instruments. One simply approaches this ensemble as one would with any chamber group, accentuating its more precise intonation and clarity of individual part. The instrumentation one may expect to have at one's disposal in the wind ensemble setting is as follows:

1st Flute
2nd Flute (doubles on piccolo)
Alto Flute (auxiliary instrument)
Bass Flute (auxiliary instrument)
1st Oboe
2nd Oboe (doubles on English horn)
1st Bassoon
2nd Bassoon
    (*or*) Contrabassoon (auxiliary instrument)
E♭ Clarinet
1st B♭ Clarinet
2nd B♭ Clarinet
3rd B♭ Clarinet
    (occasionally a 4th B♭ clarinet part is included)

E♭ Alto Clarinet
Bass Clarinet
Contra-alto Clarinet (auxiliary instrument)
Contrabass Clarinet (auxiliary instrument)
Soprano Saxophone (auxiliary instrument)
Alto Saxophone
Tenor Saxophone
Baritone Saxophone
Bass Saxophone (auxiliary instrument)
Cornets/Trumpets (3–4)
Horns in F (4)
Euphonium/Baritone
1st Trombone

2nd Trombone
Bass Trombone
Tuba
Percussion

String Bass
Piano
Harp (auxiliary instrument)

Should one wish to employ what would be considered auxiliary instruments, one should write any exposed selections for these instruments as cue notes in other suitable parts (see Chapter 14, Instrument Substitution). In tutti sections, these parts should be doubled, either in unison or at the octave, with other instruments to insure that the harmonic balance remains intact should these instruments be unavailable.

Concert Band

The inconsistency and irregularity of the available instrumentation within the concert band, particularly in the academic environment, is the most challenging problem with which an orchestrator must contend. There are several approaches that the orchestrator may employ to accommodate the variances in instrumentation. The following are but a few of the possible options:

- In the initial scoring of a selection, one may choose to assume a relatively balanced distribution of parts within the ensemble, scoring the work exactly as one wishes it to sound. One would then add cue notes in parts that would serve as a suitable substitute for instruments that may be unavailable in a given ensemble (see Chapter 14, Instrument Substitution).
- One could restrict any featured solo passages contained within the work to the most readily available instruments (i.e. 1st flute, 1st B♭ clarinet, 1st B♭ trumpet, 1st Trombone, etc.). One should note that in a rural academic environment, the availability of double reeds cannot be assumed. As such, any featured elements for members of the double reed family should be written as cue notes in other suitable parts (see Chapter 14, Instrument Substitution).
- One can avoid isolating an individual instrument by scoring all featured areas for pairs of instruments from different families, thereby insuring that all featured elements are adequately represented should a particular individual instrument be absent from the ensemble instrumentation.

Nearly all concert bands reside in the academic setting. This is a vast and viable market for the orchestrator. A large majority of schools, ranging from middle schools (junior high schools) to universities, have at least one wind band, and most will have multiple ensembles. Post-academic concert bands are generally community bands, with professional concert bands being virtually non-existent. Most professional wind bands are wind ensembles, but unfortunately, their numbers have dwindled over the years. While one should always seize the opportunity of writing for a professional ensemble, should one wish to write extensively for wind band, one's career would be best served by focusing upon the academic environment. A basic, generic instrumentation list for the university/professional-level concert band would be as follows.

Flutes (8–10, one doubling on piccolo)
Oboes (2, one doubling on English horn)
Bassoons (2, one doubling on contrabass bassoon)
E♭ clarinet (1)
B♭ clarinets (12–14)
Alto clarinets (2)
Bass clarinets (2)
Contrabass clarinet (1)
Alto saxophones (2–4)
Tenor saxophones (2)
Baritone saxophone (1)
Trumpets/cornets (8–10)

Horns in F (4–8)
Trombones (3–4)
Bass trombone (1)
Baritones/Euphoniums (2)
Tubas (2–4)
Double bass (1)
Percussion (6 players)
    Full complement
    Glockenspiel
    Timpani (4 drums)
Piano (auxiliary instrument)
Harp (auxiliary instrument)

The percussion complement available at this level will still vary from ensemble to ensemble, but with a full battery of instruments would likely include the following:

Snare Drum	Bell tree	Whip
Field snare	Wood Blocks	Sleigh bells
Tom-toms	Temple Blocks	Timbales
Bass drum	Anvil	Drum set
Hand cymbals (piatti)	Brake drums	Timpani (4 drums)
Suspended cymbals	Bongos	Glockenspiel
Finger cymbals	Congas	Xylophone
Tam-tam	Claves	Marimba
Triangle	Guiro	Crotales
Tambourine	Maracas	Vibraphone
Wind chimes	Shakers	Chimes
Mark tree	Castanets	

Since scoring for the various individual instruments and sections has been previously addressed in this text, writing for the full concert band tutti will be the focus of the remainder of this chapter. The manner in which one orchestrates and the technical boundaries within which one must work varies with the age and skill level of the ensemble. One must be cognizant of the limitations of the range, register, technical skills and, in some cases, physical abilities of the players at each level for which one writes.

PRACTICAL CONSIDERATIONS

In most cases, the melody can be doubled at the octave, as well as being doubled octavo basso. To insure a balanced and well-blended ensemble texture, one should avoid large intervallic gaps between voices. While it is acceptable to double a bass line octavo basso, it should never be doubled an octave above its original pitch.

Extreme registers rarely, if ever, yield positive results in the tutti environment. Should one choose to use extreme registers; they are best employed at louder dynamic levels. At softer dynamic levels, extreme registers will compromise the overall blend and ensemble texture. If any extreme registers are to be used, they are best approached in a step-wise manner (diatonically or chromatically) or by small intervals.

Piccolo is best used for "splashes of color" and is generally not suited for the tutti environment. Should one wish to include piccolo in a tutti section, it should be employed only in passages of rapid rhythmical contain, and avoided in slow, lyrical passages.

Though there are exceptions, flutes are usually scored in two parts for the concert band. Best results are achieved if these parts are scored in close voicing, spanning less than an octave.

Oboes are usually scored in two parts for the concert band. Best results are achieved if these parts are scored in close voicing, spanning less than an octave. If scoring for university- or professional-level ensembles, one may assume the availability of English horn, either as a double for the 2nd oboe or as a separate (3rd) member of the oboe section.

The clarinet family generally constitutes the largest family in the woodwind section. As such, one should consider it the nucleus of the woodwind texture. All elements of the tutti (melody, harmony and bass line) should be logically distributed, as completely as possible, throughout the clarinets with the largest intervals occurring between the lowest voices. Unless scoring for university- or professional-level ensembles, one should not assume the availability of contrabass clarinet. When scoring for bass clarinet or contrabass clarinet, one should avoid complex, tongued passages in the low register.

Care should be exercised when scoring the saxophone section to ensure proper harmonic balance with the remainder of the woodwind section. Generally, the saxophones are scored in tandem with the clarinets and bassoons.

Unless scoring for university- or professional-level ensembles, one should not assume the availability of multiple bassoons (or contrabassoon). While bassoons may be used for harmonic content, in the ensemble tutti they generally provide the bass line for the woodwind section. When circumstances and ranges permit, this bass line may be doubled (octavo basso) in the second bassoon (or contrabassoon) part. One should avoid intricate, tongued passages in the low register.

Trumpets/cornets sound best when voiced in closed position. Scoring trumpets/cornets in open voicings should be avoided whenever possible.

Horns sound best when voiced in close position. Scoring horns in open voicings should be avoided whenever possible.

Trombones can be scored in either open or closed voicings. However, if one desires a rich and sonorous texture from the trombones, open voicings yield the best results.

Since the brass texture will dominate the ensemble sound, all elements of the tutti (melody, harmony and bass line) should be logically distributed throughout the brass family (with the largest intervals occurring between the lowest voices). The brass section can cover any harmonic element that may be lacking in the woodwind section voicings. However, the woodwind section cannot be used to fill any gaps the may be present in the brass section voicings.

Practical Guidelines when Scoring for Wind Ensemble/Concert Band Tutti

- Instrumental and harmonic balances are critical.
- Score all instruments in comfortable registers.
- Avoid altissimo registers, especially in brass.
- Score each instrumental family is such a manner that they sound rich and full independently.
- Also be aware of the implied fundamental generated by each and every voicing.
- Learn from the *masters*! *Listen to and analyze* as many different examples of wind ensemble tutti scoring as possible.

BUILDING THE SCORE

Scoring for Wind Ensemble/Concert Band Tutti

Scoring for university- or professional-level concert band affords one expanded instrumentation in the woodwind section and solidifies the instrumentation of the brass section. One can also expect a full complement of percussion instruments at this level.

In the woodwind section one can assume the availability of E♭ clarinet, contrabass clarinet and contrabassoon. Though not particularly effective in the tutti environment, English horn, alto flute and B♭ soprano saxophone are also generally at one's disposal.

In the brass section, one generally eliminates baritones from one's instrumental palette, opting exclusively for euphoniums (bass clef only). One can also assume that a bass trombone will play the lowest trombone part.

To show the opportunities offered by the expanded wind instrumentation available in the wind ensemble (vs. the orchestra), the same SATB selection previously used will also serve for the following demonstration.

John Antes, Christ the Lord, the Lord Most Glorious, mm. 1–9.

One can approach the clarinet choir at university or professional level much in the same way one approaches it at high-school level, the only difference between the two being the addition of the E♭ clarinet and contrabass clarinet to the ensemble. Following the same process as for the high-school ensemble, the soprano line is placed in the 1st clarinets, the alto line in the 2nd clarinets, the tenor line in the 3rd clarinets and the bass line in the bass clarinet. Since, at high-school level, the 3rd clarinets are often weaker players than those in the 1st and 2nd clarinet sections, the alto clarinet can be used to reinforce the 3rd clarinet parts. For this example, the alto clarinet would yield best the results by doubling the tenor line.

The E♭ clarinet could be used in a few different ways, depending upon the range and register of a given selection. It could double a harmony part 8va, placing it above the 1st B♭ clarinets. It could double the melody in the 1st B♭ clarinets. It could double the 1st B♭ clarinets melody 8va, though this technique can be problematic as the instrument becomes quite piercing and dominates in the upper register. For this example, the E♭ clarinet would yield best the results by doubling the alto line 8va.

The contrabass clarinet is best used as an octavo basso reinforcement of the bass line. Since the original version of the bass line already exists in the bass clarinet part, the addition of an octavo basso will add stability and depth to the clarinet texture.

One could address the flutes and oboes in the same manner used for the highschool level example, placing the soprano line (8va) in the 1st flutes, the alto line (8va) in the 2nd flutes and 1st oboe, and the soprano line (in its original form) in the 2nd oboe.

At the university or professional level one could score two bassoons, or two bassoons with the 2nd bassoon doubling on contrabassoon (designated in the score simply as bassoon and contrabassoon), or two bassoons and contrabassoon. As such, one has a number of options when scoring for the bassoon section. If scoring for two bassoons, the 1st bassoon could be voiced on a harmony part above the 2nd bassoon, with the 2nd bassoon doubling the bass line. If scoring for two bassoons with the 2nd bassoon doubling on contrabassoon (designated in the score simply as bassoon and contrabassoon), one could place the bass line in the 1st bassoon and the bass line (8vb) in the contrabassoon, thereby doubling the bass clarinet and contrabass clarinet. If scoring for two bassoons and contrabassoon, one could place the bassoons on harmony parts and the bass line (original or 8vb, depending upon register) in the contrabassoon. Or, depending upon the situation, one could place the 1st bassoon on a harmony part, the 2nd bassoon on the bass line, and the contrabassoon on the octavo basso bass line. For the purposes of this example, the bass line is placed in the 1st bassoon and the bass line (8vb) in the contrabassoon (2nd bassoon doubling on contrabassoon).

The configuration of the saxophone section at the university or professional level generally consists of two alto saxophones, one tenor saxophone and one baritone saxophone, though one can expect the availability of a soprano saxophone (usually as a substitute for the top alto saxophone) at this level. If one chooses this option, one has access to all of the saxophones contained in the classical saxophone quartet. One might consider this option should the range and register of the top saxophone voice venture into the altissimo register if scored for alto saxophone. For this example, the soprano line will be placed in the 1st alto saxophone, the alto line in the 2nd alto saxophone, the tenor line in the tenor saxophone and the bass line in the baritone saxophone.

The basic brass section of the university- or professional-level ensemble is virtually identical to that of the high-school ensemble, with the exception of the baritones. At this level, euphoniums have supplanted baritones, so it is no longer necessary to accommodate the range restriction of the baritone, nor is it necessary to provide the transposed treble clef parts. As such, one may treat the euphonium as a melodic instrument, a harmonic element or as a tenor tuba used to reinforce the tuba parts. One makes that decision based upon the range, register and balance needs of the selection. For the purposes of this example, the euphonium will be used as a tenor tuba, playing the bass line in its original form.

At this level, trumpets are generally scored in two or three parts, horns in two to four parts and trombones in three to four parts (with the lowest part being designated as the bass trombone part). One decides upon the trumpet and horn configurations based upon the range and register dictated by the composition, and the ability to voice these sections primarily in close voicings. The configuration of the trombone section is determined by the harmonic complexity of the selection and ability to voice the section primarily in open voicings.

For the provided example, the following configuration would yield the best overall ensemble texture:

Soprano line:	*Alto line:*	*Tenor line:*	*Bass line:*
1st trumpets	2nd trumpets	2nd horns	bass trombone
3rd horn (8vb)	1st horns	2nd trombone	euphonium
1st trombone (8vb)			tuba (8vb)

Scoring in the manner described above results in a rich, stable and balanced sound throughout the ensemble.

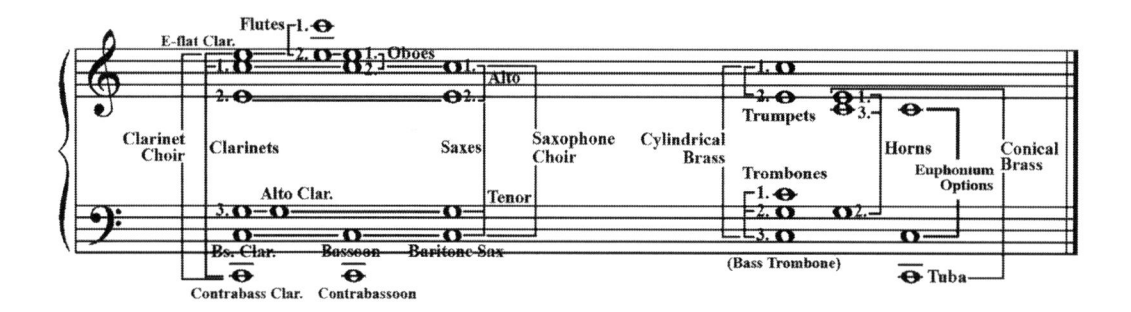

John Antes, *Christ the Lord, the Lord Most Glorious*, **mm. 1–9 (orchestrated by RJ Miller, transposed score)**

SCORING EXAMPLES

J.S. Bach, *O Haupt voll Blut und Wunden*, orchestrated by RJ Miller, concert score.

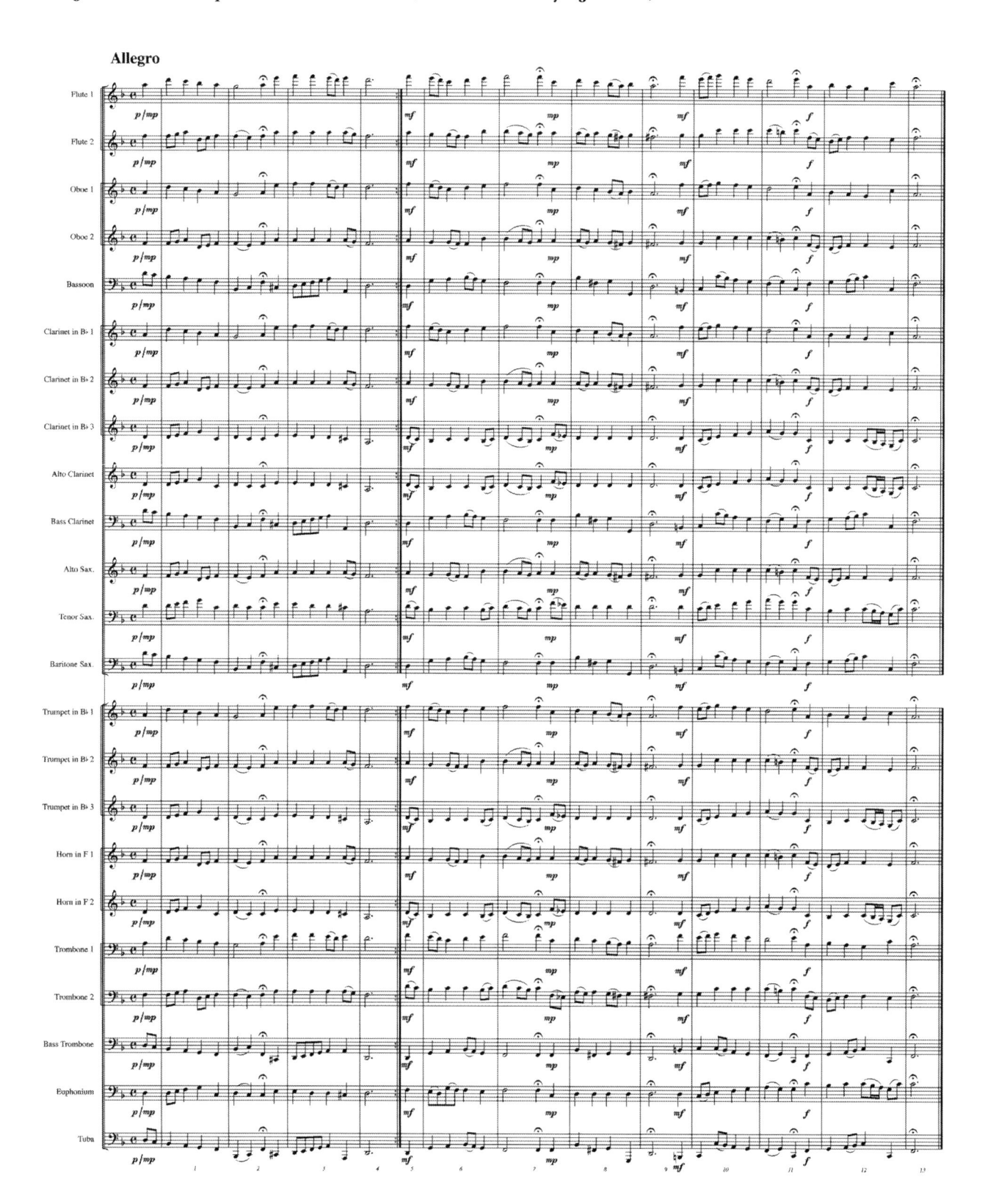

THE WIND ENSEMBLE AND CONCERT BAND TUTTI 393

RJ Miller, *Yuletide*, mm. 111–120.

Copyright © 1996 by Appassionata Music. Used by permission.

RJ Miller, *Recessional*, mm. 41–49.

Copyright © 1997 by Appassionata Music. Used by permission.

SUGGESTED EXERCISE

Using the information and guidelines presented in this chapter and in Chapter 3 (Practical Problem Solving), orchestrate the following example for wind ensemble tutti. Start by performing a harmonic analysis and ensure harmonic balance in each instrumental family.

Xaver Scharwenka, *Polish Dance*, **Op. 3, No. 1**

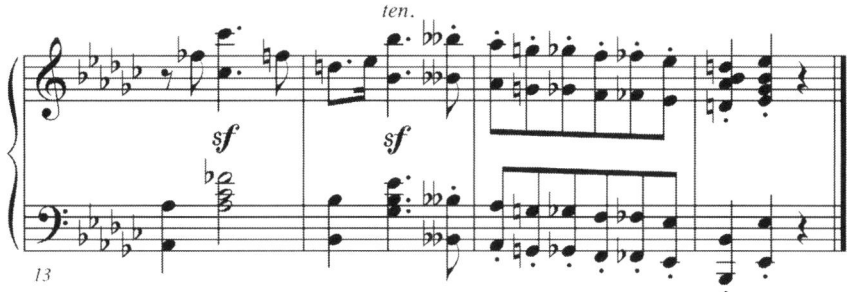

13
SCORING FOR MUSICAL THEATER

Scoring for musical theater presents challenges for the orchestrator which are not encountered in other genres. Traditional productions from the golden age of musical theater (i.e. the works of Gershwin, Rodgers and Hammerstein, Victor Herbert, Jerome Kern, etc.) were generally scored for a fairly consistent group of instruments. However, in contemporary time there is no standardized instrumentation. The instrumentation is completely dependent upon the style of the play and the economics of the production.

Attrition

Even when scoring for a traditional-style production, economics can affect the scoring process. During the run of a production the number of musicians often diminishes from that of the opening night. One may have a "full" pit orchestra on the opening night, followed by a reduction in numbers after six to eight weeks, and possibly another reduction a few months later. A skilled orchestrator will score the work with this in mind, attempting to avoid constant reorchestration throughout the run of a show. Generally, the string section is the first casualty of this economic attrition, occasionally being significantly reduced in numbers, or completely eliminated from the pit orchestra. Even if the budget allows for a few string players to remain (often no more than a string quartet), their presence in the orchestration is greatly reduced. This can be problematic for the orchestrator, as there is no viable substitute for the warmth of a full string section when accompanying vocals. Since the advent of synthesizers and samplers, what once was the realm of a dozen or more string players is now often relegated to an electronic keyboard. One cannot expect a sampled or synthetic string section to be capable of all the nuances of a live string section. Conversely, one cannot expect a live string section to perform all the functions possible from a sampled or synthetic string section. It is that responsibility of the orchestrator to be equally skilled in scoring for either configuration. Finding the common ground between these two elements will yield the most viable results.

Woodwinds and brass generally are not affected by economic attrition as they are generally scored for the minimum acceptable amount of players from the beginning of the production. The percussion section will usually begin with two players, one on drum set and one on auxiliary instruments (which may include timpani, chimes, mallet instruments, tam-tam, cymbals, etc.). This will generally be reduced to one player on drum set unless the auxiliary instruments are an intricate part of the story (i.e. chimes for church bells, tam-tam for an Asian effect, etc.).

Bandstration

Bandstration is a term one will commonly encounter in the musical theater environment. Derived from the amalgamation of "band" and "orchestration," the term has been in use since the 19th century to describe the process of orchestrating for wind band. It was most likely incorporated into the musical theater lexicon when the instrumentation of the pit orchestra evolved to more closely resemble that of a wind band than that of an operatic orchestra. Though the term has become somewhat archaic outside the theatrical milieu, it survives in accepted usage in that setting.

Books

In the pit orchestra setting, the parts for each instrument are assembled into "books." The parts are bound sequentially, in the order in which they occur during the musical. Books from musicals of the "golden age" of musical theater were configured much as one would expect in a classical orchestra, i.e. flute I, flute II, oboe I, etc. However, in contemporary times, all the woodwind players are generally expected to double on multiple instruments, and the woodwind books are referred to as "reed" books. This term applies even if a given book does not require the woodwind player to actually perform on a reed instrument.

Conductor's Score

Though it is occasionally supplied, particularly for "golden age-style" productions, a full conductor's score is not normally part of the orchestral package for musical theater production. In contemporary times, and as a direct result of economic considerations, one person generally performs the roles of music director, pianist, rehearsal pianist and conductor. As such, a combination Piano/Conductor score has become the accepted norm. This score may be constructed as elaborately as a detailed condensed score with a full piano part, or as simplistically as a vocal/piano part with instrument cues (sometimes using only text) written in the piano part. One must always bear in mind that the music director/pianist is simultaneously executing multiple responsibilities. As such, one attempts to be as concise as possible, avoiding the inclusion of elements that would cause the score to become cumbersome. For example, the pianist/conductor needs to know the exact placement for the entrance of the flutes, but doesn't necessarily need a representation of the harmony parts provided by flute II and flute III.

Instrumentation

As previously mentioned, the instrumentation for "golden age-style" productions resembles that of a small operatic orchestra. The instrumentation for *The King and I* by Rodgers and Hammerstein is an example of this style of scoring.

The King and I

Music by Richard Rodgers
Book and lyrics by Oscar Hammerstein II
Based on *Anna and the King* by Margaret Landon
Original choreography by Jerome Robbins
Licensing agent: R&H Theatricals

1—Piano/conductor score
1—Flute I
1—Flute II (doubles piccolo)
1—Oboe (optional doubling English horn)
1—Clarinet I–II

1—Clarinet III (doubling bass clarinet)
1—Bassoon
1—Horn I–II
1—Horn III
1—Trumpet I–II
1—Trumpet III
1—Trombone I
1—Trombone II
1—Tuba
2—Percussion (trap set, timpani, bells, gong, triangle, xylophone, temple blocks, oriental drum, finger cymbals, wood block, ratchet, slap stick)
2—Violin A (divisi)
2—Violin B (divisi)
1—Violin C
1—Viola (divisi)
1—Cello
1—Bass
1—Harp

Supplemental books:
Libretto-vocal books
Piano/vocal score
Two-piano arrangement (Act I, 2 Act II)

Note that a two-piano arrangement of the orchestral score is also supplied. This is not an unusual occurrence for productions that are originally scored for large instrumentation. One should always be prepared to supply a piano (or two-piano) reduction for large pit orchestras.

In musical theater terminology, the instrumentation of the above listed orchestra would be referred to as "twenty-seven, plus piano." This refers to the number of instrumentalists required for the orchestration, plus the piano/conductor part.

The instrumentation for contemporary productions incorporates the use of "reed books" that require the woodwind players to double on multiple instruments. The instrumentation for *Cats* by Andrew Lloyd Webber is an example of this style of scoring. One will note that in this production a full conductor's score is provided, in addition to a piano/conductor part. This allows the production company the option of having a dedicated conductor, or a pianist who doubles as the conductor.

Cats

Music by Andrew Lloyd Webber
Lyrics: T. S. Eliot, Trevor Nunn, Richard Stilgoe
Based on *Old Possum's Book of Practical Cats* by T. S. Eliot
Licensing agent: Really Useful Music Publishing

1—Full score—Act 1
1—Full score—Act 2
1—Piano/Conductor score—Act 1
1—Piano/Conductor score—Act 2
1—Reed I (flute, tenor sax, soprano sax)
1—Reed II (clarinet, baritone sax, flute)

1—Reed II (English horn, oboe)
1—Horn I
1—Horn II
1—Trumpet I (B♭ trumpet, piccolo trumpet)
1—Trumpet II (B♭ trumpet, flugelhorn)
1—Trombone
1—Cello
1—Guitar (electric, acoustic)
1—Bass
1—Drums
1—Keyboard I (electric piano, piano)
1—Keyboard II
1—Keyboard III
1—Percussion (bass drum, bell tree, cabasa, castanets, concert bass drum, congas, cowbell, cymbal, deep gong, glockenspiel, gong, maraca, ratchet, rattle, shake, suspended cymbal, tambourine, tam-tam, timpani, triangle, vibes, vibraslap, whip, wood block, xylophone)

Supplemental books:
Libretto-vocal books
Piano/vocal score

In musical theater terminology, the instrumentation of the above listed orchestra would be referred to as "sixteen, plus piano." Again, this refers to the number of instrumentalists required for the orchestration, plus the piano/conductor part.

Productions that stylistically align more with the genus of pop, rock, rap, etc., tend to favor instrumentation more akin to that of the given genre. The instrumentation for *Rent* by Jonathan Larson is an example of this style of scoring.

Rent

Book, music and lyrics by Jonathan Larson
Licensing agent: Music Theatre International (MTI)
Piano/conductor score Act 1
Piano/conductor score Act 2

Guitar (acoustic guitar, electric guitar, tambourine)
Guitar 2/keyboard 2 (acoustic guitar, electric guitar, keyboard/synthesizer)
Bass
Drums (drum kit, electronic percussion, garbage can lid, shaker, sleigh bells)

Supplemental books:
Libretto-vocal books
Piano/vocal score

Alternate Instrumentation

Many musicals will be scored with alternate instrumentation that either expands or delineates the original instrumentation. For example, *Oklahoma!* by Rodgers and Hammerstein is available in its "standard" instrumentation, in a version with expanded instrumentation, or as a two-piano reduction.

Oklahoma!

Music by Richard Rodgers
Book and lyrics by Oscar Hammerstein II
Original dances by Agnes de Mille
Based on the play *Green Grow the Lilacs* by Lynn Riggs
Licensing agent: R&H Theatricals

Standard Orchestration Package (18, plus piano)

1—Piano/conductor score
1—Flute (doubling piccolo)
1—Oboe (optional English horn)
1—Clarinet I–II (clarinet I doubles bass clarinet)
1—Bassoon
1—Horn I–II
1—Trumpet I–II
1—Trombone
1—Percussion (trap set, 2 timpani, wood block, bells, temple blocks, xylophone)
2—Violin a–b (divisi)
1—Viola (divisi)
1—Cello
1—Bass
1—Guitar (doubling banjo)
1—Harp

Supplemental books:
Libretto-vocal books
Piano/vocal score

Alternate Orchestration Package (24, plus piano)

1—Piano/conductor score, bandstration
1—Flute I–II (both doubling piccolo with opt flute III)
1—Oboe
1—Clarinet I
1—Clarinet II
1—Clarinet III
1—Alto clarinet
1—Bass clarinet
1—Bassoon
1—Alto sax
1—Tenor sax
1—Baritone sax
1—Trumpet I
1—Tumpet II–III
1—Horn I–II
1—Trombone I–II
1—Trombone III
1—Baritone horn
1—Tuba (optional divisi for two players)
2—Percussion (trap set, 2 timpani, wood block, bells, temple blocks, xylophone)

Supplemental books:
Libretto-vocal books
Piano/vocal score

Additional options

2—Two-piano Arrangement—Act I
2—Two-piano Arrangement—Act II

PRACTICAL CONSIDERATIONS

Practical Guidelines when Scoring for Musical Theater

- Vocals are the paramount priority.
- With the exception of overtures, exit music and incidental music, the orchestra serves a supportive role.
- Score all vocals in comfortable tessituras.
- Score all instruments in comfortable registers.
- Avoid altissimo registers, especially in brass.
- Always be aware of the "attrition factor."
- Score each instrumental family is such a manner that they sound rich and full independently.
- Also be aware of the implied fundamental generated by each and every voicing.
- Learn from the *masters*! *Listen to and analyze* as many different examples of musical theater scoring as possible.

BUILDING THE SCORE

Since one should always be aware of the attrition factor when scoring for musical theater, it is wise to construct one's orchestration in the reverse order of attrition. As one proceeds through each layer, one should strive to insure that, while each addition should add to the richness of the orchestration, the essence of the selection will not suffer should the instrumentation be lost to attrition.

To begin the orchestration process, one starts with what is essentially a lead sheet, i.e. melody, lyrics and basic harmonic structure. One then analyzes the melodic and harmonic content, locating and identifying the passing tones and/or neighboring tones. One then determines how one wishes to address these tones in the context of the orchestration.

RJ Miller, *Sarah's Song.*

Copyright © 2013 by Appassionata Music. Used by permission.

In this particular example the passing tone in measure 6 (B♮) and the upper neighboring tone in measure 7 (G♮) will both be harmonized as a suspended 9 chords. The passing tone in measure 4 (F♯) presents no harmonic inconvenience and needs no special consideration in the context of this example.

Always be cognizant of the range and register of the melody and how it falls within the tessitura of the character. The above melody will be comfortably performed if "Sarah" is a soprano, but would be less effective if the "Sarah" character is an alto. Change the key, as necessary, to place the melody in a register which is most conducive to the voice classification of the character. Vocal considerations are paramount in musical theater, and key signatures one would normally avoid in the classical orchestral settings are not uncommon in this environment. Instrumentalists in this genre are adept and proficient in keys that would be considered awkward or inappropriate in a classical genus. It is not unusual for the instrumentalist to be required to play parts written in 5, 6 or 7 sharps, or even parts that would require 8 or more sharps that are spelled enharmonically in flats.

Once all of the above considerations have been addressed, one creates a piano accompaniment part. This part should serve as both a rehearsal piano part and as a performance part (when combined with the pit orchestra). It should be somewhat simplistic in nature as the player is most likely serving multiple rolls (music director, conductor and pianist) while performing the part.

Scoring the Chorus

One approaches scoring for background vocals or chorus in musical theater differently from scoring for classical choir. Generally, one scores the accompaniment vocals in two parts—high chorus and low chorus. The high chorus part is sung by the higher female voices and the higher male voices (8vb) and the low chorus is sung by the lower female voices and the lower male voices (8vb). These parts may, on occasion and if needed, be scored divisi. However, the simpler option usually yields the best results. One must remember that the chorus parts are not being performed by a choir in a stationary position, but rather by performers who, most likely, will be moving about the stage. Normally, the less acrobatic the chorus parts are, the better and more effective the performance will be.

Though the vocal score shows a singular line in each chorus, one should always be cognizant that the parts are actually doubled at the octave (8vb). One must consider this factor as it applies to the overall harmonic balance of the piece. In performance, the above example would actually result in the following voicings:

Creating the Piano/Vocal Part

When creating the piano/vocal part, one attempts to be as concise as possible while still maintaining clarity within the parts. Merging the chorus parts into a singular line is an accepted practice and applicable for most circumstances. However, if the chorus parts contain thick harmonic textures, or contrapuntal elements, a score with the chorus parts on separate staves may eliminate the possibility of confusion. One must strive to be as clear and succinct as possible, while avoiding notation that could result in uncertainty and wasted rehearsal time.

Scoring the Rhythm Section

If this were a contemporary rock or pop production, one might only need to add the remainder of the rhythm section to complete the orchestration. Should that be the case, one would create complementary guitar, bass and drum set parts. Beginning with the guitar, one would decide if an electric, acoustic or classical guitar would best serve the orchestration, and designate the part as such in both the part and the score. Unless a specific line (melody or countermelody) is required, best results are achieved simply by providing the chord progression and designating the style of the selection.

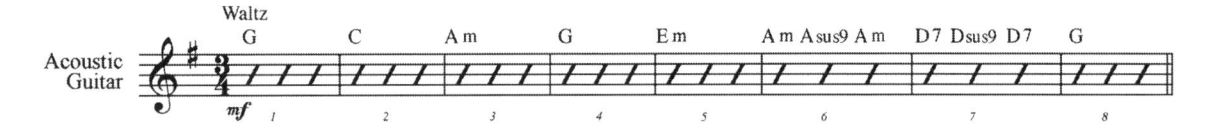

When creating the bass part, one has a several options, depending upon the freedom one wishes to extend to the bass player. If one wishes to strictly define the bass, one would notate exactly what one wishes the bass to play. (If this part were to be played on an acoustic bass, one would designate the part to be performed arco or pizzicato, as applicable.)

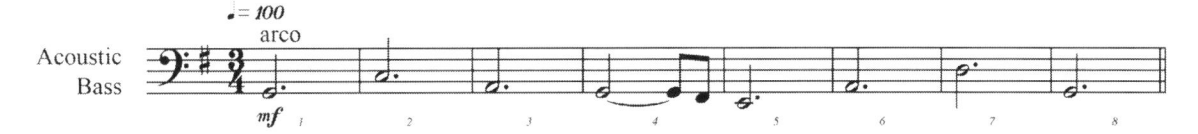

If the use of an electric bass is most appropriate for a given selection, another option is to provide the chord progression and allow the bassist to improvise the bass line within the framework of the harmonic structure. Should there be any essentials specifically required to align with other elements of the orchestration, those should be notated within the context of the chord progression, e.g. measure 4 and measure 5 in the example below. As members of the standard rock, pop, jazz, etc. rhythm section, players of electric bass are adept at providing stylistically appropriate accompaniments.

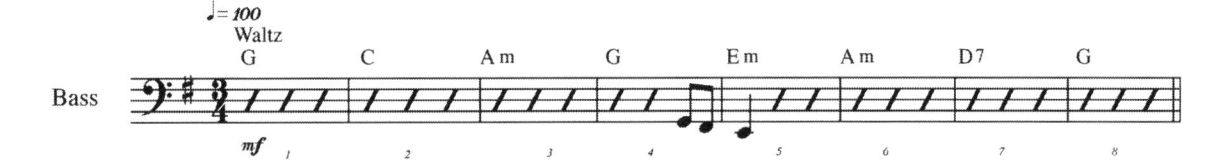

Notating every element of the drum set part is time-consuming, cumbersome for the player and will often yield rigid, less than acceptable results. Percussionists are adept at creating stylistically appropriate accompaniment, and providing the player with a framework within which to work (rather than a fully notated part) will produce a more fluid, supportive and integrated effect. One defines the style, the dynamics and the measures to which that stylistic pattern applies. Measure numbers defining the amount of repetition in the accompaniment pattern are a useful aid and should also be added to the part. Should there be any rhythmic essentials specifically required to align with other elements of the orchestration, those should be designated with supplemental notation, e.g. measure 4 and measure 5 in the example below. One should also designate (usually with text, rather than notation) any specific needs required for one's orchestral treatment of a given selection (i.e. the use of brushes or mallets instead of sticks, shaker instead of cymbals, etc.).

Scoring the Brass Section

Just as in the classical orchestra, there are a wide variety of approaches one may employ with scoring for brass in the pit orchestra environment. Since the string section is relatively small, the "fullness" of the pit orchestra usually comes from the brass section. Generally, one covers all the elements contained within the rehearsal piano part, plus (if instrumentation allows) additional parts that enhance the interest of the selection. This can be additional harmonic content, or possibly independent contrapuntal parts.

For the purposes of this example the following distribution of parts will yield successful results:

Melody: 1st trumpet
Melodic harmony part: 2nd trumpet
Accompaniment harmony: horns

It would be perfectly acceptable for the trombone to double the bass line in this configuration. However, since one should always attempt to add interest to the orchestration, the creation of a countermelody would serve this concept well. If assembled in this manner, the brass section would be scored as follows:

Scoring the Woodwind Section

While the woodwind section can add little "fullness" to the ensemble sound, they can be quite useful for adding contrapuntal/obbligato lines, and for providing textural reinforcement to significant elements of the orchestration. Since these parts are normally labeled as "reed" parts, it is always necessary to designate which instrument is required in the part and score. If a subsequent section requires the play to switch to a different instrument, it is helpful to place an appropriate direction in the part, e.g. *to bass clarinet*. It is also helpful to place the name of the instrument at the beginning of the section for which the instrument is required (see example below).

Should one wish to add an obbligato element to the orchestration, generally one identifies an area where the melody sustains a note (even if only briefly) and creates a transient melodic element that adds interest to what would otherwise be a static moment. Generally, this contrasting element should be complementary in nature, rather than distracting or dissonant. In a situation where the entire ensemble is engaged, doubling this obbligato line yields best results.

Depending upon the register of the featured vocal melody, oboe, clarinet or English horn are complementary timbres that can be used to add texture to the line by doubling it in unison (rather than at the octave). If the orchestration contains chorus parts, one could certainly choose to double those lines to thicken that texture. Should the orchestration contain a countermelody, clarinet or bassoon can add texture and reinforcement to that element.

For the purposes of this example the following distribution of parts will yield successful results:

Obbligato element: 1st reed (flute) and 2nd reed (flute)
Melody: 3rd reed (oboe)
Countermelody: 4th reed (bassoon)

Scoring the String Section

As previously mentioned, the string section is generally the first casualty of economic attrition in the musical theater setting. One must orchestrate the strings in such a manner that they are a viable textual element, while being mindful that at some point these parts could be completely eliminated from the score.

The quickest and probably most practical approach to scoring the string section is to double the elements present in other instruments of the ensemble. This approach is particularly applicable in tutti sections. However, one does not want to ignore the opportunity to employ the warmth and texture that strings afford while they are available (or should they not be lost to attrition). One accommodates this prospect by scoring the strings as one deems appropriate, and adds these parts as cue notes in other instruments that would serve as a suitable substitute.

For the purposes of this example, the following distribution of parts will yield successful results:

1st violins play the melody
2nd violins and violas play the accompaniment figures
Cello plays the countermelody

Piano/Conductor's Score

To create a piano/conductor's score (condensed score), include the lead vocal and the chorus parts (as condensed as possible). Below the vocals, include one or two auxiliary staves containing any additional parts not covered in the rehearsal piano part (with text to designate the instruments covering the musical element). Below these auxiliary parts, include the rehearsal piano part (with text to designate parts double in other instruments).

Piano/Vocal Part

As the name implies, the piano/vocal part contains the lead vocals, a condensed version of the chorus parts, and the rehearsal piano part.

Two-piano Arrangement

On occasion, one may be required to provide a two-piano score for a production. This part is similar to the piano/conductor's score (condensed score) in content, but different in layout. This part contains the lead vocal, the chorus parts (as condensed as possible) and the rehearsal piano part. Below the rehearsal piano is a secondary piano part containing any additional parts not covered in the rehearsal piano part.

Full Score

A full score contains all of the musical elements one would expect to find in an orchestral score, however the score order is unique to the musical theater genre. One places the lead vocal and chorus parts at the top of the score, following by the rehearsal piano. Following the vocals and piano, one places the woodwind, followed by the brass, followed by string sections. The rhythm section is place at the bottom of the score. One should include all cue notes in the full score. Doing so enables the musical director/conductor to determine which instruments are designated substitutes for any instruments lost to attrition.

410

SUGGESTED EXERCISE

Using the information and guidelines presented in this chapter and in Chapter 3 (Practical Problem Solving), orchestrate the following example for musical theater. Ensure that the vocals are the priority, that there is harmonic balance in each supporting instrumental family, and the final scoring will work well as it proceeds through the attrition of the production.

RJ Miller, *Lullaby for Ethan.*

Copyright © 2000 by Appassionata Music. Used by permission.

14
INSTRUMENT SUBSTITUTION AND QUICK REFERENCE GUIDES

When transcribing a selection from one genre to another (i.e. orchestra to wind ensemble, wind ensemble to orchestra, large ensemble to chamber ensemble, etc.) one will undoubtedly be required to allocate elements to substitute instrumentation. As such, it is imperative that the orchestrator has an in-depth understanding of alternate instrumentation (including both individual instruments and instrumental combinations) to call upon, depending upon the texture and context of a given selection. The following is a basic, generic list of possible substitute instrumentation:

Instrument	Register	Replacement Instrument(s)
Piccolo	high (sustained)	violin harmonics
Piccolo	high (moving)	replace (8vb) with flute, E♭ clarinet, or violin
Piccolo	middle, low (sustained)	viola harmonics, E♭ clarinet
Piccolo	middle, low (moving)	flute, E♭ clarinet, violin
Flute	high (sustained)	violin harmonics, viola harmonics, E♭ clarinet
Flute	high (moving)	E♭ clarinet, violin
Flute	middle, low	oboe, B♭ clarinet, violin
Alto flute	high	B♭ clarinet, muted horn, viola
Alto flute	middle, low	B♭ clarinet, bass clarinet, muted horn, viola
Bass flute	high	B♭ clarinet, bass clarinet, muted horn, cello
Bass flute	middle, low	bass clarinet, bassoon, muted trombone (cup or bucket), cello
Oboe	high	flute, E♭ clarinet, violin
Oboe	middle, low	clarinet, soprano sax, muted trumpet (straight or cup)
English horn	high	oboe, soprano sax, muted trumpet (cup or bucket), viola
English horn	middle, low	bassoon, alto sax, muted horn, viola, cello [clarinet with muted horn]
Bassoon	high	English horn, muted horn, viola [English horn with muted horn]

Instrument	Register	Replacement Instrument(s)
Bassoon	middle, low	bass clarinet, cello
Contrabassoon	all	contrabass clarinet, muted tuba, double bass [muted tuba with double bass]
B♭ clarinet	high	piccolo, flute, violin
B♭ clarinet	middle, low	soprano sax, muted horn, muted trumpet (cup), viola
Alto clarinet	all	alto sax, horn
Bass clarinet	high	bassoon, stopped horn, muted trumpet (cup), muted cello
Bass clarinet	middle, low	bassoon, muted trombone (cup), muted cello [bassoon with muted horn]
Contrabass clarinet	all	contrabassoon, double bass
Soprano sax	high	B♭ clarinet, oboe [B♭ clarinet with oboe]
Soprano sax	middle, low	B♭ clarinet, English horn, muted trumpet (cup), flugelhorn [B♭ clarinet with muted trumpet (cup) or flugelhorn]
Alto sax	high	B♭ clarinet, oboe, violin [flute with B♭ clarinet, oboe with violin]
Alto sax	middle, low	B♭ clarinet, English horn, horn, viola [B♭ clarinet with horn, horn with viola]
Tenor sax	high	bass clarinet, horn, baritone/euphonium, viola [bassoon with horn, B♭ clarinet with viola]
Tenor sax	middle, low	bass clarinet, baritone/euphonium, cello [bassoon with horn]
Baritone sax	high	bassoon, bass clarinet, baritone/euphonium, trombone, cello [bassoon with horn, horn with cello]
Baritone sax	middle, low	bassoon, contrabassoon, bass clarinet, bass trombone, cello [bassoon with trombone, trombone with cello]
Horn	high	alto flute, muted trumpet (cup or bucket), flugelhorn, viola
Horn	middle, low	bass flute, baritone/euphonium, cello [B♭ clarinet with cello, bassoon with cello]
Horn (stopped)	high	oboe, alto clarinet, muted trumpet (straight), viola (muted) [oboe with violin]

Instrument	Register	Replacement Instrument(s)
Horn (stopped)	middle, low	bass clarinet, bassoon, muted trombone (straight), cello [bassoon with viola, bass clarinet with viola]
Horn (muted)	high	English horn, alto clarinet, muted trumpet (straight)
Horn (muted)	middle, low	bass clarinet, bassoon, muted trombone (straight) [bass clarinet with cello]
Trumpet	high	flute, oboe, B♭ clarinet, violin [flute with oboe, oboe with B♭ clarinet]
Trumpet	middle, low	oboe, B♭ clarinet, soprano sax, horn, violin, viola [flute with muted horn, oboe with muted horn]
Trumpet (muted)	high	flute, oboe, violin
Trumpet (muted)	middle, low	English horn, B♭ clarinet, soprano sax, horn (muted), viola
Cornet	high	flute, oboe, flugelhorn, violin (muted) [flute with B♭ clarinet]
Cornet	middle, low	English horn, B♭ clarinet, flugelhorn, viola (muted) [flute with muted horn]
Trombone	high	alto clarinet, bassoon, horn, baritone/euphonium, viola [flute with violin, B♭ clarinet with oboe]
Trombone	middle, low	bass clarinet, bassoon, baritone/euphonium, cello [horn with viola, bassoon with bass clarinet or viola]
Trombone (muted)	all	bassoon, bass clarinet, viola/cello, [clarinet with English horn]
Tuba	high	bassoon, bass clarinet, bass trombone, baritone/euphonium, cello [trombone with horn]
Tuba	middle, low	contrabassoon, contrabass clarinet, bass trombone, double bass [contrabassoon with contrabass clarinet]
Violin	high	piccolo, flute, E♭ clarinet [flute with E♭ clarinet]
Violin	middle, low	flute, alto flute, English horn, B♭ clarinet [English horn with B♭ clarinet]
Violin harmonics	all	piccolo, flute

Instrument	Register	Replacement Instrument(s)
Viola	high	B♭ clarinet, English horn, muted trumpet (straight)
Viola	middle, low	bassoon, Alto clarinet, horn (muted)
Viola harmonics	all	flute, oboe, E♭ clarinet, muted trumpet (straight)
Cello	high	alto clarinet, bassoon, horn (muted) [clarinet with bassoon]
Cello	middle, low	bassoon, bass clarinet, muted trombone (cup) [bassoon or bass clarinet with muted trombone]
Cello harmonics	all	horn (muted), muted trombone (straight)
Double bass	high	bassoon, bass clarinet, muted trombone (cup)
Double bass	middle, low	contrabassoon, contrabass clarinet, tuba
Double bass harmonics	all	bassoon, bass clarinet, horn (muted), muted trombone (cup)

Practical Ranges and Registers for the Orchestral String Family

Violin

Standard Tuning

Full Range

Practical Range

Full Pizzicato Range

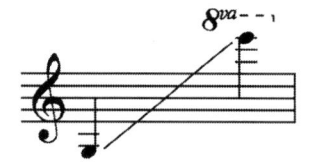

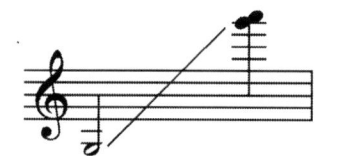

Practical Pizzicato Range

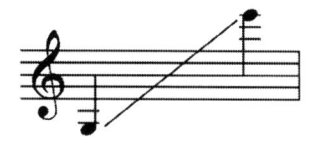

Full Harmonic Range   **Practical Harmonic Range**

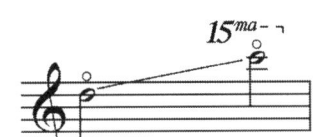

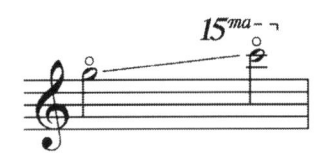

Viola

Standard Tuning

Full Range    **Practical Range**

Full Pizzicato Range    **Practical Pizzicato Range**

Full Harmonic Range 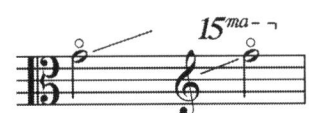   **Practical Harmonic Range**

Violoncello

Standard Tuning

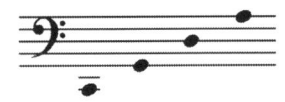

Full Range    **Practical Range**

Full Pizzicato Range

Practical Pizzicato Range

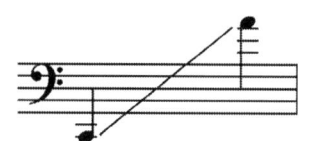

Full Harmonic Range

Practical Harmonic Range

Double Bass

Standard Tuning (4-string bass)

5-string basses have the ability to play the low C.

Concert Pitch

Transposed Pitch

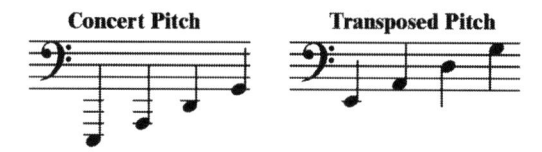

(Double Bass always appears in transposed form, even in a concert score.)

Full Range (transposed)

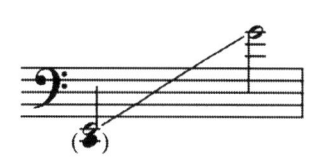

Practical Range (transposed)

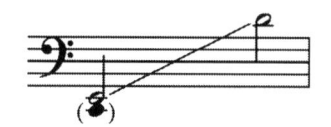

Full Pizzicato Range (transposed)

Practical Pizzicato Range (transposed)

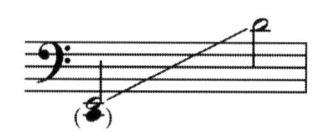

Practical Double Bass Harmonics

(Only natural harmonics are practical on a Double Bass.)

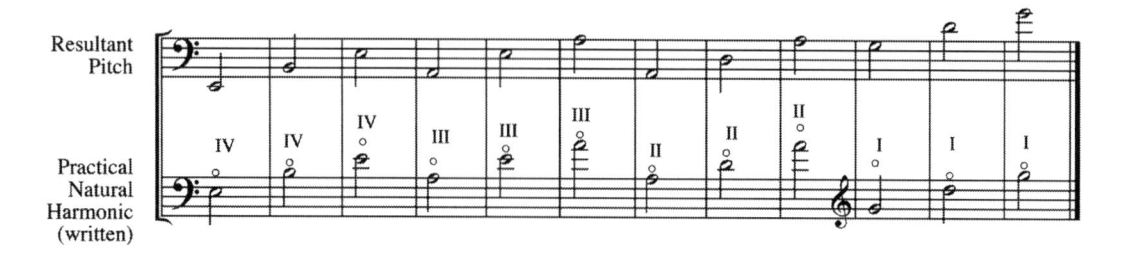

Practical Ranges and Registers for Brass Quintet

Trumpets

Practical Range (Transposed)

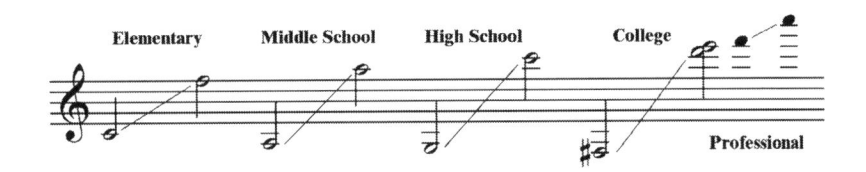

Registers (Transposed)

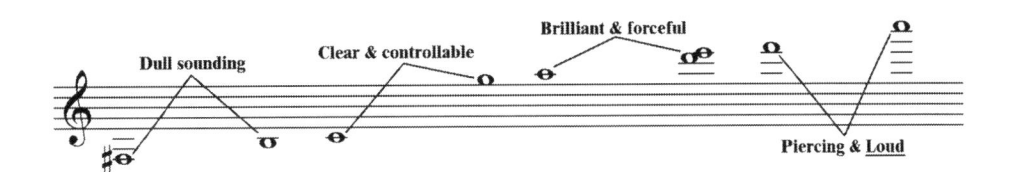

B♭ Trumpet Transposition

B♭ Trumpets sound a major 2nd below the written note. Transposed parts are notated a major 2nd above concert pitch (adding two sharps to the key signature), and always notated in treble clef.

C Trumpet Transposition

C Trumpet is a non-transposing instrument that is always written in treble clef.

Horn

Horn Range (Transposed)

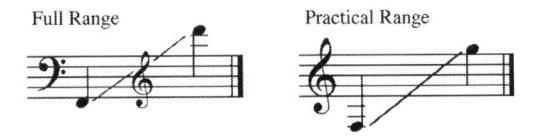

Horn Registers (Transposed)

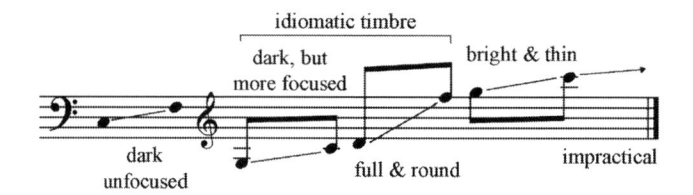

Horn Transposition

Horn parts are always written transposed up a perfect fifth from concert pitch. It is left to the player to decide which side of the horn will be utilized on any given note. While horn players are capable of reading both treble and bass clefs, it is preferable to write the parts in treble clef, reserving the use of bass clef for those occasions when the number of ledger lines become prohibitive.

Trombone

Trombone Range

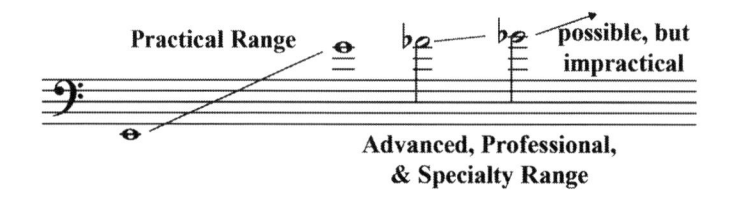

Trombone Registers

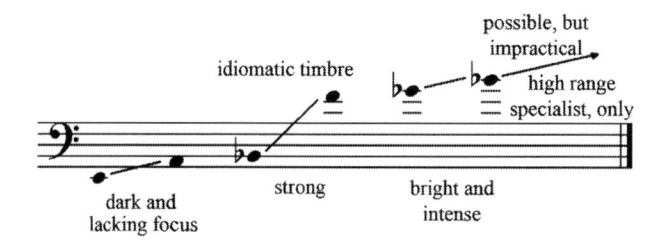

Trombone Transposition

Tenor Trombones are non-transposing instruments that are written predominantly in the bass clef. Tenor clef may be utilized for passages where the number of ledger lines becomes prohibitive. Advanced players are equally adept at reading in either clef.

Tuba

Tuba Range

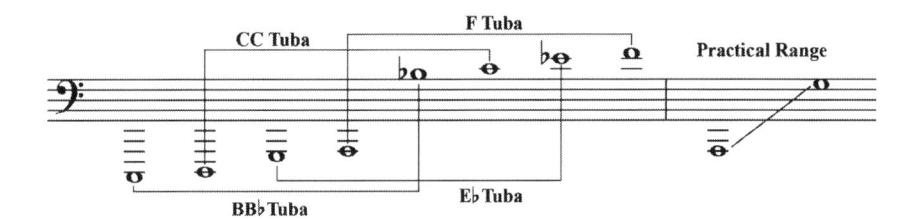

Tuba Registers

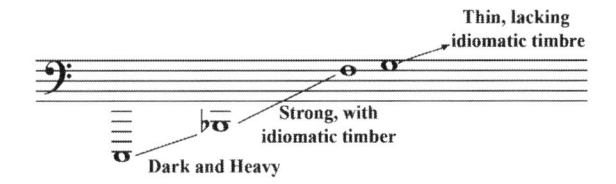

Practical Ranges and Registers for Wind Quintet

Flute

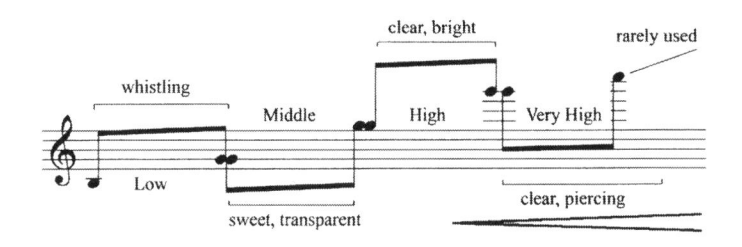

For the purposes of this assignment, please restrict your usage to the following range. Be aware that the "cautionary" range does not project, and should be used only in areas where if would be completely exposed.

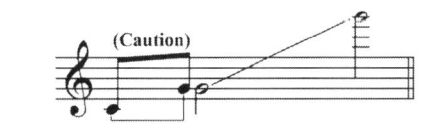

Oboe

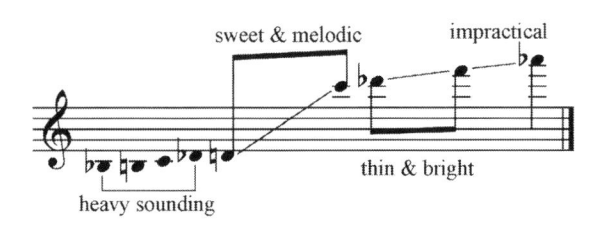

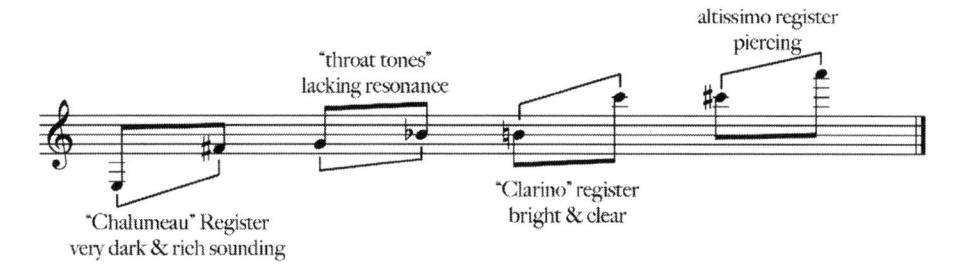

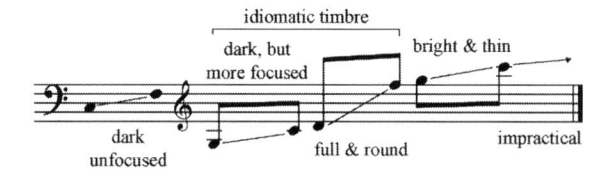

For the purposes of this assignment, please restrict your usage to the following range. Be aware that the "cautionary" range does not respond well unless approached from above. Do not start a phrase in this register.

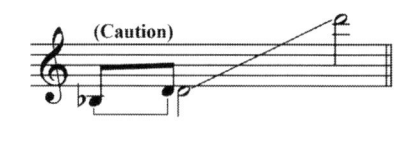

Clarinet

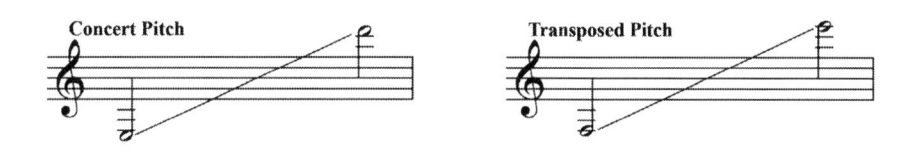

Horn

Bassoon

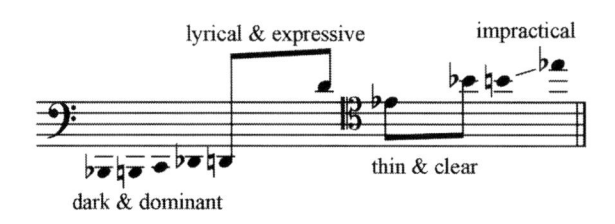

For the purposes of this assignment, please restrict your usage to the following range. Be aware that the "cautionary" range does not respond well unless approached from above. Do not start a phrase in this register.

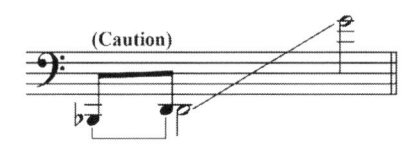

Practical Ranges and Registers for Saxophones

B♭ Soprano Saxophone

Range

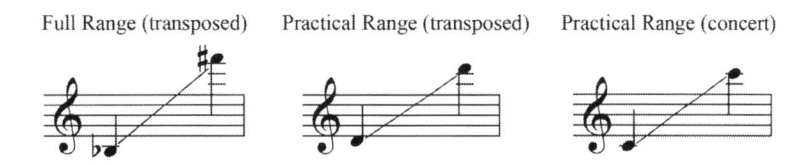

Registers (Transposed)

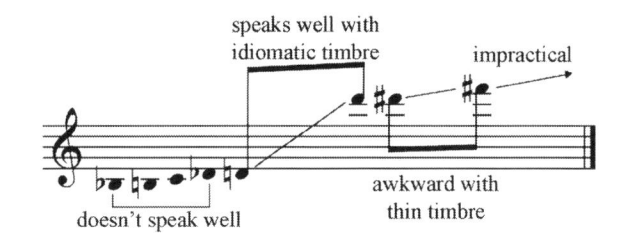

B♭ Soprano Saxophone Transposition

B♭ Soprano Saxophones sound a major 2nd below the written note. Transposed parts are notated a major 2nd above concert pitch (adding two sharps to the key signature) and always notated in treble clef.

E♭ Alto Saxophone

Range

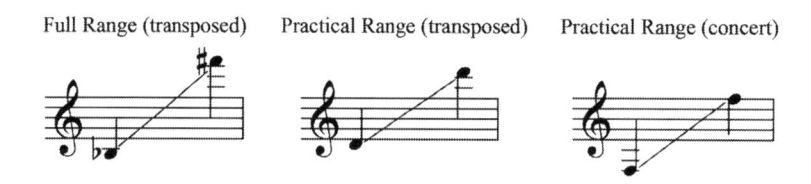

Registers (Transposed)

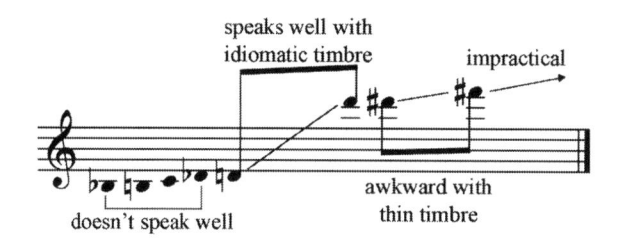

E♭ Alto Saxophone Transposition

E♭ Alto Saxophones sound a major 6th below the written note. Transposed parts are notated a major 6th above concert pitch (adding three sharps to the key signature) and always notated in treble clef.

B♭ Tenor Saxophone

Range

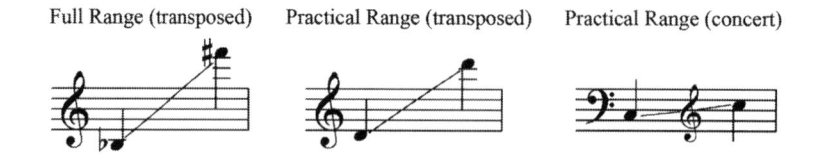

Registers (Transposed)

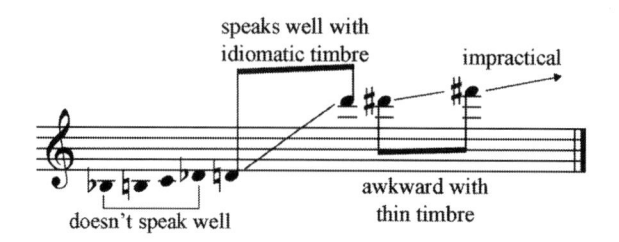

B♭ Tenor Saxophone Transposition

B♭ Tenor Saxophones sound a major 9th below the written note. Transposed parts are notated a major 9th above concert pitch (adding two sharps to the key signature) and always notated in treble clef.

E♭ Baritone Saxophone

Range

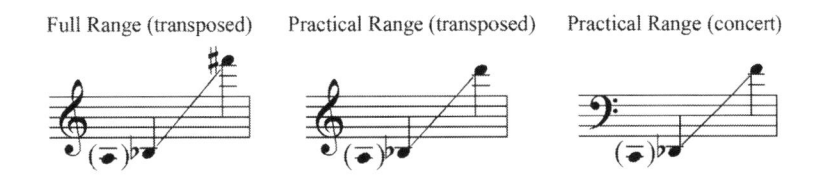

Registers (Transposed)

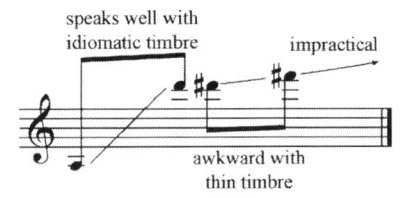

E♭ Baritone Saxophone Transposition

E♭ Baritone Saxophones sound an octave plus a major 6th below the written note. Transposed parts are notated an octave plus a major 6th above concert pitch (adding three sharps to the key signature) and always notated in treble clef. Most Baritone Saxophones are now equipped with a low A key (concert C).

Practical Ranges and Registers for the Orchestral Percussion Family

Timpani

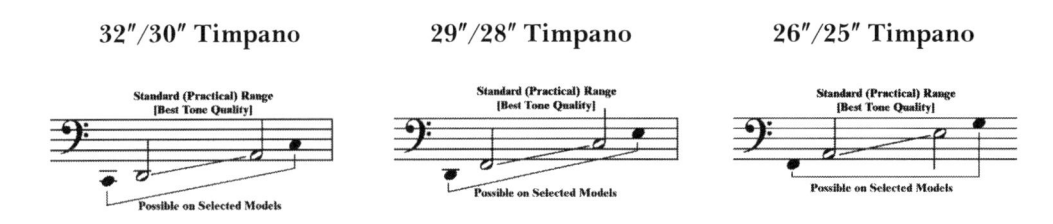

32"/30" Timpano
Standard (Practical) Range [Best Tone Quality]
Possible on Selected Models

29"/28" Timpano
Standard (Practical) Range [Best Tone Quality]
Possible on Selected Models

26"/25" Timpano
Standard (Practical) Range [Best Tone Quality]
Possible on Selected Models

24"/23" Timpano
Standard (Practical) Range [Best Tone Quality]
Possible on Selected Models

21"/20" Timpano
Standard (Practical) Range [Best Tone Quality]
Possible on Selected Models

Glockenspiel

Written Range
Standard Range 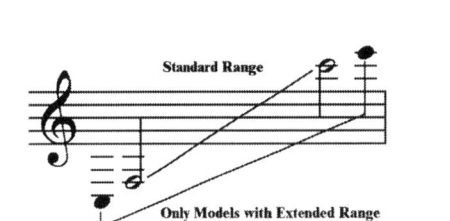
Only Models with Extended Range

Concert Range
Standard Range
Only Models with Extended Range

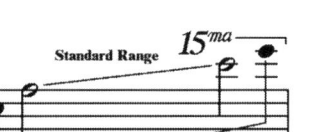

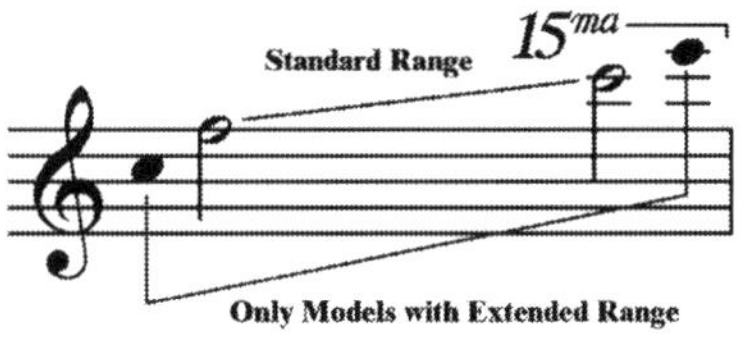

Crotales

Written Range
One Octave Set
2 Octave Set
2 1/2 Octave Set

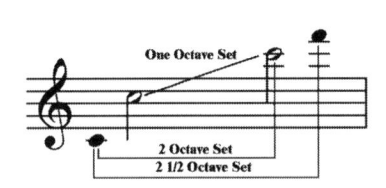

Concert Range
One Octave Set
2 Octave Set
2 1/2 Octave Set

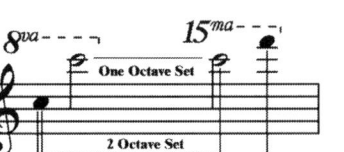

Xylophone

Written Range
3 Octave Models
3 1/2 Octave Models
4 Octave Models

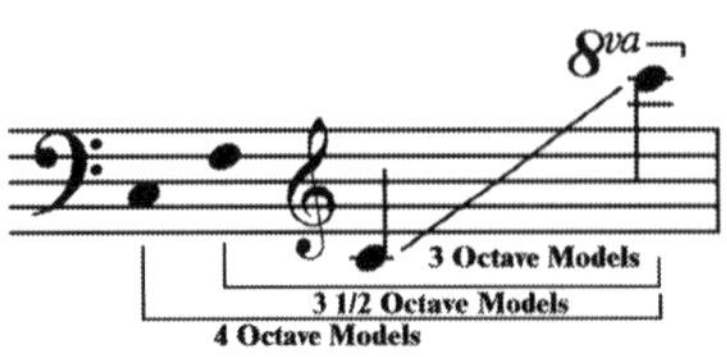

Concert Range
3 Octave Models
3 1/2 Octave Models
4 Octave Models

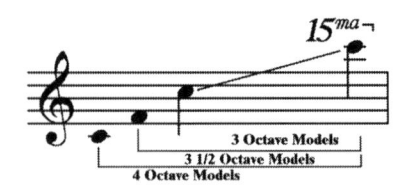

INSTRUMENT SUBSTITUTION

Marimba

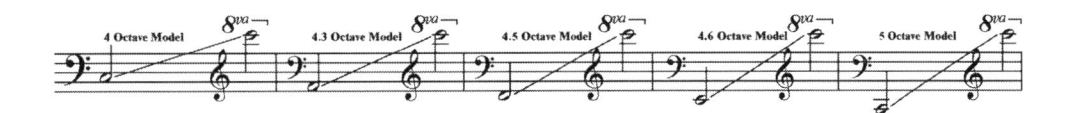

Vibraphone

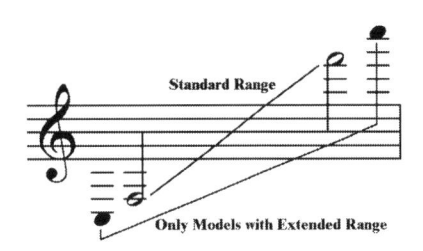

Chimes

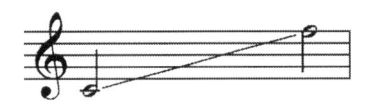

Celesta

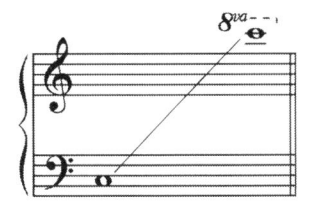

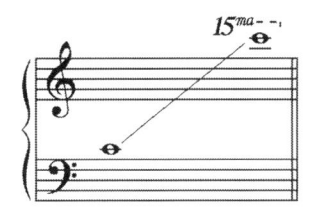

Piano

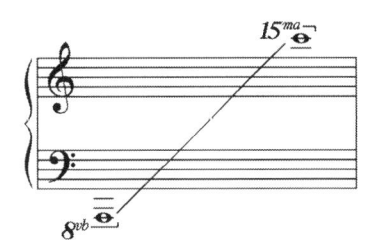

Practical Ranges and Tessitura for Voices

Adult and Adolescent Vocal Ranges

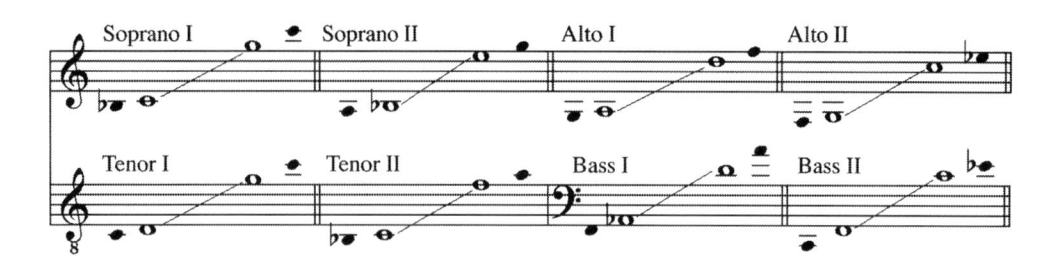

General Considerations in Arranging for Adult Voices

- Range and tessitura
- Phrases—(length/shape)
- Level of difficulty
- Vowels (vocal formants—male and female being treated differently)
- Durations

General Considerations in Arranging for Adolescent Voices

- Unusual useful range and tessitura
- Vocal quality
- Problems with register transition
- Avoid use of heavy mechanism too high in the range

Children's Vocal Ranges

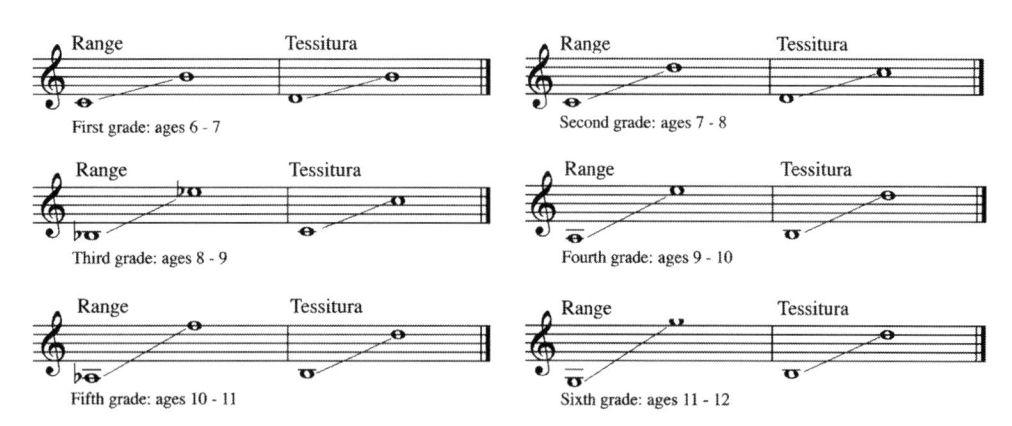

General Considerations in Arranging for Children's Choir

- Limited useful range
- Use stepwise melodic lines
- Limited breathing capacity
- Limited length of note duration
- Limited dynamic contrast
- Write simplistically
- Keep the accompaniment simple

15

SUGGESTED LISTENING AND ANALYSIS

One can greatly expand one's orchestration skills by listening to performances (both live and recorded) and analyzing orchestral scores. Since it is impossible to anticipate the specific styles of orchestration one may need to create during one's career, one should strive to encounter and intently analyze as many genres and orchestration styles as possible. Being well versed in a wide variety genres and techniques can only enhance one's skills. The following is an abbreviated list of suggested works for listening and analyzing.

Albinoni, Tomaso Giovann
    Adagio in G minor for Organ and Strings (arr. Remo Giazotto)

Bach, Johann Sabastian
    Brandenburg Concerto No. 2
    Brandenburg Concerto No. 3
    Brandenburg Concerto No. 5
    Cantata No. 56
    Cantata No. 140
    Cantata No. 147
    Cantata No. 208
    Clavier Concerto No. 3 in D
    Concerto for 2 Violins in D minor
    Concerto No. 2 for 3 Harpsichords in C
    English Suite No. 2
    Italian Concerto
    Orchestral Suite No. 2
    Orchestral Suite No. 3 in D for Orchestra
    St Matthew Passion
    Violin Sonata No. 1

Barber, Samuel
    Adagio for Strings
    Agnus Dei

Barry (Prendergast), John
    Born Free (film score)
    The Lion in Winter (film score)

Somewhere in Time (film score)
Out of Africa (film score)
Dances with Wolves (film score)
Chaplin (film score)

Bartók, Béla
Music for Strings, Percussion and Celesta
Concerto for Orchestra

Beethoven, Ludwig, van
Egmont Overture, Op. 84
Symphony No. 3 in E flat ("Eroica")
Symphony No. 5 in C minor, Op. 67
Symphony No. 6 in F major ("Pastoral")
Symphony No. 9
Violin Concerto in D major
Piano Concerto No. 5 in E flat ("Emperor")

Berlioz, Hector
Symphonie Fantastique
L'Enfance du Christ

Bernstein, Elmer
The Magnificent Seven (film score)
The Ten Commandments (film score)
The Great Escape (film score)
To Kill a Mockingbird (film score)

Bernstein, Leonard
West Side Story (musical theater/film score)

Bizet, Georges
Carmen

Boccherini, Luigi
String Quintet in E, Op. 11 No. 5

Borodin, Alexander
Polovtzian Dances from Prince Igor (for orchestra)
In the Steppes of Central Asia

Brahms, Johannes
Symphony No. 1 in C minor
Symphony No. 3 in F major
Symphony No. 4 in E minor
Violin Concerto in D
Piano Concerto No. 2 in B flat
Piano Concerto No. 1 in D minor

Bruckner, Anton
    Symphony No. 7 in E Major
    Symphony No. 9 in D Minor
    Chopin, Frédéric
    Piano Concerto No. 1

Copland, Aaron
    Appalachian Spring
    Rodeo
    Fanfare for the Common Man
    Of Mice and Men (film score)
    The North Star (film score)
    The Red Pony (film score)

Corelli, Arcangelo
    Concerto Grosso, Op.6 No.8

Crumb, George (Henry, Jr.)
    Black Angels
    A Haunted Landscape

Debussy, Claude
    Suite Bergamasque
    Prélude à l'après-midi d'un faune
    La mer, trois esquisses symphoniques pour orchestre

Delibes, Léo
    Lakmé

Dvořák, Antonin
    Concerto for Violoncello and Orchestra
    Symphony No. 9
    Rusalka: Polonaise
    Scherzo Capriccioso, Op. 66
    Slavonic Rhapsody, Op. 45 No. 2
    Slavonic Dance No. 5 in A, No. 6 in D, No. 10 in E minor

Elgar, Edward
    Cello Concerto
    Pomp and Circumstance March No. 4
    Pomp and Circumstance March No. 1
    Symphony No. 1
    Serenade for Strings

Fauré, Gabriel
    Cantique de Jean Racine
    Pavane, Op. 50
    Masques et bergamasques

Franck, César
    Symphony in D minor
    Symphonic Variations for Piano and Orchestra

Gershwin, George
    An American in Paris
    Rhapsody in Blue
    Cuban Overture

Giacchino, Michael
    Star Trek Into Darkness (film score)
    Up (film score)
    The Incredibles (film score)
    Ratatouille (film score)

Gilbert, William, and Sullivan, Arthur
    H.M.S. Pinafore
    The Pirates of Penzance
    The Mikado

Goldsmith, Jerrald King (Jerry)
    The Sand Pebbles (film score)
    Planet of the Apes (film score)
    Patton (film score)
    The Omen (film score)
    The Mummy (film score)
    Star Trek (film score)

Grieg, Edvard
    Peer Gynt Suites (Nos 1 and 2)
    Piano Concerto in A minor, Op. 16
    Two Elegiac Melodies for Strings, Op. 34

Handel, Georg Friedrich
    Concerto Grosso in B minor, Op. 12 No. 6
    Concerto No. 6 in B flat, Op. 4 No. 6
    Messiah
    Water Music Suite No. 3 in D
    Royal Fireworks Music

Hanson, Howard
    Symphony No. 2
    Symphony No. 7, "A Sea Symphony"

Haydn, Franz Joseph
    Symphony No. 94 in G Major, ("Surprise")
    Symphony No. 101 in D Major, ("Clock")
    Symphony No. 104 in D Major, ("London")
    Die Schöpfung (The Creation)

Concerto for Trumpet in E flat Major
The Seasons (oratorio)

Herrmann, Bernard
Psycho (film score)
Vertigo (film score)
Citizen Kane (film score)
The Day the Earth Stood Still (film score)
North by Northwest (film score)

Holst, Gustav
The Planets
First Suite in E flat for Military Band, Op. 28 No. 1
Suite No. 2 in F for Military Band, Op. 28 No. 2
A Somerset Rhapsody, Op. 21 No. 2

Howard, James Newton
King Kong (film score)
The Sixth Sense (film score)

Ives, Charles
The Unanswered Question
Three Places in New England (Orchestral Set No. 1)

Janácek, Leoš
Idyll for Strings
String Quartet No. 1
String Quartet No. 2

Jarre, Maurice-Alexis
Doctor Zhivago (film score)
Lawrence of Arabia (film score)
The Man Who Would Be King (film score)
Shogun (film score)
A Passage to India (film score)
Dead Poets Society (film score)

Khachaturian, Aram
Gayaneh Suite No. 1
Gayaneh Suite No. 3
Symphonic Pictures from Spartacus

Korngold, Erich Wolfgang
Violin Concerto, Op. 35
Captain Blood (film score)
The Prince and the Pauper (film score)
The Adventures of Robin Hood (film score)
The Sea Hawk (film score)
The Sea Wolf (film score)

Ligeti, György Sándor
    Atmosphères
    Cello Concerto
    Requiem, for soprano, mezzo-soprano, 2 mixed choirs and orchestra

Liszt, Franz
    Concerto No. 1 in E flat major for Piano
    Eine Faust-Symphonie in drei Charakterbildern, S. 108
    Mahler, Gustav
    Symphony No. 1 in D Major
    Symphony No. 4 in G Major
    Symphony No. 9 in D Major

Mancini, Henry
    Touch of Evil (film score)
    Breakfast at Tiffany's (film score)
    Days of Wine and Roses (film score)
    The Pink Panther (film score)
    Charade (film score)
    A Shot in the Dark (film score)
    Victor Victoria (film score)

Mascagni, Pietro
    Cavalleria Rusticana
    Messa di Gloria in F major for soloists, chorus and orchestra

Massenet, Jules
    Thaïs
    Fantasy for Cello and Orchestra

Mendelssohn, Felix
    Hebrides Overture
    Violin Concerto in E minor
    A Midsummer Night's Dream
    Piano Concerto No. 2
    Quintet in B flat, Op. 87

Messiaen, Olivier
    O Sacrum Convivum
    Quatuor pour la fin du temps
    L'ascension

Mozart (Johann Georg), Leopold
    Cassation in G major for toys, 2 oboes, 2 horns, strings and continuo

Mozart, Wolfgang Amadeus
    Concerto for Clarinet
    Don Giovanni
    Concerto No. 20 in D minor for Piano, K. 466

Sinfonia Concertante in E flat major for Violin and Viola, K. 364
Flute Concerto No. 1
Serenade in G Major for Strings, K. 525
Piano Concerto No. 21
Quintet in E flat
Requiem
Symphony No. 40
Symphony No. 41 in C Major, K. 551
Die Zauberflöte

Mussorgsky, Modest Petrovich
Night on the Bald Mountain
Pictures at an Exhibition (orchestral adaptation by Maurice Ravel)

Offenbach, Jacques
Orpheus in the Underworld
The Tales of Hoffmann

Orff, Carl
Carmina Burana

Pachelbel, Johann
Canon and Gigue in D major for 3 Violins and Basso Continuo

Pärt, Arvo
Cantus in Memory of Benjamin Britten
Te Deum
Arbos for brass and percussion

Paganini, Niccolò
Violin Concerto No. 2

Penderecki, Krzysztof
Cello Concerto
Canon for 2 string orchestras and tapes
Threnody for the Victims of Hiroshima

Prokofiev, Sergei Sergeyevich
Alexander Nevsky
Cinderella
Lieutenant Kijé Suite
Peter and the Wolf
Romeo and Juliet

Puccini, Giacomo
La Bohème
Gianni Schicchi
Tosca
Madama Butterfly

Purcell, Henry
    Dido and Aeneas
    Fantasias for Strings

Rachmaninoff, Sergei Vasilievich
    Concerto No. 2 in C Minor for Piano, Op. 18
    Concerto No. 3 in D Minor for Piano, Op. 30
    Rhapsody on a Theme of Paganini

Ravel, Joseph-Maurice
    Bolero
    Daphnis et Chloé

Respighi, Ottorino
    Le fontane di Roma (The Fountains of Rome)
    I pini di Roma (The Pines of Rome)
    Feste Romane (Roman Festivals)

Rimsky-Korsakov, Nikolai Andreyevich
    Scheherazade
    Capriccio Espagnol

Rodrigo, Joaquín
    Concierto de Aranjuéz

Rossini, Gioachino Antonio
    Guillaume Tell
    Il bariere di Siviglia
    Otello

Rózsa, Miklós
    Violin Concerto, Op. 24
    Cello Concerto, Op. 32
    Spellbound (film score)
    The Asphalt Jungle (film score)
    Ivanhoe (film score)
    Lust for Life (film score)
    Ben-Hur (film score)
    King of Kings (film score)
    El Cid (film score)

Saint-Saëns, Charles Camille
    The Carnival of the Animals
    Symphony No. 3
    Danse Macabre

Schubert, Franz Peter
    Ave Maria, Op. 52 No. 6
    Symphony No. 2 in B flat Major

Symphony No. 5 in B flat
Symphony No. 8 in B Minor ("Unfinished")
Symphony No. 9 in C ("Great")
Piano Trio in E flat, D. 929 Op. 100
Piano Trio in E flat, D. 897 (Notturno Op. Posth. 148)

Schumann, Robert
Concerto in A Minor for Cello and Orchestra, Op. 129
Concerto in A Minor for Piano and Orchestra, Op. 54
Symphony No. 1 in B flat major, Op. 48, *"Spring"*

Shore, Howard Leslie
Lord of the Rings (3 film scores)
Hugo (film score)

Shostakovich, Dmitri Dmitrievich
Piano Concerto No. 2
Symphony No. 5
Symphony No. 8
Festive Overture

Sibelius, Johan Julius Christian (Jean)
Finlandia
Symphony No. 1 in E Minor, Op. 39
Symphony No. 2 in D Major, Op. 43
Symphony No. 5 in E flat Major, Op. 82

Silvestri, Alan
The Polar Express (film score)
Contact (film score)
The Abyss (film score)

Smetana, Bedřich
String Quartet No. 1 in E Minor
Vltava

Strauss, Jr., Johann (Strauss the Younger)
On the Beautiful Blue Danube Waltz
Tales from the Vienna Woods

Strauss, Richard
Also Sprach Zarathustra
Der Rosenkavalier Suite, Op. 59
Don Juan, Op. 20
Till Eulenspiegel, Op. 28

Stravinsky, Igor Fyodorovich
The Firebird Suite
The Rite of Spring
Petrushka

Tchaikovsky, Pyotr (Peter) Ilyich
    The Nutcracker Suite
    Piano Concerto No. 1 in B flat minor, Op. 23
    Swan Lake
    Violin Concerto in D major, Op. 35
    Symphony No. 6 in B Minor ("Pathetique")
    Romeo and Juliet (Overture-Fantasia)
    1812 Overture

Vaughan Williams, Ralph
    Fantasia on a Theme by Thomas Tallis
    Fantasia on "Greensleeves"

Verdi, Giuseppe Fortunino Francesco
    Requiem
    La Traviata
    Il Trovatore

Vivaldi, Antonio Lucio
    The Four Seasons
    Double Mandolin Concerto in G
    L'estro armonico

Wagner, Wilhelm Richard
    Lohengrin
    Tannhäuser
    Die Walküre

Webern, Anton
    Five Pieces for Orchestra, Op. 10

Weill, Kurt
    The Threepenny Opera
    Suite for Orchestra

Williams, John Towner
    Concerto No. 1 for Violin and Orchestra
    Superman (film score)
    Close Encounters of the Third Kind (film score)
    Star Wars (film score)
    Indiana Jones and the Last Crusade (film score)
    Schindler's List (film score)
    Harry Potter and the Sorcerer's Stone (film score)
    Memoirs of a Geisha (film score)
    The Book Thief (film score)

Wintory, Austin
    Journey (video game score)

16
PARTING THOUGHTS

Common Sense

Common sense is one of the greatest attributes an orchestrator can possess. Using a practical, reasonable, learned approach to one's orchestrations will always yield favorable results. An extensive knowledge of scoring techniques and instrument capabilities, tempered with common sense, empowers one to produce superior orchestrations that will be enjoyed by both the audience and the performers.

Step One

Performing a harmonic analysis of the selected work should *always* be the first step in creating an orchestration. Quite simply, one cannot create a well-balanced, well-executed orchestration without intimate knowledge of the harmonic content of the selection. Virtually every problem-solving decision an orchestrator must make is dependent upon the harmonic content. A harmonic analysis provides the element necessary for competent decision-making. Failure to perform a harmonic analysis will inevitably doom one's orchestration to the realm of mediocrity (or worse).

Awareness of Acoustical Balances

One should be vigilant in addressing acoustical balances within one's orchestrations. Every note, every chord, every passage and every combination of instruments should be written in such a manner as to ensure blend and acoustic balance. Be attentive to how balances change, depending upon registers and dynamic levels. One should strive to use acoustics to one's advantage. Application of one's knowledge of the overtone series and its application to the acoustical environment should always be a significant element in one's orchestrations.

Scoring for Orchestral Tutti

When scoring for a full orchestral tutti, ensuring proper harmonic balance within each instrumental family yields a balanced and full-sounding ensemble. When listening to each instrumental family independently, one should experience the full harmonic content (either present or acoustically implied), appropriately balanced throughout the family. This concept applies even if the harmonic voicings vary from family to family. If a suitable harmonic balance is present within each family, the combined ensemble will also exhibit proper harmonic balance.

Cross-voicing of Like Timbres

Cross-voicing melody and harmony with instruments of like timbre can result in an obfuscation of the melody line. Often one must alter the register of the accompaniment instrument to accommodate range restrictions. However, one should avoid cross-voicing if the net effect results in a (perceived) altered melody. If one imagines the following played by two violins (or two B♭ clarinets, B♭ trumpets, etc.), one can see how the listener's perception of the melody is unintentionally altered.

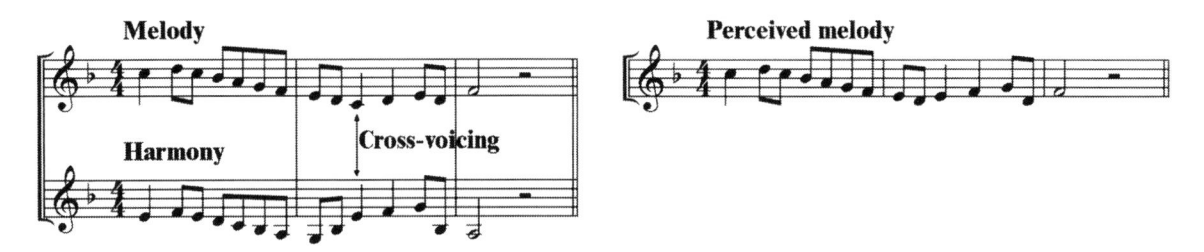

Though usually viewed as an undesirable consequence of a poor scoring technique, one should not completely discard the effect as it can be used to create a novel effect and interest within the parts. However, this technique should only be used when the net effect does not result in the perception of an altered melody.

RJ Miller, *Concerto for Unaccompanied Trumpet Trio*, **movement II, mm. 36–40.**

Copyright © 1987 by RJ Miller and Appassionata Music.

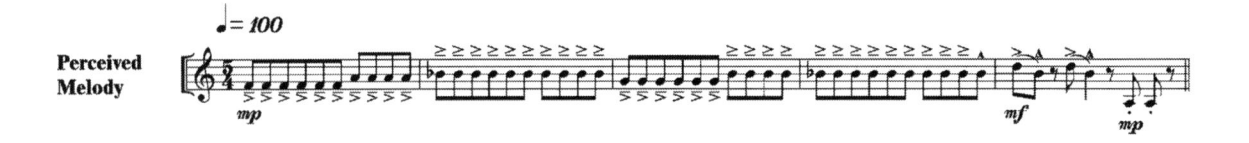

Cover the Seams

While there are exceptions, one would generally desire one's orchestrations to flow logically and smoothly from beginning to end. To accomplish this "flow" one should overlap or "dovetail" sections. Metaphorically, one is attempting to create a continuous, flowing line of sound as opposed to a series of sonic blocks placed end-to-end (resulting in a sonic "seam" between sections).

RJ Miller, *Berceuse* (for String Quartet and Piano), mm. 13–20.

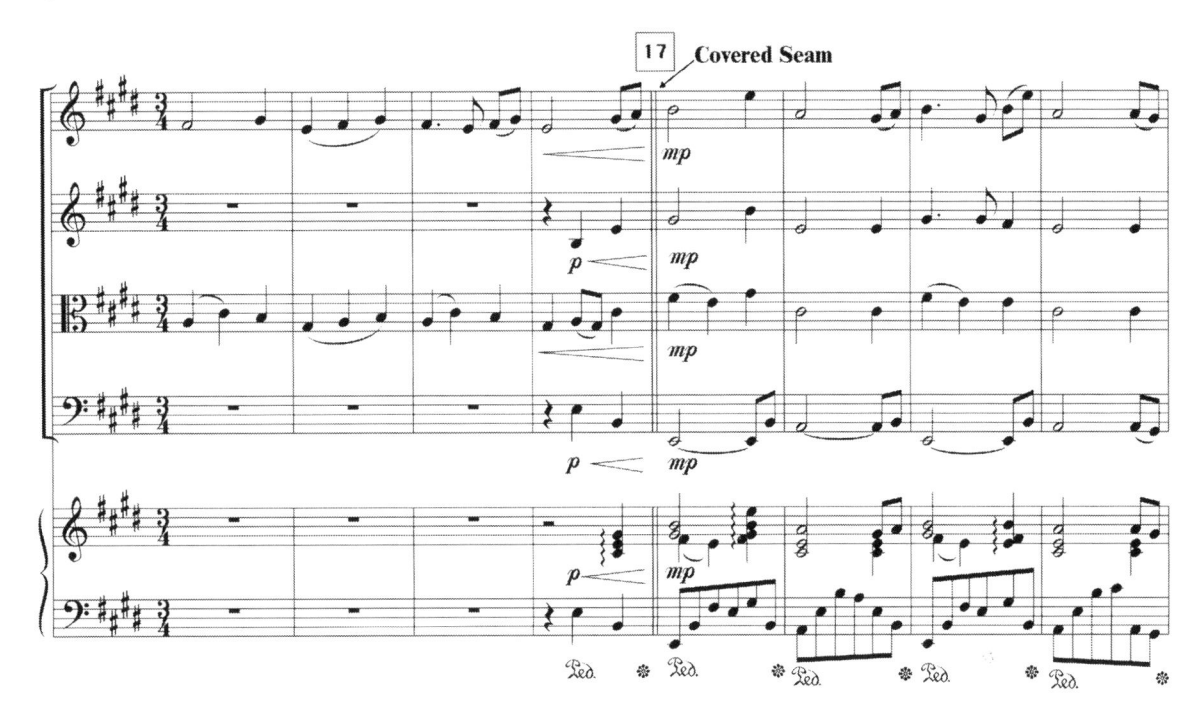

Copyright © 2004 by Appassionata Music. Used by permission.

Passing Melodies from Instrument to Instrument

When the baton is passed from runner to runner in a relay race there is a brief moment when both runners are in contact with the baton. A similar concept should be applied when passing melodies from part to part. Overlapping parts at the point of exchange results in fluid exchange of melody with the added benefit of rhythmical security and a continuous, flowing melody line.

Marie Auguste Durand, *Valse*, Op. 83 No. 1, mm. 223–231 (for piano).

Marie Auguste Durand, *Valse,* **Op. 83 No. 1, mm. 223–231 (orchestrated for string quartet by RJ Miller).**

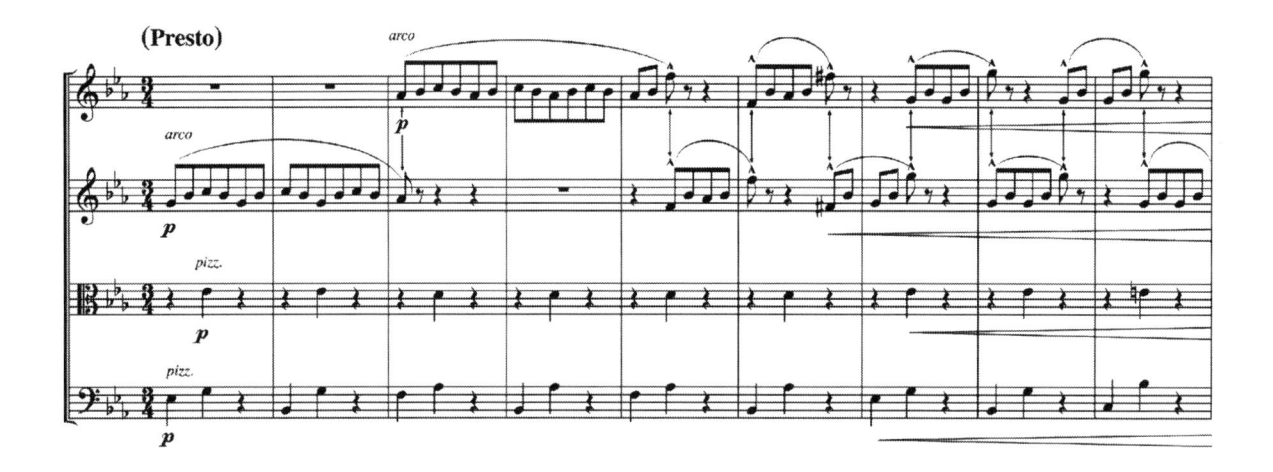

Not Everyone Needs to Play All the Time

The natural tendency when scoring for small ensembles is to use all of the instruments all of the time. Often the original composition is written in four-part harmony. When translating this type of composition to a quartet of instruments (i.e. string quartet) it would seem logical to assign one instrument to each of the four existing parts. However, in practice this results in a static-sounding orchestration with little interest and no variance of overall timbre. By using the overtone series to determine the appropriate chord members to be deleted from a given chord, one can usually reduce each chord to as little as two or three notes. Doing so results in the opportunity to rest certain parts, pass the melody from instrument to instrument, or trade melody or harmony between instruments of different timbre, thereby adding significant interest and variety to the orchestration. This is a particularly valuable approach when scoring for brass, as it presents viable options needed to accommodate embouchure endurance considerations.

Avoid Exact Repeats

While repeated sections were standard practice during the Classical period (and very common in solo piano music), one should make every effort to avoid exact repeats of orchestrated sections. One should always attempt to add interest to sections that were written as exact repeats in the original composition. One should view a repeated section as an opportunity to add interest to an orchestration by altering the instrumental timbres involved, thinning or thickening the texture, altering the bowing technique or resonance for strings (i.e. pizz., arco, muted, etc.), using mutes for brass, shifting to different registers, etc.

Importance of Voice-leading and Rhythmic Interest Within Parts

It is a natural tendency to focus one's attention upon the voice leading contained within the featured melody line. However, one should strive for proper voice leading within each and every voice. The internal parts, while admittedly subservient to the melody, should be treated with equal importance. Internal parts should have a logical contour. Jagged, illogically contoured accompany parts are not only difficult to sight-read, but often jump from register to register, resulting in blending and balance issues. Revoicing the harmony, usually through the use of chordal inversions, can result in a far more intuitive and "playable" part that interacts more smoothly and logically with the featured melody line.

Additionally, one should focus on the melodic/rhythmic interest contained within the accompaniment lines. Avoid writing parts that contain endless arpeggios, constant off-beats or continuous rhythmic repetition. A lack of interest within a part will result in a lack of interest from the player. Trading repetitive figures from instrument to instrument, dividing an arpeggio between multiple instruments and altering the melodic contour of an accompaniment figure (without altering the harmonic content) are just a few of the viable options.

Importance of Clear/Clean Notation

Perception has always been a part of the musical environment. A conductor and/or ensemble begins to form their perception of the orchestrator before a note is played. Their initial opinion is formed the moment they see the score and parts for the first time. Ambiguous, imprecise or poorly executed notation demonstrates a lack of understanding of professional standards. If one's score and parts are not of a professional stature, the inference is that the orchestration will likely not meet professional expectations. As stated earlier in this text, ease of reading and clarity of part should always be a priority when creating one's scores and parts. Any inexactness or obfuscation will result in additional (wasted) rehearsal time, additional studio costs and a perception that may be detrimental to one's professional career. Spending the appropriate time necessary to produce clear, concise and easily readable scores and parts will allow the orchestrations (as well as the orchestrator) to be judged on their merits without preconceived prejudice.

Know the Capabilities and Limitations of Every Instrument

The more one knows about a given instrument, the more competently one may employ that instrument within one's orchestration. While an orchestration text may serve as a functional general guide to the usage of a particular instrument, it is no substitute for the practical knowledge gained by playing the instrument. Enrolling in college practicum/instrumental and choral techniques classes will greatly enhance one's orchestration skills. Even though these classes are generally designed for training music educators, an orchestrator can gain an invaluable understanding and appreciation for the capabilities and limitations of the instrument that directly relates to one's writing. If enrolling in such classes is not a viable option, spending time with a skilled instrumentalist/vocalist and asking specifically directed questions about the idiosyncrasies, detailed capabilities and precise limitations of the instrument can also produce adequate results.

Ask a Player

Often the most valuable and salient information can be garnered from professional musicians. Professional musicians know far more about the capabilities and idiomatic use of their instrument than one can ever acquire from an orchestration text. When one has doubt about a particular passage, one can only benefit from seeking the learned input of a professional performer. One should never allow one's ego to foil an opportunity to gain insight that may advance one's skills.

Think Like a Player

One should endeavor to view one's scores through the eyes of a conductor. Similarly, one should strive to view one's parts through the eyes of a player. When examining one's work from this perspective, flaws in one's layout and notation become readily evident. Contour of line, voice leading and lack of interest within the parts are also easily observed. This process presents the opportunity to readdress issues that could be problematic if presented to the ensemble. One should embrace this process as an opportunity to transform a potentially mediocre orchestration into an excellent orchestration.

Know What to Avoid

Knowing what *not* to write is often more important than knowing what to write. One should know the fingerings (or slide positions), performance techniques, registers, idiosyncrasies and limitations of every instrument for which one writes. There are always ways to solve scoring problems that may arise from the nature of each instrument. However, one cannot solve these problems if one isn't aware that they exist.

Learn from Your Mistakes

At some point everyone writes something that doesn't work, or at least doesn't work in the manner anticipated. Writing something that doesn't work is one of the greatest learning tools available. It is unlikely that one will ever repeat this type of mistake, especially if it occurs in the professional environment. Ultimately, one learns to orchestrate by orchestrating. Learning from one's mistakes is simply part of this pragmatic process. One should never be dispirited by a mistake, but rather embrace it as an educational experience.

Find Your Voice

Over the course of one's career one will incorporate (both consciously and subconsciously) various techniques into one's writing that eventually become identifiable as one's individual style (or "voice"). Finding one's voice is a journey. Every new work one encounters has the potential to influence one's style. One should listen to everything, analyze everything one finds appealing, absorb the techniques and approaches that one finds artistically pleasing or interesting, and write, write, write. It is through this process that one's "voice" ultimately evolves.

Seven Traits of a Great Orchestrator

A great orchestration can make a mediocre composition sound exceptional. An inferior orchestration can make an exceptional composition sound mediocre.

A Great Orchestrator Employs a Practical Modus Operandi

Ultimately, one is orchestrating for the instrumentalist. As such, the hypothetical capabilities of a given instrument are always less important than the actual capabilities of the instrumentalist. A practical approach to ranges, registers and technique will always yield better results than writing to the technical extremes of the instrument.

A Great Orchestrator has a Thorough Understanding of Both the Technical and Emotional Content of the Composition

It is imperative that an orchestrator conveys the emotional intent of the composer. One generally must infer this intent through a meticulous analysis of the selection. A great orchestrator never embarks upon an orchestration without a detailed analysis of all aspects of the composition. Only when one understands the technical characteristics of the work can one approach the emotional content.

A Great Orchestrator is Ever Mindful of Acoustical Balances

While it is technically possible to achieve acoustical balance through the manipulation of dynamic levels, it is always preferable to accomplish this goal through the use of appropriate instrumentation. A great orchestration will guide the audience to the melody, with other simultaneously sounding elements (counterpoint, harmony, etc.) scored in supportive symmetry to evoke the desired emotional response.

A Great Orchestrator Manipulates the Extensive Variety of Orchestral Timbres to Augment the Emotional Content of the Music

One's skillful use of creatively varied timbres and textures defines one's career as an orchestrator. A good orchestrator has an extensive understanding of all instruments within the orchestral palette. A great orchestrator possesses an extensive and intimate knowledge of both standard orchestral instruments, and instruments from other genres and cultures. Employing the appropriate instrumentation for the emotional content should always be the goal of the orchestrator. While this can often be accomplished within the confines of the standard orchestral palette, a great orchestrator will not hesitate to exploit expertise beyond this boundary.

A Great Orchestrator Exploits the Wide Dynamic Scope of the Orchestral Palette

Many (if not most) of the orchestrations one creates are based upon piano music. While the piano is capable of a wide range of dynamics, it pales (as any singular instrument does) in comparison with the dynamic scope of the orchestra. Be it through subtlety or through power, a great orchestrator exploits these extended dynamic capabilities to enhance the emotional impact of the work.

A Great Orchestrator is Ardently Focused on Musical Details

Musical details, such as phrasing, dynamics (and dynamic shaping), articulations, etc., transform notation into music. Supporting details, such as double bars, rehearsal marks, measure numbers, etc., aid greatly in both rehearsals and performances. While these elements are often lacking in the original version of the composition, it is the orchestrator's responsibility to add these musical elements to the orchestration. An orchestration lacking in musical detail will sound inert and lack-luster. An orchestration rich in musical detail will sound vibrant and radiant.

A Great Orchestrator is Ever Cognizant of Professional Courtesies

As previously stated, one is ultimately orchestrating for the instrumentalist. As such, a great orchestrator continually exercises deference for musical tradition and respect for the player. One should always be cognizant of necessary notational practices and avoid those that would be considered insulting by the instrumentalist.

CREDITS

Chapter 2

RJ Miller, *Callisto* (from *The Galilaen Moons of Jupiter*, Movement II), mm. 1–11. Copyright © 2006 by Appassionata Music. Used by permission.

RJ Miller, *Io* (from *The Galilaen Moons of Jupiter*, Movement I), flute part, mm. 1–40, 61–68. Copyright © 2006 by Appassionata Music. Used by permission.

RJ Miller, *The Processional*, violin part, mm. 1–55. Copyright © 1997 by Appassionata Music. Used by permission.

Austin Wintory, *Captain Abu Raed* (score), mm. 1–11. Copyright © MMVII by Austin Wintory. Reprinted with permission of the composer.

Austin Wintory, *Captain Abu Raed* (violin parts), mm. 1–11. Copyright © MMVII by Austin Wintory. Reprinted with permission of the composer.

RJ Miller, *Moments*, mm. 1–17. Copyright © 2007 by Appassionata Music. Used by permission.

Chapter 4

RJ Miller, *Elegy*, mm. 23–41. Copyright © 2002 by Appassionata Music. Used by permission.

RJ Miller, *The Wilderness Suite*, Movement VIII (*The Balance of Nature*), mm. 56–65. Copyright © 1992 by Appassionata Music. Used by permission.

Chapter 5

Cecil Effinger, *Silver Plume*, mm. 107–114. Copyright © 1961 by Elkan Vogel, Inc. Used by permission of the Cecil Effinger estate, Corinne Effinger Owen, Executor.

H. Owen Reed, "Mass," Movement II from *La Fiesta Mexicana*, mm. 68–84. Copyright © 1954 (renewed) Beam Me Up Music. All rights controlled and administered by Alfred Music. All rights reserved. Used by permission of Alfred Music.

RJ Miller, *The Summit*, mm. 12–30. Copyright © 2004 by Appassionata Music. Used by permission.

Chapter 6

George Gershwin, *Rhapsody in Blue*, mm. 1–5, orchestrated by Ferde Grofé (transposed solo B♭ clarinet part). Copyright © 1924 (renewed) WB Music Corp. All rights reserved. Used by permission of Alfred Music.

Alfred Reed, *A Sacred Suite*, mm. 1–22 (transposed score). Copyright © 1962 by Edwin F. Kalmus. Used by permission of EF Kalmus/LMP.

Norman Dello Joio, *Fantasies on a Theme by Haydn*, mm. 37–54. Copyright ©1968 by Edward B. Marks Music Company. Copyright renewed. This arrangement copyright © 2014 by Edward B. Marks Music Company. International copyright secured. All rights reserved. Used by permission. Reprinted by Permission of Hal Leonard Corporation.

Vaclav Nelhybel, *Chorale*, mm. 72–86. Copyright © 1965 Franco Columbo, Inc. Copyright assigned to and renewed by Belssin-Mills Publishing Corp. All rights controlled and administered by Alfred Music. All rights reserved. Used by permission of Alfred Music.

Vaclav Nelhybel, *Festivo*, mm. 43–63. Copyright ©1968 Franco Columbo, Inc. Copyright assigned to and renewed by Belwin-Mills Publishing Corp. All rights controlled and administered by Alfred Music. All rights reserved. Used by permission of Alfred Music.

Chapter 7

RJ Miller, *Ba-Da-Ka-Dup!*, mm. 1–17. Copyright © 2004 by Appassionata Music. Used by permission.

RJ Miller, *The Circus is in Town* (marimba part), mm. 72–80. Copyright © 2001 by Appassionata Music. Used by permission.

RJ Miller, *Zounds*, mm. 1–22. Copyright © 2009 by Appassionata Music. Used by permission.

Alan Hovhaness, *October Mountain*, Op. 135. Movement I, mm. 1–80. Copyright © 1957 by C.F. Peters. Used by permission of C.F. Peters Corporation.

RJ Miller, *Yellowstone*, mm. 165–181. Copyright © 2001 by Appassionata Music. Used by permission.

RJ Miller, *Cadence #1*, mm. 1–12. Copyright © 2008 by Appassionata Music. Used by permission.

RJ Miller, *Your Heart's Desire*, mm. 1–69. Copyright © 2001 by Appassionata Music. Used by permission.

Chapter 8

Dimitri Bortnianski, *Cherubic Hymn*, m. 1–38. Copyright © 1977 by Hinshaw Music, Inc., edited by Ray Robinson and available from Hinshaw Music, Inc. (www.hinshawmusic.com) as HMC323. Used by permission of Hinshaw Music, Inc.

RJ Miller, *Good Tidings*, mm. 1–13. Copyright © 2008 by Appassionata Music. Used by permission.

Chapter 10

Antonio Vivaldi, *Concerto in D major*, Movement I, transcribed and edited by Alex Komodore. Copyright © MMXIV by Alex Komodore. Used by permission.

Ferninando Sor, *Sonata in C Major for Guitar*, Op. 15b, transcribed and edited by Alex Komodore. Copyright © MMXIV by Alex Komodore. Used by permission.

RJ Miller, *Zoot Suit* (guitar part), mm. 1–40. Copyright © 2004 by Appassionata Music. Used by permission.

Chapter 11

RJ Miller, *Promises*, from *The Wedding Suite*, mm. 98–105. Copyright © 2010 by Appassionata Music. Used by permission.

RJ Miller, *Celebration Waltz*, from *The Wedding Suite*, mm. 73–105. Copyright © 2010 by Appassionata Music. Used by permission.

Franz Schubert, *Symphony in C Major*, Movement IV, Op. posth., mm. 15–25. Public domain.

RJ Miller, *Processional*, mm. 5–11. Copyright © 1997 by Appassionata Music. Used by permission.

Chapter 12

RJ Miller, *Yuletide*, mm. 111–120. Copyright © 1996 by Appassionata Music. Used by permission.

Chapter 13

RJ Miller, *Sarah's Song*, mm. 1–8. Copyright © 2013 by Appassionata Music. Used by permission.

RJ Miller, *Lullaby for Ethan*, mm. 1–16. Copyright © 2000 by Appassionata Music. Used by permission.

Chapter 16

RJ Miller, *Concerto for Unaccompanied Trumpet Trio*, Movement II, mm. 36–40. Copyright © 1987 by Appassionata Music. Used by permission.

RJ Miller, *Berceuse*, mm. 13–20. Copyright © 2004 by Appassionata Music. Used by permission.

INDEX

½-valve glissando 109
40 International Drum Rudiments 251

accelerando 37
achtel 38
achtelpause 39
acoustical balances 439
acoustical physics 1
acoustics 1
Adagio 36
Adagietto 36
adolescent voice 297, 428
adult vocal ranges 296, 428
adult vocal registers 296, 428
aerophones 237, 277–278
afuche-cabasa 275–276
agogo bells 274–275
Albinoni, Tomaso Giovann: *Adagio in G minor for Organ and Strings* 429
Allegretto 36
Allegro 36
alternate beaters 256
alto clef 41
alto flute 32, 171, 413; range 171; registers 171; transposition 172
alto ophicleide 33
alto recorder 32
alto trombone 33, 123; range 124; registers 124
am griffbrett 61
am steg 60
Amati 57
amplitude 1
Andante 36
Andantino 36
anreissen 61
Antes, John: *Christ the Lord, the Lord Most Glorious* 364–369, 387–391
anvil 273
archetier 65
arpa 35
arraché 61
artificial harmonics 62–63
ask a player 443
attrition 397

B♭ bass clarinet 32, 34, 179, 414; range 179; transposition 179
B♭ bass saxophone 32, 185; range 186; registers 186; transposition 186
B♭ bass trumpet 33, 117; range 118; transposition 118
B♭ clarinet 32, 177, 414; range 177, 422; transposition 177, 422
B♭ contrabass clarinet 32, 180; range 181; transposition 181
B♭ cornet 33, 113, 415; transposition 113; range 113; registers 113
B♭ soprano saxophone 32, 181; range 181, 423; registers 182, 423; transposition 182, 423
B♭ tenor saxophone 32, 183; range 183, 424; registers 183, 424; transposition 183, 425
B♭ trumpet 33; range 112, 419; registers 112, 419; transposition 112, 419
B♭ tuba 138
Bach, J. S.: *Acknowledge me, my Keeper* 207; *Brandenburg Concerto No. 2* 429; *Brandenburg Concerto No. 3* 429; *Brandenburg Concerto No. 5* 429; *Cantata No. 56* 429; *Cantata No. 140* 429; *Cantata No. 147* 429; *Cantata No. 208* 429; *Clavier Concerto No. 3 in D* 429; *Concerto for 2 Violins in D minor* 429; *Concerto No. 2 for 3 Harpsichords in C* 429; *English Suite No. 2* 429; *Italian Concerto* 429; *Orchestral Suite No. 2* 429; *Orchestral Suite No. 3 in D for Orchestra* 429; *St. Matthew Passion* 429; *Violin Sonata No. 1* 429; *O Haupt voll Blut und Wunden* 392
back-row cornets 134
bandstration 397–398
banjo 33
Barber, Samuel: *Adagio for Strings* 429; *Agnus Dei* 429
baritone 33, 126, 135; clefs 126; range 127; registers 127; transposition 126
baritone clef 42
baritone oboe 188; range 189; transposition 189
Barry (Prendergast), John: *Born Free* 429; *Chaplin* 430; *Dances with Wolves* 430; *Out of Africa* 430; *Somewhere in Time* 430; *The Lion in Winter* 429

Bartok pizzicato 62
Bartók, Béla: *Concerto for Orchestra* 430; *Music for Strings, Percussion and Celesta*, 430
bass clef 41
bass clef ottava 42
bass clef ottava bassa 42
bass drum 34, 256
bass flute 32, 172, 413; range 172; registers 172; transposition 172
bass guitar 33
bass oboe 188
bass ophicleide 33
bass recorder 32
bass trombone 33, 122, 136; range 122; registers 122
bass viol 79
bassist 79
bassklarinette 34
bassoon 32, 34, 189, 413; range 189, 422; registers 189, 422–423; transposition 189
Baton 39
BB♭ tuba 127
becken 34
Beethoven, Ludwig van: *Egmont Overture*, Op. 84 430; *Gloria*, from Mass in C Op. 86 305–308; *Piano Concerto No. 5 in E Flat* 430; *Prayer*, Op. 48 No. 1 213–214; *Quartet in B♭ major*, Op. 130 93; *Quartet No. 8 in E minor*, Op. 59 No. 2 91; *Symphony No. 3 in E Flat* 430; *Symphony No. 5 in C Minor*, Op. 67 430; *Symphony No. 6 in F Major* 430; *Symphony No. 9*, Op. 125 223–224, 430; *Violin Concerto in D Major* 430
bell tree 272
Berlioz, Hector: *L'Enfance du Christ* 430; *Symphonie Fantastique* 430
Bernstein, Elmer: *The Great Escape* 430; *The Magnificent Seven* 430; *The Ten Commandments* 430; *To Kill a Mockingbird* 430
Bernstein, Leonard: *West Side Story* 430
biscroma 38
Bizet, Georges: *Carmen* 430
blanche 38
blocci de legno cinese 34
blocci de leno coreano 34
blocs de bois 34
Boccherini, Luigi: *String Quintet in E*, Op. 11 No. 5 430
Bohm, Carl: *La Zingana* 144–146
bongos 259
books (musical theater) 398
Borodin, Alexander: *In the Steppes of Central Asia* 430; *Polovtzian Dances from Prince Igor* 430; *String Quartet No. 1*, Scherzo 94
Bortnianski, Dimitri: *Cherubic Hymn* 303–304
bow 57
bowing 58
Brahms, Johanne: *Piano Concerto No. 1 in D Minor* 430; *Piano Concerto No. 2 in B Flat* 430; *Symphony No. 1 in C Minor* 430; *Symphony No. 3 in F Major* 430; *Symphony No. 4 in E Minor* 430; *Violin Concerto in D* 430
brake drum 273–274
brass chamber ensembles 129
brass embouchure 111
brass glissandi 109
brass instruments 107
brass quintet 129
bratsche 35
breve 38
breve rest 39
brevis 38
bridge 57
British-style brass band 131–139
Bruckner, Anton: *Symphony No. 7 in E Major* 431; *Symphony No. 9 in D Minor* 431
bucket mute 111
bull fiddle 79
buzz roll 243

C attachment 81
C trumpet 32; transposition 112, 419
cabasa 275–276
caisse claire 35
calano 37
campanelli 34
capabilities and limitations (instruments) 443
capane tubolari 34
carillon 34
carrée 38
castagnettes 34
castanets 34, 276
Cats 399–400
CC tuba 127
celesta 278, 427
céleste 35
celli 75
cellist 75
cello 75, 416
cello harmonics 416
cembalo 35
cent-vingt-huitième 38
cent-vingt-huitième de soupir 39
centoventottavo 38
chamber strings 82
chamber woodwinds 194–195
children's vocal ranges 297, 428
chimes (tubular bells) 33, 34, 267, 427
choir with keyboard 300
choir with orchestra 300
choir with wind ensemble 300
choo-choo 252
Chopin, Frédéric: *Piano Concerto No. 1* 431; *Prélude* 84–86
chordaphones 237, 278–280
cimbalini 34
cimbasso 33, 124; range 124; registers 125
clarinet choir 192–193
clarinet in A 32, 178

clarinet quartet, 194
clarinet-cello-piano trio 194
clarinet-viola-piano trio 194
clarinet, violin, piano 194
clarinets 34, 176–181; registers 176
clarinette 34
clarinette basse 34
clarinetto 34
clarinetto basso 34
classical guitar 337
clavecin 35
claves 34, 275
clear notational 443
clefs 41–42
coach's whistle 277
col legno 62
common sense 439
con sord. 62
concert band 384–385
concert band brass 130
concert band percussion 280–281
concert band tutti 387–390
concert band woodwinds 195
concert score 21
concertmaster 83
condensed score 22–23
conductor's score (musical theater) 398
conga 259
conical brass107
conical woodwinds 165
contra-alto flute 32, 173; range 173; registers 173; transposition 173
contra octave 41
contrabass 79
contrabass flute 32, 173; range 174; registers 174; transposition 174
contrabass recorder 32
contrabassoon 32, 34–35, 190, 414; range 190; registers 190; transposition 190
contrafagotto 34
contrebasse 35
contrebasson 34
Copland, Aaron: *Appalachian Spring*, 431; *Fanfare for the Common Man* 431; *Of Mice and Men* 431; *Rodeo* 431; *The North Star* 431; *The Red Pony* 431
copyist 35
cor 34
cor anglais 34
Corelli, Arcangelo: *Concerto Grosso* Op.6 No.8 431
corno 34
corno inglese 34
cover page 14
covering seams 441
cowbells 274–275
crash cymbals 34
crécelle 34
Cremona 57
croche 38
croma 38

cross-voicing 440
crotales 33, 34, 263–264, 426
crotali 34
crotchet 38
crotchet rest 39
Crumb, George (Henry, Jr.): *Black Angels* 431; *A Haunted Landscape* 431
cup mute 110
cylindrical brass 107
cylindrical woodwinds 165
cymbale suspendue 34
cymbales 34
cymbales antiques 34
cymbales digitales 34

D♭ piccolo 175; range 175; registers 175
D trumpet 32 115; range 115; registers 115; transposition 115
de Mesquita, Carlos: *Esmeralda* 333–334
de Vilac, Renaud: *Adeste Fideles* 232–233
Debussy, Claude: *La mer, trois esquisses symphoniques pour orchestre* 101, 431; *Prélude à l'après-midi d'un faune*, 431; *Suite Bergamasque*, 431
Delibes, Léo: *Lakmé*, 431
Dello Joio, Norman: *Fantasies on a Theme by Haydn* 228
demi-pause 39
demi-soupir 39
demisemiquaver 38
demisemiquaver rest 39
détaché 58
deviled egg 252
diddle rudiments 242, 246
division of horn parts 120
doghouse bass 79
dominant 7th 4
doppel pause 39
doppeltakt 38
double bass 33, 79, 416; harmonics 80, 416; multiple stops 80, 418; pizzicato range 80, 418; range 80, 418; transposition 79, 418; tuning 79, 418
double bass ophicleide 33
double contrabass flute 174; range 174; transposition 175
double croche 38
double drag tap 250
double flam drag 252
double flam Swiss triplet 252
double horn 119
double paradiddle 246
double quartet 82
double ratamacue 251
double reed instruments 166, 186
double stops 63
double tenor clef 42
double wind quintet 130, 195
double-stroke roll 244
double-stroke rudiments 242–243

double-tonguing 108, 167
double-whole note 38
double-whole rest 39
down-bow 58
drag 249
drag paradiddle #1 250
drag paradiddle #2 250
drag rudiments 242, 249
drop 2 scoring 301
drum set 261–262
drumsticks 255
Durand, Marie Auguste: *Valse*, Op. 83 No. 1 441–442
Dvorák, Antonin: *Concerto for Violoncello and Orchestra* 431; *Rusalka: Polonaise* 431; *Scherzo Capriccioso*, Op. 66 431; *Slavonic Dance No. 5 in A* 431; *Slavonic Dance No. 6 in D* 431; *Slavonic Dance No. 10 in E Minor* 431; *Slavonic Dances*, Op. 46 No. 4 in F Major 152; *Slavonic Rhapsody*, Op. 45 No. 2 431; *Symphony No. 9* 431

E♭ alto clarinet 32, 178, 414; range 178; transposition 179
E♭ alto horn (mellophonium) 33
E♭ alto horn (tenor horn) 125, 134; range 125; registers 125; transposition 125
E♭ alto saxophone 32, 182, 414; range 182, 424; registers 182, 424; transposition 183, 424
E♭ baritone saxophone 32, 184; range 184, 425; registers 184, 425; transposition 184, 425
E♭ bass trumpet 33
E♭ clarinet, 32, 176; range 177; transposition 177
E♭ contrabass saxophone 32, 186
E♭ contralto clarinet, 32, 180; range 180; transposition 180
E♭ cornet 33
E♭ sopranino saxophone 32, 184; range 185; registers 185; transposition 185
E♭ soprano cornet 117, 132; range 117; registers 117; transposition 117
E♭ trumpet 32
E♭ tuba 127, 138
edge-blown aerophones 166
Effinger, Cecil: *Silver Plume* 154
eggbeater 252
eighth note 38
eighth rest 39
eleven-stroke 245
Elgar, Edward: *Cello Concerto* 431; *Pomp and Circumstance March No. 1* 431; *Pomp and Circumstance March No. 4* 431; *Serenade for Strings* 431; *Symphony No. 1* 431
Englisches horn 34
English horn 32, 34, 187, 413; range 187; registers 187; transposition 188
euphonium 33, 126, 137; range 126; registers 126
exact repeats 442

F alto horn, mellophonium 33
F tuba 127–128
fagott 34
fagotto 34
Fauré, Gabriel: *Cantique de Jean Racine* 431; *Masques et bergamasques* 431; *Pavane*, Op. 50 92–93, 431
fiddler 66
Field, John: *Nocturne* 202–206
fifteen-stroke 245
find your voice 444
finger cymbals 34, 269
fingered tremolos 60
fingerzimbeln 34
first page (parts) 24
first page (score) 16
five-line octave 41
five-stroke roll 244
flam 247
flam accent 247
flam drag 249
flam paradiddle 248
flam paradiddle-diddle 248
flam rudiments 242, 247
flam tap 247
flamacue 247–248
flamadiddle 248
flautando 60
flauto 34
flauto piccolo 34
flessatono 34
flexaton 34
flexatone 272–273
flöte 34
flugelhorn 33, 114, 134; range 114; registers 114; transposition 114
flûte 34
flute (C flute) 32, 34, 169, 413; range 169, 421; registers 170, 421; transposition 170
flute choir 191
flute orchestra 191
flute quartet 194
flute, viola and harp 194
flutes 169–175
flutter-tonguing 108, 167
four-line octave 41
four-stroke ruff 251–252
Franck, César: *Symphonic Variations for Piano and Orchestra* 432; *Symphony in D Minor* 432
Franz, Robert, and Müller, Wolfgang: *Widmung* 296
French bow 81
French horn 118
French violin clef 42
frequency 1
frog 57
front-row cornets 133
fundamental 2

ganze 38

ganze pause 39
ganze takt 38
geige 35
German bow 81
Gershwin, George: *An American in Paris* 432; *Cuban Overture* 432; *Rhapsody in Blue* 168, 432
Giacchino, Michael: *Ratatouille*, 432; *Star Trek Into Darkness* 432; *The Incredibles* 432; *Up* 432
Gilbert, William, and Sullivan, Arthur: *H.M.S. Penifore* 432; *The Mikado* 432; *The Pirates of Penzance* 432
glissandi 168
glissando 61
glocken zimbeln 34
glockenspiel 34, 426
Goldsmith, Jerrald King (Jerry): *Patton* 432; *Planet of the Apes* 432; *Star Trek* 432; *The Mummy* 432; *The Omen* 432; *The Sand Pebbles* 432
gran cassa 35
grand martelé 58
Grave 36
great bass recorder 32
great octave 41
Grieg, Edvard: *Arietta* 16–18; *Peer Gynt Suites (No. 1 & No. 2)* 432; *Piano Concerto in A Minor*, Op. 16 432; *Spring Dance*, Op. 38 No. 5 197–201; *Sylph*, Op. 62 No. 1 208–212; *Two Elegiac Melodies for Strings*, Op. 34 432
grosse caisse 35
grosse trommel 35
Guarneri 57
guiro 276
guitar 33; chords 339–347; harmonics 347–349; notation 338–339; range 337; transposition 337
guitar ensemble 349
guitar orchestra 349

halbe 38
halbe pause 39
halbe takt 38
half note 38
half rest 39
half-tube brass 108
hand cymbals 268
Handel, Georg Friedrich: *Concerto Grosso in B minor* Op. 12 No. 6 432; *Concerto No. 6 in B♭*, Op. 4 No. 6 432; *Messiah* 432; *Royal Fireworks Music* 432; *Sarabande* 90; *Water Music Suite No. 3 in D* 432
hängendes becken 34
Hanson, Howard: *Symphony No. 2* 432; *Symphony No. 7* 432
hard mallets 254
harfe 35
Harmon mute 110
harmonic balance 439
harmonics 62–63

harp 33, 34; arpeggios 317–318; enharmonics 317; glissandi 318, 320–331; harmonics 319; pedal changes 316; pedal diagrams 316, 320–331; pedals 315–316; repeated notes 319; scales 320–331; sustain 318
harpe 35
harpsichord 34
hautbois 34
Haydn, Franz Joseph: *Concerto for Trumpet in E♭ Major* 433; *Die Schöpfung* 432; *Symphony No. 94 in G Major* 432; *Symphony No. 101 in D Major* 432; *Symphony No. 104 in D Major* 432; *The Seasons* 433; *Gipsy Rondo* 216–217; *Symphony No. 100 in G Major*, Movement I 220; *Symphony No. 101 in D major* (Hoboken 1/101) 94–95
heckelphone 32
heel 57
hemidemisemiquaver rest 39
hemidemisemiquaver 38
Herrmann, Bernard: *Citizen Kane* 433; *North by Northwest* 433; *Psycho* 433; *The Day the Earth Stood Still* 433; *Vertigo* 433
hertz 1
hoboe 34
Hollaender, Victor: *Canzonetta* 360–361
Holst, Gustav: *A Somerset Rhapsody* Op. 21 No.2 433; *First Suite in E♭ for Military Band* Op. 28 No. 1 433; *Suite No.2 in F for Military Band* Op. 28 No.2 433; *The Planets* 433
holzblöke 34
holzstab 34
horizontal alignments 43
horn (French horn), (horn in F) 33, 34, 118, 414; notation 119; range 120, 419, 422; registers 120, 420, 422; transposition 119, 420
horn trio 129
Hovhaness, Alan: *October Mountain*, Op. 135 285–286
Howard, James Newton: *King Kong* 433; *The Sixth Sense* 433
huitième de soupir 39
hundertundachtundzwanzigstel 38
hundertundachtundzwanzigstelpause 39
hybrid rudiments 251
hybrid studio scores 28

idiophones 237, 263–276
Ilyinsky, Alexander: *Cradle Song* 102–103
implied fundamental 6–8
"In the stand" 111
incalzando 37
inside cover page 15
instrument names and abbreviations 34–35
instrument transpositions 32–33
instrumental balances 9–12
instrumental combinations 10–12
International Horn Society 118
intero 38
inverted flam tap 249

Ives, Charles: *The Unanswered Question* 433; *Three Places in New England* 433

Janácek, Leoš: *Idyll for Strings* 433; *String Quartet No. 1* 433; *String Quartet No. 2* 433
Jarre, Maurice-Alexis; *A Passage to India* 433; *Dead Poets Society* 433; *Doctor Zhivago* 433; *Lawrence of Arabia* 433; *Shogun* 433; *The Man Who Would Be King* 433
jeté 58
Jeu des claches 34

Karganov, Genari: *Arabeske* 141–143
kastagnetten 34
kavier 35
Khachaturian, Aram: *Gayaneh Suite No. 1* 433; *Gayaneh Suite No. 3* 433; *Symphonic Pictures from Spartacus* 433
The King and I 398–399
Kjerulf, Halfdan: *Berceuse* 234–235
klarinette 34
kleine flöte 34
kleine trommel 35
kontrabass 35
kontrafagott 34
Korngold, Erich Wolfgang: *Captain Blood* 433; *The Adventures of Robin Hood* 433; *The Prince and the Pauper* 433; *The Sea Hawk* 433; *The Sea Wolf* 433; *Violin Concerto*, Op. 35 433

Lack, Theodore: *Cabaletta* 162
Larghetto 36
Largo 36
last page (parts) 26
last page (score) 18
learn from your mistakes 444
legato 58
legato (tenuto) 40
legato-staccatissimo 40
legato-staccato 40
lentando 37
Lento 36
lesson 25 rudiment 250
Ligeti, György Sándor: *Atmosphères* 434; *Cello Concerto* 434; *Requiem* 434
Liszt, Franz: *Concerto No. 1 in E♭ Major for Piano* 434; *Eine Faust-Symphonie in drei Charakterbildern) S.108* 434
long roll 244
louré 58
luthier 65

MacDowell, Edward: *The Brook* 310–312; *The Flow'ret* 104–106
Mahler, Gustav: *Symphony No. 1 in D Major* 434; *Symphony No. 4 in G Major* 434; *Symphony No. 9 in D Major* 434
major 2nd 2
major 3rd 3

major 6th 3
major 7th 3–4
Major Orchestras Librarians' Association 13
mallets 254
Mancini, Henry: *A Shot in the Dark* 434; *Breakfast at Tiffany's* 434; *Charade* 434; *Days of Wine and Roses* 434; *The Pink Panther* 434; *Touch of Evil* 434; *Victor Victoria* 434
maracas 275
marcato 40, 58
marcato-legato 40
marcato-staccatissimo 40
marcato-staccato 40
marimba 33, 34, 265–266, 427; mallets 257
marimba mallets 257
marimbaphon 34
mark tree 271
martelato 40
martelato-legato 40
martelato-staccatissimo 40
martelato-staccato 40
martellato 58
martelé 58
Mascagni, Pietro: *Cavalleria Rusticana* 434; *Messa di Gloria* 434
Massenet, Jules: *Fantasy for cello and orchestra* 434; *Last Dream of the Virgin* 314; *Thaïs* 434
measure numbers 19
medium mallets 254
membranophones 237, 253–262
Mendelssohn, Felix: *A Midsummer Night's Dream* 434; *Hebrides Overture* 434; *Piano Concerto No. 2* 434; *Quintet in B♭*, Op. 87 434; *Violin Concerto in E Minor* 434; *War March of the Priests* 87–89
meno mosso 37
Messiaen, Olivier: *L'ascension* 434; *O Sacrum Convivum* 434; *Quatuor pour la fin du temps* 434
metà 38
mezzo-soprano clef 42
Miller, RJ: *Akumal* 262; *Ba-Da-Ka-Dup!* 238–240; *Cadence #1* 290; *Callisto* 21–23; *Celebration Waltz* 373–379; *Concerto for Unaccompanied Trumpet Trio* 440; *Elegy* 91–92; *Good Tidings* 309; *Io* 24–26; *Lullaby for Ethan* 411; *Moments* 28–29; *Processional* 381; *Promises* 370–372; *Recessional* 394; *Sarah's Song* 402–410; *The Circus is in Town* 265; *The Processional* 30; *The Summit* 156–157; *The Wilderness Suite* 100; *Yellowstone* 287–289; *Your Heart's Desire* 291–293; *Yuletide* 393; *Zoot Suit* 359; *Zounds* 282–284
minim 38
minim rest 39
minima 38
Moderato 36
Moszkowski, Moritz: *Spanish Dance*, Op. 12 No. 1 382

Mozart, (Johann Georg) Leopold: *Cassation in G* 434
Mozart, Wolfgang Amadeus: *Concerto for Clarinet* 434; *Concerto No. 20 in D Minor for Piano* 434; *Die Zauberflöte* 435; *Don Giovanni* 434; *Flute Concerto No. 1* 435; *Piano Concerto No. 21* 435; *Quintet in E♭* 435; *Requiem* 435; *Serenade in G Major for Strings* 435; *Sinfonia Concertante in E Flat Major for Violin and Viola* 435; *Symphony in G Minor*, K. 550, 96; *Symphony No. 40* 435; *Symphony No. 41 in C Major*, K. 551, 435
multiple stops 81
multiple-bounce roll 243
multiple-bounce rudiments 242–243
musical theater instrumentation 398–402
Mussorgsky, Modest Petrovich: *Night on the Bald Mountain* 435; *Pictures at an Exhibition* 435
mute 62
muted trombone 415
muted trumpet 415
mutes 110

natural harmonics 62–63
Nelhybel, Vaclav: *Chorale* 229; *Festivo* 230–231
nine-stroke 244
noire 38
non-pitch clef 42
norm. 61

oboe 32, 34, 186–187, 413; range 187, 421; registers 187, 421; transposition 187
oboe d'amore 32, 188; range 187; transposition 188
Offenbach, Jacques: *Orpheus in the Underworld* 435; *The Tales of Hoffmann* 435
Oklahoma! 401–402
one hundred twenty-eighth note 38
one hundred twenty-eighth rest 39
one-line octave 41
orchestra bells 33, 34, 263
orchestral brass 130
orchestral percussion 280–281
orchestral tutti 363–379
orchestral woodwinds 195
ord. 61
Orff, Carl: *Carmina Burana* 435
organ 34
organo 35
orgel 35
orgue 35
ottavino 34
ottavo 38
overtones 2–8

Pachelbel, Johann: *Canon and Gigue in D Major* 435
Paganini, Niccolò: *Violin Concerto No. 2* 435
paradiddle-diddle 246
part preparation 23–26
Pärt, Arvo: *Arbos for brass and percussion* 435; *Cantus in Memory of Benjamin Britten* 435; *Te Deum* 435

partials 2–8
passing melodies 441
pataflafla 248
pauken 34
pausa di biscroma 39
pausa di breve 39
pausa di centoventottavo 39
pausa di croma 39
pausa di minima 39
pausa di semibiscroma 39
pausa di semibreve 39
pausa di semicroma 39
pausa di semiminima 39
pause 39
pause de brève 39
pedal harp 313–319
Penderecki, Krzysztof: *Canon for 2 string orchestras and tapes* 435; *Cello Concerto* 435; *Threnody for the Victims of Hiroshima* 435
percussion 139
percussion ensemble 280
percussion score order 238–241
Percussive Arts Society 251
perdendosi 37
perfect 4th 3
perfect 5th 3
perfect octave 4
petite flûte 34
phrasing 43
piano 33, 34, 278–280, 427
piano and wind quartet 129, 194
piano and wind quintet 129, 194
piano and wind trio 129, 194
piano quartet 82
piano sextet 82, 194
piano trio 82
pianoforte 35
piatti 34, 268
piatto sospeso 34
piccolo 32, 34, 170, 413
piccolo range 170
piccolo registers 171
piccolo trumpet 32, 115; range 116; trumpet in A 32; trumpet in B♭ 32; transposition 116
Pierrot ensemble 82, 194
piu mosso 37
pizzicato 61
pizzicato secco 62
Poldini, Ede: *In the Wood* 159
portamenti 168
portamento 61
portato 58
posaune 34
Prestissimo 37
Presto 37
principal players 83
Prokofiev, Serge: "Noces de Kijé" 153; *Alexander Nevsky* 435; *Cinderella* 435; *Lieutenant Kijé Suite* 435; *Peter and the Wolf* 435; *Romeo and Juliet* 435

Puccini, Giacomo: *Gianni Schicchi* 435; *La Bohème* 435; *Madama Butterfly* 435; *Tosca* 435
Purcell, Henry: *Dido and Aeneas* 436; *Fantasias (for Strings)* 436

quadruple croche 38
quadruple stops 64
quart de soupir 39
quarter note 38
quarter rest 39
quarto 38
quasihemidemisemiquaver 38
quaver 38
quaver rest 39
quintuple croche 38

Rachmaninoff, Sergei Vasilievich: *Concerto No. 2 in C Minor for Piano*, Op. 18 436; *Concerto No. 3 in D Minor for Piano*, Op. 30 436; *Rhapsody on a Theme of Paganini* 436
raganella 34
rainstick 276
rallentando 37
Rameau, Jean-Philippe: *Tambourin* 149
ratatap 250
ratchet 34, 271
ratios 2–4
ratsche 34
Ravel, Joseph-Maurice: *Bolero* 436; *Daphnis and Chloe* 436
recording studio parts 29–31
recording studio scores 27
Reed, Alfred: *A Sacred Suite* 227
Reed, H. Owen: "*Mass*" 155
registers 41
rehearsal marks 19, 43
Reicha, Anton: *Two Andantes and Adagio* 217–218
Rent 400
repiano cornet 133
Respighi, Ottorino: *Feste Romane* 436; *I pini di Roma* 436; *Le fontane di Roma* 436
rhythmic interest 442–443
rhythmic subdivisions 43–45
rim shot 256
Rimsky-Korsakov, Nikolai Andreyevich: *Capriccio Espagnol* 436; *Scheherazade* 436
ritardando 37
Rodrigo, Joaquín: *Concierto de Aranjuéz* 436
röhrenglocken 34
roll rudiments 242
ronde 38
Rosetti, Antonio: *Quintet in E flat* 219
rosin 58
Rossini, Gioachino Antonio: *Guillaume Tell* 436; *Il bariere di Siviglia* 436; *Otello* 436
rotary valves 118
Rózsa, Miklós: *Ben-Hur* 436; *Cello Concerto*, Op. 32, 436; *El Cid* 436; *Ivanhoe* 436; *King of Kings* 436; *Lust for Life* 436; *Spellbound* 436; *The Asphalt Jungle* 436; *Violin Concerto*, Op. 24 436
rudiments 242

Saint-Saëns, Charles Camille: *The Carnival of the Animals* 436; *Danse Macabre* 65, 436; *Symphony No. 3* 436
saltando 58
samba whistle 277
sampled sounds 237–238
sassofono 34
saxophon 34
saxophone mouthpieces 166
saxophone quartet 194
saxophone subtone 169
saxophones 34, 181–186
Schubert, Franz Peter: *Ave Maria*, Op. 52 No. 6 436; *Marche Militaire*, Op. 51 No. 1 160–161; *Piano Trio in E Flat*, D. 897 437; *Piano Trio in E Flat*, D. 929 437; *Symphony No. 9 in C* 437; *Symphony in B Major*, Op. posth. 96, 221–222; *Symphony in C Major* 380; *Symphony No. 2 in B♭ Major* 436; *Symphony No. 5 in B Flat* 437; *Symphony No. 8 in B Minor* 437
Schumann, Robert; *Concerto in A Minor for Cello and Orchestra*, Op. 129 437; *Concerto in A Minor for Piano and Orchestra*, Op. 54 437; *Symphony No. 1 in B♭ Major*, Op. 48 437
Schütt, Eduard: *En Bercant* 335
scordatura 65
score in C 21
score order 19
score preparation 13–23
sechzehntel 38
sechzehntelpause 39
sedicesimo 38
seizième de soupir 39
semibreve 38
semi-brève 38
semibiscroma 38
semicroma 38
semihemidemisemiquaver 38
semihemidemisemiquaver rest 39
semiminima 38
semiquaver 38
semiquaver rest 39
senza sord. 62
serpent 33
sessantaquattresimo 38
seven traits 444–445
seven-stroke 244
seventeen-stroke 245
shakers 271
shakes 109
Shore, Howard Leslie: *Hugo* 437; *Lord of the Rings* 437
Shostakovich, Dmitri Dmitrievich: *Festive Overture* 437; *Piano Concerto No. 2* 437; *Symphony No. 5* 437; *Symphony No. 8* 437

Sibelius, Johan Julius Christian (Jean): *Finlandia* 437; *Symphony No. 1 in E Minor*, Op. 39 437; *Symphony No. 2 in D Major*, Op. 43 437; *Symphony No. 5 in E♭ Major*, Op. 82 437
Silvestri, Alan: *The Abyss* 437; *Contact* 437; *The Polar Express* 437
single drag tap 249
single dragadiddle 250
single horn 118
single paradiddle 246
single ratamacue 251
single reed instruments 166
single-flammed mill 248
single-stroke four 242
single-stroke roll 242
single-stroke rudiments 242
single-stroke seven 243
single-tonguing 108, 166
siren 278
six-stroke roll 244
sixteenth note 38
sixteenth rest 39
sixty-fourth note 38
sixty-fourth rest 39
sizzle cymbal 269
sleigh bells 271
slentando 37
slide whistle 277
slurs 108, 167
small octave 41
Smetana, Bedřich: *String Quartet No. 1 in E Minor* 437; *Vltava* 437
snap pizzicato 62
snare drum 34, 255–256
soft mallets 254
solo cornet 133
solo horn 135
sopranino recorder 32
soprano clef 42
soprano recorder 32
soprano sax 414
Sor, Ferninando: *Sonata in C Major for Guitar*, Op. 15b 355
sordino 62
soupir 39
sousaphone 33, 128; *range* 128; *registers* 129
spiccato 58
staccatissimo 40
staccato 40, 58
step one 439
stick shot 256
stopped horn 111, 414–415
Stradivari 57
straight mute 110
Strauss, Jr., Johann: *On the Beautiful Blue Danube Waltz* 437; *Tales from the Vienna Woods* 437
Strauss, Richard: *Also Sprach Zarathustra* 437; *Der Rosenkavalier Suite*, Op. 59 437; *Don Juan*, Op. 20 437; *Till Eulenspiegel*, Op. 28 437

Stravinsky, Igor Fyodorovich: *The Firebird Suite* 437; *Petrushka* 437; *The Rite of Spring* 437
string bass 79
string octet 82
string orchestra 82
string quintet 82
string sextet 82
string trio 82
stringendo 37
sub contra octave 41
subcontrabass flutes 174: *range* 174; *transposition* 174
subsequent pages (parts) 25
subsequent pages (score) 17
sul G 61
sul ponticello 60
sul tasto 61
Sullivan, Arthur: *The Lost Chord* 147
Händel, Georg Friedrech: "*Largo*" 148
sur la touche 61
sur le chevalet 60
suspended cymbal 34, 268–269
Swiss Army triplet 248
synthetic sounds 237–238

tam-tam 34, 270
tambour de basque 35
tamburin 35
tambourine 34, 257–258
tamburo basco 35
tamburo piccolo 35
Tchaikovsky, Peter Ilyich: *1812 Overture* 438; *Capriccio Italien* 150–151; *Chanson Triste* 48–56; *Nutcracker Suite* 225–226, 438; *Piano Concerto No. 1 in B♭ minor*, Op. 23 438; *Romeo and Juliet* 97–100, 438; *Swan Lake* 438; *Symphony No. 6 in B Minor* 438; *Violin Concerto in D major*, Op. 35 438
tempel-blöcke 34
tempel-blocs 34
temple blocks 34, 270
tempo (terminology) 36–37
tempo blocks 270
ten-stroke 245
tenor banjo 33
tenor clef 41–42
tenor drum 258
tenor recorder 32
tenor sax 414
tenor trombone 33, 121; *range* 121, 420; *registers* 121, 420; *transposition* 122, 420
think like a player 444
thirteen-stroke 245
thirty-second note 38
thirty-second rest 39
three-line octave 41
thunder and cannons 257
thunder sheet 274
timbales 260

timbales (timpani) 34
timpani 33, 34, 139, 253–255, 426
tip, 57
tom-toms 258
traditional: *Auld Lang Syne* 301–302; *Greensleeves* 350–354
transposed score 22
treble clef 41
treble clef octava 42
treble clef quindicessima 42
tremolos 60, 168
trentaduesimo 38
triangle 34, 268
triangolo 34
trills 60, 108, 167
triple croche 38
triple horn 119
triple paradiddle 246
triple ratamacue 251
triple stops 64
triple-stroke roll 243
triple-tonguing 108, 167
tromba 34
trombones 34, 136, 415; glissando 109; slide positions 122
trompete 34
trompette 34
trumpet 34, 111, 415; range 112, 419; registers 112, 419
tuba 33–34, 127, 415; range 128, 421; registers 128, 421
tuba-euphonium quartet 130
two-line octave 41

unaccompanied choir 299–300
up-bow 58
upright bass 79

valve tremolo 109
valve trombone 123; range 123; registers 123; transposition 123
Vaughan Williams, Ralph: *Fantasia on "Greensleeves"* 438; *Fantasia on a Theme by Thomas Tallis* 438
Verdi, Giuseppe Fortunino Francesco: *Il Trovatore* 438; *La Traviata* 438; *Requiem* 438
vertical alignments 42
vibrafono 34
vibraphon 34
vibraphone 266–267, 427
vibraslap 273
viertel 38
viertelpause 39
vierundsechzigstel 38
vierundsechzigstelpause 39
viola 33, 70, 416–417; double stops 72–73; harmonic range 71, 417; harmonics 71–72, 416; pizzicato range 70, 417; quadruple stops 74; range 66, 417; triple stops 73–74; tuning 70, 417

violas da braccio 57
violin 33, 66, 415; double stops 68; harmonic range 66, 417; harmonics 66–67, 415; pizzicato range 66, 416; quadruple stops 69–70; range 66, 416; triple stops 68–69; tuning 66, 416
violin, clarinet, cello and piano 194
violine 35
violinist 66
violino 35
violist 70
violon 35
violoncell 35
violoncelle 35
violoncelli 75
violoncello 33, 75; clef changes 75; double stops 77; harmonic range 75, 418; harmonics 76–77; pizzicato range 75, 418; quadruple stops 78–79; range 75 417; triple stops 78; tuning 75, 417
viols 70
Vivace, 37
Vivaldi, Antonio: *Concert in D major* 356–358; *Double Mandolin Concerto in G* 438; *The Four Seasons* 438; *L'estro armonico* 438
vocal notation 295–296
vocal voicings 298–299
voice-leading 442–443
voice, clarinet and piano 194
voice, horn and piano 129
von Weber, Carl Maria; *Prayer* 163
vowel considerations 297–298

Wagner, Wilhelm Richard: *Die Walküre* 438; *Lohengrin* 438; *Tannhäuser* 438
wah-wah mute 110
WB 58
Webern, Anton: *Five Pieces for Orchestra*, Op. 10 438
Weill, Kurt: *Suite for Orchestra* 438; *The Threepenny Opera* 438
Westbrook, W. J.: *Pleyel's Hymn* 158
what to avoid 444
whole note 38
whole rest 39
whole-tube brass107
Williams, John Towner: *Close Encounters of the Third Kind* 438; *Concerto No. 1 for Violin and Orchestra* 438; *Harry Potter and the Sorcerer's Stone* 438; *Indiana Jones and the Last Crusade* 438; *Memoirs of a Geisha* 438; *Schindler's List* 438; *Star Wars* 438; *Superman* 438; *The Book Thief* 438
wind and string nonet 82, 130, 195
wind and string octet 82, 130, 195
wind and strings quintet 194
wind and string septet 82, 130, 195
wind chimes 272
wind ensemble 383–384
wind ensemble brass 130
wind ensemble percussion 280–281
wind ensemble tutti 387–390

wind ensemble woodwinds 195
wind instrument and string trio 194
wind octet 195
wind quintet 129, 193
wind sextet 129, 194
Wintory, Austin: *Captain Abu Raed* 27, 31; *Journey* 438
wire brushes 256
wolf tone 65
woodblocks 34, 270
wooden mallets 254
woodwind ensembles 191–195
woodwind instruments 165

wool beaters 257

Xaver Scharwenka: *Polish Dance*, Op. 3 No. 1 395
xilofono 34
xylonphon 34
xylophone 33, 264–265, 426

Zeisler, Fannie Blumenfeld: *Près de L'Eau*, Op. 38 No. 3 215–216
zurückhaltend 37
zweiunddreißigstel 38
zweiunddreißigstelpause 39

eBooks
from Taylor & Francis
Helping you to choose the right eBooks for your Library

Add to your library's digital collection today with Taylor & Francis eBooks. We have over 50,000 eBooks in the Humanities, Social Sciences, Behavioural Sciences, Built Environment and Law, from leading imprints, including Routledge, Focal Press and Psychology Press.

Choose from a range of subject packages or create your own!

Benefits for you
- Free MARC records
- COUNTER-compliant usage statistics
- Flexible purchase and pricing options
- 70% approx of our eBooks are now DRM-free.

Benefits for your user
- Off-site, anytime access via Athens or referring URL
- Print or copy pages or chapters
- Full content search
- Bookmark, highlight and annotate text
- Access to thousands of pages of quality research at the click of a button.

ORDER YOUR FREE INSTITUTIONAL TRIAL TODAY

Free Trials Available

We offer free trials to qualifying academic, corporate and government customers.

eCollections
Choose from 20 different subject eCollections, including:
- Asian Studies
- Economics
- Health Studies
- Law
- Middle East Studies

eFocus
We have 16 cutting-edge interdisciplinary collections, including:
- Development Studies
- The Environment
- Islam
- Korea
- Urban Studies

For more information, pricing enquiries or to order a free trial, please contact your local sales team:

UK/Rest of World: **online.sales@tandf.co.uk**
USA/Canada/Latin America: **e-reference@taylorandfrancis.com**
East/Southeast Asia: **martin.jack@tandf.com.sg**
India: **journalsales@tandfindia.com**

www.tandfebooks.com

Made in the USA
San Bernardino, CA
01 September 2017